STRATEGIES FOR ASIA PACIFIC: BEYOND THE CRISIS

Philippe Lasserre
and
Hellmut Schütte

palgrave

Published by
PALGRAVE
Houndmills, Basingstoke, Hampshire RG21 6XS and
175 Fifth Avenue, New York, N.Y. 10010
Companies and representatives throughout the world

PALGRAVE is the new global academic imprint of
St. Martin's Press LLC Scholarly and Reference Division and
Palgrave Publishers Ltd (formerly Macmillan Press Ltd).

ISBN 0–333–73582–X

This book is printed on paper suitable for recycling and made from fully managed and sustained forest sources.

A catalogue record for this book is available from the British Library.

10   9   8   7   6   5   4   3
08   07   06   05   04   03   02   01

Printed and bound in Great Britain by
Antony Rowe Ltd, Chippenham, Wiltshire

Contents

Acknowledgements

The gestation period for this book has been a long one. After more than twenty years of working, teaching and researching in Asia, we wrote together the book *Strategies for Asia Pacific* which appeared in 1985 and was consequently published in French, German and Japanese. We continued to benefit from spirited classroom discussions and interaction with hundreds of senior managers both in Asia and the West, often focusing on topics taken up in the book. Taking these comments into account and the changed economic circumstances, we got together to produce an up-to-date and revised version now sub-titled 'beyond the crisis'. We acknowledge with gratitude that this new book like the former one has been very much influenced by many of our contacts and is the fruit of our discussions with them. Unfortunately, these managers are too numerous to mention by name.

We owe a debt of gratitude to INSEAD and its Euro-Asia Centre whose support enabled us to constantly travel between Asia and Europe. The idea for such a book, indeed the very existence of the Euro-Asia Centre, would never have come into being without the vision and persistence of Henri-Claude de Bettignies, who had the foresight to recognise the importance of Japan and Asia Pacific long before the region gained its present reputation and who pushed us to learn about Asia and pass that knowledge on to others.

We are grateful to Jocelyn Probert for her continuing collaborative research on which some of the chapters are based. Her hand in the final editing of the text is appreciated. Without the valiant attempts of Joan Lewis to organise us, her energy and her patience in the face of all the 'final' changes to the text, this book would never have seen the light of day.

Finally, while acknowledging the assistance and support of the organisation and other colleagues, the responsibility for all that is presented here lies solely with the authors.

The editors and publishers also acknowledge with thanks permission from the following to reproduce copyright material.

McKinsey Quarterly, for Figure 1.6 from D. Turcq, 'The Global Impact of Non-Japan Asia', *Long Range Planning* (February 1995).

Harvard Business School Press, for Figure 9.3, from C. Bartlett and S. Ghoshal, *Managing Across Borders: The Transnational Solution* (1989).

Every effort has been made to contact all the copyright holders, but if any have been inadvertently omitted the publishers will be pleased to make the appropriate arrangement at the earliest opportunity.

Introduction

The West cannot expect to compete successfully with Asia as long as the Asians know more about the West than the West knows about Asia.

THE ASIA PACIFIC REGION: THE LIMITS OF GLOBAL MANAGEMENT

In the space of four decades up to 1997, Asia, long referred to in the West as the 'Far East', has emerged as one of the growth poles of the world economy. Japan's transformation from post-war ruin into economic superpower was followed by the awakening of South Korea and Taiwan, which further accelerated the growth of the entire Asia Pacific region. In the 1970s and early 1980s rising foreign investment and de-regulation in Indonesia, Malaysia, and Thailand spurred this momentum, with the entrepreneurial city-states of Singapore and Hong Kong acting as the region's growth poles. China's tentative opening to the West in 1979, followed by its bold free market reforms in the late 1980s, led to unprecedented economic growth rates in the 1990s. Together these countries form the Asia Pacific region, a formidable force that is drawing in the residual non-capitalist economies of Vietnam and Laos. In the 1990s, the Asia Pacific region became increasingly self-sufficient in terms of intra-regional trade and investment. Then financial turmoil hit the region, leading it towards a recession with characteristics closer to that of a structural crisis than of a cyclical downturn.

At the beginning of the 1990s, Western firms started to perceive Asia as an opportunity for exploiting emerging markets and for actively sourcing from there. This turned in the following years into a scramble for Asia that had many companies aiming to double or triple their activities within a relatively short time-span. At the end of the 1990s the situation had again turned around. Faced with huge overcapacities in most industries and slack demand in most markets, the firms' own operations in Asia had become a threat to the overall profitability and well-being of Western companies.

In this book we have tried to keep a truly strategic, that is, longer-term perspective on management issues in Asia. We have therefore tried to stay away from quick advice on situations amidst turmoil. Such advice is either so general and shallow that it is not worth mentioning (for example 'cut costs'), or has to be so specific to a given firm, industry or country at a given moment that it cannot be dealt with in a book aimed at a broad audience.

If there are any lessons to learned from the 'Asian Crisis', they are twofold. First, nothing is better than solid, fact based and planful management. Therefore a strategic approach rather than an opportunistic one is needed, today even more so than in the past. Secondly, while the crisis does challenge the superiority of Asian, particularly Japanese management over Western ideas and systems, Western managers must continue to accept and respect that fundamental differences exist between their home territories and the Asia Pacific region. This remains a precondition for the success of their firms over the long term. In Asia, relationships usually count more than contractual transactions, groups and networks matter more than individuals, and wealth creation for society as a whole, over the long term, takes priority over short-term profit motives. Even the narrowly defined, rational self-interest of *homo economicus* must be questioned in light of Asia's very different cultural and business contexts.

For the Western firm, doing business in the Asia Pacific region often demonstrates the limits of global management and the universality of Western strategic thinking. As Western managers and firms set up and expand operations in Asia, and as they compete and cooperate with Asian firms in a rapidly evolving market, they now confront a part of the world that in both geographical and economic terms is no longer the exotic, marginalised 'Far East', but an important part of the global economy.

It is possible, and even necessary, to generalise about Asia's business cultures and environments without denying the enormous differences that exist between its countries and sub-regions. Only by challenging the universality of Western assumptions about both management and competitive practice will Western managers and firms be able to seize opportunities and ensure future success, both in the Asia Pacific region and the rest of the world.

In writing this book the authors have in mind the large number of corporations and executives whose ambition it still is to increase their presence in this region over time, but who would like a road map to help them. The book is designed primarily for action oriented managers and students who feel that they need an overall grasp of the task of building a business and competing in Asia Pacific. To this end, the authors have made series of conscious choices.

First, the book does not present a catalogue of country characteristics and opportunities. This can be provided more easily by the various publications of the Economic Intelligence Units, among others. The choice has been to look at the commonalities rather than the differences, and therefore to analyse the various strategic and managerial aspects that Western managers are confronted with when approaching the region. When necessary, differences are taken into consideration and for that reason the region has been divided into four major blocks: Japan, the Newly Industrialised Economies of Korea, Taiwan, Hong Kong and Singapore, the rapidly developing countries of ASEAN, and China.

The second deliberate choice has been to cover a broad range of issues relevant for business managers rather than to attempt to present a deep and academic analysis and discussion of each topic. In so doing, the authors are aware that for each topic covered they can be criticised by the specialists. The cultural scientists, the economists, the sociologists, the industrial analysts or the Japanese scholars will probably find that presentations of the cultural traits, of the economic factors, of the industrial policies of governments or of the business behaviour of Japanese or Overseas Chinese groups are somewhat rudimentary. This book is not written for specialists. The authors give reference in the bibliography to some scholarly works to which the reader who is hungry for deeper knowledge can refer.

Finally the book is based on a series of research, some originating with the authors themselves, some drawn from the experience and research of others. The book does not pretend to develop a new management theory, but provides new insights in complex problems and alternative views on issues which are mistakenly taken for granted. The intention is to give to experienced and future managers a synthesis of what, in the authors' view, constitutes the essential ingredients of knowledge and analysis needed to approach the region. As Montaigne, the French philosopher said in the sixteenth century, 'Il vaut mieux une tête bien faite qu'une tête bien pleine' (A well rounded mind is better than an overcrowded one). The purpose of the book is to help managers to be well rounded about Asia rather than to overcrowd them with bare facts.

The content of the book is structured around two major types of subject matter: one, dealing with the external environment, is addressed in Chapters 1, 3, 4, 5 and 11, and the other, which discusses the firm's internal environment, is covered in Chapters 2, 6, 7, 8, 9 and 10.

Chapter 1 gives an overview of the region. It defines the Asia Pacific region and sub-regions, and discusses the weight of the region in the world economy. It then looks at the impact of the crisis on growth prospects and the consequences for companies. In Chapter 2 the authors propose a framework for the formulation of strategy and describe its main components. Chapter 3 analyses the market characteristics of the three main sub-regions – Japan, the industrialising and developing economies of South-East and East Asia, and China – and focuses on market segmentation and consumer behaviour. The major non-Western players in the region, the Japanese *kaisha*, the Korean *chaebol* and the Overseas Chinese conglomerates, as well as other national companies, are the subject of Chapter 4. Their managerial culture and organisational practices are discussed in this chapter, while Chapter 5 concentrates on the roles which governments, culture and society play in shaping competitive behaviour and business practices. Chapter 6 debates the various entry strategies in the region as well as some of the problems arising in collecting information. As acquisitions have become a more viable option for firms for expansion in the region, this issue is newly taken up in this part of the book.

Chapters 7 and 8 discuss the strategic and managerial issues involved in the planning, negotiating and managing of joint ventures and strategic alliances. Chapter 7 focuses on the joint ventures which are designed to establish a business within the boundaries of a particular country, while Chapter 8 centres the discussion on global strategic alliances between Western and Asian, mainly Japanese, partners.

Chapter 9 concentrates on the organisational aspects of developing and managing businesses across the region. It argues that organisational practices have to be significantly adapted if a company is to cope with the demands of the Asian competitive environment. It also debates the various roles that regional headquarters can play in supporting country strategies. The management of human resources is the subject of Chapter 10. Two major issues are discussed in this chapter: first, the recruitment, development and retention of local personnel, and second, the management of expatriates. This chapter finishes with a discussion of the main cultural traits affecting the interface between Westerners and Asians.

The eleventh and final chapter identifies the major trends which shape the future of the region. It draws heavily on the current debate concerning the crisis and the renaissance of growth in the region. It also looks at the political framework within which business is conducted in Asia and the assertiveness of an Asian identity and its implications for the Western world.

The best hope of the authors is that this book will contribute (modestly but significantly) to a better understanding of this fascinating part of the world and will provide a road map for increasing cooperation between Western firms and their Asian counterparts.

List of Abbreviations

AFTA	Asian Free Trade Association
APEC	Asian Pacific Economic Cooperation
ASEAN	Association of South-East Asian Nations (Indonesia, Malaysia, Philippines, Thailand, Vietnam)
DC	developed country
EAEC	East Asian Economic Caucus
EDB	Economic Development Board
ETDZ	Economic and Technical Development Zone
EU	European Union
GDP	gross domestic product
GNP	gross national product
GSP	Generalised System of Preferences
HDI	Human Development Index
IMF	International Monetary Fund
INSEAD	Institut Européen d'Administration
IPF	Islamic Pilgrim Funds
JETRO	Japan External Trade Organization
LDC	less developed country
MFN	Most Favoured Nation
MITI	Ministry of International Trade and Industry
MOF	Ministry of Finance
NGO	non-governmental organisation
NIE	Newly Industrialised Economy
OCC	Open Coastal City
OECD	Organisation for Economic Cooperation and Development
OEM	original equipment manufacturing
P&G	Procter & Gamble
PPP	purchasing power parities
RHQ	regional headquarters
ROI	return on investment
SAR	Special Administrative Region
SBU	strategic business unit
SEZ	Special Economic Zone
UNCTAD	United Nations Conference on Trade and Development

UNDP	United Nations Development Programme
VP	vice-president
WOFE	Wholly Owned Foreign Enterprise

1 The Strategic Importance of Asia Pacific

ASIA PACIFIC AS A REGION

From the Far East to Asia Pacific

During the first decades of the twentieth century, Asia was still called the Far East and was seen as being very far away, if not on the periphery of a world dominated by the European colonial powers and the USA.

The Far East provided raw materials. In exchange some manufactured goods were shipped to the region. Daring trading houses (which had started operations during the last century) expanded, and the first manufacturers sent their own representatives to Japan, China and other countries in order to set up factories. Despite these activities, the Far East did not gain much importance in the world economy, or at least not in the minds of those whose thinking was influenced by a colonial mentality and centred on the Atlantic.

Japan became an industrial country in the 1920s and 1930s, by which time it was already exporting massive quantities of cheap watches and textiles to the West. In 1941 Japan felt it had sufficient technical capabilities to attack the world's most powerful nation, the USA; but Japan was the exception in the region. China, hundreds of years previously a leader in many technologies, was in a shambles, and most other Asian countries were being exploited rather than developed by their colonial masters.

After the war, at the beginning of the 1950s, Japan's manufacturing base was destroyed and half of its workforce was employed in the agricultural sector. Shanghai had been taken over by the communists under Mao, and entrepreneurs were driven out to Taiwan and Hong Kong. Korea, with an average income below that of Sudan, saw a devastating war which led to the division of the country. Manila, Rangoon and Saigon, however, were flourishing and promised a new era in Asia.

Much has changed since then. Japan has become a highly developed country challenging American leadership in a number of industries. The group of Newly Industrialised Economies (NIEs – South Korea, Taiwan, Hong Kong and Singapore) became the most successful economies in the world with sustained growth rates of 7–8 per cent over long periods, doubling the

1

size of their gross national product (GNP) each decade and leaving the leading Latin American countries, such as Brazil and Argentina, far behind. In 1998, in spite of the recent financial crisis, the NIEs represent probably the only economies in the developing world which seem likely to catch up with the industrialised countries of Europe and North America in terms of technology, infrastructure and income per capita in the foreseeable future.

Behind the NIEs, four member countries of the Association of South-East Asian Nations (ASEAN) – Indonesia, Thailand and Malaysia and to some extent the Philippines – have shown a consistently good economic performance which is matched by very few other developing countries in the world. By reducing their dependency on raw materials and agriculture, they have built up substantial manufacturing capacities and capabilities, backed up by an improving infrastructure. Today, the standard of living in these countries compares favourably with that of the overwhelming majority of people living in the Third World. Vietnam, which more recently joined the ASEAN group, has shown equally high growth rates in the 1990s and is trying to catch up with the other members.

Comparing its own stagnation with economic developments in neighbouring countries, China decided at the end of the 1970s to open up and welcome foreign technology, foreign traders and foreign investors. With pragmatism increasingly overruling ideology, China became the fastest growing economy in the region during the 1980s and 1990s (though admittedly starting from a very low base).

Japan, the NIEs, the five ASEAN members, the four mentioned above plus Vietnam (the ASEAN 5), and China represent for us Asia Pacific. It is this group of countries which enticed a number of observers to talk about the coming 'Pacific Century'. This group of countries is slightly broader than that of the high-performing Asian economies which the World Bank used for its major study of *The East Asian Miracle*.[1]

The term Asia Pacific is now widely used by economists, journalists and business professionals, though it is often unclear which countries are referred to. Admittedly, it stretches geographic credibility considerably to imply that Singapore lies on the shores of the Pacific, while it is in fact thousands of miles away, but the overall acceptance of the term is convenient for this book.

The eleven countries in our definition of Asia Pacific do not cover the whole geographic area of Asia which is closest to the Pacific. North Korea, Laos, Cambodia, Papua New Guinea, Brunei and Macao have been omitted from this study either because their economies are too small or because the experience of foreign firms in them is too limited.

The division of Asia Pacific into the four groups (Japan, NIEs, the ASEAN 5 and China) reflects economic development patterns rather than political affiliations. Singapore is a member of the ASEAN, but has characteristics more like those of a newly industrialised country. We therefore group this nation together with South Korea, Taiwan and Hong Kong, though the latter are increasingly considered parts of what is called Greater China.

Asia Pacific by no means represents a group of homogeneous economic or political systems. National and business cultures vary significantly and macro-economic data show extreme differences. In 1996 Indonesia had 197 million people with an income per capita of US$1080; neighbouring Singapore had a population of three million with an average income of US$30 550. Japan represents 17 per cent of the global economy, but has only 2.2 per cent of the world's population; China's population, on the other hand, makes up more than a fifth of the world's population but contributes only 3.0 per cent to the world's economy. Officially at least, government socialist principles still determine the fate of the Chinese economy, while Hong Kong's *laissez-faire* policies have turned its economy into a capitalist's paradise.

In no other part of the world does one find such variations, whether in Europe, Latin America or Africa; yet, despite all these differences, common characteristics can be found. First, in all societies there is the will to improve the individual's economic well-being through one's own efforts. This can be seen in a high degree of entrepreneurship in the region, an apparent determination to progress, high savings rates and substantial private investment in assets and in education. Second, business-oriented and outward-looking governments support wealth creation through moderate intervention and economic growth-oriented policies. Third, effort and results are shared within the nation, the local community, the firm or the family. This is documented in relatively even income distribution (compared to Latin America, for example) and achieved through consensus-oriented policy making mechanisms. Fourth, there is a vaguely defined emerging feeling of 'Asianness' which can be best described as not being Caucasian, African or Latin American. The increasing cultural, economic and political links among Asian societies support this trend, which is facilitated by regional media and growing contacts between the various communities.

It is this cultural dimension which justifies the exclusion of Australia and New Zealand from the Asia Pacific region. Economically, these two countries have become deeply intertwined with the region but cannot claim to be Asian in culture or to show many of the other characteristics of Asia Pacific. On the other hand, because of its lack of close economic and political ties with the region India is not considered part of Asia Pacific, and in geographical terms its inclusion would create conceptual problems, too. Like China, India has been inward-looking for many decades and has opened up towards the outside world only fairly recently. Lacking the extensive family ties of the

Chinese across Asia, however, India has not shown much interest in becoming more closely involved in the developments of Asia Pacific.

Western firms, like economists, find it difficult to determine which countries to include in the region. Some follow our rather narrow definition of Asia Pacific, whereas others include Australia and New Zealand (although less out of conviction that they are part of the region than due to the lack of other linkages). Alternatively, the much broader term of 'Asia' is used. There is no consensus, however, on what comprises such a region geographically, politically or economically. For some European observers Asia begins with Turkey and ends with New Zealand to the south and Japan or even Siberia to the north. If the new nations such as Kyrgystan and Kazakhstan are included, this could be taken as Asia in the broadest sense. From a business perspective such a broad definition does not seem to be practical.

In this book we will therefore deal only with Asia Pacific. It is only a part, though by far the most dynamic part, of Asia; and it is in itself extremely large. With 1835 million inhabitants, the region represents 32 per cent of the world's population. Geographically, it reaches from the cold deserts in the north of China to the tropical belt covered by the ASEAN countries. A direct flight from Singapore to Tokyo takes more than seven hours; the distance from Paris to New York is shorter than a trip from one extremity of Indonesia to the other. As the millennium nears its end, Asia Pacific represents, however, only 25 per cent of the world's output. This figure is bound to increase, but not overnight.

Intra-regional cooperation

In comparison with Europe and North America, Asia Pacific has had much less success in institutionalising economic cooperation, let alone political collaboration. Historical legacies, gross disparities between the countries and different ties with nations outside the region have hindered the emergence of a common voice in international negotiations and of a consensus on a broad range of important issues.

Among the many initiatives towards closer cooperation the APEC (Asia Pacific Economic Cooperation) grouping has recently gained some weight. Structured as a debating club whose decisions are not binding for anybody, rather than as a negotiating body, it is a rather toothless institution. Representing 50 per cent of the world's population, 50 per cent of the world's output and 40 per cent of world trade it is closer to a mini-World Trade Organisation than a regional forum based on common interests. Its membership includes the USA and Canada, heavyweights in their own right and certainly not Asian, thus denying APEC the status of a truly Asia Pacific body. No wonder that some Asians, and the government of Malaysia in particular, feel that their efforts to promote greater Asian unity have been hijacked.

ASEAN was formed in 1967 and for many years comprised Thailand, Malaysia, Singapore, Indonesia, the Philippines and Brunei. Set up as a group for economic, social and cultural cooperation, it evolved as a tightly knit anti-communist group, effective mainly in security matters. Despite manifold attempts to foster intra-ASEAN trade and investments, the countries in this sub-region continue to do most of their foreign business with outside partners and not with each other. If trade with Singapore is excluded, the ASEAN countries conduct only 5 per cent of their trade with each other. With communism fading and Vietnam shortly to become a new member rather than a common enemy, ASEAN at the beginning of the 1990s ran the risk of becoming irrelevant. It therefore launched AFTA, the ASEAN Free Trade Association, which is supposed to convert the area into a free trade zone within 15 years. As many exceptions and exemptions have been built into the last agreement, AFTA cannot be expected to give much of a boost to the economies concerned or to greatly influence the investment decisions of firms. The admittance of two more new members (Myanmar and Laos) did not add to the clout of ASEAN. On the contrary, the strong opposition of the outside world to human rights abuses in Myanmar and the strict adherence of the group to non-interference in the internal affairs of member states have weakened ASEAN's standing in the world community.

The failure of politicians and government officials to bind their countries together contrasts sharply with the increase of business activities across borders. Growing intra-regional trade and investments have led to a *de facto* economic interdependence in Asia Pacific which was neither anticipated nor is fully appreciated by bureaucrats. The close links between China, Taiwan and Hong Kong are the best example of the conflicting interests between governments and business communities.

The leading forces of the economic integration of the region are the Overseas Chinese with their nationless enterprises and multinational firms, mainly of Japanese and more recently also of Korean and Taiwanese origin. The Overseas Chinese are the dominant foreign investors in China, and Hong Kong and China are each other's largest trading partner. Taiwanese and Korean firms are important investors in Vietnam, while Singaporeans play a major role in Malaysia and the Philippines. Overall, Japan's multinationals, originally led by the general trading houses, are the largest foreign investors in Asia Pacific, supplying most manufactured imports and buying large quantities of goods from the region, though not necessarily for import into Japan. Statistics show that these intra-regional activities are growing considerably, a trend which leads some observers to talk about the emergence of a third regional bloc in the world.

A careful interpretation of trade and investment data in Asia Pacific does not entirely support such a view.[2] While intra-regional activities are growing, so are foreign trade and investment with other parts of the world. The US remains by far the most important export market for most of the countries in the region, and will probably remain so for quite some time to come. The economic exchanges with European countries often still exceed those with neighbouring countries. Japan's engagement in the region is vital for most of developing Asia, which has become increasingly dependent on its funds and technology. But Japan, still geared towards the USA in terms of exports and foreign investment, is much less dependent on the region. The role of Singapore and Hong Kong as trans-shipment centres also leads to artificially high intra-regional trade figures. Any increase of activity within the growth triangle of Singapore, Johore (Malaysia) and Batam (Indonesia) would be seen as a boost of intra-Asian trade and investment, when in reality it is just an integration of adjacent localities. Similarly, the intensification of exchange between Hong Kong and southern China is statistically an increase in foreign trade, but *de facto* is a prologue to the full integration of Hong Kong into China.

Much of the trade and investment flow within Asia Pacific today is based on a division of labour in the sense that certain activities of the value chain are carried out in one country, and other activities in a different country. Frequently, the country of destination and final consumption is a third one, more often than not the USA. For example, Matsushita's 14 plants in Malaysia are financed by the Japanese and induce the exports of machinery, parts and components from Japan, although their main objective is the establishment of a 'triangle trade' to the USA in order to capitalise on Malaysia's Generalised System of Preferences (GSP) status and the absence of quotas for certain products from Japan. While statistically such investments and the exports from Japan count as intra-regional trade, it is questionable whether such projects truly lead to closer integration of the region.

Defining sub-regions

Dividing Asia Pacific into sub-regions helps us to avoid making statements which are too generalised and highlights the differences between the sub-regions themselves. At the same time such division provides a better base for comparing countries within a sub-region and for delineating those features which distinguish them. From a strategic point of view, sub-regions also make it easier to think about implementation issues.

While a common (and natural) feature of groupings is geographical proximity, this is by no means the only criterion which should be used. It is the underlying purpose of the sub-region which determines the other criteria to be applied. The identification of similar purchasing patterns requires a different sub-regional categorisation from the choice of a regional manufacturing site or the possibility of sharing scarce human resources in research or accounting across several countries. To facilitate understanding of the region, pure economic criteria allow us to divide Asia Pacific into four sub-regions (although in Chapter 3 we will reduce this from a marketing point of view to three sub-regions).

As no criterion is universally effective, firms take a pragmatic approach to the issue of sub-regions. In most cases internal reasoning (reducing costs or shared experience) supersedes the macro-economic and political rationale (similar economic stage or political system). But the division of Asia Pacific into sub-regions is rarely non-controversial. There is no argument about Japan being different from the rest of Asia and therefore constituting a sub-region on its own. When Australasia (Australia and New Zealand) is included in the region, it is equally treated as a separate sub-region. There is also relative clarity about South-East Asia as a sub-region which generally includes Singapore, often Vietnam, sometimes Myanmar, but not necessarily the Philippines. The case of China is much more difficult to deal with. Its size and complexity would justify treating China as a separate sub-region. The 'Chineseness' of Hong Kong and Taiwan and their increasing economic and political integration might well warrant a grouping of all three economies as a sub-region called Greater China. In this case, Korea will be isolated, whether as South Korea or in combination with the North or as part of a more distant future grouping together with some northern parts of China and the Russian East. Linking Korea with Japan is a possibility in some industries such as shipbuilding, but one which neither the Koreans nor the Japanese accept easily. Alternatively, the region can be sub-divided into South-East and North-East Asia, the latter including or excluding Japan.

As can be seen, sub-regionalisation does not lend itself easily to neat or durable solutions. Overlaps are the rule, as are disputes over the exclusion or inclusion of particular countries in a given sub-region. Firms will have to remain flexible, finding solutions which fit their own needs and changing groupings as their own requirements shift.

Links with the outside world

During the first half of the twentieth century much of Asia Pacific was under colonial rule, or at least very strong foreign influence. Malaysia and Singapore, then still united as Malaya, were British; Indonesia was ruled by the Dutch. The Americans governed the Philippines, the French Vietnam, and the Japanese Korea and Taiwan. Colonial rule came to an end in the decade after the Second World War throughout the region except for Malaya, from which the British withdrew at a later stage, and Hong Kong, which they left in 1997.

While the Europeans have generally retreated from the region, the USA has expanded its influence further, primarily through political and military means. Japan, which occupied most of Asia during the war, had to withdraw completely. Since the 1960s and 1970s it has re-established itself in the region through trade and investment links.

Relationships between the now independent countries and their former rulers are mixed. The Dutch had difficult times in Indonesia, as did the Americans in the Philippines. While the British found cooperation with Malaysia difficult at times, the Japanese are occasionally exposed to unfriendly gestures in Korea. As a new generation replaces those with direct experience of colonial times and occupation, relationships are more influenced by today's economic and political realities, and shaped by international media and tourism. Dutch and French have become irrelevant languages in Indonesia and Vietnam, just as Spanish did a long time ago in the Philippines. English remains the dominant language of business in Asia Pacific even among Asians, just as the US dollar has remained the most frequently used currency in the region.

This is a paradox, bearing in mind the overwhelming influence of Japan on most of the countries. Japan is the largest foreign investor in the region; the largest exporter to most of the countries; and the largest provider of technology, foreign capital and foreign aid. Among the foreign firms in Asia Pacific, the Japanese employ by far the largest number of locals. But the USA remains economically strongly committed, too. About 50 per cent of all foreign investment in Japan comes from the USA, and in many other countries in the region the Americans are ranked among the three largest foreign investors (see Table 1.1).

Exports have for a long time been a major contributor to growth in the region. Since 1965 exports have increased by 10 per cent per annum, at a rate faster than recorded anywhere else in the world. As a result Asia Pacific's share in world exports grew from 11 per cent in 1965 to 25 per cent in 1996. Japan remains by far the largest exporter from the region, though its share in total Asian exports is dropping. This is due to the trade activities of Korean and Chinese firms on the one hand, and to the shift of export-oriented manufacturing operations from Japan into other countries of the region, on the other (Table 1.2).

Table 1.1 Ranking of Foreign Investors in Asia Pacific*

Host country	No. 1 foreign investors	No. 2 foreign investors	No. 3 foreign investors
Japan	USA	Netherlands	Switzerland
South Korea	Japan	USA	Netherlands
Taiwan	Japan	USA	Netherlands
Hong Kong	Japan	USA	UK
Singapore	USA	Japan	UK
Indonesia	Japan	USA	UK
Thailand	Japan	USA	UK
Malaysia	Japan	USA	UK
Philippines	USA	Japan	UK
China	Japan	USA	UK

*Cumulative Direct Foreign Investment; the picture is somewhat distorted as regional investors (from Hong Kong, Taiwan, China and Singapore) are excluded, though they play a very important role as investors in Hong Kong, China and all the ASEAN countries. The true origin of such neighbourly investment is often unclear. Foreign investment is often redirected domestic investment.[3]

Table 1.2 Country Shares in World Trade in Goods (1996)

World	Exports (US$ billion) 5 266	Share of World Trade 100.00
Hong Kong	181	3.4
China	151	2.9
Taiwan	116	2.2
South Korea	131	2.5
Singapore	125	2.4
Malaysia	78	1.5
Thailand	56	1.1
Indonesia	48	0.9
Philippines	21	0.4
Developing Asia	907	17.2
Japan	411	7.8
Asia Pacific	1 318	25.0

Data include re-exports, thereby considerably inflating the figures for Hong Kong and Singapore.

SOURCE: IMF, *Direction of Trade Statistics Yearbook*, 1997.

By far the most important export destination outside the region has been the USA, which runs a major trade deficit with Asia Pacific, while Japan, as the largest exporter to the region, runs a major trade surplus (see Table 1.3). Because of the market opportunities which the USA has to offer, the Americans exert significant power over the trade policies of the countries in the region. The endless trade disputes between Japan and the USA are the most prominent example of US pressure and influence. Past arguments over the extension of the Most Favoured Nation (MFN) status of China, intellectual property rights in Taiwan and Thailand, and labour unions in Indonesia have demonstrated the dependence of these countries on the USA for purely economic gain.

Table 1.3 Main Trading Partners (1995)

Imports		*Exports*	
Into:	*From:*	*From:*	*To:*
Japan	USA	Japan	USA
S. Korea	Japan	S. Korea	USA
Taiwan	Japan	Taiwan	USA (Hong Kong)
Hong Kong	China (Japan)	Hong Kong	China (USA)
Singapore	Japan	Singapore	USA
Malaysia	Japan	Malaysia	USA (Singapore)
Indonesia	Japan	Indonesia	Japan
Thailand	Japan	Thailand	USA
Philippines	Japan	Philippines	USA
China	Japan	China	Hong Kong (Japan)

NB: Second largest trading partners shown in brackets.
Source: Asian Development Bank, *Key Indicators*, 1996, IMF, *Direction of Trade Statistics Yearbook*, 1997.

As the only remaining superpower at the turn of the millennium and with a major military presence in Japan and South Korea, the USA also provides security to Asia Pacific. As such the USA balances the influence of Japan and the growing assertiveness of China. This gives Americans additional weight in government negotiations and explains why their taking a leading role in APEC has been accepted.

The strong influence of the USA also casts a shadow over any attempt by Asian leaders to oppose the West, and the Americans in particular, on fundamental issues. It is in the cultural, not the economic or the political sphere, where Asia may start to establish itself as being different and independent from the West. We shall explore this further in Chapter 11 at the end of the book.

THE ROLE OF ASIA PACIFIC IN THE WORLD ECONOMY

Economic size compared

The easiest way to compare the size of economies is to look at their gross national product (GNP). This is basically derived from adding up all the income

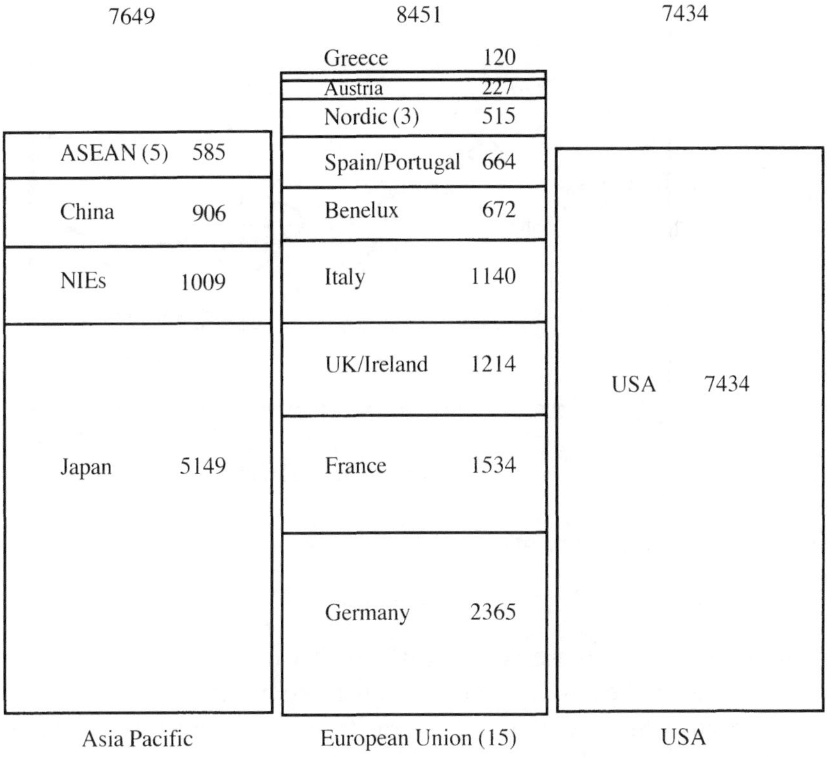

SOURCE: World Bank, *World Development Indicators* (1998).

Figure 1.1 Total GNP 1996 in US$ billion

which the various participants in the economy receive in terms of wages and salaries, rents, interest, profits and so on, during the course of the year. This income is spent on private or public consumption, or on investments, or is saved. Consumption and investments represent the demand for products and services in the economy. Income saved is channelled back as demand, as long as the savings are given to financial institutions which in turn lend to domestic creditors. This simplified economic model allows us to use the data on GNP as overall indicators of demand in a given country.

According to the World Bank, the total GNP of the Asia Pacific region in 1996 amounted to about US$7.65 trillion. This is about 3 per cent more than the GNP of the USA, or 10 per cent less than the sum of the GNP of all the 15 members of the European Union (see Figure 1.1).

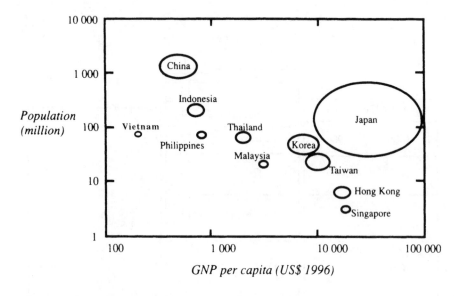

GNP per capita (US$ 1996)

SOURCE: World Bank, *World Development Indicators*, 1998.

Figure 1.2   Economic Size of Asia Pacific Countries (1996)

The problem with these comparisons is that the USA is a reasonably homogeneous market, and even the European countries can be considered fairly unified, while the eleven Asia Pacific markets remain distinct and separate. Geographic distances and differences in industrial sophistication, purchasing power and consumer behaviour are substantial. In Asia Pacific, the multinational firm is faced with eleven, instead of one unified or a few combined, markets.

On the chart (shown in Figure 1.2) the markets are positioned according to income per capita and size of population. These are the two most important criteria, at least as far as demand for consumer goods is concerned. The size of the ellipse for each country indicates the total size of the economy (GNP).

Two observations can be made. First of all, nine out of the eleven countries more or less follow a line which begins with China in the upper left-hand corner and descends to Singapore in the bottom right-hand corner. The exceptions are Japan and Vietnam. This demonstrates that most of the individual Asian countries either have a large population, but not much money to spend, or have a small population with more purchasing power.

Second, the size of the individual economies is relatively small. Japan is again the exception, representing two-thirds of Asia Pacific's GNP. The GNP of Singapore or Malaysia would probably turn out to be not much larger than that of a German city such as Cologne or Munich, and Indonesia's economy is probably smaller than that of Paris would be if any of these cities existed as independent units and produced the appropriate statistics.

These two observations do not render Asia Pacific an attractive region for the Western firm, always excepting Japan which, however, is often perceived as a market closed to foreign firms. Small separate markets with a unique market structure and organised by a set of specific government rules often make local independent operations infeasible due to the high management attention required and consequent high overheads.

There are, however, several reasons why the above observations do not give a complete and therefore correct assessment of the region. Figures such as these have to be interpreted with great care, even if they are produced by international institutions such as the World Bank, the International Monetary Fund (IMF) or the Asian Development Bank. We will look at this point again later on. In addition, the prospects for growth, particularly in the developing countries of Asia Pacific, call for a long-term perspective rather than a static view. This will be discussed in the following section. There is also the trend towards regionalisation in Asia which may reduce some of the 'separateness' of the individual economies. This will also be explored later on.

Finally, the value of an economy is not only derived from the size of its market. Asia Pacific remains an important supplier of natural resources such as tin, rubber, edible oil, crude oil and gas. Human resources in the form of cheap labour are increasingly gaining in importance and form the second supply base. A third source, technology in the broadest sense, is recently emerging, though concentrated in Japan for the time being. Purely competitive reasons may also call for a heavy commitment to the region which is the home territory of Asian competitors who are increasingly becoming household names in the USA and Europe. And as the attractiveness of the region is reassessed among global companies the need to pre-empt, match or follow competitors is growing. These strategic issues will be taken up in further chapters.

Purchasing power parities

Only four of the eleven economies of Asia Pacific are considered high income economies by the World Bank, and only two, Japan and Korea, are currently members of the Organisation for Economic Cooperation and Development (OECD), the club of the rich countries. China and Vietnam are low income economies with the rest belonging to the middle income category. As a rule, countries at a lower stage of development have a larger informal sector than the rich countries. This is the part of the economy in which products and services are exchanged without monetary equivalent or without being recorded in official statistics. An example would be farmers or part-time farmers producing for their own family or community (a common feature in China but exceptional in Japan or Hong Kong). As a consequence, government statistics of developing countries tend to underestimate economic activity. There may be an additional tendency for these countries deliberately to underreport their economic size, as lower income figures make them more eligible for foreign aid and international trade concessions. Both phenomena call for an upward adjustment of official data.

To compare national economies with one another, all statistics collected in local currencies have to be converted into one single currency, normally the US dollar. Countries with soft currencies but high growth rates may therefore see their dollar-denominated GNP in international statistics go down despite an impressive growth record. China, for example, despite a dramatic growth in output and demand which has continued for more than a decade, shows up in World Bank statistics as a stagnating economy from the beginning of the 1980s to the beginning of the 1990s.

Theoretically, when economies open up for international trade, exchange rates will start to move towards a point where price levels across countries are more or less in line, at least over longer periods. In practice, this equalisation effect may occur for prices of internationally traded goods, but not for non-traded goods such as housing, transport services or education. As a result we observe major price differentials for those essential goods across countries. By and large, price levels in developing countries are lower than in developed countries, because governments have a vital interest in keeping prices for essential products and services low, and may even subsidise them. A hundred dollars in local currency in Jakarta or Shanghai will therefore buy considerably more local goods than the same amount in Japan or the USA.

To correct these shortcomings international institutions like the United Nations Development Programme (UNDP), the IMF and the World Bank have recently started to recalculate income and GNP figures using purchasing power parities (PPP). The results show staggering deviations from the figures published so far based on traditional data, especially for countries such as China and Indonesia (Table 1.4).

On the whole, the wide income differentials between the rich and the poor are narrowing considerably, although they do not disappear entirely. Returning from income calculations to the size of the economy as a whole, the need for a reassessment of the traditional data, especially of developing countries, is becoming apparent (see Figure 1.3). Taking PPP into account, China is judged by the World Bank to be already the second largest economy in the world (behind the USA and ahead of Japan). The calculation of PPP data is difficult due to a number of methodological and statistical problems. However, even if the new PPP data are somewhat inaccurate, they still describe the activities in developing countries better than the former international statistics. In fact, taking into account China's consumption of commodities such as steel and cement, or various food items and consumer durables such as bicycles and television sets, its ranking as one of the largest economies in the world seems to be appropriate. Similarly the revaluation of the size of the Indonesian, Thai or Philippine economies seems justified, as would be the devaluation of the size of the Japanese economy.

Table 1.4 Income Comparison 1996 in US$

Country	GNP per Capita	GNP per Capita PPP
Japan	40 940	23 420
Singapore	30 550	26 910
Hong Kong	24 290	24 260
Taiwan*	14 000	N/A
South Korea	10 610	13 080
Malaysia	4 370	10 390
Thailand	2 960	6 700
Philippines	1 160	3 550
Indonesia	1 080	3 310
China	750	3 330
In comparison:		
Switzerland	44 350	26 340
USA	28 020	28 020
France	26 270	21 510
India	380	1 580

*Authors' estimates.
SOURCE: World Bank, *World Development Indicators* (1998).

The assessment of the size of an economy based on PPP conversion basically measures comparable quantities of output. For the foreign firm this is the first indication of the volume of business to be expected in a given country. It also allows for a more useful comparison of per capita consumption between countries. According to PPP data, the average Greek, for example, earns about 20 per cent more than the average Malaysian, while measurements based on traditional data suggest that the Malaysian earns less than 40 per cent of the income of a Greek.

While these considerations are important in estimating local production and sales volumes, PPP statistics lose their relevance once local profits have to be converted into home country currencies. At this point current exchange rates matter, and a lower price level in the host economy no longer counts. A similar situation exists when imports into a given country have to be paid

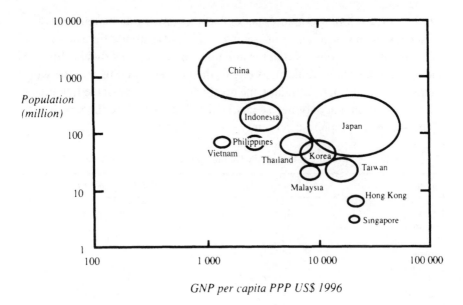

GNP per capita PPP US$ 1996

Source: World Bank, *World Development Indicators* (1998).

Figure 1.3   Economic Size of Asia Pacific Based on PPP

for in hard currency, or investment decisions have to be taken based on revenues and expenses linked with both local and foreign currencies. In other words, traditional statistics do underestimate the real size of the economies of the developing countries of Asia Pacific considerably. PPP statistics make appropriate upward adjustments and are useful for measuring economic welfare, but accounts of multinational firms cannot accept anything other than values based on current exchange rates.

Growth as a driver

By any standard of comparison, the economies of Asia Pacific have grown very fast over the last decades. The notable exception has been the Philippines which complies least with what we have described as the typical societal characteristics of the region; it is sometimes called a group of Latin American islands which drifted over to Asia. The other special case is Japan which grew dramatically in the 1960s and 1970s, showed a good performance in the 1980s, but lost its growth momentum in the 1990s. Over the long period 1965–96, the country nevertheless was number 12 in the ranking of the fastest growing economies of the world. Seven of the Asia Pacific countries were listed by

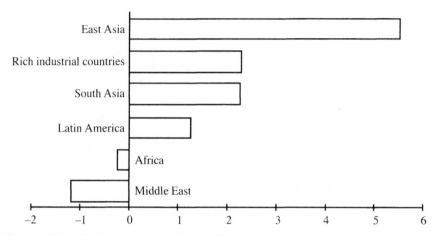

SOURCE: World Bank, *Development Report* (1998).

Figure 1.4   GDP Per Person – Annual Average % Change, 1965–96

the World Bank among the 'Top Ten'. Taiwan, omitted from all World Bank statistics for political reasons, would have been the eighth.

High growth rates are generally seen as positive, as long as they are not so high as to cause an economy to overheat, a phenomenon which occurred in the mid-90s in a number of Asian countries and arguably led to the start of the Asian crisis in 1997/8. During the years 1965–96, a period of more than three decades, Asia Pacific grew considerably faster than any other region in the world. A long-term rate of over 7.2 per cent, which would allow the total size of an economy to double within a decade, was seen as normal in developing Asia, though unrealistic for Japan or any other mature economy in the world.

Income growth per capita is smaller due to population growth. However, as population growth has decreased in the region over the last few years, the differences between the two growth rates are less prominent than in other parts of the world, such as Africa or Latin America. On a per capita income base the differences between East Asia (excluding Japan) and other parts of the world were thus even more impressive (see Figure 1.4).

For business, the prospects for the future are at least as important as past performance. In a rare show of unity, international institutions, Asian governments, business forecasters and scholars around the world were optimistic about the region's future in the middle of the 1990s. The World Bank, for example, foresaw growth in the developing countries of Asia Pacific of nearly 8 per cent a year until 2005. Any growth projection of this kind implied that Asia Pacific as a region would overtake both the USA and the European Union within the next few years. Based on PPP statistics, it already had.

At the end of the 1990s such growth scenarios had become unpopular, with the exception perhaps of those comparing China with the USA. Governments, businessmen and academics were concerned about the crisis and the prospects for countries and companies to recover from the negative growth rates experienced and losses suffered (see the discussion in the section below).

The timing of the return to high growth rates is not a macro-economic or political question only. It is of immediate relevance for competitors and their strategies.

High growth rates in an economy or in a specific industry often lead to a reduced level of rivalry in the marketplace. Firms rarely resort to cut-throat competitive behaviour when sales grow fast and all suppliers show a satisfactory profit performance. As a consequence, industry-wide price cutting or advertising battles remained exceptions in Asia Pacific in the past. This contrasts with fierce competition in stagnating or shrinking markets where the gains of one firm lead to the losses of another. Everything else being equal, firms in fast growing markets should therefore be able to reap higher profits than comparable operations in stagnating markets.

High growth rates also lead to rapid changes in the constellation of the market, be it the structure of competition, the market segmentation, or the use of the marketing mix. This volatility creates new market openings (that is, opportunities for outsiders to enter a market at a later stage). There are far fewer such opportunities in a stagnating or shrinking market in which participants pursue defensive strategies and fight off new participants vigorously.

The effects of growth on different parts of the economy differ considerably, with some parts benefiting disproportionately. In consumer goods, the growth rate influences the speed with which thresholds of consumption are reached by new groups of households or individuals. A higher rate of income growth will move consumers faster from transistor radios to television sets and video equipment, or from bicycles to motorbikes and cars. A slower growth rate will still result in volume increases for given items such as soap, but the upgrading towards shampoos or other products of a higher order will take place much more slowly.

Growth in the domestic market provides opportunities for local production which will experience scale effects as soon as large volumes can be achieved. This enables suppliers to lower the prices of products and services, thereby moving the threshold of consumption closer to the income level of the consumer. It acts as a growth accelerator for certain markets and can lead to explosive growth rates for certain goods (see Figure 1.5). Industrial goods, whether raw materials, parts and components or machinery, which are needed

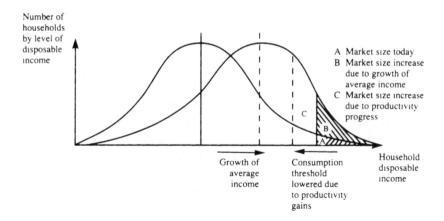

SOURCE: *McKinsey Quarterly* (1995).

Figure 1.5 Emerging Consumption Curve

to produce those fast growing consumer goods markets, are similarly benefiting from reaching new thresholds quickly.

To restart growth and to enable growth to be sustained, governments in Asia Pacific have realised that substantial infrastructure investments are needed in the sectors of energy, transportation and telecommunications. Starting from a low base, all countries in the region except Japan have first of all to make up for past neglect of their infrastructure. As they assume growth will accelerate again, they also need to provide for additional demand for electricity, aircraft, railways and roads, and communication services. As a consequence products and services which can unblock these bottlenecks and help further development have priority on the shopping list of most governments in the region even in difficult times. In OECD countries, on the other hand, the infrastructure is mainly in place and does not need substantial expansion due to low growth rates. Not surprisingly, most suppliers of infrastructure equipment or services are vying for participation in this market, which in many sectors makes up for more than 50 per cent of the world demand. For these firms, absence from the region is not an option.

THE ASIAN CRISIS

The unravelling of the miracle

While for most observers the Asian crisis started with the unpegging of the Thai baht from the US dollar on 2 July 1997, the causes triggering the spectacular events of the following year are to be found at a much earlier period.

In 1985, under the Plaza Accord, the G7 nations decided to halt and reverse the US dollar's rise against the major currencies, the yen and the Deutsche Mark. The foreign exchange markets duly followed and the dollar declined steadily over the next ten years. As most of the currencies of the Asian developing countries were closely linked to the dollar, these currencies softened as well, making their exports more competitive. The resulting high growth in exports led automatically to a boom in the export-oriented economies of Asia Pacific. This was accelerated by the increasing value of the Japanese yen. Japanese consumers finally started to import more from other Asian countries, and Japanese manufacturers increasingly shifted their now uncompetitive export operations from Japan to Asia, thereby contributing to the build-up of production facilities in the region.

The boom in developing Asia and the prospects for future growth created an environment of over-optimism and over-investment. Success which had come relatively easily was now – in the second half of the 1990s – taken for granted. Foreign banks and foreign investors poured money into the region in search of higher yields, thereby enabling domestic banks and investors to finance their projects easily. Financial deregulation which had been introduced gradually in a number of countries made the massive transfer of funds possible.

In January 1994, the Chinese government devalued the renminbi in conjunction with a simplification of the foreign exchange system. In 1995 the dollar finally hit the bottom and started to increase in value once more while the Japanese yen began to soften. Asian exports consequently became relatively more expensive and their growth slowed. At the same time the boom in the region sucked in ever increasing imports – from machinery and elevators, to Mercedes Benz cars and French cognac.

In the first half of 1997, foreign exchange traders launched their first attacks on the Thai baht, but only on 2 July that year did the Thai government realise that the peg linking the baht to the dollar had become unsustainable in view of a large current account deficit and shrinking foreign exchange reserves.

From Thailand financial turmoil quickly spread to Malaysia, Indonesia, the Philippines and later South Korea. The immediate effect in these countries was a severe devaluation of currencies and a massive drop in stock market values.

More importantly, many of even the most prominent financial institutions, conglomerates and stand-alone firms found themselves in a sea of debt. As it turned out, many of their loans and projects had been undertaken without due consideration of market risks. The result was the build-up of enormous over-capacities in many industries across the region, from empty office blocks to idle car factories. In raising money for their new investments businessmen had neglected the basic rules of financial risk management: debt/equity ratios of 4:1 had become the norm rather than the exception. Funds borrowed short term were invested long term. In addition a large percentage of those funds were raised in foreign currency, particularly US dollars, but were invested in domestic projects expected to produce a stream of income denominated in local currency.

All of this worked well – until the moment that banks, especially foreign banks, refused to roll over short-term funds any longer. The depreciation of Asian currencies inflicted a heavy toll on both the financial and corporate sectors which did not have incoming cash flows in foreign currencies to match their foreign debt service obligations. The domestic currency value of their foreign debt had ballooned dramatically and led to substantial losses.

Equity investments from abroad which had flooded into these five countries – Thailand, Malaysia, Indonesia, the Philippines and Korea – slowed down when the currencies started to slide and the banks stopped financing. Direct investment in 1997 remained at almost the same level as in the preceding year. Portfolio investment, however, that previously had exceeded direct investment flows by almost 100 per cent, turned negative. Commercial banks, attracted by high growth rates and pressured by peers not to miss out on the Asian boom, had provided the region with easy credit of more than US$50 billion in both 1995 and 1996. The same banks in 1997 took fright and withdrew US$27 billion.

Governments, themselves caught in the strong belief in an ever expanding economy, had neglected good housekeeping. Current accounts were out of control, and supervision of the financial sector was weak or non-existent. The link between their currencies and the dollar had been falsely taken as a quasi-government guarantee to keep rates steady. Senior officials' vested interests in the economy made governments reluctant to undertake corrective measures quickly. The IMF and World Bank, hanging on to their earlier assessment of the region as the 'Asian miracle', reacted late and imposed harsh austerity and tight money policies with high interest rates on Thailand, Indonesia and South Korea, thereby deepening the financial crisis.

The immediate impact and consequences

In the second half of 1998 the situation in Asia Pacific was looking grim. What had still been considered a short-term problem by the IMF in November 1997 had turned into a major structural financial crisis. Asia was drowned in debt. In both South-East Asia and South Korea the combination of high debt/equity ratios, reliance on foreign denominated loans and massively devalued local currencies had rendered a very high percentage of large financial institutions and manufacturers effectively bankrupt, though only a few admitted to it. The term 'negative equity' became widely used in Asian capitals.

Interestingly, the debt problem was mainly centred on the private sector, though governments were implicated through governmental banks and guarantees. Funds flowing in from the IMF and World Bank were also the responsibility of the public sector. Up to mid-1998 many companies had continued to evade bankruptcy through the reluctance of lenders to initiate legal proceedings to enforce repayment or closure, the lack of suitable bankruptcy laws, and the application of creative accounting techniques.

As time passed the financial crisis had evolved into an economic crisis. Financial institutions, themselves burdened with many bad loans and heavy foreign exchange losses, stopped lending and shortened credit lines even to their best customers with impeccable debt service track records. Manufacturers ran out of working capital. Foreign banks refused to assist even those who exported to hard currency countries. Operations were reduced or came to a standstill, workers were dismissed. The Asian crisis started to inflict social pain on large parts of the population in terms of falling standards of living. The first hunger crisis for decades was reported in South-East Asia. After unprecedented high growth rates over three decades, unprecedented high negative growth rates were forecast for the year 1998.

In May 1998, the IMF predicted for the first time moderately negative growth rates for the affected ASEAN countries and South Korea. For 1999 positive growth rates of 2.5 per cent and 4.1 per cent were forecast.[4] Later in 1998, however, most observers considered those views as too optimistic. World-wide financial repercussions were beginning to be felt, and negatively affecting confidence in other developing countries as far apart as Russia, South Africa and Brazil. The impact on the advanced economies, however, was modest due to solid growth, particularly in the USA.

Assessing the debt situation, it became increasingly clear that countries like Indonesia would not be able to return all the loans they had absorbed. As borrowers were private institutions or individuals, the support of the World Bank and IMF was necessarily limited, whether or not they had sufficient funds. In other words, foreign lenders could see that they had to write off a substantial amount of loans and offer debt relief. Simply lengthening maturities and rolling-over loans would not be enough. Lenders facing these losses were primarily European and Japanese banks, the latter themselves in deep trouble at home.

The amount of bad loans accumulated by Japanese banks was unprecedented. In comparison, the problems in South-East Asia and South Korea appeared almost insignificant. The Japanese debt crisis was similar to that in Asia, in that it was the result of reckless lending particularly to real estate developers and construction companies during the 'bubble economy' in Japan at the end of the 1980s. But it was also different, as Japanese banks had lent to Japanese companies without much involvement of foreign institutions or foreign currencies. It was, thus, a home-grown problem of epic proportion. But Japan, unlike the rest of Asia, can boast other strong economic indicators. The country has the largest current account surplus and the highest foreign exchange reserves in the world. It owns more than half of the world's net savings.

Even if we assume a very large debt write-off by foreign lenders, the fundamental question to be raised is how long it could take the economies of the affected countries to pay off the remaining debt. For South-East Asia and South Korea the repayment of debt will determine medium-term, if not long-term, prospects. The money paid to lenders abroad cannot be spent on consumption and investment, thereby holding back growth-inducing demand. In Japan, the question concerns the distribution of the debt burden rather than the affordability of debt repayment itself. Financial institutions have to be kept afloat even if the government, and thus taxpayers, have to pay for it.

The end of the crisis in developing Asia will be in sight only when funds from private investors start to flow back into the region. Partial debt forgiveness has to come beforehand. Efforts must also be made to start repaying a substantial part of outstanding foreign loans. The amount of capital needed to lead into a true recovery and a subsequent return to growth is, however, too large to be generated domestically, even bearing in mind the high saving rates and newly positive trade balances in the respective countries. Potential sources of funds may include new loans by foreign banks, portfolio investments by foreign investment houses or individuals, and direct foreign investment by multinationals. To see such funds flowing back, Asian governments have to carry out major reforms at home, that is, improvement of financial regulation and supervision; less preferential treatment for those close to the government; increased transparency for the benefit of all; and a more welcoming attitude towards foreign investment. Improvements were apparent in 1998, in some countries more than in others. A change in political leadership has helped to accelerate progress and to cut the links with the less fortunate past. But much more has to be achieved to bring back the trust and the confidence in foreign investors in the medium- and long-term future of Asia Pacific.

Asia Pacific beyond the crisis

Bearing in mind the severity of the crisis described above, it is easy to dismiss the coming of the 'Pacific Century' as a dream, or at least as a dream postponed for decades. There is also the argument which says that the Asian crisis proved Asian politicians, bureaucrats and businessmen are incompetent and are thus unable to lead the region into a prosperous future.

Such statements carry elements of malice but also of truth. They disregard three decades of extraordinary growth, and forget that the 'Asian miracle' was not a pipe dream, but a reality. At the same time they remind us that, indeed, many shortcomings in Asia Pacific that became visible during the crisis had been covered up during the boom years. They can also serve as a reminder that even after recovery, that is, beyond the crisis, there remain many other basic problems to be solved.

When assessing the crisis and its impact on the long-term future of Asia Pacific, three points have to be taken into account.

1. The size of the affected countries

The four South-East Asian countries to suffer from the collapse of their currencies were Thailand, Malaysia, Indonesia and the Philippines. Their economies are relatively small. The fifth country affected, South Korea, has an economy not much smaller than that of the four South-East Asian countries combined. Together these five 'crisis countries' have economies which are still smaller than those of China and Hong Kong. Neither of the latter has suffered any currency depreciation, and nor do they have a net debt exposure towards foreign lenders. We can add to these 'healthy' economies those of Taiwan and Singapore. Both have seen their currencies soften, but they are not indebted to foreigners at all.

This leaves Japan, a totally different economy with very different problems. Its domestic debt is much larger than all the debt which the rest of Asia has accumulated over the years, but the resources of Japan to solve its financial crisis are also of a different, much greater magnitude than those of all others. Among other features, Japan has no net debt. It provides more funds to the outside world than any other country.

Putting the five 'crisis countries' into the context of the whole of Asia Pacific, they represent only 14 per cent of its total created wealth. To extrapolate from this small part of Asia to the whole of the region may therefore be an exaggeration, or at least premature.

Put into a different perspective: Asia Pacific's future beyond the crisis will be determined by Japan and China, not by the other economies of the region.

2. The fundamentals

Will Asia look different once the crisis is over? To some extent this will be the case. Governments and businessmen will have learned from their mistakes. More transparency, greater competence, fewer market distortions can be expected. As the fundamental strength of Asia Pacific will still be there, an improved legal and technocratic framework may well lead to a higher degree of international competitiveness. Consequently the IMF, despite its criticism of governments in Asia in 1998, spoke of the 'strong underlying growth potential' of the region in its forecasts published in May that year.

The fundamental strength of the region compares well with other parts of the world and is characterised by:

- High savings rates
- Entrepreneurship
- Low taxes
- Young population
- High work ethic
- Flexible labour markets
- Emphasis on education

Due to the heterogeneity of the regions these characteristics do not, and cannot, apply equally to all countries, but to most of them.

With respect to savings rates, eight of the Asia Pacific countries rate among the top ten in the world, but the Philippines, for example, has a fairly low rate. Entrepreneurship flourishes in the Chinese communities in the region, but less so in Korea and in Japan. Hong Kong, Singapore and China levy the lowest taxes on their people, and consequently government budgets and their direct influence on the economy are limited. A large proportion of the population of Indonesia and Malaysia is below the age of 15 years but Japan is ageing rapidly, raising worries about future welfare and pension payments. Work ethics are high everywhere in Asia Pacific, particularly in Japan, Singapore and Hong Kong, less so in Indonesia and Thailand. Climatic conditions rather than cultural factors may be the reason for the differences within the region. Labour markets are highly flexible in Hong Kong and Singapore, but much less so in Japan and Korea. Finally, the emphasis individuals, families, governments or society at large puts on education is high everywhere in the region, but higher in the Confucian-influenced countries of the NIEs and Japan than in South-East Asia.

It is education as a means of investing in future generations which represents the most fundamental strength of Asia Pacific. As value creation takes place less and less on the farm and in the factories, information and knowledge is becoming more important. A recent international survey of 13-year-old school children across 41 countries tested their average score in the two areas of mathematics and science.[5] In mathematics, of the five participating Asian countries, Singapore, South Korea, Japan and Hong Kong were ranked number one to four. Thailand ranked 20th among the 41 countries. In science, three were ranked among the top four countries, and Thailand and Hong Kong were placed 21st and 24th. As we begin to talk about knowledge industries becoming the driving forces of the next century, it seems that academic achievements resulting from investments in education are the best hope for success in an increasingly borderless and ever changing future.

3. The limits of growth

If the fundamentals are still in place, is there enough evidence for high growth to return to Asia Pacific? It was in the 1970s that the Club of Rome warned that the world would soon reach the limits of growth. Then Asia Pacific demonstrated to the rest of the world the growth of limits. During the crisis years some countries of Asia Pacific painfully discovered their own limitations. Some of them, related to the financial sector and the debt problem, will hopefully be overcome over time. But there are also fundamental problems in the region which have existed for many years and will continue to have an impact on Asia far beyond the years of the crisis. They concern the business environment.

The lack of basic services and facilities has long negatively affected businesses in a number of countries. While governments have been eagerly working on improving the infrastructure of their economies, the crisis has led to further delays or cancellations of projects designed to ease bottlenecks. It is not clear whether the improvements being implemented and planned will still be 'too little, too late'.

Closely linked with the shortcomings in infrastructure is the dramatic deterioration of the environment, both in urban centres and in certain parts of the countryside. Bangkok's traffic congestion is legendary, as is industrial pollution in Seoul and Taipei, and even more so in the industrial centres of China. As the trend towards further industrialisation and further urban agglomeration continues, there is not much hope that living conditions will improve markedly in the foreseeable future.

In the rural areas aggressive logging and expansion of arable land have led to widespread deforestation and soil erosion with consequent flooding, and even changes in weather patterns. This has negatively affected the earning potential of farmers and accelerated the move from the farms into the cities, which in turn become overcrowded and unmanageable. As recent forest fires in Indonesia and consequent smoke clouds over Singapore, Malaysia and Thailand have shown, environmental degradation has a major negative impact on living conditions of large parts of Asia's population. It also scares away tourists and the dollars they bring.

Population growth, while low in percentage terms in comparison with other parts of the world, increases population density, thus testing the patience of the people. China adds 16–18 million people to its population per year, the equivalent of the entire current population of Scandinavia. Indonesia grows by 3–4 million people a year, a figure which equals the total population of New Zealand.

More careful use of energy is needed in order to sustain growth and save vital natural resources. Both China and Indonesia are on the way to becoming energy importers, thus joining Japan, the Asian NIEs and the Philippines in their dependence on oil supplies from the Middle East and setting in train serious consequences for their foreign exchange balances.

Periods of crisis bring misery to many, but also create opportunities for a few to get rich quickly. Similarly rapid growth of income enhances perceived unfairness in income distribution. Ostentatious consumption will be envied or detested, the achievement of materialistic gains questioned. Industrialisation and liberalisation of markets will bring efficiency gains and productivity increases, but also the danger of growing un- and underemployment, as can be witnessed in China and Indonesia. Governments have to work hard to maintain the delicate balance between economic growth and the risk of social upheaval.

Notes and references

1. World Bank (1993).
2. World Bank (1994a).
3. Probert (1992). The paper gives some idea of the difficulties of gathering reliable investment data.
4. International Monetary Fund, *World Economic Outlook*, May 1998, pp. 24–5.
5. International Study Center at Boston College, *Third International Mathematics and Science Study*, 1997, Boston.

2 Formulating Strategies for Asia Pacific

A STRATEGIC FRAMEWORK FOR ASIA PACIFIC

The formulation of strategies for Asia Pacific can be organised around four major issues. First, what is the firm's ambition for the region? An ambition is what the firm wants to achieve both qualitatively (mission, vision) and quantitatively (specific market and financial-related objectives) during a strategic time-horizon. For Asia Pacific the definition of strategic ambition relies on determining the anticipated future importance of the region in the corporate portfolio relative to the existing one. Second, how should businesses be positioned? Positioning is the selection of businesses or market segments in which the firm wants to compete and the type of competitive profile it wants to adopt. In Asia, positioning means selecting the various countries in which a company wants to operate, in which form and in which segments. Third, what kind of capabilities need to be created? Creating capabilities calls for three basic forms of strategic investment. The first of these is access to external resources: accessing raw materials or components, human resources, financing, information, various types of external supports (lobbying, contacts, and so on). Then come investments in assets such as product development, plants, equipment, distribution networks, information systems, logistics, brand names and reputation. Next are investments in competences (the development of technological and managerial know-how required to compete successfully in the region. Fourth, how should the region be organised? Organisation covers not only formal structure, but also the various processes and systems which will govern the distribution of power; rules and procedures; internal communication; evaluation and rewards; coordination mechanisms; and the management of a corporate culture fitting the requirements of the region).

These four components are depicted in Figure 2.1 and are referred to as the strategic framework. This framework can typically be applied at different levels: at the level of the total corporation or at the level of a product division. It is important, however, to consider a firm's Asian strategy, or strategies, as an interdependent part of its overall, world-wide strategic effort.[1]

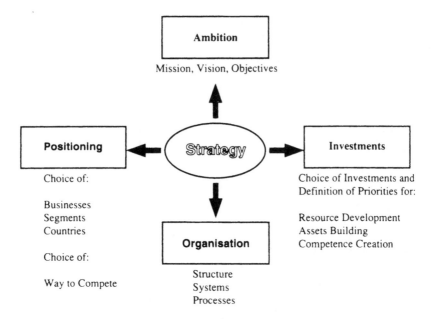

Figure 2.1 Strategic Framework

AMBITION FOR ASIA PACIFIC

Taking into account both overall corporate vision and mission, and specific, long-term objectives for global businesses, there are three critical questions to address. How important is it for the future of the company to be a player in the Asia Pacific region? What are the key countries in Asia Pacific which play and will play a major role in the various industries in which the corporation is involved, in terms of markets, sources of competition and resource bases? What share of the business – expressed in terms of sales and assets – does the company want to achieve in the Asia Pacific region over the next ten years relative to its operations in Europe and North America?

For a company, the Asia Pacific region may be considered as strategically important for three reasons: its market prospects, the quality and cost of its resources, and the learning which can be gained from a regional presence.

The importance of Asia Pacific as a market

In 1995, Asia Pacific generated 25 per cent of the world's total output. In certain sectors the region already represents more than 25 per cent of world sales (Table 2.1) and this proportion will increase over time.

Table 2.1 Share of Asia Pacific in Selected Industries

Industry	Industry Demand Asia/World (*)
Construction Materials (Cement...)	40%
Electrical Power	35/40%
Telecommunication Equipment	35/40%
Telecommunication Traffic	35%
Transport Infrastructure	35%
Elevators	50%
Consumer Electronics	30%
Industrial Electronics/Defence	30%
Automobiles	30%
Detergents	25%
Foods	25%

SOURCE: (*) Authors' estimates.

However, most Western firms barely achieve more than 10 per cent of their direct or export sales in this region. Figure 2.2 shows the relative importance of the Asia Pacific region measured in terms of sales for selected major European and North American companies. From a global perspective, Asia is underrepresented in the portfolio of these companies.

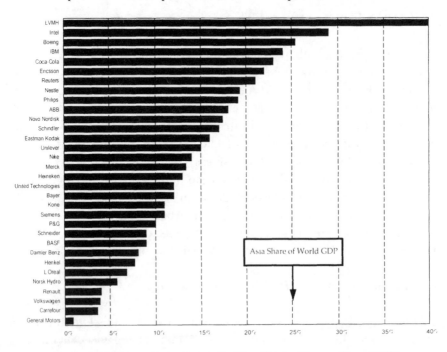

Figure 2.2 Share of Sales in Asia Pacific of Major Western Firms (1997)

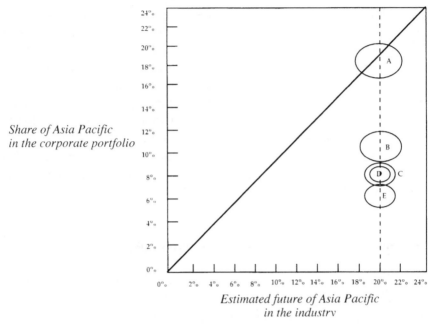

Note: A, B, C, D, E are companies in the chemical industry.
Bubbles represent the size of sales in Asia.

Figure 2.3   Asia Pacific Grid

Companies, or individual businesses in multi-business corporations, could start their strategic thinking process by charting their position on a grid similar to that shown in Figure 2.3. This grid indicates where the company or the business stands internally *vis-à-vis* Asia Pacific by comparison both with the industry as a whole and with its competitors. A business positioned on the diagonal achieves sales in Asia Pacific proportional to the region's weight in the industry. Businesses above the diagonal are more involved in Asia Pacific as a region than in the industry, a rare situation for the majority of Western companies. Finally, businesses below the diagonal are the ones in which Asia is underrepresented.

The advantage of such a chart is that it measures the gap between an existing position, the theoretical position represented by the industry's share in Asia share, and an industry's future position.

This evaluation process does not imply that a firm should conduct a percentage of its activities equivalent to the weight of the Asia Pacific region in this sector. Rather, such a process is a means of encouraging managers to benchmark the company position against the industry and to reflect upon the costs and benefits of such a position in both the short and long term.

In addition to a purely quantitative approach one should also consider the qualitative benefits to be gained from an Asian market presence. In the Asia Pacific region, the qualitative aspects of demand are as important as, if not more important than, the quantitative ones. Due to the demanding nature of the Asian customer, many Asian markets – especially the Japanese market – may provide Western firms with an opportunity to increase their overall corporate goodwill. For example, the fact that a Western automobile components firm is accepted as a supplier for Toyota or Nissan gives the company a reputation for quality that can be exploited elsewhere and applied to other markets. More and more companies have used a successful presence or position in Asian markets as a benchmark or reference in other countries or regions.

The importance of Asia Pacific as a resource base

The Asia Pacific region offers a vast reservoir of natural, human and tech-nological resources which can reinforce the global competitive advantages of firms. Figure 2.4 gives a pictorial representation of the various types of resources which can be obtained from the countries of Asia Pacific and the types of competitive advantage they can reinforce.

The south-eastern part of the Asia Pacific region is rich in a wide range of natural resources which serve as raw materials for many mineral processing industries (bauxite, tin, manganese, natural gas, petroleum) as well as agro-

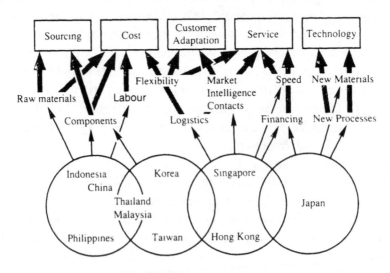

Figure 2.4   Asia Pacific as a Resource Base

based sectors (timber, palm oil, rubber, fisheries, cocoa, coconuts). As an example, by the year 2000 the region is expected to provide the majority of the world reserves in edible fats and in timber.

In terms of human resources, Asian governments perceived the comparative advantage of their region as early as the 1960s, when they established export processing zones in order to attract foreign investment. These zones, originally established in Singapore (Jurong, Ang Moh Kio, Toa Payoh, Bedok), Korea (Masan, Kumi, Inchon), Malaysia (Penang, Klang, Johore), Indonesia (Batam, Surabaya, Jakarta), Philippines (Bataan, Cebu) and Taiwan (Kaohsiung, Taichung) served as models for China's Special Economic Zones (SEZs). In these industrial estates, foreign companies can benefit from a labour market in which wages fall far below Western standards. The productivity and discipline of labour is variable, but these zones have generally succeeded in attracting labour-intensive industries such as electronic assembly, textiles, and shoe manufacturing. To cite just one example: Matsushita Electric Industrial has 29 different manufacturing sites in South-East Asia: fourteen in Malaysia, three in Indonesia, three in Thailand, one in the Philippines and eight in Singapore.

Western companies can benefit from low labour costs either directly through investment in manufacturing and assembly facilities, or, as is increasingly the case, through long-term components manufacturing contracts or original equipment manufacturing (OEM) contracts.

Technological resources are another key resource which can be drawn from the Asia Pacific region. Until recently, Japan was the only Asian location where Western firms sought to establish research and development centres to access scientific infrastructure and capabilities. Now, a number of Asian locations have attracted the attention of Western firms as potential bases for laboratory facilities. Similar in their physical design to the industrial parks or export processing zones mentioned above, the first Scientific Park was installed in the Taiwanese city of Hsinchu in 1980, and was followed by Kent Ridge in Singapore in 1984. Asian governments have used these parks to attract Western research laboratories by offering both infrastructure and technically skilled personnel at reduced costs.

This combination of resources and availability enhances the attractiveness of the region with respect to the four major attributes of competitive advantage: cost, quality, time and flexibility. To cite one example, a Boston Consulting Group study conducted in Singapore for an American printing manufacturer found that productivity was 30 per cent higher, time to market 50–100 per cent faster, quality 10–15 per cent better, and the number of models 2–3 times higher there than in an equivalent plant in the USA.[2]

The importance of Asia Pacific as a source of learning

For the Western firm, the advantage of establishing and maintaining a presence in Asia Pacific does not just depend on the region's economic growth and resource potential. Advantages should also be measured in terms of the experience and competitive advantage which are to be gained by being present in one of the world's most important and fast-paced industrial battlefields. Through confrontation with talented competitors, exposure to demanding customers and contact with a large variety of suppliers of components and services, Western competitors will be forced to maintain their corporate fitness and test their capabilities. Market and competitive dynamism are sources of competitive innovation and fitness. In a sense, Asia Pacific is a permanent industrial Olympics where first-class competitors compete side-by-side with a wide array of newcomers and mavericks. To use the terminology of Michael Porter,[3] some Asian markets can be referred to as 'global platforms' where any company that wants to be 'in the race' has to be present. Japan obviously holds first place among these 'global platforms' in a certain number of sectors, most notably new materials, opto-electronics, biotechnology or mechatronics. However, other Asian countries are also candidates: Indonesia for petrochemicals and process engineering, Thailand for food processing and Hong Kong for financial engineering. Long-term profitability cannot be secured unless a company establishes strong competitive capabilities which in turn derive from permanent fitness acquired through competition in a demanding, diverse and constantly changing business environment such as the Asia Pacific region.

Asian business philosophy and enterprise cultures, and Asian competitive approaches, may force Western companies to re-evaluate and, in some cases, adapt their own traditional business strategies and concepts. Success in Asia depends to a large extent on the capacity to learn new repertoires and new approaches to doing business. Operating in Asia is a learning experience, whether this takes the form of new kinds of liaison with suppliers, a new approach to the management of human resources, innovative ways of packaging a tender to establish a long-term relationship with customers, or different ways of thinking about consumer behaviour. The example of Procter & Gamble (P&G) in Japan, which after much painful experience was able to renew its approach to the design and marketing of nappies, is an object lesson for other Western firms. The advantage of accumulating learning from the Asia Pacific is that lessons learned there – particularly those concerning customer services, flexibility, total quality and human resources management – can be transferred back to the parent company in Europe or North America.

POSITIONING IN ASIA PACIFIC

The Western firm's ambition for Asia Pacific determines the scope and intensity of its future business operations in the region. This corporate ambition must be concretely reflected in the choice of products and markets. The company must also differentiate itself from its competitors both in the manner in which it chooses to establish a regional presence and in the way it competes. This set of choices – referred to as positioning – consists of determining whether the company is interested in accessing resources, or market, or both; deciding on the countries in which it wants to operate; deciding on an entry mode (whether the company will go it alone via wholly-owned subsidiaries, or in partnerships such as joint ventures, licensing and franchising arrangements); defining the type of activities it plans to establish, the segments in which it wants to compete and a competitive approach which will differentiate it from its competitors; and deciding to integrate activities regionally or country-by-country.

Resources-based versus market-based strategies

As indicated earlier, the Asia Pacific region offers business opportunities in terms of both its markets and its resources. The first element of regional positioning is the selection of the appropriate mix of markets and resources.

In the case of a strategic orientation based on access to resources, the firm should concentrate its activities in the countries which have the cheapest and/or best sources of supply. They should also establish sourcing offices and offshore production plants in low labour-cost areas such as south China, or in raw material processing areas like Sumatra or Borneo. During the 1960s and 1970s, certain Western companies, mainly from the USA, focused exclusively on Asia's resources, setting up offshore assembly plants in the region's export processing zones. Today, however, the limits of this strategy are obvious. First, a narrow focus on resources neglects the full range of potential the region has to offer in terms of markets, learning and competitiveness. Second, an exclusive focus on resources is risky due to rapid changes in conditions: Asian labour costs are likely to increase, as they did in Singapore in the late 1970s. In 1976 Thomson Consumer Electronics established a factory at Toa Payoh, an industrial estate in Singapore, on the basis of low-cost labour, only to find that by 1982 Singaporean costs were no longer so competitive. More importantly, Asian natural resource producers are most likely to move quickly to fill the vacuum left in the markets by investing in downstream sectors. The evolution of the plywood industry in Indonesia illustrates this point: when the Indonesian government decided to

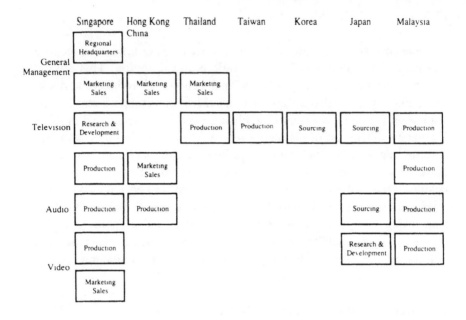

Figure 2.5   Thomson Consumer Electronics: Asia Pacific Mosaic (1990)

ban the export of logs in the late 1970s, Western companies, which had relied on these supplies and suddenly found themselves without any local processing facilities or markets, were squeezed out. In practice, however, Western firms are not forced to make an 'either/or' choice between resources and markets, but to determine an appropriate mix of the two.

In the case of a market-based strategy, the company will set up local marketing and occasionally manufacturing activities, either wholly-owned or with local partners. The choice will depend on market potential, the competitive climate, government policies and the company's competitive capabilities.

As mentioned above, a firm's regional strategic positioning should be a combination of resources and market-based orientations which will lead to a mosaic of activities spread over the region, some purely resources-oriented, some purely market-oriented and some both. Figure 2.5 shows as an example the mosaic of Thomson Consumer Electronics in the region in the early 1990s.

Choice of countries

Country selection depends on the relative attractiveness of each country. Attractiveness is a function of three factors: market attractiveness (size, growth, segmentation, sophistication of demand, intensity and nature of

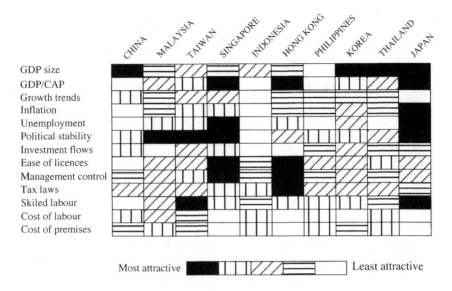

Figure 2.6 Country Attractiveness in a Financial Services Company

competition); resource attractiveness (availability, quality and cost of raw materials, labour cost, productivity and attitudes, supplier networks, quality of information, financing, buildings, general infrastructure and logistics); political/regulatory and operational attractiveness (political stability, monetary stability, administrative practices, operational flexibility, price and exchange controls).

Such an assessment is obviously industry specific, while political and economic developments have also made some countries more fashionable than others. Each company will find it necessary to design its own criteria. Figure 2.6 shows how a financial services company might evaluate countries in the region in 1998. This kind of assessment is frequently made in two steps: first the evaluation of the political and regulatory climate through what is known as country-risk analysis; then a business analysis which covers both market and resources attractiveness for specific business projects or business plans within a specific country.

Choice of entry mode and pathway to strategic development

Decisions about entry modes are concerned with the types of operation that should be established in order to penetrate targeted regions and countries. After entering, further decisions will have to be made in order to develop (and later consolidate) the business. The particular entry and pathway to development chosen will depend upon the company's prior experience and capabilities and the particular strategic attractiveness of an industrial sector or country.

As will be further discussed in Chapter 6, the typical choice on entering a market is between going it alone with wholly-owned operations (greenfield operations or acquisitions), or entering partnerships (for instance, joint ventures, licensing, franchising, long-term contractual agreements). Entry mode choices, for Western firms considering the Asia Pacific region, should generally be determined by the following five factors: the overall attractiveness of the market; the costs; the timing and internal ability of the firm to enter and develop the necessary resources, assets and competences; government requirements; and finally, the competitive situation and the political and operational risks involved.

The countries in Asia Pacific roughly divide into five types: platform, emerging, growth, maturing and established. Platform countries such as Singapore or Hong Kong can be used at the start of the entry process as bases for gathering intelligence and initiating contacts; they can become the hub for regional coordination later on. Medium-sized companies with no prior experience in the region could begin by establishing a listening post in these countries. This was the case for Gemplus, a medium-sized French company, and a leader in the field of smart cards. One of this company's first moves was to set up a joint venture with Singapore Technology. From Singapore the managing director of the joint venture can develop contacts and initiate further partnerships in the region.

The task in emerging countries such as Vietnam and (in the near future) Myanmar or Cambodia is to establish an initial presence through a local distributor and a representative office which will take charge of building the necessary relationships in order to prepare the establishment of either a direct local operation or a joint venture. In growth countries such as China and the ASEAN 5 a significant presence has to be established urgently in order to capitalise on the opportunities generated by the rapid economic development of those countries. Maturing and established countries such as Korea, Taiwan and Japan already have a significant economic infrastructure and well-established local and international competitors. The task here at the entry phase is to find a way to access the operational capability necessary to catch up with competitors, either through joint venture, acquisition or massive investment.

Firms which have identified a potentially very attractive market with space for competition might select one of these countries and then develop their presence from this stronghold. This was the case for Bell Alcatel which set up the first telecommunication equipment operation in China, and now uses China as its centre of expertise for developing Asia.

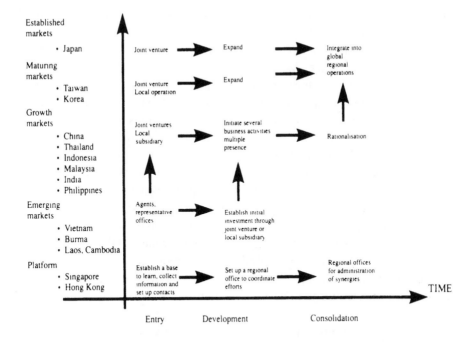

Figure 2.7   Entry Modes and Development in Asia Pacific

Figure 2.7 illustrates different potential entry pathways, taking into account the extent of prior experience, and using the countries classification outlined above.

Choice of business segments and competitive approach

Business segmentation in Asia Pacific is extremely complex, since the region can be broken down into a variety of very diverse marketing environments. At one extreme is Japan, with its highly sophisticated and unique segmentation, and at the other is Indonesia or the Philippines, where markets are still very pyramidal with masses of consumers still living in rural economies. In the middle are Asia's NIEs, where segmentation is becoming more and more similar to Western markets. Finally, China and Vietnam are a category apart; they are just beginning to shed their limitations as non-market economies, with market segmentation still in its infancy but changing very rapidly.

Traditional strategic management literature, academic scholarship and consulting research have all advocated a dualistic 'either/or' approach to competitive strategy. Either a company positions itself as the cost leader of its particular industry, and aims to win the game by underpricing its competitors, or it differentiates itself and aims to win by offering better technology, quality or services. However, this dualistic approach appears inadequate when applied to the complex and demanding nature of Asia Pacific's markets and consumers. On the whole, Asia Pacific markets do not tend to be 'either/or' but rather 'and/and': in other words, to compete in the region a Western firm has to provide low prices *and* good quality, *and* good service, *and* a short response time, *and* proper financing, and so on. Obviously, this is a general proposition and competitive profiles need to be designed on a case-by-case basis, but it is useful to remember that, *ceteris paribus*, Asian customers tend to exhibit a much larger repertoire of demands than Western firms are accustomed to in their traditional markets. In Japan, customers tend to be highly sophisticated and demanding in terms of certain attributes of product and service quality, while in other countries in the region customers will try to get the best of both worlds: great price and great performance. However, in yet other countries, 'relationships', combined with indirect services, will be the prime determinant of competitive approaches. The Western manager needs to demonstrate flexibility in designing competitive strategies.

Orientation: regional strategy versus country-by-country strategy

In positioning a business in the region a company will decide whether it is going to adopt a regional approach or a country-by-country approach. The implications of this choice are described in Table 2.2.

Table 2.2   Regional versus Country-by-Country Positioning

	Region	*Countries*
Innovation	• Regional research • Coordination of technological intelligence	• Local laboratories
Production	• Specialised plants serving the world and/or the region • High level of intra-regional flow	• Plants tailored for national markets • Little intra-regional flow
Marketing	• Marketing research coordinated by region • Coordination of marketing programmes	• Marketing research done for local markets • Local marketing programmes
Financing	• Regional pooling of cash flows • Regional financial engineering	• Local borrowing • Local cash flows
Human resources	• Regional careers • Regional training	• National careers • Local training

The extreme diversity of the Asia Pacific region means that there is as much difference between Japan and Indonesia as there is between Germany and Tunisia. Because of this diversity, both in terms of economic development and cultural orientation, Asia Pacific's only regional economic organisation, ASEAN, is still far from achieving the coordinated political will needed to forge the beginning of a regional common market comparable to the EU. The differences in traditions, religions, public policies and government regulations have created and maintained solid barriers around country borders within the Asia Pacific region. From the point of view of the Western firm, a homogeneous or purely regional approach is likely to be ineffective; strategies should be a mix of regional perspective and country-by-country approach.

The need to adopt a regional approach is reinforced by a number of economic factors. First, it can be argued that certain business functions – notably strategic intelligence, financial engineering, research and development, training, and specialised services – can only reap the benefits of economies of scale by being located somewhere from where they can service the whole region. Second, it is still possible for Western firms to achieve a regional or a sub-regional coordination of certain flows, most notably components, spare parts and semi-finished products. Third, certain industries are obliged to serve regional customers (corporate banking, for instance) and to confront regional competitors in order to make a regional strategy worthwhile. Finally, in many large Western corporations, managers find that there is internal pressure to represent the region as a whole in order to obtain an adequate allocation of investment resources. Boards of directors of large Western corporations are unaccustomed to thinking in terms of individual countries, and prefer to think in terms of aggregates such as North America or Europe. Therefore, many managers operating in the Asia Pacific region may find that in order to be heard they will have to present a regional perspective rather than a collection of country strategies.

CREATING CAPABILITIES THROUGH INVESTMENTS IN RESOURCES, ASSETS AND COMPETENCES

The most critical part of any strategy process comes when corporate ambition is confronted with the investments required to transform it into reality. In the Asia Pacific region the qualitative aspect of the investment effort is almost more important than the quantitative aspect. The diversity of enterprise cultures in Asia Pacific, the tenacity of certain cultural traditions and ways of doing business, make this complex qualitative dimension crucial to the success of Western ventures in the region. Research and Western business experience in Asia Pacific have shown the most salient characteristics of doing business in the region to be the following.[4]

Marketing and strategic information is sparse or unreliable and therefore difficult to obtain in the region. Consequently, forecasting market demand, assessing competitors, and the search for local partners are clearly perceived by Western managers to be more difficult in Asia than in the USA or Europe.

Building contacts and relationships is a prerequisite to any strategic development in the region; but relationship-building and networking in Asia require time, effort and perseverance beyond what Western managers and corporations are used to.

Success requires long-term effort and commitment and the ability to invest cash, time, people and management attention, with the expectation that the pay-off will come beyond what is considered a normal time horizon in Western countries.

Asian business practices and enterprise culture are often difficult for Westerners to understand, either because of the complexity of cultural norms or because of the inaccessibility of ethnic or informal networks.

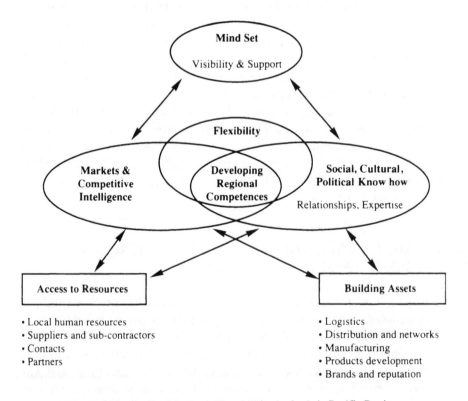

Figure 2.8   Required Strategic Capabilities in the Asia Pacific Region

As a consequence, Western firms need to build capabilities in the Asia Pacific region which will demand additional and specifically tailored strategic investments in resources, assets and competences, as illustrated in Figure 2.8.

Development of resources

In practice there are six major strategic resources which constitute the basis of competitive advantage: finances, people, supplies, information, location and sponsorship. Table 2.3 lists the relative advantages and disadvantages of Western firms *vis-à-vis* local Asian firms in terms of access to five of these types of resource. There is evidence that Western firms operating in Asia Pacific are at a relative disadvantage in all six of the above-mentioned categories, most particularly people and information. The development of those resources requires continuous and systematic investment in the soft areas of business: forming links with schools and universities, cultivating relationships with journalists, making contacts, gathering information, lobbying, financing scholarships, sponsoring social and cultural events, compiling and updating intelligence reports, and so on. All these activities constitute cash outflows for which it is difficult to estimate a return and for which results take a long time to materialise.

Western companies sometimes complain that they are also at a disadvantage in the Asia Pacific region because of the biased treatment they receive from Asian governments, who tend to favour and protect local companies. In a 1997 INSEAD Euro-Asia Centre survey on the competitive climate in the Asia Pacific region, the majority of respondents, with the exception of those Western executives based in Hong Kong and Taiwan, agreed with the statement that 'local governments grant preferential advantages to local firms'. It is important, however, not to exaggerate the frequency of this preferential treatment. It is understandable, at least as far as the less developed Asian countries are concerned, that governments will extend incentives to local enterprises. Western firms can often compensate for this bias by taking advantage of subsidies and preferential treatment accorded by their own governments in the form of export credits, political support, tax exemptions, and so on.

In terms of financing, the major issue is more a question of internal commitment than of cost of capital. One may occasionally find that a local or Japanese competitor has privileged access to cheap financing. This has to be balanced against the fact that Western firms, in many instances, benefit from government subsidised loans.

Table 2.3   Relative Advantages and Disadvantages of
Western Firms in Accessing Resources in Asia Pacific

Resources	Western firms	Asian firms
Finances	• Reliance on central headquarters	• Japanese firms supposedly benefit from cheaper cost of capital
	• Access to offshore financing based on corporate credit rating	• Korean firms benefit from subsidised funds
	• Influence of Western stock markets on cost of capital	• Most local governments tend to give preferential treatment to local firms
	• Constraints on local borrowing in some cases	
Human resources	• Western firms often lack the public visibility needed to attract the best local talent	• In some cases local graduates prefer to work for local firms
	• Difficulties in creating loyalty among local employees	• Loyalty is stronger
Supplies	• At par for international supplies	• In certain countries, like Japan or Korea, local firms have privileged access to some suppliers
	• Some difficulties penetrating local networks	
	• Some advantages derived from a multinational network	
Information	• Weak information base	• Long-standing information network
	• Lack of insider's sources	• Implicit information
Sponsorship	• Some Western governments subsidise exports and foreign investments	• Governments encourage national champions
	• Very often lack of commitment from central headquarters	• Granting of privileges

Building assets

Building up tangible and intangible assets is the bread and butter of any strategic development in Asia, just as it is in any other area of the world. However, the specific demands of operating in the Asia Pacific arena necessitate a focus on two key areas: the transfer of technology and the building of marketing assets.

Establishing a presence in Asia Pacific requires a transfer of technology to the local operation, whether it is a fully-owned venture or a partnership. In the developing areas of Asia Pacific, this aspect is critical. Other aspects of this process which require particular attention are: the down-scaling of operational infrastructure; the adaptation of technology to local conditions; and the need to emphasise the software part of the investment. Down-scaling is often crucial because individual Asian markets are generally far smaller than the world efficient scale. As mentioned earlier, the diversity of the markets in the Asia Pacific region makes it difficult – and at times impossible – for Western firms to establish specialised plants, and hence to benefit from large economies of scale. A case in point was the investment made by a Western aluminium producer, Alcan, in a Malaysian rolling mill in the late 1970s. The size of the Malaysian market, even taking into account its considerable growth potential, was insufficient to justify investment in a state-of-the-art plant. The company encountered great difficulty in designing a small-scale plant because engineers in North America and Europe were used to thinking big. Finally, after 18 long months of internal struggle, a down-sized plant was designed by engineers brought from the parent corporation's Indian subsidiary.

Marketing assets are commonly the most difficult of assets to accumulate and develop, particularly goodwill and distribution networks. Goodwill, in consumer segments, depends upon both image and reputation for quality and services, while in industrial segments it depends upon the quality of relationships with customers. Asian consumers are acutely sensitive to image and services; as a consequence, Western firms will have to make a long and consistent effort to develop the kind of reputation that Asian markets require. The complexities of building distribution networks and personal relationships are related to the fact that Asian markets have already been widely cultivated by local and multinational traders, Japanese and Western industrial and services firms who began investing in the region in the 1970s and 1980s.

Creating competences

The role of competences in strategy has been described as one of the most powerful in creating competitive advantages.[5] This is probably more true for the Asia Pacific region than anywhere else. In addition to classical competences such as project management, time-to-market or system integration, three sets of competences are of particular importance for success in Asia Pacific: intelligence building (the ability to invest in decoding the particularities of the business, political and sociological environment and to translate them into significant business recommendation); flexibility (decision-making process adapted to analysing problems and coming up with solutions which may be specific to Asia and at variance with the core organisational norms or accepted practices of the corporation); and networking (the ability to partner and manage relationships with Asian firms and within different cultural contexts).

These three sets of competences can be derived from a whole range of investments: first, investment in cultural understanding (language, history and sociology). Asian cultures are at the crossroads of a variety of cultural streams: Confucianism, Buddhism, Taoism, Islam, Shintoism, Hinduism and Christianity. China, with its 50 centuries of historical heritage, and the rich traditions and social norms of Japan, Korea, Thailand and the Indonesian islands, have always fascinated Western traders, poets and warriors. Diplomatic services in the UK and France had a specially trained force for Oriental postings. However, modern professionally trained business executives, coming from schools of engineering or business, very often lack the cultural sensitivity and multicultural background necessary to understand and operate effectively in such a culturally complex region. The task of developing an appropriate Asia-sensitive corporate culture – mixing cultural, technical and business skills – depends on the leadership of the corporation. This is a dual task: first the firm must develop in its managers specific competences for the region; then the firm must create an organisation-wide understanding and respect for these competences so that Asian strategies will be accepted by corporate and business managers at headquarters.

Second, there is a need for investment in information gathering. The paucity and unreliability of publicly available sources of information virtually force firms to invest in intelligence. This requires more than the purchase of a database or the sub-contracting of market research; it needs a network of contacts and systematic cross-checking of unstructured information, calling for physical representation and an investment of time.

The third investment required is in relationships. Doing business in Asia Pacific calls, perhaps more than any other region in the world, for a unique set of competences in developing partnerships, and creating and managing a network of contacts. Building relationships with suppliers, distributors, partners, officials and other contacts is often a slow process, particularly in Asia, where great importance is attached to the personalisation of business contacts. Building competences in relationships is not only a matter of individual talent; it relies also on the ability to institutionalise a relationship's culture. This requires time and an appropriate personnel development policy, as well as the creation of an internal regional network of communication and cooperation among managers operating in various countries.

ORGANISATIONAL CAPABILITIES

When Western firms come to the point where they need to translate strategic decisions regarding the proper organisational mechanisms for the region, the following questions are likely to arise. What is the proper organisational structure: geographical, global or regional? Should the company set up a regional headquarters? Should Asia Pacific be represented as a region at board level? What degree of autonomy should country managers enjoy in product, production and marketing decision-making? To what extent should planning, budgeting and performance evaluation systems be adapted or transformed to fit regional specifications? How should local managers be recruited and trained? How should expatriate managers be managed?

It can be argued that the weakness of Western companies in Asia stems from a lack of proper organisational mechanisms.[6] Given the small percentage of Western business activities currently carried out in Asia (see Figure 2.2), the obvious conclusion is that top Western management is unfamiliar with the region. This is unsurprising, considering that top managers have traditionally come from businesses and countries which are heavily weighted in the corporate portfolio. It is also likely that corporate norms, systems and procedures have not been properly adapted to Asian business and cultural contexts. Therefore, vicious circles have tended to develop: a relatively weak presence fails to lead to cumulative internal knowledge of the region, and tends to perpetuate *ad hoc* and inappropriate business systems which in turn fail to generate adequate institutional and financial support for the region at corporate headquarters. This circle inevitably perpetuates a weak presence.

Organisational facilitators should be designed for implementing Asian strategies. Such facilitators include: the appointment of a powerful senior executive in charge of the region; the creation of a regional orientation through regional networking and sometimes, although not always, the establishment of one or more regional headquarters; the development of a regional spirit, sometimes referred to as the 'missionary spirit', an orientation which encourages managers to build and act on a sense of mission in a particular country or region; the creation of a local managerial elite rapidly and thoroughly trained to spearhead the corporation into the region; and lastly (and most importantly) the ability to instigate a complete transformation in the way in which corporations structure problems, and make and implement decisions.

When managing businesses across borders, companies are confronted with three sets of problems. The first could be described as problems of adaptation: ensuring that local operations develop the skills and attitudes needed to adapt strategies to local contexts (for example, how to fit with local legal requirements, adapt business practices to local social norms and translate corporate language into a local one). A British company setting up an operation in China will need to adapt its literature to the Chinese language and encourage its managers to follow the social codes of the Chinese business establishment.

Another set of problems are those of modification: how to develop different business paradigms or mental models. Modifications are required when the conceptual distance between the dominant business logic of the corporation is far from the one required in the host country. For instance, a British firm setting up a subsidiary in India may not find contextual adaptation too difficult, linguistically or even institutionally, but may need to make fundamental changes to its business approach.

When these two sets of problems are combined, a transformation (that is to say, a complete overhaul of management practices and business logic) is required. Asia Pacific countries typically fall into this category, where Western firms have not only to speak differently but also to think differently (see Figure 2.9). Asia Pacific, as a region, requires more than just an adaptation to different cultural contexts; it requires a paradigmatic transformation. It is no longer enough for Western firms and managers to learn how to speak Japanese in order to become players in the Japanese market. Increasingly, they are having to learn how to play Japanese in a Japanese game and

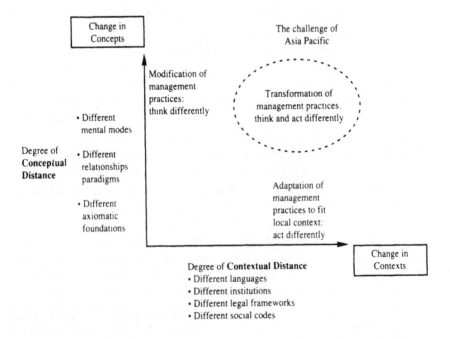

Figure 2.9   Transforming Management Practices for Strategic Success in Asia

according to a strategic logic which is often at odds with the prevailing business philosophy or strategic logic of their parent company. A good example of such a transformation is provided by P&G in Japan. P&G had successfully developed and marketed products in the USA and Europe during the 1960s and 1970s. P&G core competences were undoubtedly based on the mastery of market research, consumer analysis, mass merchandising and product launch. A marketing manager who had worked for P&G was practically guaranteed future job offers. When P&G entered Japan, after a series of unsuccessful trials with a joint venture partner, it installed a local subsidiary and started to apply P&G marketing expertise. The results were so catastrophic that P&G was forced to consider the complete cessation of its Japanese operations. After transforming its approach, P&G Japan became successful and is now a model of innovation and a source of profit for the whole group.[7]

Interviews with Western expatriate managers based in Japan and other Asian countries support the view that the prevailing rules of the game inside both North American and European companies are ill-suited to the requirements for success in the Asia Pacific region. Similarly, it can now be argued that the competitive edge of the emerging Asian global players, although still primarily Japanese, has been their ability to create new, highly flexible strategic capabilities which, when compared to traditional Western corporate strategy, are better suited to the shifting and fast-paced Asian competitive climate.

This flexibility is one of the core competences Western firms will need to learn and deploy in order to operate efficiently in the region. As they formulate strategies for Asia Pacific, Western managers should look carefully and realistically at their firm's accepted norms and business practices.

HOW DOES THE FINANCIAL CRISIS AFFECT ASIA PACIFIC STRATEGIES?

In 1998, confronted with what appears to be an economic disaster, Western companies have adopted a variety of attitudes. Some companies have retrenched, some have revised their plans but are firmly committed to the region, and others have seized the opportunity presented by the crisis to increase their presence through acquisition.

The retrenchment strategy consists of closing operations or running them at a minimum level. Just to give an example, a distributor of office equipment who was selling more than 150 machines a month in Thailand has seen his sales volume plunge to two machines in January 1998. Mercedes Benz has announced that it has closed all its plants in South-East Asia. Daihatsu has closed definitively its plant in Thailand. The retrenchment strategy is based on the assumption that it will take a long time for these economies to recover.

The second approach consists of revising downward forecasts for the region but maintaining operations and even sticking to the investment plans designed before the crisis. Carrefour, the French mass retailer, is planning to open more than ten new stores in the region including one in Jakarta. The company expects a decrease in revenues and in certain cases even losses during the next three years, but thinks that it is strategically important to establish itself properly in order to operate at full strength when the turmoil is over. Accor has repatriated all the expatriates it employed in Indonesia and is running its hotels with a minimum number of local staff. This kind of strategy is based on the assumption that the crisis will last for two to three years and that the region will rebound thereafter.

The final strategy takes the position that the fall in local currency values, coupled with local firms' need for cash, make acquisitions an attractive proposition for companies who believe that the future of Asia is still promising. A certain number of acquisitions and equity participations have already been announced. ABN Amro is buying the Bank of Asia in Thailand, Volvo acquired Samsung Heavy Industries' excavator division, Procter & Gamble bought Ssangyong Paper, and the Finnish group UPM Kymmene has injected US$235 million into the April group, an Indonesia-based pulp and paper group.

A survey conducted by the International Chamber of Commerce and UNCTAD in March 1998 revealed that only 12 per cent of 198 multinational companies (MNCs) were planning to reduce their investment in the region, while 62 per cent planned to maintain and 12 per cent to increase their investment. European companies represented 34 per cent of the MNCs in the last category. Altogether 94 per cent of respondents were positive about the long-term prospects of the region.

In terms of the framework proposed in this chapter, the crisis changes little. Of the four factors constituting the strategic framework, the most affected is probably Positioning. Prospects for some countries have to be scaled down, at least in the short term: ambitions are affected in Indonesia, Malaysia and Thailand, particularly with regard to marketing targets in consumer goods and in industrial goods related to domestic demand. Conversely, all activities linked to exports and to raw material processing for exports are still growing. China still holds great potential in consumer, industrial and infrastructure goods. The downside of China's attractiveness is intense competition and, in certain sectors, significant overcapacity.

In terms of the cultural transformation we suggested earlier, it is possible that the crisis may reduce somewhat the distance between Western management practices and the requirements of the local environment. A certain number of 'good practices' such as financial controls, sound procedures and profit orientation will be more readily accepted by Asian partners, employees and shareholders. However, we maintain that for European, American and Australian managers and companies, conducting business in Asia will still require a strong dose of flexibility and adaptiveness.

The financial crisis does not change fundamentally the strategic importance of the region. Western firms need to adopt a long-term view of events, and most of them are indeed doing so.

The practical implications are:

1. Strategies need to be revised but long-term goals of presence in the region should be maintained.
2. Resources need to be readjusted and expansion plans temporarily down-scaled or delayed, but not abandoned. Particular attention has to be given to the preservation of human resources and of business partnerships.
3. Commitment to the region has to be demonstrated to governments, employees, partners, suppliers and distributors. Past efforts put into building external credibility could be ruined by a short-term opportunistic attitude.
4. Specific intelligence capabilities have to be enhanced.
5. Flexibility and adaptability remain key competences and should be preserved or enhanced.
6. New opportunities offered by potential acquisitions have to be seriously considered. (We will devote a section later in the book to acquisitions, now that they are more feasible.)

Notes and references

An earlier version of this chapter has been published in *Long Range Planning*, Vol. 28, No. 1 (February 1995), pp. 13–30.
1. In most instances managers use the concept of 'strategic planning' to describe the frameworks and the processes by which strategy is formulated. One should make a clear distinction between this formal aspect of strategy formulation, which is nothing more than a methodology, and the concept of a strategic framework used here. While it is critical to have a strategic framework, it may not be necessary to have formal strategic plans in the Asia Pacific region. Academics like Richard Pascale (1990) and Tom Peters (1987) argue that strategic planning hampers real strategy formulation by its excessive focus on quantitative aspects. Henry Mintzberg (1990) advances similar arguments. In an earlier article, one of the authors developed the argument that a formal approach to strategy formulation in the developing countries of the Asia Pacific region was inappropriate. See Lasserre (1983), pp. 37–41.
2. 'Competition in Asia', *Asian Business*, October 1992, p. 4.
3. Porter (1986), p. 39.
4. The characteristics indicated in the figures come from two surveys done with European executives operating in the region. See Lasserre and Probert (1994a) and Lasserre (1993a).
5. Hamel and Prahalad (1990).
6. Lasserre (1988b).
7. Yoshino (1990).

3   Asia as a Market

As discussed in Chapter 1, 25 per cent of the world's wealth is created in Asia Pacific. This wealth is in turn spent, through consumption or through investment. This expenditure represents the market for goods and services in the region.

High growth in wealth creation basically stimulates high growth in demand. With the arrival of the Asian crisis and the first experience of negative growth rates in 1998, demand has started to fall dramatically in a number of the ASEANIEs.[1] In Japan markets are stagnating, while in China the growth of demand is slowing down – which should, however, not be mistaken for a decline in demand.

The impact of the Asian crisis on manufacturers and service providers is significant. Demand from private individuals, companies, or governments is dependent not only on present income. It is also influenced by expectations of future income. This psychological element in purchasing decisions leads to wide fluctuations in demand. In times of sombre mood, demand may shrink much more than macro-economic growth data would suggest. This is clearly the case in Japan where, despite the continuing high degree of wealth creation, over-pessimistic consumers are reluctant to spend, and investors in turn see no new demand emerging to justify new investments. The worst results of such a mood are large increases in savings - not necessarily channelled back to others in need of funds – and transfers of money out of the country.

The influence of sentiment on buying decisions, however, also has a positive side. Once the mood in an economy changes, the result may be a sudden surge in demand which in turn will spur investment activity.

Changes in demand do not affect all product segments equally. The market for daily necessities tends to remain stable even in times of economic downturn. Products and services bearing elevated prices, but without a strong positioning, are the ones which suffer most. Buyers, whether individuals or firms, tend to opt for cheaper solutions when they have doubts about the true benefits. Basic products, thus, may enjoy growth and profitability during difficult times. At the same time, strong brands at the upper end of the product spectrum can benefit from the uncertainty in the mind of the consumer. As witnessed in Japan during the period of 1997–8, products 'caught-in-the-middle' were hit, but the true premium brands were not.

In response to the crisis, consumption and investment decisions for many goods and sources may be delayed, but they are not cancelled. Cars have to be replaced at some stage, and machinery wears out or becomes technologically obsolete and thus needs renewing or upgrading.

Finally, the specific features of the Asian markets, roughly divided into Japan, the ASEANIEs and China, will not change dramatically. Japan will remain a difficult market for foreign firms, despite further liberalisation and deregulation. Buying behaviour will remain group oriented in Japan, as in the rest of Asia. The ASEANIEs and China are largely inefficient markets burdened by strong government interference. We do not expect major changes, in spite of pressure from institutions like the IMF to move towards free competition. The weakness of many local companies *vis-à-vis* strong multinational corporations will give the latter more muscle. However, we should not expect governments to welcome foreign firms indiscriminately and allow local companies to fade away. The following sections discuss the markets in Japan, then the ASEANIEs and China.

JAPAN

Open market, closed society

With more than 120 million affluent customers and a manufacturing industry that has outgrown its own large economy and expanded abroad, Japan should be every marketing manager's dream. But in fact Japan is still perceived by many foreign firms as a nightmare. The majority of Western firms find it difficult to come to terms with the intricacies of an environment where the rules appear to be both different and rigged against them.[2]

There are, of course, successful foreign firms in Japan. From the late 1980s to the early 1990s, IBM could boast annual profits of US$1 billion. Taken as a group, Western pharmaceutical firms and oil companies have also performed well. Even McDonald's hamburgers have now conquered Japan, an achievement that ran counter to all expectations. In the 1980s, French luxury goods and German car manufacturers witnessed surging demand for their products and, by the 1990s, US software suppliers had finally established viable operations in Japan.

However, on average Western firms have generally been less successful in Japan than in other comparable markets. Manufacturers of international class – including those firms cited above – have rarely been able to match the level of their market shares in the USA or Europe. They have often had to settle for less than half of their normal share, even in industries where Japanese firms were initially unable to equal the standards of their Western competitors.

The frustration of Western firms operating in Japan, paired with Japan's consistently high trade surpluses with the rest of the world and the USA in particular, have led to the public conviction that the Japanese market is in reality less open to Western firms than American and European markets are to their Japanese counterparts. As a consequence, serious trade disputes have dominated the international agenda with Japan for more than a decade.

After Japan initiated a series of market opening measures in the 1980s, it became apparent that the country's classic tariff and non-tariff barriers were in fact lower than those in certain Western countries. Faced with this reality, American trade negotiators shifted their demands to focus on the dismantling of 'structural impediments' which they identified as being disadvantageous to foreign firms in Japan. By doing this, the USA implicitly recognised that while the Japanese market was essentially open, Japanese society remained closed. The closed nature of Japanese society to foreign firms is due to a number of exclusionary phenomena: networks of Japanese firms buying from each other; invisible and subtle administrative guidance distinctly favouring local firms; the complexities of the distribution system; closed-door bidding for construction contracts; and bureaucratic and regulatory obstacles, especially in high-tech sectors.

It is interesting to note that the Japanese government has moved towards the gradual reduction of even these remaining impediments. For example, the Japanese telecommunications company NTT has been persuaded to purchase a portion of its equipment abroad. Japanese science institutions have acquired American super computers, and the Japanese electronics industry is buying a sizeable number of American semiconductors. Also, and despite the international hue and cry, Japan can now claim to be the only country in the world which officially exhorts its citizens to buy imported goods, which provides special loans for imports and which has a government agency (JETRO) charged with the mission of helping foreign exporters from rival industrial countries find a Japanese market for their goods.

Experience has shown, however, that success in Japan can rarely be achieved by exporting alone without substantial direct involvement in the country. Moreover, such involvement requires a commitment of major resources over a long period. The perception of foreign firms that success in Japan is difficult to achieve represents an important psychological entry barrier, creating a vicious circle of risk aversion, lack of commitment, and failure.

Commitment and competition

Many Japanese observers point to lack of commitment rather than to the existence of a closed market or closed society as the main reason for the dismal performance of foreign firms in their country. The minimal presence of Western firms speaks for itself: the number of all foreign businesses in Japan is only a fraction of the number of Japanese businesses operating abroad. Taken on a per capita basis, foreign investment in Japan is extremely low when compared with other industrialised countries. However, these asymmetries may be attributable not so much to lack of Western interest but to the very restrictive foreign investment policies of the past, the difficulty of market entry and the prohibitive costs of keeping expatriate staff in Japan today. Investing in Japan is extremely expensive, particularly in view of the high land prices; it also requires considerable time, since opportunities for acquisitions remain rare, and companies are forced to build up their operations from scratch.

Corporate commitment is not merely defined in quantitative terms (that is, by the amount of money flowing into Japan and the expectations of a payback within a given period); it is also indicated by the degree to which foreign firms are prepared to change their own ways of running a business to suit the Japanese environment. Commitment must also be judged by Western efforts to satisfy the exigencies of Japanese customers, especially in terms of quality and service. Finally, commitment should be judged by the degree to which the Western firm seeks to adjust its marketing-mix to the peculiarities of the Japanese market.

The prevailing corporate rhetoric about the globalisation of markets and consumers may have actually hindered foreign firms in their approach to the Japanese market.[3] Western firms have too often tried simply to replicate in Japan strategies that have proved successful in Europe and the USA. In the process, they have often overlooked the fact that differences can matter more than similarities in a market.

It took P&G 11 years to realise that their American imported marketing strategies did not work. Similarly, though without accumulating massive losses, Club Med had to learn that the concept of easy-going, somewhat hedonistic holiday-making had appeal for only a tiny number of Japanese customers. By introducing more structure to the club experience, and by emphasising opportunities to learn new kinds of sports, Club Med finally was able in the 1990s to increase its clientele in Japan substantially.[4]

The mistake of overestimating a foreign firm's own strengths is inseparable from the mistake of underestimating local competition in Japan. In the case of P&G, as in many other instances, Western firms were lulled into a false sense of security by what they perceived to be a rather too cosy relationship between Japanese government and industry and an unusually high degree of collusion among Japanese firms. As a result, foreign companies tended to look down on the capabilities of their Japanese competitors, particularly local firms that were unknown outside Japan. But the reality is very different.

Competition in Japan in many sectors is very intense and, contrary to Western assumptions, close cooperation among Japanese firms has not prevented them from simultaneously competing with each other. Nowhere else in the world will the foreign business person find the degree of transparency that exists in Japan, where newspapers regularly publish market shares of a large number of companies in industries ranging from steel to advertising. In no other country of the world will the foreign firm find more than 10 local manufacturers of air-conditioners, cameras, copiers, audio or video equipment and trucks; nowhere else will the Western firm find 9 national car manufacturers, 6 mainframe computer producers or 34 semiconductor companies, all competing both with each other and against foreign firms in their own local market.

Western firms often find it difficult to understand the precise nature of Japanese competition which, while very intense, does not always manifest itself in expected ways. For example, many are baffled by the fact that even in Japan's embattled markets, the price wars so common in the West are the exception rather than the rule. This was at least true until recently, but is changing now due to the emergence of aggressive retail chains. In general, however, competition in Japan is still measured more qualitatively. The constant flow of new or improved products into the market, and unrelenting attempts by Japanese firms to differentiate their offerings in terms of performance, quality and service, are more accurate indicators of the intensity of rivalry in a given industry. Even at the beginning of the 1990s, more than 1000 new soft drinks were launched in Japan each year, and leading producers of television sets have been known to have up to one hundred different models on the market at any given moment in order to capture all market opportunities. Both strategies are very clear signs of the acute levels of competition. In the West, price wars and noisy advertising battles are seen as indicators of intense competition. Their absence in Japan may explain the failure of Western firms to take accurate measure of Japanese rivalry. In Japan, competitive pressure is often judged according to qualitative criteria which foreign firms may overlook, considering them 'too soft' to be important.

Foreign firms usually enter the Japanese market with new products and services or with goods promising superior performance and prestige. There is no point in offering 'me-too' products, since foreign companies normally operate with higher costs and thus cannot afford to sell these undifferentiated products at lower prices, except, as in the case of Belgian beer or Agfa's films, in close cooperation with retail chains. However, market success achieved on the basis of new or superior product offerings can only be sustained if these products are constantly and rapidly upgraded. Local Japanese competitors study their foreign challengers carefully and can be expected to seize the first opportunity to counter any new product introductions from abroad, either with improved versions or similar products that have more appropriate specifications and a lower price. Strengthened by their reliance on a dedicated distribution network and long-term suppliers who are willing to cooperate closely with them to ensure common survival, the responses of local Japanese companies can be devastating for the foreign firm. This is especially the case if the foreign firm is unprepared, because of false expectations, for the nature, speed and sophistication of the counterattack.

Buyer–supplier relationships

As every economics student is taught, a market is a place where buyers and sellers agree to meet at a certain price. Buyers try to obtain products and services from whoever gives them the lowest price; sellers will try to find buyers who offer the highest price. However this might be descriptive of Western realities, this concept is in many ways inappropriate for describing Japanese markets. In Japan, a transaction is carried out after a relationship has been established, and price is considered only one ingredient in a complex recipe of expectations and interactions. This is, of course, also true in Europe and, to a lesser degree, in the USA. But, by and large, in the West pricing has been and still is the most important factor in the conclusion of a business deal. In Japan, on the other hand, this rarely holds true. This is not to say that pricing is irrelevant, or that it may not gain importance in the future, particularly in Japan's rapidly-changing consumer markets. However, as a general rule, in Japan, relationships matter more than a good price, which is rarely allowed to define a relationship or a social obligation.[5] This rule is particularly applicable to sales to Japanese industrial customers, or to individuals who attach great importance to the image of the manufacturer, or who have high expectations of after-sales service. The easily identifiable *keiretsu*, or enterprise groups, are the best known examples of industrial cliques, described in more detail in Chapter 4. Understanding the links between the various members of these groups and the way they grant each other preferential treatment is vital for calculating an individual firm's chances of success in a given market. But close relationships do not guarantee the conclusion of a contract, not even within the *keiretsu*. Business links are becoming more loose, and selling to and buying from competitors is becoming more common, even on an OEM basis. But Japanese buyers will continue to define the quality of their relationships with existing suppliers, customers and other supporting enterprises as a competitive advantage at least as important as an outsider's ability to offer the right product or service at the right time at the right price.

Consumer behaviour

Consumer behaviour is strongly influenced by cultural and social factors. These factors give marketers the first indications for segmenting their target group and positioning their products and services. Until recently, two distinct features characterised Japanese consumer behaviour. First, the historical separateness of Japan from the rest of the world and the strong Japanese belief in the uniqueness of their culture and society meant that Japanese consumer behaviour differed greatly from that found in other world markets. One striking example of this is the long-standing Japanese emphasis on service rather than price. Second, within the Japanese market, differences in behaviour are almost insignificant. The overwhelming majority of the Japanese still consider themselves members of the middle class, if not the middle of the middle class. Small wage disparities, similar living conditions in largely urban areas, a lack of minorities and sub-cultures, a generally high degree of education and the rapid spread of new trends throughout Japan by the omnipresent media; all these characteristics led to a society whose members enjoyed a uniquely homogeneous standard of living and who tended to act in conformity with the group.

Today, however, the growing integration of Japan in the world economy, the presence of foreign products and services and the exposure of Japanese consumers to foreign cultures and values through the media or foreign travel have blurred the previously clear demarcation between what was 'Japanese' and what was 'foreign'. Today, Western firms offer typical Japanese goods with Japanese specifications and Japanese names, while Japanese firms sell foreign novelties under foreign names. The confusion of product origin, brand images and perceptions has created, at least superficially, a sense of internationalisation in both the Japanese marketplace and the mind of the Japanese consumer.

Not all Japanese consumers, however, are open to these new influences. Not surprisingly, the younger generation has eagerly followed new trends and has tried to distinguish itself from the older generation by a different type of consumer behaviour. Traditional Japanese values are being increasingly questioned and have been replaced with more modern values, which have many similarities with Western values but are nevertheless not exactly the same. Figure 3.1 sets out some shifts in values and behaviour.

In Japanese terms, the *shinjinrui* (rebellious youth) exhibit a very untraditional type of consumer behaviour. They represent the first generation of Japanese who have lived neither in a wartime society nor in a post-war reconstruction society, with their emphasis on frugality and sacrifice to future generations. The *shinjinrui* came of age in a relatively affluent society, where ownership of consumer durables was already widespread, and where the future appeared financially secure. Consequently, and in marked contrast to their parents and elders, this younger generation has been much less hesitant to purchase on credit, or to spend money easily on fads and fashions, entertainment and leisure. Conditioned by this new type of consumer, Japanese markets have become more fickle and product lifecycles have become extremely short.

Traditional	*Modern*
Work	Leisure
Diligence	Quality of life
Thrift	Conspicuous consumption
Deferred gratification	Instant gratification
Non-material	Material
Conformity	Differentiation
Collectivism	Individualism
Loyalty	Independence
Security	Risk taking
Age	Youth
Position	Performance
Dedication	Detachment
Japaneseness	Ecletic/imitative

Figure 3.1   Values in Japan

Consumption for this particular consumer group is in general very lifestyle oriented and strongly influenced by the specialised media. In this context, consumption has become more conspicuous, more expressive of individuality, and more concerned with impressing the consumer's immediate peer group. From the marketing perspective, two separate and clearly defined target groups stand out: young men prior to the acceptance of their first career ladder job, and young women, often referred to as Office Ladies, prior to marriage and/or childbearing. Within these groups, consumption patterns exhibit, again, a high degree of conformity.

The new trend towards consumption and even superficial individuality does not necessarily herald the dawning of a new era in Japan. Much depends on whether the new generation will turn back to traditional Japanese values once they become *shakaijin* (that is, full members of society with responsibilities towards their families or firms). There are indications that this may well be the case.

In Japan, as in Korean and Chinese societies, group conformity and face-saving remain extremely strong driving forces in consumer markets, even among the two target groups mentioned above. Most decisions are strongly influenced by the group with which the individual interacts and by fear that the individual will lose face if social expectations are not met. Brand, price and packaging of presents, for example, must accord with the status of both the giver and the recipient.[6]

In Japan, as in many other East Asian societies, the individual is not judged by his or her own personality, behaviour or performance, but by his or her relationship to other members of the group. As a result, ego-driven consumption which thrives on self-fulfilment is generally considered to be a Western behavioural pattern and is rarely found in Japan. This cultural pattern implies that consumption will continue to be driven by socially-acceptable or socially-driven needs; more specifically, by the individual's desire – and need – to establish and enhance positive images of him- or herself through the prestige value of certain consumer goods. The success of Western prestige brands such as Louis Vuitton, Waterman and BMW in Japan as well as in other Asian countries supports this claim.[7]

The counterargument is that Japan is witnessing the emergence of a new category of lifestyle-oriented consumers with a strong desire to assert their independence from the surrounding society. These new consumers, it is argued, will be the trend-setters for future generations. However, according to this same view, it is premature to expect a truly Western type of individualism. A third perspective posits that in Japan, self-fulfilment can be defined as a more socially-oriented desire to enhance one's position by contributing to society. In contrast to this the Western notion of self-fulfilment is seen as purely egotistical, accumulative individualism with no regard for society. The question remains unresolved. But this disparity in the interpretations of Japan's consumer trends should serve as a caveat to foreign firms. They may find that the Japanese market challenges many common and largely unexamined Western assumptions about the functioning of collectivism and individualism in the market place.

Market trends

The maturation of the Japanese economy, increased competition in many industries, shifts in the political landscape, and the impact of foreign pressure on the country will all change Japan's markets dramatically in the future. In general, we can expect to see barriers to foreign influence dismantled even further. The most persevering of foreign firms will attain insider status, although the increased sophistication of the Japanese market – a direct result of exposure to foreign firms and experience in world markets – will not make it any easier to achieve success on Japanese soil. Japanese government policy, which in the past has been more concerned with the welfare of its industries than of its consumers, may help to convert markets into demand- rather than supply-driven systems, but this again will translate into increased pressure on competing firms.

There are four more specific trends which will shape the future of the Japanese market. First, the country is experiencing a rapid ageing of its population. Though the average age of the population in the 1990s is still lower than that of most other industrial countries, by the second decade of the twenty-first century, the percentage of the population over 65 years old will be the highest in the world. It is the rapidity of this transition, rather than the future demographic profile it produces, which raises a host of challenging questions. Will the rapidly growing 'silver generation' be as active a driver of markets as it has been in the USA, for example, or will its members remain the passive consumers they have traditionally been in Japan? What will be the impact of this change on saving rates, health insurance and pensions? How will housing and special health care services be affected?

Second, despite the commonly accepted image of a staunchly middle-class Japan, the rich are now numerous enough to represent a new market segment. This elite group comprises entrepreneurs, doctors and artists, as well as those who got rich in the 1980s when their real estate investments soared in value. Among the latter are farmers who sold their land at the right time, as well as ordinary middle-class people who were lucky enough to have purchased the right house or apartment before the onset of asset inflation in the mid-1980s. These households have significant disposable income available for conspicuous consumption on goods which look 'special' (that is, non-Japanese) and which carry a high prestige value.

The third trend stems from the changing role of women in Japanese society. Today, women make up more than 40 per cent of Japan's workforce. Labour participation is 70 per cent among young women, a figure that falls when women marry and concentrate on raising children, and then rises again after the children have left school and university and entered professional life themselves. These figures will probably increase in the future. The stereotype of the caring Japanese housewife waiting for her family to return from school and work no longer reflects reality. Japanese women have traditionally been in charge of the family's finances; this power is even more considerable now that they control most of the financial decision-making and also contribute an increasing share to the budget themselves. This has important implications, specifically that in the future fewer and fewer purchasing decisions are likely to be made or even influenced by Japanese men. Because of increasing time constraints on women, who now have a dual role as wage earners and housewives, it is expected that the demand for supporting services and convenience products will continue to accelerate.

The increased purchasing power and financial clout of Japanese women will also accelerate change in the Japanese distribution system. The Japanese have traditionally lived within easy reach of a small Mom-and-Pop store supplied in turn by one or more very small wholesalers. This system evolved in response to the lack of retail space. Retailers needed frequent supplies of small quantities from small wholesalers who were located close by. These would buy from larger, regional wholesalers who in turn were supplied by primary wholesalers often working exclusively with manufacturers or importers. Relationships between the various partners were very close and were built over years, if not decades. The services provided not only included the extension of credit, but also sales promotion support, and reimbursement of returned goods.

While this system suited neighbourhood customers who liked to shop on foot, it drove up prices and perpetuated exclusionary practices. For some years, these old-fashioned shops have been declining and increasingly replaced by large chains of highly efficient convenience stores. With the change in the retail law in 1990, larger firms such as Toys'R'Us have moved into Japan, squeezing out layers of middlemen and their related costs. Finally, new discount stores have opened up which, rather than forging close links with manufacturers or importers, purchase from the lowest cost sources, do not offer any services and use price to undercut their competitors.

The emergence of larger buying units is likely to facilitate the entry of newcomers into the Japanese market; if it does so, this will mark the first shift in the balance of power from manufacturers to distributors, a trend observed in Western markets for over a decade. Nevertheless, it is unlikely that the deeply-rooted traditional retail sector will go out of business overnight. Instead, it can be expected to co-exist with modern forms of distribution for the foreseeable future.

ASEANIEs

Demographic changes

Of all the data used to describe and evaluate a country, demographic data are often the most reliable. Demographic characteristics permit relatively safe forecasts, not only in terms of total population number, but also in terms of age, household size, geographic and racial distribution, and so on. Dramatic demographic changes can be expected to occur in the ASEANIEs over the next few decades. As a result of the rapid economic development of Asia's recent past, they will have a decisive impact on future market opportunities.

The most important demographic change is the decline in population growth. However, this does not mean that the size of Asia's populations is stabilising. As Table 3.1 shows, Indonesia's population will increase from 201 million in 1995 to 283 million over the next 30 years.

Table 3.1   Actual and Projected Population Size in Millions

Country	1990	1995	2025
Indonesia	184	201	283
Philippines	62	69	105
Thailand	55	58	72
South Korea	43	45	50
Malaysia	18	20	31
Hong Kong	6	6	7
Singapore	3	3	3
China	1153	1238	1540

SOURCE: *World Research 1994–95*, World Research Institute, Oxford University Press, 1994.

Declining population growth is primarily due to reduced childbearing. However, this phenomenon is partly compensated for by reduced infant mortality and longer life expectancy. As a consequence the structure of the population is changing and the percentage of young people is shrinking (see Table 3.2). While Japan has by far the oldest population in Asia, the NIEs follow, with the ASEAN countries representing the youngest populations.

Table 3.2   Percentage of Population 25 Years and Older

Country	1995	2020
Hong Kong	67	76
Japan	69	75
Singapore	62	69
Taiwan	58	69
South Korea	58	69
China	56	66
Thailand	50	61
Indonesia	46	59
Malaysia	44	59
Philippines	42	53

SOURCE: *World Population Register: Estimates on Projection, Cult Related Demographic Statistics 1994–95*, World Bank, Johns Hopkins University Press, 1994.

As a result of these shifts, three major changes now taking place will have a direct impact on consumption patterns. First, due to the increasing numbers of young adults with disposable income, the number of households will go up sharply. These nest-building households will be considerably smaller and will need to be accommodated and equipped. Demand for housing and consumer durables will therefore remain strong for the foreseeable future. Second, relative spending power is slowly shifting from the younger to the more mature households who have completed their family. In these units the demand will change from daily necessities to transportation, better housing, entertainment and education. Third, as women are freed of their maternal responsibilities, they will increasingly join the workforce. This will in turn create a higher demand for labour-saving goods and restaurant-going.

In addition, the trend towards urbanisation can be expected to continue. This will lighten the task of marketing products and services as consumers are within easier reach, in terms of both logistics and communication. Urban dwellers, while on average much better off financially than their rural counterparts, will nevertheless pay much higher prices for housing, leaving them with less disposable income than their total income would indicate. Traffic congestion in the main cities will worsen and the existing infrastructure will be put under extreme stress. Governments will be forced to spend heavily just to keep up with the demand for utilities and public services. Smaller families with fewer children will allow households to save more for their retirement – a system already obligatory in Singapore – and will also force parents to rely less on their children as a source of security in their old age. But as an increasing percentage of the adult population reaches retirement age, adults will begin to draw on their savings rather than accumulating more wealth. This could have the effect of reducing the net saving rate.

Consumer segmentation

Demographics, income levels and distribution, expenditure and saving rates, geographic dispersion of the population, psychographic and behavioural characteristics; all of these variables influence the make-up of segments for consumer goods. These segments have to be defined differently for each of the ASEANIEs and for each product category.

Market research firms generally divide the consumer population into segments A, B, C, D and E, thereby using relative income levels as the main criteria for differentiation.[8] It is obvious that in developing countries with a low average income the top segments are very small, while the overwhelming majority of people still live in relatively poor circumstances and have only very limited purchasing power. The simplified segmentation shown below

(Figure 3.2) for a less developed country (LDC) may be typical of Indonesia. It looks quite different from a typical segmentation in an NIE such as Singapore, where a large group of relatively affluent spenders has emerged, while the majority of the population still has limited purchasing power. It must be noted here that segments always relate to each other within one given country: a member of the E-segment in Singapore is probably better off than the C- or even B-consumer in Indonesia.

It is only when a country has reached the status of a developed country (DC), such as the USA or Germany, that the segmentation takes the shape of a diamond, with the majority of consumers belonging to the middle-class, and a similar percentage of the population either above or below that level. The Scandinavian countries represent the extremes of middle-class countries due to high taxes on the rich and welfare payments to the poor. Almost everyone lives on a similar net income. It is interesting to note that the development of a capitalist society from the status of an LDC to an NIE, and

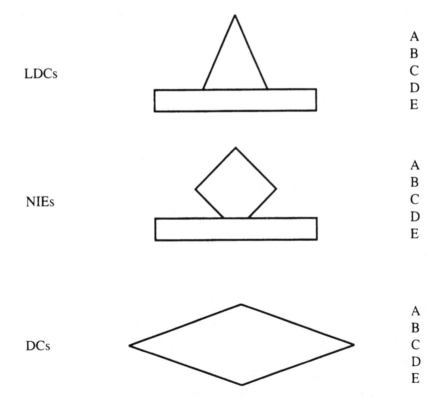

Figure 3.2 Class Structures in Development Stages

later to a DC, does not occur through a rapid growth of the D-segment, but rather through the growth of B- and C-consumers (on account of the D-segment), while the relative fate of the E-segment remains unchanged in relative terms for quite some time.

Bearing in mind the heterogeneity of the economies and markets in the ASEANIEs, a segmentation into three types of consumer may suffice for a first overview:

- The elite segment
  (where money does not matter);
- The transition segment
  (where things are changing); and
- The traditional segment
  (where one gets through the day).

The elite segment consists of a tiny minority of business, government and military leaders who, by any Western standard, are rich. They live in the capital, but travel frequently abroad. Their consumer behaviour and tastes do not differ significantly across borders and they are on the whole similar to those of the rich in the West and Japan. Although their total number is small, their frequent public appearances and their role as trend-setters in these societies make them important in marketing terms.

Those who have benefited from the economic growth of recent years represent the transition segment. The members of this segment have above-average incomes and live mainly in urban areas. They are open-minded, active, consumption-oriented and modern without necessarily being Westernised. They live in a world which is entirely different from the one their parents knew 20 or 30 years ago. They have neither inherited nor accumulated substantial wealth but possess managerial and technical skills which their parents may not have had. For this reason, this segment is not yet called middle class (a term which implies a certain degree of stability over generations).

Members of the transition segment are well educated, often thanks to sacrifices their parents made, and belong to the sector of the workforce which is currently most in demand in the ASEANIEs. A majority of Singaporeans belong to this segment (Singapore, in fact, is a country in transition) and perhaps 10 per cent of all Indonesians. The percentages for the other ASEANIEs lie between these extremes.

The demand from the transition segment creates the most dynamic markets in the region for products ranging from up-market clothing to motorbikes and cars, and services such as insurance and travel. These product markets of non-essentials aiming to improve the quality of life benefit more than others from the growth in income of the transition segment. This purchasing pattern confirms the economic law which states that as income increases the percentage spent on food will decrease and the percentage spent on housing and household operations will stay roughly constant, while other purchases will increase. The number of people belonging to this segment is also increasing as a higher percentage of the population becomes better educated, moves into urban areas, or is absorbed into the workforce of the modern sector.

In the traditional segment income is limited to the purchase of daily necessities and the occasional acquisition of cheap consumer durables. Most of the people in the countryside belong to this segment, but so do the poor masses living in urban areas. Modernisation and industrialisation of the country have hardly affected them. The members of this segment are very price-conscious and are laggards in the adoption of new products.

For Western firms who aim exclusively at the small elite segment it is not essential to make a major marketing effort in each country. The high prestige value of brands themselves creates the necessary pull. Regional promotional activities, combined with a controlled distribution of products in Singapore and Hong Kong, may suffice, as brands with a strong appeal will find their way into the other countries through indigenous channels, thereby avoiding high tariff barriers.

More marketing effort over time will be required to cater to the transition segment. The sales response function of Figure 3.3 shows the shape of the

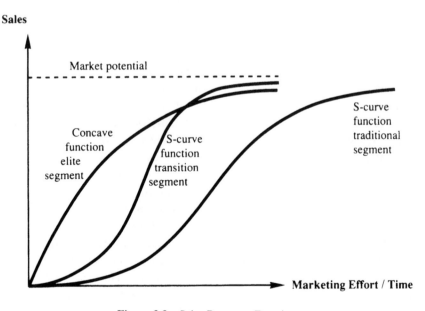

Figure 3.3 Sales Response Function

classical S-curve. Adaptation of the marketing-mix to the respective characteristics of the markets is usually necessary, and positive results can only be
achieved over time. Those who have started to cultivate the market at an early
stage will have a considerable head start over latecomers. Western firms
have most firmly established themselves in the fields of food, cosmetics and
pharmaceuticals. In consumer durables, product offerings are almost exclusively
Japanese, with competition emerging from Korean and Taiwanese producers.

For the traditional segment the sales response function again follows an
S-curve, but it is flatter and more stretched. In this segment, consumers are
reluctant to switch to new products because their limited purchasing power
makes them extremely averse to taking risks. They are also more loyal to
traditional products (preferring tea to soft drinks, for example). Foreign
firms need to keep their costs well under control to penetrate this segment.
They also have to build up elaborate distribution systems to reach the
consumers in the countryside; this involves a major effort which will only
show results over a considerable amount of time.

The distribution revolution

Nowhere in the markets of the ASEANIEs has change been as dramatic and
as visible as in the distribution sector. Japanese department stores dominate
the shopping areas of Singapore and Hong Kong, Bangkok and Malaysia,
hypermarkets attract large crowds in Taipei, and shopping malls become entertainment centres in Manila, with everything from ice-skating rinks to cinemas.
The traditional sector, consisting of small family-run shops, market traders
and itinerant vendors, is in retreat, at least in the urban centres.[9]

Growth in purchasing power, the increasing mobility of the consumer, and
interest in a wider choice of products and services under one roof have been
the driving forces behind this trend. Shopping has also become an important
social activity. Shopping centres are combinations of department and speciality
stores, restaurants and fast-food stalls, art galleries, discos and cinemas.
Lack of capital and expertise has prevented the small traditional Mom-and-
Pop shops from competing with these new types of outlets. In this respect,
family-run businesses fall short in terms of both scope and scale.

The concentrated buying power of chain stores and the increased use of
information technology in the outlets make up for their higher overheads. In
suburban neighbourhoods and country villages, however, the new economics
of distribution have not yet led to major changes. It is unlikely that these areas
will experience modernisation in the near future. Here, as in Japan, the
emphasis is on having a shop close by where one can buy fresh daily
necessities in small quantities and carry them home easily. It is the personal

relationship with the store owner which matters, and the credit one can enjoy without the need for a credit card.

Along with the modernisation of the retail sector, the wholesale trade is being streamlined. In the past, low entry and exit barriers in trade led to myriad middlemen selling to other middlemen before the products reached the retailers. The professionalisation of the trade, and the increased purchasing power of the larger retailers, have led to a decrease in the number of wholesalers.

Chinese distributors who dominate the wholesale sector in South-East Asia have traditionally defined their business as the management of cash rather than the buying and selling of products. They obtain their goods from manufacturers against payment after two or three months. These goods are then sold to retailers either against cash or credit at very high interest rates. This very high asset turnover (assets/sales) allows them to add either a very low margin or no margin at all to the products channelled through them. Interest earned from granting credit, or the return on investment made with cash raised through wholesale activities in real estate or the stock markets, is enough to achieve an overall profit on activities. With one party interested in pursuing long-term marketing strategies and the other interested in raising funds, relationships between manufacturers and wholesalers are often difficult to manage.

Western manufacturers operating in Asian countries other than Singapore and Hong Kong are usually prevented from going into distribution. They are often forced to use local distributors and have to limit themselves to sales promotions at the point of sale. Most countries, however, have already taken steps towards the liberalisation of the distribution sector.

Western distribution companies face similar restrictions. Nevertheless, through franchise operations, licensing and joint venturing a number of firms have been able to overcome these barriers. Benetton (Italy), Esprit (USA) and Marks and Spencer (UK) sell garments in most ASEANIEs; IKEA (Sweden) and Habitat (UK) have started distributing their furniture in Singapore and Hong Kong, where the French *grands magasins*, Galeries Lafayette and Printemps, compete head-on with Japanese department stores. In convenience stores 7-Eleven (USA/Japan) leads across the region. American fast-food chains such as McDonald's and Kentucky Fried Chicken count their Asian outlets among their most successful ones. Carrefour (France) introduced hyper-markets in Taiwan and has expanded from there into other countries. Makro (Netherlands) brought the cash-and-carry concept to Thailand before starting operations in other ASEANIEs. Amway (USA) in Korea evaded restrictions on distribution activities by engaging customers to sell its products to friends and neighbours for a commission. The Singaporean bookstore chain, Times Publishing, formed a joint venture in Singapore in which an Indonesian partner holds the majority. This company now operates the first foreign bookstores in Indonesia.

Relationships between foreign manufacturers and appointed importers are bound to run into trouble when products enter the latter's exclusive territory through parallel channels and are sold by unauthorised agents at a lower price. This happens rather frequently in the ASEANIEs. As the official importers shoulder the costs for sales promotions and advertising, they cannot compete with parallel imports which are often bought from the cheapest sources world-wide and then brought through customs without paying full duty. To stop this, manufacturers have had to check their own order processing procedures and keep track of their products. In trying to limit differential price policies, Western firms can reduce or prevent arbitrage opportunities.[10]

Industrial markets

Growing demand from the transition and traditional segments in the domestic markets of Asia Pacific, coupled with steady foreign demand for the export of manufactured goods, has led to a rapid increase in sales of raw materials and semi-manufactured goods. The demand for plants and equipment is created by the need to replace existing equipment, to expand capacity to satisfy increasing demand by import-substitution programmes in the more inward-looking countries, and the ever-increasing export drive in all the countries of the region.

Large-scale turnkey projects in extractive industries and the processing of raw materials represent further opportunities for the sale of capital goods. The urgent need for the development and upgrading of the infrastructure requires investment in road construction equipment, power plants, telephone systems, port facilities, and so on. The total demand for industrial products in the ASEANIEs far exceeds that in industrial countries of similar economic size.

In terms of purchasing behaviour, four different market segments can be observed in the ASEANIEs:

- The government and state-owned enterprises
- Leading local firms and non-Japanese multinationals
- Japanese firms
- Backyard operators

The government plays a major role in the purchasing of industrial products, either as a direct buyer, or indirectly through government-owned enterprises. In most countries of the region the public sector still dominates the industrial scene, although tentative and carefully-monitored attempts at privatisation have been made. Political considerations often influence purchasing decisions, and as a rule preference is given to local over foreign suppliers. To a certain extent competitive bidding controls political interference and corruption, and this in turn ensures more objective decision-making. Successful bids have often been prepared for by extensive information-gathering well in advance of the official announcement of a tender. Consultants who determine the technical specifications of a project play an important part in the complex process of marketing to government institutions.

Through the formulation of policies, setting of standards, granting of licences, provision of foreign exchange and credit or more subtle ways of exerting pressure, Asian governments also have a major influence on purchasing decisions in the private sectors of the region. Industry associations and chambers of commerce provide help in coming to grips with those factors.

There is very little difference between the purchasing processes in the leading local or regional firms and the subsidiaries of Western multinationals. In both cases technical staff are local and act as gatekeepers, specifiers and influencers. However, important purchasing decisions will be made by the chief executive who is often the founder or owner of the local firm. Subsidiaries of Western firms may have to refer major decisions back to their headquarters or regional office, or at the very least coordinate with them. Expatriate staff are often involved in the decision process, introducing a certain bias toward purchases from suppliers of the same national origin. Whether this arises from greater familiarity with home country firms or better personal relationships with one's own countrymen, such a bias is rather weak, and does not lead to the exclusion of other suppliers.

In the case of the subsidiaries of Japanese multinationals, the bias tends to be much stronger. By and large the Japanese prefer to deal with proven suppliers, which usually means Japanese companies. This is due to the very close relationships established at home between the main Japanese companies and their sub-contractors, as well as the strong influence which headquarters exert on subsidiaries. The closed nature of Japanese communities abroad adds to exclusive tendencies among Japanese firms. There is, however, also a structural element in preferring home country suppliers. Most of the Japanese manufacturers in the region are set up as joint ventures with local firms. In many cases, the large Japanese trading houses, or *sogo shosha*, have been involved in setting up ventures and have taken a small equity participation in them. With their enormous product portfolio and strong representation in all ASEANIEs, the *sogo shosha* can basically supply every additional requirement to ventures which is not already delivered by proven suppliers from Japan. As a consequence, there is not much room left for non-Japanese suppliers except for those dealing in niche products, such as special chemicals. The number of actively-producing Japanese subsidiaries in the region now amounts to several thousand and therefore represents an important but problematic segment. Marketing efforts often have to be directed at headquarters rather than at the operating unit in the specific country.

The backyard operators represent for the Western firm another difficult segment. These are local companies with a very low level of technical expertise and limited purchasing power. They play a useful role in the domestic economy with the small-scale manufacturing of simple consumer goods aimed at the traditional segment. Many of these firms operate outside major cities and are difficult to contact without local intermediaries. While overall they form a major economic factor, it is difficult and expensive to deal with them as single units directed by entrepreneurial owners. This segment may not be important to Western firms whose product line is either too sophisticated or too expensive. However, this same segment represents a more attractive market for sellers of second-hand machinery or suppliers of commodity products from Taiwan and Korea.

By and large, Western managers will find that Asian technical expertise in selecting industrial products has improved dramatically in recent years. Differences in quality between products destined for the domestic market and for exports are slowly disappearing. In buying equipment, however, there has been a visible tendency to prefer a more capital-intensive process than is justified by Asia's existing labour rates. Quality consciousness, the perception that machines are more easily managed than workers, the expectation of a future rise in labour rates or impending labour shortages are often-cited reasons for this. Prestige, however, also plays a role in impressing both customers and suppliers.

In many of the industrial sectors in the ASEANIEs, the provision of services is considered to be at least of equal importance for the buyer as price and payment terms. The degree to which a supplier is prepared to provide services is perceived by many Asians to be a strong indicator of commitment to the country, market or customer. Service starts with supplying sufficient information and a certain willingness to adapt products. It requires extensive local representation, after-sales service on the spot, and local warehousing to ensure on-time delivery. Traditional Western trading houses are said to have lost out against Japanese competitors by relying too heavily on contacts and commercial expertise, while the Japanese *sogo shosha* provide service and technical expertise.

The manufacturers from the ASEANIEs have been categorised into different technological and developmental stages. Each of these stages requires very different marketing strategies.[11] The first stage is the implementors who assemble a limited product range and who are at the first phase of the learning process. They search for new product and production opportunities. In general, implementors prefer to be offered a complete package consisting of raw materials, components, and capital equipment. This is the case for the medium-sized Indonesian cigarette manufacturer Sumatra Tobacco, which at the beginning of the 1980s decided to diversify into instant coffee. Western firms have to adjust to this bundling and put emphasis on marketing technology rather than products.

The second stage is the assimilators, those who have learned fast from their phase as assemblers and have moved toward the additional production of first components. The assimilators put more emphasis on quality and specific technical know-how. Assimilators do not require technical expertise across the whole product range, but advice on specific products and processes which need up-grading. An analysis of the operations of the potential buyer is required to provide better solutions (a less essential service in industrial countries). The Filipino brewer San Miguel does not need any more advice on brewing; however, the company works closely with Japanese and Western firms to improve its bottle production.

The third stage is the improvers, who manufacture more sophisticated products. They are interested in boosting their productivity and becoming world-class producers. In-house expertise helps in extending their product range through new product development. Aspiring improvers look for advanced technologies similar to those in industrial markets. Expertise on the supplier's side is taken for granted and full service is expected. Competitive bids are the rule for any rebuy. The Taiwanese PC-manufacturers Acer and Mitac, for example, pursue such policies.

Manufacturers at all three of these stages can be found in each of the countries of the ASEANIEs. Countries such as Korea or Singapore, however, tend to have more improvers, while in Indonesia and the Philippines implementors play a more important role.

Table 3.3 shows the main buying decision criteria used by the firms in their specific development stage when they buy equipment and materials for the first time, buy again in a modified form and simply repeat the order.

Depending on the will of the foreign parent company to transfer technology, subsidiaries of foreign firms and joint ventures will quickly move from the stage of being a technological implementor to that of an assimilator. There is, however, less interest in pushing subsidiaries in the ASEANIEs to the more advanced improver stage. Local or regionally operating firms will move through the stages more slowly.

Table 3.3   Buying Decision Criteria

	First buy	*Modified rebuy*	*Repeat order*
Implementor	Packaged technology	Reliability Training	Reliability Price
Assimilator	Specific technology	Quality Service	Value
Improver	Advanced technology	Delivery Price	Price

CHINA

The shift from state planning to market forces

Of all the countries in the Asia Pacific region, China presents the Western firm with the extreme case of a country in flux. When China opened its economy to the West in 1978–9, foreign businessmen declared the country to be the biggest remaining unexploited market in the world.

Reforms began in the agricultural sector and the resulting increase in output and productivity ensured a stable supply of food for the country's vast population and an increase in income for its rural communities. More than 70 per cent of Chinese live in rural communities. These communities moved eagerly into light manufacturing and, with their high savings rates, were able to finance part of the reforms in industry.

The opening of the country to foreign investment – particularly in the SEZs – brought in technological expertise and links with the outside world. The latter were urgently needed in order to export and earn foreign exchange. The influx of foreign exchange allowed imports to come in, though in a strictly regulated fashion.

Major reforms of industry were initiated in the mid-1980s, slowly phasing out mandatory and guidance planning in an increasing number of sectors, reducing the influence of the state's centralised administration, and moving towards market prices that reflected supply and demand. By any criteria, the results have been spectacular. The standard of living in China has visibly improved and the country has become a major player in world trade. The objective to quadruple its GNP within 20 years by the year 2000 was reached much earlier (an achievement considered impossible by economists and China experts at the beginning of the 1980s).

However, China's move towards economic pragmatism still contradicts its political ideology. Its reform goal is an open-ended one, shifting from a 'planned economy with the market as auxiliary regulator' and 'socialism with

Chinese characteristics' towards a totally undefined 'socialist market economy' within the space of just a few years. The direction of change seems to be clear as long as the economy maintains its momentum. Nevertheless, temporary setbacks cannot be ruled out. Some 50 million party members and 30 million state bureaucrats may perhaps have given up their beliefs, but it will not be easy to convince them to slacken their grip on the reins of influence and power. Dramatic growth has produced a large number of winners, particularly in the urban areas. Peasants, on the other hand, who represent the overwhelming majority of the Chinese population, may object to feeling left behind when they notice rising income differentials.

Even from this brief portrait, it is obvious that China presents extremely attractive market opportunities, but it is also a country rife with unpredictability and uncertainties. The immense size of the population and land mass raises the question of whether China should be considered as a single market or a number of warring provinces, competing for scarce resources, and eager to promote their own well-being (if not self-sufficiency). An investment in booming Guangdong, for example, does not guarantee access to markets in the hinterland of China; a plant in Shanghai does not necessarily ensure preferential treatment from a Beijing bureaucrat, who may choose to favour an importer from Japan or Europe. In contrast to the tendency towards decentralisation stands the development towards a Greater China, integrating the economies of Hong Kong and Taiwan. In the future, this could require a much more coordinated strategy from the Western firm.

The move away from bureaucratic allocations and targets towards market mechanisms, and China's lack of clear rules and regulations, raises doubts about who among the government officials is still in charge of certain industries, and to what degree. The lack of information and the tendency of officials to declare basic economic data state secrets make feasibility studies, market research and planning difficult. China's willingness to provide information is improving, though data remain unreliable and are quickly outdated by the speed of change mentioned above.

The ever-changing regulations and the weak system of justice in the country provides flexibility for those who are able to use their influence or who can massage the system. But by and large the legal situation has improved, though the enforcement of contracts remains at times difficult.

Stratification of the consumer

Until recently, communist ideology had ensured that income differentials in China remained small. Because of this, the segmentation used to describe the ASEANIEs is inappropriate, at least at the current phase in China's history. To cite one example: China's most highly qualified specialists still earn about the same as its unskilled workers, and have a similar standard of living. However, the very high income growth rates in the SEZs, in Guangdong province and in the urban areas of the coastal belt have created a group of 60–80 million people who are estimated to have about three times the income of the average Chinese. These relatively affluent consumers have reaped the lion's share of the benefits from the country's rural and urban reforms, and are now almost comparable to what has been identified as the transition segment in the ASEANIEs.

There is also a small group of people who have made enough money as entrepreneurs or speculators be able to afford to buy a car or expensive electronic gadgets. Estimates of their number range from a few hundred thousand to five million, though it is impossible to verify these estimates given the fact that conspicuous wealth still carries the residual risk of persecution if the political winds change. At the other end of the spectrum is a group of people living in poverty, either in isolated rural areas, or unemployed.

Unemployment has grave consequences for the individual in China's urban areas, where the state and the communist party still use a comprehensive social welfare system to control freedom of movement and residence to a degree unimaginable in the West. Estimates therefore range from 50–150 million people but, again, official data are not available, since the government maintains the claim that it provides the population with an 'iron rice bowl', or basic food and shelter.

This still leaves the marketing man with about one billion average income Chinese (see Figure 3.4) who over the last few years have shown a surprisingly strong appetite for consumer durables such as bicycles, watches, television sets and cameras. These consumers are moving up the income ladder and are now acquiring video recorders, air-conditioners and motorcycles.

Consumption of soft drinks, more up-market food products, cosmetics, toys and ready-to-wear apparel – all of which are frequently sold at relatively high prices – has also grown substantially. While Japanese manufacturers have tried to capture the demand for consumer durables, Western firms such as

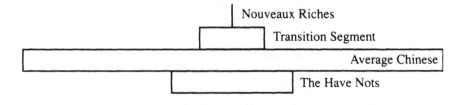

Figure 3.4   Income Segmentation in China

Nestlé, Pepsi-Cola, P&G, Wella and Unilever have built up major operations in China in order to exploit the market for consumer goods. Foreign firms, mostly in joint venture with Chinese companies, must charge much higher prices than their local competitors. This is due, in part, to very high duties on imported goods, parts, components and raw materials, but also to the higher cost of operating in China.

Chinese consumers have shown a willingness to accept these higher prices in exchange for better product presentation and quality. This is surprising considering that the World Bank calculates an average Chinese income of only US$750 per annum. Various studies have tried to come to grips with this phenomenon.[12] They conclude that in quantitative terms the low income figures grossly underestimate the purchasing power and the standard of living in China for a number of reasons, including the fact that housing, health, education and transportation are either entirely financed or heavily subsidised by the state. In terms of quality of life, greater consumer choice and improved distribution have increased consumer satisfaction. However, diminishing economic security, increasing environmental degradation and unequal access to education and medical care have negatively influenced the welfare of the people since the beginning of the reforms.

As the Chinese market becomes more sophisticated through the activities of foreign firms, local producers will find it increasingly difficult to compete. This is especially true for Guangdong province where the largely urban consumers are strongly influenced by Hong Kong's consumption patterns via exposure to Hong Kong television and radio stations and constant contact with Hong Kong Chinese.

The Hong Kong-isation of Guangdong – already very visible in the Shenzhen SEZ – represents an extreme caricature of Chinese consumerism matched only by the emergence of yuppies with their portable phones in Shanghai. For the moment these must still be considered exceptions since they are not at all representative of the overall state of the Chinese consumer market. While some Chinese consumers may be very open-minded and keen to opt for new, modern and foreign brands, the vast majority still show more conservative consumer behaviour by sticking to proven and traditional Chinese products (see Figure 3.5).

There are also important differences in purchasing behaviour. While some people want to flaunt their wealth and differentiate themselves from their neighbours and colleagues, others still adhere to egalitarian principles and restrain themselves from conspicuous luxury consumption. As Maoist political ideology fades, these latter will probably become increasingly rare.

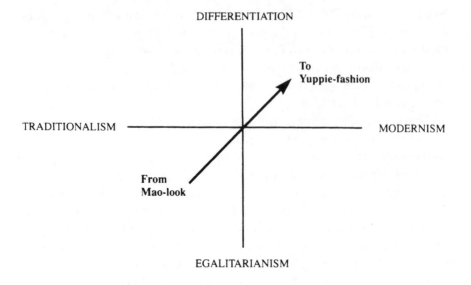

Figure 3.5   Psychographic Segmentation in China

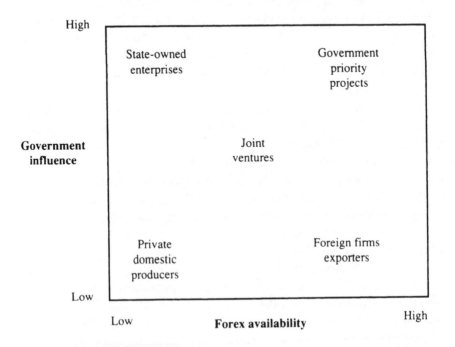

Figure 3.6   Industrial Customer Segmentation in China

Industrial markets

Industrial products are sold to the government or to producers of other industrial or consumer products. Two major criteria can be used to classify these customers: the degree to which they are dependent on the government, and the degree to which they are able to pay in foreign exchange. Both criteria influence the chances of foreign suppliers selling into the country (see Figure 3.6).

As a general rule, China's existing import substitution policies create disadvantages for foreign suppliers *vis-à-vis* local Chinese producers, since Western firms invariably want to be paid in foreign exchange and imports are normally more expensive due to high import duties. These constraints, however, can be partly overcome when the products in question have been identified as a strategic priority by the Chinese government, army or party hierarchy (for example, infrastructure projects in telecommunications) and where there is either insufficient or poor quality local supply. In trying to sell to the government or government-dependent enterprises it is vital for the Western firm not only to identify the potential customer and the urgency of the need, but also to find out the degree to which potential competitors are willing to offer their products against the local currency.

China's move away from central planning has made the identification of potential customers much more difficult. For Western firms, this often requires much more intensive and extensive research than in other countries in the region. In China, buyers exist at the national, provincial and municipal levels. However, most Chinese industries are vertically oriented, with the result that decisions made at one level can be influenced by bureaucrats at another level. State import and export companies, formerly unavoidable, are still useful in some instances, but in other situations may only add to the general complexity and cost of operations. In the electronics industry, for example, a number of different ministries, departments and bureaux are involved, often with overlapping and ill-defined responsibilities. Bureaucrats are normally reluctant or unable to disclose who has decision-making power, who has influence, and who has the right to specify technical requirements. They are very often unclear about the situation themselves. The experience of many Western firms shows, however, that power resides where the funds are, and this is increasing in the provinces.

The growing willingness of China's state-party bureaucracy to move profit responsibility to the enterprises themselves has concentrated purchasing decisions in the hands of managers. However, approval is often needed from higher authorities, particularly when foreign exchange allocations are required or when major deals are concluded with long-term commitments from the

Figure 3.7 Typical Industrial Marketing Procedure

Chinese side. In any case, foreign suppliers of industrial products deal with a multitude of contacts, requiring both persistence and a good feel for the interdependencies of the various players.

Numerous reports show that Chinese bureaucrats and managers try to limit their risks when making decisions. This has meant that they prefer to deal with well-known companies and individuals with whom they have previously established a good relationship. Western firms therefore have to create an initial awareness of their company and products before starting to develop personal relationships (*guanxi*)[13] with individuals in the various bureaucracies. This can then be followed up with a more detailed provision of technical details, often in the form of a seminar in China. Should more concrete interest in an agreement emerge, the Chinese partners will often insist on an invitation to the supplier's overseas plant or headquarters. Only after these steps have been taken can serious negotiations begin (see Figure 3.7).

Marketing instruments

Price controls in China are being increasingly phased out and limited to the most essential products. This development, which started with a two-tier pricing policy in the early 1980s, allows the seller the freedom to set the price. But exploitation of product scarcity through high pricing by foreign firms risks inviting retaliation from the Chinese government, which is now well aware of market prices abroad. Low pricing, on the other hand, does not guarantee high sales for industrial products. Purchasing decisions are not always taken on the basis of economic considerations, and political arguments may weigh heavily. In bids for major projects, financial terms are becoming more important. China has shed its reluctance to become indebted to foreigners, and foreign governments tend to support their national suppliers with the offer of cheap finance.

There is a general aversion in China to paying for software and services, such as training and consultancy. As a result foreign suppliers often try to bundle the various parts of their offer into a single package with a lump sum price. This procedure, which is resented in other parts of Asia, is actually appreciated by Chinese buyers. They expect both to obtain a favourable overall price discount and to reduce bureaucratic interference and influence by asking for funding and/or approval only once.

Due to the emphasis on quantitative targets rather than qualitative aspects of output, product quality has always been extremely low in China. For several decades, service virtually did not exist. Progress has been made since 1979, but the gap between China's quality standards and those in the rest of Asia, and especially Japan, is astounding. Foreign products are expected to be of better quality and carry a high-status image. Consumer satisfaction with the product and a good reputation associated with either the manufacturer or the brand can lead to exceptionally high brand loyalties. The prestige which accompanies a given product is highly valued, even in industrial markets. This may explain why the Chinese often purchase advanced machinery, though less sophisticated equipment could be cheaper, easier to handle and therefore more feasible. Service is now expected to be provided, normally free of charge or against low fees.

There are few restrictions on Chinese advertising, which makes heavy use of television, radio, magazines and newspapers. The national television station, Central TV, claims an audience of 600 million for its evening news, and advertising hoardings can be seen everywhere in the countryside. The first direct mail campaigns have recently been carried out. Advertising rates have increased but are still reasonable. Foreign firms are charged higher prices and must pay in foreign currency. Joint ventures pay in local currency but still pay more than local firms.

Due to the overall lack of information and reading material, advertising is followed with great interest. Simple explanatory messages seem to work better than sophisticated image campaigns. Besides creating awareness and preferences among the consumers, advertising has to influence bureaucrats and convince them of the usefulness of the offer for the Chinese. Word-of-mouth is important, as is the recommendation of a certain product by a direct salesman or employees in department stores. Avon's use of part-timers to sell its cosmetics directly to the consumer – primarily via the traditional Chinese network of friends and neighbours – has been very successful in southern China.

Distribution is the most critical and limiting marketing-mix factor for the foreign firm in China. The problems relate to both logistics and channel structure. The large distances, provincial self-interest, the overburdened transportation and telecommunications infrastructure and the lack of independent flexible transport companies make physical distribution extremely difficult. It takes three or more days to drive newly-built Volkswagen Santanas on bad roads from the Shanghai plant to customers in the Sichuan province. When they arrive they are in need of a good overhaul if they are not to be considered used cars. It is easier to ship coal from Australia to the coastal regions of China than to transport it on the one single railway from the hinterland.

The distribution channels are no less chaotic. While formerly the government was in charge of allocating output from the factories to a network of state wholesalers and retailers, a new breed of private distributor has emerged in recent years. This gives Western firms the opportunity to bypass some of the bureaucratic organisations. But the evaluation of channel alternatives is difficult and the process of streamlining channels is slow due to the importance of *guanxi*, the system of personal interrelationships and mutual obligations.

For most products, several distribution systems now exist in parallel. Some state-owned department stores take part of their deliveries directly from the producers, bypassing their own ministries or related wholesalers. Cooperative stores run by local governments compete with factory outlets and an increasing number of specialised private retailers. Joint ventures by Nike, Esprit and Benetton are beginning to sell through their own retail outlets, and chain stores such as 7-Eleven and department stores such as Yaohan may be well established across China within the next few years.

Notes and references

1. This is the group of middle-sized developing and industrialising countries made up by the ASEAN group and the NIEs.
2. Fields (1989).
3. Fields (1989).
4. Schütte and Ishida (1990).
5. Schrage (1991).
6. Lee (1990).
7. Schütte with Ciarlante (1998).
8. Roberto (1987).
9. Malayang (1988).
10. Palia and Keown (1991).
11. Wortzel (1983).
12. Chai (1992).
13. The concept of *guanxi* will be discussed in Chapter 5.

4   The Players

The large number of different business players and the variety of their approaches has made the Asia Pacific region a dynamic competitive arena with intensive rivalry. As Figure 4.1 shows, competition in most sectors comes not only from global players (the 'traditional' multinationals and the 'new' multinationals from Korea and Taiwan) but also from regional firms such as the Overseas Chinese, the *hongs* (formerly colonial trading houses) and various local companies. The basis of their competitive advantage differs considerably. Asian firms therefore cut across a huge range of technologies, markets and management philosophies, from the global Japanese *kaisha* to the high-tech clones of Taiwan and Hong Kong, and the diversified trading and manufacturing *chaebol* conglomerates of South Korea.

Until the 1960s successful Asian corporations were viewed as exploiters of cheap labour or imitators of outdated technologies. This perception started to change in the 1970s *vis-à-vis* Japanese corporations and more recently *vis-*

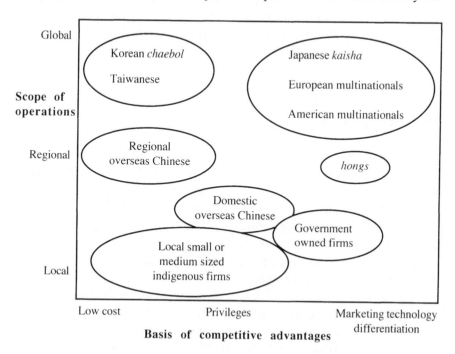

Figure 4.1   The Players in the Asia Pacific Competitive Arena

à-vis Korean and Taiwanese firms. Still other players, such as the Overseas Chinese, remained relatively unknown.

Shaped by different societal cultures and different economic and political home environments, firms in Asia have developed unique management styles which are often an eclectic mix of traditional, Confucian-inspired Asian ethics, entrepreneurship and Western professional management. In terms of organisation and business logic, they can be divided into very distinct groups: Japanese *kaisha*, Korean *chaebol*, and Overseas Chinese family-owned and managed conglomerates, with additional players such as the *hongs* and state-owned enterprises. Indigenous, non-Chinese private companies in the ASEAN countries have also gained prominence in the region without developing their own specific management style. In their often opportunistic diversification policy they resemble Overseas Chinese firms, but rely on the recruitment of a country's best talents rather than on family members. San Miguel in the Philippines, the Bakrie Brothers in Indonesia or Siam Cement in Thailand are good examples of such companies.

The Asian crisis has revealed the weaknesses of many Asian players: lack of transparency, over-diversification, speculation, poor financial discipline, dangerously high gearing ratios, and an overall lack of intrinsic competitiveness in the absence of government protection. In this chapter we discuss the origin, management styles, strategic development and logic of the various Asian players. In the final section we look towards their future.

JAPANESE *KAISHA*

Devoted employees and patient capital

As Japan's economy stands out among the others in the region in terms of size and sophistication, so do the Japanese firms (which are usually referred to by the Japanese name *kaisha*). Three-quarters of the largest companies in Asia Pacific are of Japanese origin, and in 1998 no fewer than 112 Japanese firms were listed among the Fortune 500, a ranking of the largest companies in the world. Many of them are 100 years old and more, compete in world markets and spend a considerable amount on research and development. Very few other firms in Asia can match their standing.

As a result of their importance and the threat many of them pose to firms in the West, much has been written about Japanese firms, their strategic behaviour and management practices.[1] This chapter, therefore, focuses only on the characteristics which may be useful to understanding Japanese competitive behaviour, inside as well as outside Japan. This is strongly influenced by the domestic resources on which Japanese companies base their strength: devoted employees and patient capital. The formative influence of the home environment justifies some generalisation while not denying that individual firms may differ substantially from each other and from what is normally described as 'typically Japanese'. The strong grounding in domestic resources is particularly true for Japanese firms which typically have developed initially within the Japanese context, and only much later ventured abroad. It should also be borne in mind that what is said here about Japanese firms applies to large, well-known corporations and not necessarily to the millions of small- and medium-sized Japanese companies. As a rule, these do not compete with Western firms and can therefore be omitted from the present discussion.

The devotion of Japanese employees to their *kaisha* is the result of two factors. On the one hand there is the strong desire of the Japanese to identify with a group rather than striving for individual achievement. This cultural trait is complemented by economic behaviour. In joining a company as a member of a group, an employee is implicitly offered life-long employment in exchange for life-long commitment and loyalty. In return it is expected that the employee will do his or her best to make the company succeed. The employee's future is closely tied to the well-being of the firm as life-long employment not only offers job security, but also reduces lateral job mobility.

This gives employees a strong incentive to look after the interests of their firm, reduces potential conflict between employees and other stakeholders, and brings a certain amount of harmony into the firm. Japanese managers have been able to convert this group spirit into a strong commitment to the objectives and the vision of the firm and devotion to the ultimate task, winning in the market. This ambitious 'strategic stretch', which is often out of all proportion to existing resources and capabilities, is pursued at all levels of the organisation and is now recognised as one of the most important features of globally successful firms.[2] Life-long employment and life-long loyalty also make heavy investment in learning and skills development worthwhile, not only because better-trained employees produce better results in knowledge-intensive industries, but also because employees rarely leave the firm. High investment in education, combined with a willingness to share information, leads to the development of an overall competence in the workforce. This competence can be used in different applications, combined in new configurations, and exploited in a wide variety of markets.

Patient money has been the other important source of strength of the Japanese *kaisha*, but also the seed of complacent financial management. It is estimated that 70 per cent of the equity of all the large companies quoted on the Japanese stock markets is held by long-term investors, often affiliated to companies. Banks play an important, but not as dominating, a role as they do, for example, in Germany. Long-term investors do not insist on high financial returns. Consequently, Japanese firms do not have to worry much about dividends, share prices or the recommendations of security analysts. Instead, they can concentrate on developing new products and new markets. Freed internally from the 'tyranny of accountants', they are able to pursue strategies which either have a very long time-frame or are very risky.[3]

The direct influence of shareholders on the companies they own is negligible. Rarely do they have seats on the board, or any real chance to raise objections against management during the annual assembly. The board consists of senior managers who have spent their whole life in the firm as employees.[4] Their interest is primarily in seeing the firm succeed, which is different from increasing shareholders' value as seen in the USA. As such, their job definition is that of the management of their employees to the benefit of all stakeholders. Shareholders nevertheless expect rewards – not necessarily in terms of high dividends, on which a high tax has to be paid, but through long-term capital gains in the share price on which no tax is payable. Alternatively, shareholders expect business as the pay-off for their long-term commitment. Such business may come in the form of purchasing orders for manufacturing firms, agency representation for trading houses, loans for banks, or insurance contracts for insurance companies. This explains the economic reasoning behind long-term share holdings in the absence of high dividends. From a financial perspective these expectations have led to lower costs of equity complemented by low-cost debt available to domestic firms (due to consistently lower interest rates in Japan than in the rest of the world).

As a consequence of the tradition of devoted employees and patient capital, Japanese firms can pursue long-term strategies: that is, invest in developing markets which do not promise any immediate return or in technologies of questionable benefit. The basis for these long-term strategies is provided by the rigorous application of economies of scale, scope and speed over the last decades.

Economies of scale, scope and speed

After the Second World War, cheap labour was just about all Japanese firms had to offer the world. By the 1960s, however, labour costs had increased to such a level that the Japanese began to lose out in major industries. Textiles, Japan's largest industry at the time, was just one victim of this. In order to boost productivity, the Japanese invested in large and capital-intensive facilities, and output increased substantially. This led to enormous economies of scale (in other words, a lowering of unit costs by a certain percentage each time production volume doubled). In this way competitiveness was restored and even sharpened. In the 1970s, Japanese firms made major inroads into international markets by combining scale effects with concentration on a very limited number of standardised products, often at the lower end of the product range. Less focused Western competitors found it difficult to muster an adequate response.

At the beginning of the 1980s, Japanese firms realised that their focused approach both limited their growth potential and was unable to satisfy increasingly sophisticated and differentiated demand. Reorganising their factories with the help of flexible manufacturing systems and a network of related and supporting industries, they moved towards economies of scope, increasing the variety of a firm's products without losing the benefits of mass production. Advantages of scope were thus added to those gained in terms of scale. This process was partly achieved by extending product ranges (simply offering a large number of variations on the same base model). Increasingly, however, a broad spectrum of very different segments was covered with entirely different products. Competitors began to see Japanese firms introducing new products at every level of the market, as witnessed in the car industry. Shiseido even entered Western cosmetics markets exclusively from the top end.

At the end of the 1980s, Japanese firms added yet another level to their competitiveness by trying to speed up response to customer demands. The result was economies of speed, benefits from shorter development and production cycles, and closer relationships with customers. At the beginning of the 1990s, providing a large variety of products for the lowest cost in the shortest length of time was considered the new pattern for success.[5] Japanese firms were well positioned to exploit this new phenomenon in competition: just-in-time systems had been in place for years, and both employees and the network of suppliers could easily be rallied around new campaigns. Sharing of information within the organisation, the emphasis on action rather than analytical problem-solving, and a high degree of competence at all levels, all these characteristics made the Japanese firm highly responsive to time-based competition.

Other features of Japanese life also proved extremely useful as competitive weapons, such as the service orientation of suppliers towards customers and attention to detail. This enabled Japanese department stores, supermarkets and hotel groups to make major inroads into Asia Pacific markets while Western observers were still pointing at Japan's outdated and uncompetitive service sector.

The gains in the world markets of the 1970s and 1980s led the Japanese *kaisha* to believe that success could only be achieved through high growth.

Growth thus became a dogma. Survival and victory could only be ensured by establishing and maintaining a 'winner's competitive cycle'. This cycle required faster growth than that of competitors through higher investment on a continuous basis.[6] This investment went towards the build-up of additional capacities or the development of new markets and products, and was geared towards market share and long-term competitiveness.

As a logical consequence of this thinking, financial indicators such as return on investment (ROI) were not given high priority in measuring the feasibility of projects or the success of the firm. The final judgement could only be derived from the markets in which the firm operated, both in terms of sales (as an absolute measure) and market share (as a relative measure). In hotly contested markets, such as consumer electronics, the strong focus on competitors led to 'product churning' and 'product covering', or the constant outpouring of new models at breakneck speed and at any cost in order to stop others from taking the lead, even in the most minuscule market segment. Should a firm miss out on an opportunity to introduce a new product variant, it would very quickly cover its risk of losing market share by launching a product equivalent to that of its competitor. In such an environment, time-consuming market research and long-lasting analyses were discarded in favour of market experimentation, and the inevitable failures were considered learning opportunities for the future.[7]

At the beginning of the 1990s, after the Japanese 'bubble' economy burst, the *kaisha* found itself in a stagnant environment both at home and in its major export markets in the USA and Europe. The unexpected change left it stranded with substantial overcapacity, overstaffed offices, infeasible diversifications and acquisitions abroad on which too much money had been spent and which were difficult to manage. The consequent soul searching gave cost-cutters the edge over growth maniacs.

After the bubble burst in the early 1990s, and in the aftermath of the Asian crisis, the Japanese *kaisha* have come to realise that the productivity of their capital is far below that of comparable firms in America and Europe. Shareholders who no longer see the huge stock appreciation they enjoyed in the 1980s are demanding better returns. The return on Japanese shares is way below what people expect in the USA. Some of the leading *kaisha* have announced that they will pay more attention to shareholder value. We will not know until later whether this difficult period will lead to a major reorientation of the *kaisha*, or whether the dream of being number one, *ichiban*, will resurface. This is an all-pervasive dream and relates to the importance of the positioning of the firm in the strictly hierarchical order of Japan.

Keiretsu

As most Japanese describe themselves in terms of their place in a network of relationships rather than as individuals, so does the Japanese firm define its role and status through its relationship with other firms rather than as a stand-alone organisation. Most of the larger firms are connected with affiliated companies with whom they form a *keiretsu* system whereby companies maintain long-standing business ties with each other that are sometimes, but not always, cemented by mutual ownership of some of each other's shares.

Japan's industrial landscape is dominated by six very large *keiretsu*: Mitsubishi, Mitsui, Sumitomo, Fuyo, Daiichi-Kangyo and Sanwa. About 60 per cent of all companies quoted on the Tokyo stock exchange are affiliated with these groups in some way. The first three are successors of the pre-war *zaibatsu* (family-dominated groups with a long history, organised around a holding company). The other three were formed after the Second World War. All groups consist of a large number of firms operating in the most important industrial sectors and fiercely competing within these sectors with the affiliates of the other *keiretsu*. Because of this spread across various industries, this type of industrial group is called a 'horizontal' *keiretsu* (see Table 4.1).

As the American occupying forces disallowed holding companies after the war, the links between affiliated companies are no longer based on one relationship between main or holding companies and subsidiaries. The older pre-war *keiretsu* are centred around a core of a main bank, a general trading firm (also called *sogo shosha*), and one or two major manufacturing firms. The other three groups are dominated by financial institutions. Share holdings or cross-share holdings exist, but are often small. Banks are not allowed to own more than 4.9 per cent of the equity of any industrial company but even the smallest share holding creates the feeling of a common purpose, or common history. Exchange of personnel, monthly meetings of the heads of the largest affiliated firms or the use of a common name (especially in the most closely knit group, Mitsubishi) serve to foster a common spirit. Each individual firm remains largely independent and a mutual respect for management autonomy is maintained. It participates, however, in the group's overall strategy formulation and its cooperation efforts.

Apart from these horizontally organised groups, so-called 'vertical' *keiretsu* are also found in Japan. These are agglomerations of a large number of small- and medium-sized firms under the umbrella of a major manufacturing or assembly-type company. The best known example is the Toyota production system, which involves more than 10 000 sub-contractors. Other vertical *keiretsu* are formed by companies like Matsushita or Shiseido to

Table 4.1 Horizontal *Keiretsu*

	Mitsubishi	Mitsui	Sumitomo	Fuyo	DKB	Sanwa
Group members (FY 92)	187	154	173	154	135	124
Council Members (Sep 93)	28	26	20	29	48	44
Finance & Insurance	Bank of Tokyo – Mitsubishi Mitsubishi Trust & Banking Meiji Mutual Life Tokio Marine & Fire	Sakura Bank Mitsui Trust & Banking Mitsui Mutual Life Mitsui Marine & Fire	Sumitomo Bank Sumitomo Trust & Banking Sumitomo Life Sumitomo Marine & Fire	Fuji Bank Yasuda Trust & Banking Yasuda Mutual Life Yasuda Fire & Marine	Dai-Ichi Kangyo Bank Asahi Mutual Life Taisei Fire & Marine Fukoku Mutual Life Nissan Fire & Marine[1] Kankaku Securities Orient	Sanwa Bank Toyo Trust & Banking Nippon Life Orix
Electronics & Electrical Equipment	Mitsubishi Electric	Toshiba	NEC	Oki Electric Industry Yokogawa Electric Hitachi[1]	Fujitsu Fuji Electric Yasakawa Electric Mfg. Nippon Columbia[1] Hitachi[1]	Iwatsu Electric Sharp[1] Nitto Denko Kyocera Hitachi[1]
Transportation Machinery	Mitsubishi Motors Mitsubishi Heavy Industry	Toyota Motors[1] Mitsui Engineering & Shipbuilding Ishikawajima-Harima Heavy Industries[1]		Nissan Motors[1]	Isuzu Motors Niigata Engineering Iseki Ebara Furukawa	Daihatsu Motor Hitachi Zosen Shin Maywa Industry
Trading & Retailing	Mitsubishi Corp	Mitsui & Co Mitsukoshi Hokkaido Colliery & Steamship	Sumitomo Corp	Marubeni	Itochu Nissho Iwai[1] Kanematsu Kawasho Itoki[1] Seibu Department Stores[1]	Nissho Iwai[1] Nichimen Iwatani International Takashimaya

Food & Beverages	Kirin Brewery	Nippon Flour Mills		Nisshin Flour Milling Sapporo Breweries Nichirei		Itoham Foods[1] Suntory[1]
Construction	Mitsubishi Construction	Mitsui Construction Sanki Engineering	Sumitomo Construction	Taisei	Shimizu	Toyo Construction Obayashi Sekisui House Zenitaka
Iron & Steel	Mitsubishi Steel Mfg	Japan Steel Works	Sumitomo Metal Industries	NKK	Kawasaki Steel Kobe Steel[1] Japan Metals & Chemicals[1]	Kobe Steel[1] Nakayama Steel Works Hitachi Metals[1] Nisshin Steel
Non-ferrous Metals	Mitsubishi Materials Mitsubishi Aluminium Smelting Mitsubishi Cable Industries Mitsubishi Shindoh	Mitsui Mining & Smelting	Sumitomo Metal Mining Sumitomo Electric Industries Sumitomo Light Metal Industries		Nippon Light Metal Furukawa Electric	Hitachi Cable[1]
Real Estate	Mitsubishi Estate	Mitsui Real Estate	Sumitomo Realty & Development	Tokyo Tatemono	Tokyo Dome	
Petroleum & Coal	Mitsubishi Oil			Tonen	Showa Shell Sekiyu[1]	Cosmo Oil
Rubber & Glass	Asahi Glass		Nippon Sheet Glass		Yokohama Rubber	Toyo Tire & Rubber
Chemicals	Mitsubishi Chemical Mitsubishi Gas Chemical Mitsubishi Plastics Industries	Mitsui Toatsu Chemicals Mitsui Petrochemical Industries Denki Kagaku Kogyo[1]	Sumitomo Chemical Sumitomo Bakelite	Showa Denko Kureha Chemical Industry NOF Corp	Kyowa Hakko Kogyo[1] Denki Kagaku Kogyo[1] Nippon Zeon Asahi Denka Kogyo Sankyo[1] Shiseido Lion	Ube Industries Tokuyoma Corp Hitachi Chemical[1] Sekisui Chemical Kansai Paint Fujisawa Pharmaceuticals

Table 4.1 cont.

Fibres & Textiles	Mitsubishi Rayon	Toray Industries		Nisshinbo Industries Toho Rayon	Asahai Chemical Industry[1]	Unitika Teijin
Pulp & Paper	Mitsubishi Paper Mills	New Oji Paper		Nippon Paper Industries[1]	Honshu Paper	
Mining & Forestry		Mitsui Mining	Sumitomo Forestry Sumitomo Coal Mining			
Machinery	Mitsubishi Kakoki		Sumitomo Heavy Industries	Kubota NSK	Kawasaki Heavy Industries NTN Ishikawajima-Harima Heavy Industries	
Precision Machinery	Nikon			Canon	Asahi Optical	Hoya
Cement		Onoda Cement	Sumitomo Cement	Nihon Cement	Chichibu Cement[1]	Osaka Cement
Shipping & Transportation	Nippon Yusen Mitsubishi Warehouse & Transportation	Mitsui OSK Lines[1] Mitsui Warehouse	Sumitomo Warehouse	Showa Line Keihin Electric Express Railway Tobu Railway	Kawasaki Kisen Shibusawa Warehouse Nippon Express[1]	Navix Line Hankyu Nippon Express[1]
Service Industry	Mitsubishi Research Institute					

[1]Companies are strictly speaking independent or have affiliations with more than one group.

SOURCE: *Industrial Groupings in Japan*, Dodwell Marketing Consultants, 1994.

organise their distribution systems. As a rule the smaller firms depend almost entirely on the umbrella firm, which in turn prioritises its connections with those which show long-term commitment. This system of vertical affiliation fosters exchange of information, joint product development, and simplified and speedy delivery procedures based on low transaction costs.

The complexity of the Japanese *keiretsu* system is increased by the fact that many of the vertical *keiretsu* are part of a horizontal group. It therefore seems justifiable to look at Japan's industry as an integrated network of firms rather than as a large number of independently operating *kaisha* in a culturally homogeneous environment.

The subject of the Japanese *keiretsu* has – like the topic of Japanese management – attracted a large number of foreign observers and produced a flood of publications.[8] Many of them, particularly those of American origin, have political overtones, interpreting the close intra-firm relations of the *keiretsu* as indicative of collusive practices, and considering the *keiretsu* system as just another entry barrier to the Japanese market. This criticism implies that the *keiretsu* system provides the Japanese firm with an unfair competitive advantage.

These interpretations and arguments need qualification. Undoubtedly, the provision of preferential buying and selling opportunities to affiliated firms represents discriminatory, if not collusive behaviour. Whether the competitiveness of the participating firms is enhanced by these practices is, however, questionable. To start with, not all large and successful Japanese *kaisha* belong to a *keiretsu*. Sony, Honda, Kao and Kyocera are not part of a horizontal *keiretsu*, though due to their sheer size they may have started to build up their own vertical group. Second, cooperative behaviour does not exclude intra-*keiretsu* competition among affiliated firms within the group. In addition, affiliated suppliers are often pitted against rivals from other *keiretsu* or from outside (independent *kaisha* or foreign suppliers). Intra-*keiretsu* contracting cannot be taken for granted. As a matter of fact, it is relatively modest and its importance is grossly overrated by outsiders.

Third, granting each other privileges or being forced to buy from each other does not necessarily provide firms with a competitive advantage. As the whole debate about make-or-buy has shown, in-house purchasing led to inefficiencies in many Western firms which in turn started to favour outsourcing and increasingly squeeze their outside sub-contractors very hard. As the 1990s progress, it seems that the Japanese see more clearly than ever the disadvantages of a system in which relationships can be used to cover up a lack of competitiveness. There is a growing trend towards more flexibility in the relationships between *keiretsu*, and even more competition within individual *keiretsu*.

Mini-Japans and *sogo shosha* abroad

The effects of the *keiretsu* system are not limited to Japan, they are also felt abroad. As the main foreign investment flows of the 1990s are redirected from the USA to the Asia Pacific region, three aspects of Japanese cooperative behaviour are becoming increasingly apparent.

The first relates to the vertical *keiretsu* and the tendency of the leading manufacturer/assembler to buy only from its own network of suppliers. In moving assembly operations offshore, companies such as Matsushita, Toshiba and Hitachi have continued to rely on their traditional suppliers in Japan shipping parts and components to plants located in Asia. As most production was originally destined for other parts of the world, only one part of the value chain was shifted abroad without breaking up the *keiretsu* system.

Over time local sales have become more important and with this has come the need – often enforced by the local government – to increase local content. Instead of turning to local suppliers, many Japanese firms have responded by asking their suppliers to move to Asia too, and to build factories in their vicinity. As a result, the vertical *keiretsu* is replicated abroad with mini-Japans emerging in most of the ASEANIEs as well as in China. The high yen in the mid-1990s forced manufacturers to reduce their costs in Japan, and they in turn put great pressure on their suppliers to cut prices. Many, however, had reached their limits in high-cost Japan. Sourcing from abroad, particularly from the developing countries of Asia, became an alternative option for leading manufacturers. However, this did not mean buying from Korean or Taiwanese companies. Instead, the affiliated Japanese firm was advised to move abroad and to supply its traditional customer from there. By keeping the *keiretsu* system alive across national borders, Japan enhanced the view that it remains a closed society.

The second aspect refers to the ability of the horizontal *keiretsu* to muster sufficient support within the group to bid for even the largest and most risky projects in a region, such as energy systems in China or the exploitation of raw materials in Siberia. Complete packages are offered to the countries concerned, backed up by Japanese development aid. The package is then parcelled out to affiliated companies; industrial firms provide the technology, engineering firms handle the construction, banks provide the financing, the insurance company covers the risks, the shipping branch transports the equipment, and so on. Not all jobs, however, remain within the specific *keiretsu*. Affiliates from other groups or foreign firms are increasingly included in the consortia.

Who remains in charge among the *keiretsu* is determined by the *sogo shosha*, which processes information and coordinates the bidding process.

These *sogo shosha* spearhead many of the international activities of Japanese firms with which they are affiliated. Their central role as trader, information provider and project organiser cannot be overrated and represents the third and probably most important aspect of the *keiretsu* abroad.

With sales of between US$102 and 142 billion, Mitsui and Co., Mitsubishi Corp., Itochu, Marubeni and Sumitomo Corp. occupied five of the top ten places in the rankings of the world's largest companies in terms of sales in 1993, far ahead of any trading house from either the USA or Europe. Each of these *sogo shosha* employs about 10 000 people scattered in more than 200 offices around the world. Much of their strength is based on their ability to collect and disseminate information. This has made them into some of the world's largest private intelligence networks, comparable only to the CIA or the KGB.

Activities are divided between domestic business, exports and imports, and offshore trading, and cover every conceivable product and service from commodity trading to satellite leasing. The diversification of the activities of the *sogo shosha* away from their traditional export/import trade was underlined in 1993 by an offer from Mitsui Europe in London to organise an investment promotion trip to Vietnam for European companies.

The missionary role of the *sogo shosha* within their *keiretsu*, their pervasive presence and their wealth of local know-how and contacts have led each of them to invest in hundreds of projects abroad. Many of these investments do not exceed 5 or 10 per cent of the equity, but they ensure that any cross-border business with which the venture is involved will be discussed with the *sogo shosha*. A typical example would be the setting-up of a local automobile assembly plant or glass manufacturing project in Indonesia or Thailand. An industrial firm from Japan will tie up with a local investor, often after an introduction from the *sogo shosha* in the same *keiretsu*. The *sogo shosha* will enter the joint venture as a third, minor partner. Machinery, raw materials, parts and components will be imported from affiliated companies in Japan with the help of the trading firm, and transported to the destination on affiliated shipping lines. Output will again be channelled through the *sogo shosha* and shipped abroad. Because of the extent of the products and services offered by the trading house and its *keiretsu*, it is almost impossible for an outside firm to offer its goods successfully to any joint venture with *sogo shosha* participation in Asia Pacific.

Kaizen instead of restructuring

When Japan unexpectedly went from boom to stagnation at the beginning of the 1990s, the Japanese *kaisha* were caught sitting on massive overcapacity and overvalued assets. Combined with frequently overpriced acquisitions abroad, the investments during the bullish 1980s now called for large write-offs and depreciation. While the financial viability of well-known Japanese firms was not called into question, profits began to deteriorate. Soft markets in the USA and in Europe, and the strengthening of American competitors in particular, made it difficult to compensate for lost growth in the domestic market through expansion abroad.

The ever appreciating yen had risen from 260 yen to the US dollar in 1985 to 85 in 1995, an increase in currency value which few Western export-oriented firms would have survived. In addition, relationships with suppliers and customers had become too cosy. It also became apparent that the efficiency of Japanese factories was not matched by that of the offices. A substantial surplus of white-collar workers produced high costs and bureaucracy but failed to create added value.

A situation as dramatic as this would have called for a radical dose of restructuring, re-engineering, down-sizing, de-layering and other remedies of modern management in almost all Western firms. Not so in Japan, where the latest management gospels were followed with interest, but not found suitable (at least not in their harsher applications). *Kaizen*, the continuous effort by everybody to improve everything,[9] was pursued rigorously instead. Managers and staff who had become complacent during the bubble era regained their former rigour.

Painful cost-cutting measures, particularly in the white-collar sector, began with early retirement, reduced recruitment, bonus and overtime cuts and transfers to affiliated companies among the core group of employees. Managers without subordinates became a new feature, and temporary staff contracts were not renewed. Overall, though, large-scale lay-offs were avoided and serious attention was paid to maintaining the reciprocal loyalty between firm and employee.

Pressure was also exerted on suppliers and other business partners to cut costs. This resulted in a certain shift of manufacturing abroad, the reduction of component numbers, and sharing of models between competitors. Products of one car manufacturer, for example, are now sold under its competitor's name (an arrangement unthinkable just a few years ago). While some less competitive suppliers are closing down, close attention is again paid to keeping the overall industrial structure and the *keiretsu* system intact. Some cross-share holdings were reduced, but interdependencies were not. As a rule shares are sold to other members of the same industrial group, not to outsiders, and only after consultation with the firm concerned.

Production processes continue to be improved through *kaizen*. Product development cycles continue to be shortened, while product lifecycles are extended and the number of product varieties reduced. Flexible pricing, once shunned, has been forced on manufacturers by large distributors and has thus become acceptable. Outright discounting, on the other hand, is still excepted. Contrary to outside expectations, spending on research and development remains very high. The strategic direction for the future points to a concentration on core activities rather than further diversifications and acquisitions. Foreign investment will slow down as long as the yen stays at a relatively low level in comparison with the US dollar and the European currencies. Substantial devaluation in the developing countries of Asia will not be reason enough to increase investments there. Local demand will have to recover considerably before the need for new capacities will arise.

As Japan is changing, so is the Japanese *kaisha*. But the whirlwind of change on the surface should not be mistaken for a break with the past or a move towards a Western, often Anglo-American, model of the firm. The Japanese model is being improved and adjusted, but not discarded.

THE KOREAN *CHAEBOL*

Characteristics

While the term *chaebol* means 'financial clique', it is used to describe a large business group, originally created by a talented entrepreneur and still largely family controlled, and spread over many diversified areas.[10] The total turnover of the ten largest *chaebol* is equivalent to 53 per cent of Korea's GNP (Table 4.2). Among the 1998 Fortune 500 are 12 Korean groups who rival the major Western firms. For instance, Samsung's consolidated turnover was equivalent to 5 per cent of Siemens' in 1975; as the world's fourteenth largest firm Samsung had overtaken the German giant in 1993 (but currency devaluation in 1997 pushed it way behind Siemens again).

The *chaebol* are the offspring of Korea's forced industrialisation. In the 1960s the Korean government identified talented, export-oriented entrepreneurs and systematically sponsored them by granting them preferential credit, import licences, tax advantages and domestic protection. With a liberal financial policy and astute financial engineering based on cross-equity exchange and high leverage, the *chaebol* were able to sustain an average growth rate of about 30 per cent a year during the 1970s and the 1980s.

These groups originally developed through privileged access to resources: those granted by the government plus the tapping of managerial talents and of a low-cost, disciplined, hard working labour force. This allowed the *chaebol* to gain competitive advantage in labour-intensive manufactured products, mainly sold on the export market as OEM goods. The cash flow generated by these activities, amplified by leveraged financing, was reinvested in modern equipment. This strategy, combined with aggressive pricing, has generated sufficient volume to achieve global economies of scale. More recently, in the mid-1980s, the *chaebol* started to move on to more value-added products, developed their own technology and promoted their own brand on the world markets. Korean *chaebol* are globally significant players in shipbuilding, construction, steel, semiconductors, consumer electronics and cars.

Table 4.2   The Ten Largest Korean *Chaebol*

Group	Business sectors	Turnover (1996 US$bn)	Total Assets (1996 US$bn)
HYUNDAI	Motor vehicles, electronics, oil, heavy industries, engineering, machinery, construction materials	63.3	59.6
SAMSUNG	Electronics, aerospace, chemicals, semiconductors, food, textiles, services	58.7	57.4
LG	Electronics, chemicals, oil, insurance, telecommunication, engineering, instruments	37.2	42.6
DAEWOO	Motor vehicles, machinery, electronics, distribution, shipbuilding, construction, finance	33.9	39.4
SSANGYONG	Motor vehicles, cement, oil	17.4	18.3
SUNKYONG	Energy, chemicals, distribution, shipping	15.5	25.5
KIA	Motor vehicles, machinery, steel	10.0	15.9
HANJIN	Airline, shipping, machinery, construction	8.5	15.9
HANWHA	Energy, petrochemicals, distribution	9.1	12.2
HYOSUNG	Chemicals, synthetic fibres, machinery, leather goods	4.3	4.6
Total 10 largest *chaebol*		258.0	291.4
Korea GNP 1996		490	
% Turnover/GNP		53	

SOURCE: *Korea Money*, May 1997.

Korean *chaebol* are widely diversified, ranging from electronics and shipbuilding through construction and industrial equipment, but as with Overseas Chinese firms their managerial styles reflect the personal style of their founder-chairmen. The development of the *chaebol* has followed a marked pattern of gradual upgrading of competitive advantages (Figure 4.2).

The strategic development of Korean conglomerates hit a crisis point in the late 1980s when local labour costs shot up and the Korean currency, the won, rose sharply. The conglomerates responded by setting up offshore plants in South-East Asia and by investing in higher value added, know-how-intensive sectors. During the 1980s the Korean government attempted to rationalise the business portfolio of the *chaebol* by forcing them to concentrate on a limited number of sectors. Similar moves had failed in the past, but in 1993/4 the government announced that financial support would be given only to groups which concentrated on core businesses.

It became obvious in 1997 that this rationalisation effort had failed. The *chaebol* had continued their race towards growth and overcapacity. The most conspicuous example was the massive investment by Samsung in the automobile sector, an industry plagued by world-wide overcapacity. When the crisis came, the *chaebol* were caught holding huge debts and unproductive

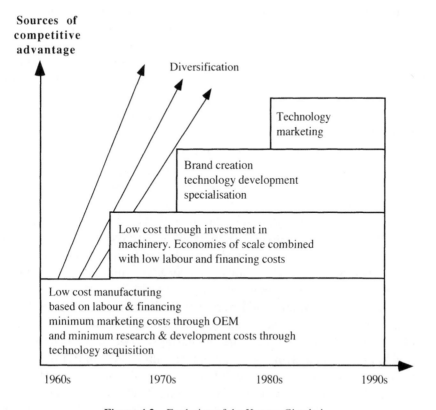

Figure 4.2 Evolution of the Korean *Chaebol*

assets. Their reaction was a 'nationalistic' stand, blaming the IMF instead of their own grandiose strategies. The new president, Kim Dae-Jung, has announced that the *chaebol* will have to restructure or die and has allowed foreign companies to take equity stakes in Korean firms as well as make straight acquisitions. At the end of 1998, the *chaebol* were still showing reluctance to comply with orders to restructure, despite the lack of other options. Ultimately, restructuring and rationalisation will only take place through the opening of the Korean economy and with the stimulus of competition.

Managerial culture

Although a genuine Korean management style is still in the embryonic stage, it is clear that the Korean *chaebol*, both in terms of managerial culture and corporate structure, is a hybrid of Confucian values and Japanese group loyalty. The *chaebol* is run as an extension of the feudal family network, providing lifetime employment and a range of benefits which in turn exact a high level of loyalty and sacrifice from the employee.

The *chaebol* resembles the Chinese firm insofar as it is characterised by a top-down authoritarian style and an extreme paternalism on the part of the *chaebol* owner, the chairman or *Whoe-Jang*, who is either the founder of the group or his direct descendent. The *Whoe-Jang* demands the emotional loyalty of his employees, recruits executive managers from among family members and passes the company on to his sons. This loyalty is so extreme that corporate culture in Korea is often equated with the glorification of the chairman's beliefs and his prescriptions for conduct.

Cohesion and coordination at the top are enhanced by an elitist recruitment policy thanks to which alumni from prestigious institutions such as the Seoul National University or the Military Academy share a common set of values and social practices.

In stark contrast to Western corporate cultures, Korean culture relies heavily on intangible, abstract concepts such as harmony and challenge. The Korean *chaebol* taps a virtually inexhaustible resource: nationalism. At least one *chaebol*, Samsung, reflects this in its corporate motto: 'We do business for the sake of nation-building.'

As *chaebol* like Hyundai and Daewoo make the transition from companies moulded in the image of their traditional, charismatic founder to more institutionalised corporations, they are increasingly conscious of the need to provide more visible symbols of corporate culture, like uniforms, to their employees. Most observers predict that the critical management challenge will come not from abroad, but from home, where a new generation of Western-educated Korean managers finds the authoritarian culture frustrating and demoralising. High rates of voluntary turnover are just one sign that this management style may no longer be viable. It is interesting to note the managerial evolution of the Samsung group, which in the early 1990s was promoting a managerial style based on Western concepts,[11] applying the principles of rationalisation, de-layering and re-engineering. Lee Kun-He, the son of the company's founder who became chairman after his father's death, began to rationalise the portfolio of activities by concentrating on three core sectors. He considerably reduced the size of the chairman's office, trying to push decision-making down the chain of command.

Paradoxically, the very diversification of *chaebol* has led to a problem of identity and the challenge of instituting a binding, corporate culture. Samsung's business, for example, ranges from ships to shirts to microchips, and lacks the focus of Toyota, a name synonymous with cars, or IBM, which for some has come to mean computers. Even abstract concepts like self-sacrifice or harmony can no longer be relied upon as effective corporate cement. Lucky-Goldstar's *Inhwa*, or 'Harmony among the people', a slogan which has guided the company for more than 30 years, is now seen as too insular and has been criticised for serving as a shield to cover personal mistakes.

The Korean *chaebol* in Asia

The traditional international strategy of Korean firms was to concentrate on exports and their foreign investments were largely made to support their export drive, either to circumvent trade barriers or to control distribution channels, particularly in North America. In the early 1990s, 40 per cent of Korean foreign investments were in North America while 38 per cent were in South-East Asia. More recently, Asia Pacific countries received greater attention as bases for low-cost manufacturing and markets for Korean products. As latecomers, lagging behind Japanese and Western firms, Korean firms have targeted their approach by focusing on key sectors across the region (construction, heavy engineering, chemicals, electronics) or by entering emerging markets at an early stage: Vietnam, northern China, Mongolia, Myanmar. As competitive tools, Korean firms in Asia use their traditional low-pricing strategies enhanced by a marketing approach highlighting their 'non-Japaneseness'.

THE OVERSEAS CHINESE CONGLOMERATES

The third distinctive type of regional and local Asian players is the Overseas Chinese business conglomerate, or those companies created and run by entrepreneurs of Chinese origin scattered across South-East and East Asia (the so-called *hua qiao* or Overseas Chinese).

The Overseas Chinese have a population of around 50 million people, slightly below that of France or the UK (Table 4.3). Some estimates put the collective GNP of this population at somewhere around US$700 billion, close to the GNP of 1.2 billion Chinese living in the People's Republic. Per capita income is significantly higher than that of the countries of South-East Asia. The wealth of the Overseas Chinese outweighs the wealth of the indigenous population, which is a factor of latent resentment. These 50 million people share a common cultural background, and even if they become citizens of the country where they live, they still keep their language and traditions.

Table 4.3   The Overseas Chinese in Asia

Country	Millions of Overseas Chinese		GNP (US$bn)	
Hong Kong	6	(98%)	114	(80%)
Singapore	2	(76%)	61	(76%)
Taiwan	21	(99%)	247	(95%)
Malaysia	6	(32%)	48	(60%)
Indonesia	7	(4%)	105	(55%)
Philippines	1	(1%)	29	(40%)
Thailand	6	(10%)	88	(55%)
Vietnam	1	(1%)	4	(20%)
Total	50		696	
PRC	1200		745	

SOURCE: Based on data from the World Bank, 1997.

Historical origins

The Chinese diaspora began in South China with different waves of emigration starting as early as the seventeenth century and accelerating during the nineteenth and twentieth centuries. The most important development of the Overseas Chinese diaspora occurred in the nineteenth century, when many Chinese fled the poverty and political convulsions of the Manchu Empire, establishing large immigrant communities throughout South-East Asia. Confident of their eventual return to the Chinese mainland, these immigrants avoided investing in illiquid assets, preferring to specialise in commerce and service occupations. Their trading networks grew and at certain stages succeeded in providing an alternative, parallel framework to the colonial European multinationals and trading companies. The communist revolution in China triggered another wave of the ethnic Chinese diaspora, with many established Chinese capitalists fleeing to Hong Kong and Taiwan. This group has been more inclined towards industry and manufacturing and has gradually linked up with an existing Overseas Chinese network (see Table 4.4).

Table 4.4 Major Overseas Chinese Groups in Asia Pacific

Group name (person in charge)	Activities
Indonesia	
Salim (Liem Sioe Liong)	Cement, automobiles, flour, foods, chemicals, banking, property, insurance
Sinar Mas (Eka Tjipta Wijaya)	Paper, pulp, chemicals, agribusiness, finance, property
Astra (founder W. Soeryadjaya)	Automobiles, heavy equipment, office equipment, agribusiness, property, finance
Malaysia	
Kuok Group (Robert Kuok)	Plantations, edible oils, flour, shipping, hotels, mining, computer services, retail, film distribution
Hong Leong (Quek Leng Chan)	Banking, insurance, car distribution, construction, building materials, manufacturing
Genting Group (Lim Goh Tong)	Hotels, casinos, resorts, plantations, property, paper mill, power generation
Thailand	
Charoen Pokphand (Dhanin Chearavanont)	Feedmills, poultry, chemicals, automobiles, telecommunications, textiles, property
Bangkok Bank (Chartsiri Sophonpanich)	Banking, insurance, financial services
Siam Motors (Khunying Phornthip)	Automobiles, musical instruments
Philippines	
Fortune Tobacco (Lucio Tan)	Cigarettes, beer, banking, hotel, pig farming, airline
J.G. Summit Holdings (John Gokongwei)	Food, textiles, hotels, property, power generation, telecommunications, media, banking, airline
SM Prime Holdings (Henry Sy)	Retailing, banking, property
Singapore	
Hong Leong (Kwek Leng Beng)	Finance, property, hotels, trading, manufacturing
United Overseas Bank (Wee Cho Woo)	Banking, insurance, property, trading, manufacturing
Oversea-Chinese Banking Corporation (Lee Seng Wee)	Banking, insurance, hotels, shopping centres, property, trading, manufacturing, media
Taiwan	
Formosa Plastic (Wang Yung Ching)	Chemicals, plastics, fibres, yarn, textiles, plywood
President Enterprises (Kao Chin Yen)	Food, retailing, banking, property, pharmaceuticals
Acer Group (Stan Shih)	Computers, semiconductors, chips, publications
Hong Kong	
Hutchison Whampoa & Cheung Kong Hong Kong Electric (Li Ka Shing)	Property, construction, cement, container terminals, manufacturing, telecommunications, media, energy, finance
Sun Hung Kai (Kwok Brothers)	Property, engineering, finance, insurance
New World (Cheng Yu Tung)	Property, hotels, container terminals, telecommunications, broadcasting, construction, power plants, highways

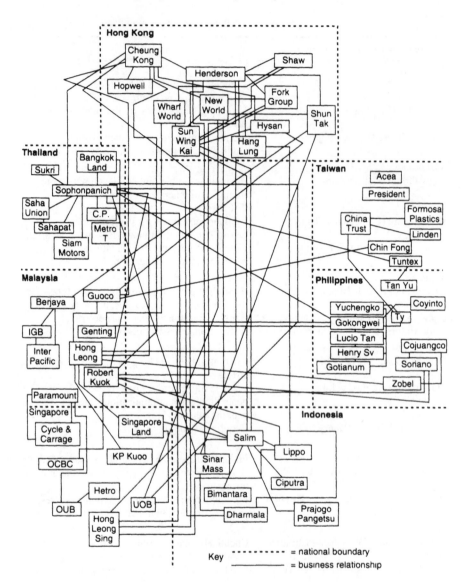

Figure 4.3   Cooperation Relationships in Business Deals Among Overseas Chinese
Major Companies, 1990–4 (China deals excluded)

Being barred, with a few exceptions, from the agricultural and public
administration sectors, Chinese immigrants concentrated on economic
activities related to trade, finance and services. In most South-East Asian

countries they became middlemen traders and financiers. On various occasions Chinese middlemen have been accused by the local population of exploiting their economic power, and members of the Chinese community have involuntarily played the role of scapegoats and frequently been the victims of public outbursts. Anti-Chinese feelings are highest in countries with a large Muslim population, such as Indonesia or Malaysia. This has generated a sense of insecurity among the Chinese, which in turn has reinforced their desire to keep their capital relatively liquid and easily transferable.

The Overseas Chinese used their rapid accumulation of capital, business networks and entrepreneurial spirit, as well as their mastery of marketing information, to gain control of industrial activities, often in partnership with Western and Japanese investors. As a result, the Overseas Chinese now exert a high degree of influence over the private sector in South-East Asia. Outside the state sector, ownership of manufacturing, banking and distribution is often concentrated in the hands of the Overseas Chinese, even in countries where they represent a small minority. This capitalistic concentration has reinforced the resentment of the local population against them and was the justification for the forced redistribution of wealth in Malaysia in the 1970s through implementation of the New Economic Policy. Nowadays anti-Chinese resentment emerges from time to time in Indonesia, as in the May 1998 riots in Jakarta and other cities across Java, and it is latent in Malaysia. However, the ethnic Chinese business community network is increasingly perceived by the governments of South-East Asia as an enormous strategic asset for their countries' economic development, establishing informal regional alliances where attempts at political consensus have failed. While the nine ASEAN governments have made slim progress in establishing formal economic groupings to compete with Japan, Europe and North America, the ethnic Chinese network is weaving powerful, albeit informal links between the region's disparate economies. The cohesiveness of the Overseas Chinese network is evidenced in Asia's surging intra-regional trade (see Figure 4.3).

Characteristics of the Chinese family business

The Overseas Chinese firm is characterised by a number of distinctive features:[12] patriarchal leadership, autocratic and centralised leadership, informal structures, the compartmentalisation of activities, a network of personal contacts and the use of different financial levers.

Paternalistic, family leadership is a trait characteristic of young enterprises all over the world. The crucial difference in Overseas Chinese enterprises appears to be a greater tendency to retain this patriarchal character, or extended family structure. It is likely that this is a response to external environmental and political uncertainty.

The structure of the Overseas Chinese enterprise is highly predictable. The patriarchal founder-owner in a Chinese enterprise is generally surrounded by an internal network of clan members who occupy all key positions. The most important financial and legal posts will generally be held by family members or trusted outsiders, who may not shine by their technical competence but who are nevertheless expected to act as the custodians of confidential business information. It is important to note that the foreign businessperson will never be considered part of this inner circle, though he or she could become part of the larger constellation of relations and contacts founded on mutual interest and personal relationships. Only a clan or family link gives a foreigner access to the inner circle of the conglomerate.

The autocratic, centralised style of the Overseas Chinese enterprise is both a function of the family character of management and a response to the hostility of the external environment. The overweening power of the state in most Asian societies means that all important business decisions require a consensus at the highest levels of government. The need for absolute discretion during this delicate process and the risk of leaks or blackmail, for example, make it impossible to include the lower echelons of the enterprise in decision-making. Large-scale decision-making is generally executed and controlled from above.

The classic method of centralised management is modelled on the ancient Chinese principle of the secretariat. The director of the enterprise is surrounded by a handful of trusted advisers without defined positions who are expected to oversee the operations of a vast array of subsidiaries. Virtually all decisions of any strategic or even operational importance are filtered through these advisers and passed back up to the director. In this way, Indonesian-Chinese billionaire Liem Sioe Liong and his son Anthony, for example, rely on 14 advisers to oversee more than 300 firms in the Salim Group.

Management structures are informal and managerial methods for planning and control are seldom utilised. Very often, the Chinese businessperson simply does not believe that the future can be planned. As a result, the decision-making process is often limited to a kind of deal-making mentality. Given certain information, an opportunity presents itself and must be seized quickly. To do this, one must have capital reserves (hence the obsession with staying liquid). In general, the Chinese entrepreneur likes to seal a deal almost immediately and reap a short-term profit.

Compartmentalisation of business activities is another way in which these groups protect themselves against the risk of take-overs, bankruptcies or expropriation. The history of Chinese communities in South-East Asia is filled with periods of overt hostility, during which pogroms, expropriation, scapegoating and persecution of ethnic Chinese minorities have been a safety valve for social and political tensions. The logic of the Chinese enterprise is, therefore, that it is better to lose a piece of the patrimony than to put all one's eggs in the same basket.

The network of family and personal contacts is the principal channel through which Chinese entrepreneurs obtain and test information crucial for the development of their companies and to the forging of new business alliances. The networking skills of the Overseas Chinese have provided them with the ability to enter a variety of business ventures with a variety of indigenous local partners, government officials and foreign companies.

Finally, Chinese entrepreneurs have an excellent mastery of financial levers. Overseas Chinese are generally highly geared, often to an extreme limit. They compensate for the lack of government backing through assistance from other Overseas Chinese groups. In their daily business dealing, they pay close attention to cash management.

Traditionally, the ethnic Chinese conglomerates of South-East Asia have deliberately blurred the distinction between their public and private assets. Typically, these conglomerates group their family holdings in what has been described as a squat pyramid.[13] In this pyramid, a handful of publicly-listed companies form a broad base, but the most profitable enterprises still belong to, and are controlled by, the family.

Strategic development

The business development of Overseas Chinese firms is based upon a combination of entrepreneurial skills and the systematic use of market imperfections. The initial fortune will have been built on an accumulation of 'deals'.[14] A deal is a self-liquidating business based on the utilisation of an opportunity arising through privileged contacts or non-publicly available information. The entrepreneur provides the initial financing, often highly leveraged, and enjoys the cash flow which is reinvested in another deal. Since most of their business development is based on taking advantage of scarcity and market imperfections, Overseas Chinese groups have rapidly moved into a large variety of business activities following a typical pattern, as described in Figure 4.4.

The number and variety of activities in which they are engaged make these groups typical entrepreneurial conglomerates whose driving force is not the valuation of shares on the stock exchange but rather the entrepreneurial energy of their leaders. It is difficult to draw the exact boundaries of these sprawling family businesses since their firms rarely consolidate accounts and

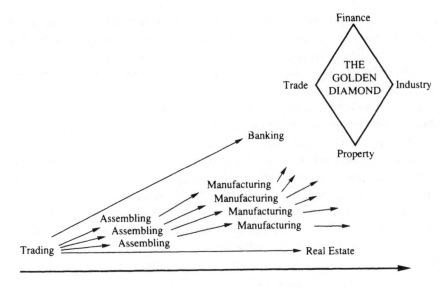

Figure 4.4 Typical Evolution of an Overseas Chinese Group

are dominated by the often idiosyncratic managerial style of their patriarchal founder-owners. Since figures and annual reports are not available, it is also extremely difficult to assess the absolute size of these businesses.

The structure of private enterprises of the conglomerate type is not unique to Asian societies, but can be viewed as a general feature of the type of enterprise which emerges in developing countries. The need to mobilise scarce resources in order to build the capital base necessary to attract investment has led either to state-controlled capitalism or an entrepreneurial capitalism led by conglomerates, or both, as is the case in Indonesia. The same phenomenon has repeated itself in Malaysia, Thailand, and the Philippines, Hong Kong, Taiwan and, in certain cases, Singapore, which has also relied on state holdings and foreign multinationals.

Most of the great Indonesian Chinese family fortunes – Liem's Salim Group, the Astra Group originally founded by the Soeryadjaya family, and the Wijaya family's Sinar Mas Group – were built through the exploitation of exclusive licences for the import or manufacture of goods for the domestic economy. Liem started with a monopoly for the trade of cloves used in the manufacture of Indonesia's fragrant *kretek* cigarettes, and his companies control the domestic flour and cement industries. The Astra Group dominates the car and motorcycle market behind a wall of high tariffs, and Sinar Mas has expanded through its monopoly on the production of cooking oil.

Most of the conglomerates have since diversified away from their monopolistic roots. The Salim Group has interests in banking, automobile assembly, processed foods, steel and other areas; Astra is investing in agribusiness, and chemical and glass exports; and Sinar Mas is involved in banking, pulp and paper production, and pig farming. These diversifications have been encouraged by Jakarta's technocratic government leadership, who have both pushed export-oriented production through credit incentives and dismantled some of the monopolies which enabled the Indonesian-Chinese families to expand. In Thailand, the Charoen Pokphand Group has diversified from agriculture into many other areas, such as telecom services. The diversification efforts of Li Ka Shing's group from Hong Kong have been less successful. Consequently his companies continue to stick to real estate and related businesses.

The Asian crisis was partly due to the speculative activities and lack of financial discipline in some Overseas Chinese groups. The crisis has revealed some of the intrinsic weaknesses of these groups: their dependence on domestic protectionism and their lack of genuine competitive advantage. With the exception of firms engaged in export-related businesses, many Overseas Chinese conglomerates have some serious restructuring to do.

The Taiwanese firm: a breed apart?

Unlike their Chinese counterparts in other Asian countries, the Taiwanese operate in a supportive and almost purely Chinese business environment, with no competition from other ethnic groups. The management style of Taiwanese companies is a distinctive hybrid of American and Japanese corporations. Japanese colonisation and the government's pro-American and export expansion policies have been the two most formative elements in the development of local Taiwanese firms.

The vast majority of Taiwanese firms are family-owned and managed. On a certain scale, owner-management can be an advantage in the sense that it creates strong cohesion among employees and a high level of commitment to the business. As Taiwanese companies increase in scale, however, family management can bring risks, such as uncontrolled management decisions by owners, the placing of personal interest above the company, *ad hoc* diversification into unfamiliar businesses on the basis of family ties, insider trading and real estate speculation.[15] Small- and medium-sized companies dominate the industrial landscape of Taiwan, where very few companies boast a turnover higher than US$100 million.

The Taiwanese government has played a pivotal role in helping Taiwanese firms tap into technologies that are beyond their research and development capability. For example, the government organises research consortia to undertake large-scale projects and then transfers the results to the private sector at low cost when commercialisation is feasible. This has been obvious in integrated circuit (IC) chip design and manufacturing, automation and development of liquid crystal display (LCD) technology. As a result Taiwanese firms spend on average less than 1 per cent of sales on research and development, since they can rely to some extent on private contacts and public research programmes.

In terms of decision-making, human resource practices and organisation, the Taiwanese company falls somewhere between the two imported corporate models.[16] In some practices, such as horizontal specialisation, and in their emphasis on a high level of technical or general education in the recruitment of employees, Taiwanese firms resemble American subsidiaries. In other practices, however, such as vertical specialisation and the importance of past performance and seniority for promotion, as well as a preference for recruiting family members of current employees, Taiwanese firms are closer to the Japanese prototype.

Despite their hybrid nature and sophistication, Taiwanese firms continue to share one salient characteristic with their Overseas Chinese counterparts: the importance of personal ties in promoting managers to high ranking positions.

The competitive strategy of Taiwanese firms can be described as 'early follower strategy', based on low cost and narrow product focus. As a rule, Taiwanese companies do not pioneer new products, and they enter the market only after Japanese or American firms have proved their potential. By doing this, Taiwanese firms benefit from the leader's experience, from lower research and development costs, and from market responses. For example, Acer, the Taiwanese computer company, only introduces a new product after the leader's product has been well received by the market. At this point, a Taiwanese firm can concentrate on serving specialised customer groups as the industry matures and low manufacturing costs become a crucial factor.

Regional activities of Overseas Chinese firms

From their beginnings as essentially domestic players, several Overseas Chinese firms became true regional players in the 1980s. This started with the expansion of Taiwanese companies, which set up offshore manufacturing plants in ASEAN countries in order to compensate for increasing labour costs at home. The movement generalised and amplified with the progressive opening of China, where the Overseas Chinese became by far the most important investors, ahead of Western and Japanese multinational firms. Gordon Wu's Hopewell Group from Hong Kong is involved in major infrastructure projects, and the Kuok family from Malaysia trades in hotels and similar sectors. Arguably the most active investor in China is the Charoen Pokphand Group from Thailand, which is involved in a large number of joint ventures in manufacturing and agribusiness. The Overseas Chinese increasingly offer their services as partners to Western and Japanese firms for regional strategic development.[17]

THE OTHER PLAYERS

The former colonial trading houses

Many of the former European colonial trading houses are still operating in Hong Kong, Singapore, Malaysia and Thailand, and are playing a distinctive, regional role. The strengths of these trading houses still reflect their historical function when they served as the major trade and commercial links between European countries and their Asian colonies. Their present day successors still remain predominantly in the traditional areas of trading, agency representation, transportation, insurance and property.

In most countries the trading houses have lost their former prominence and influence or have converted themselves into local trading and marketing companies. This applies to a number of previously well-known companies from Denmark, the Netherlands, Germany and Switzerland. The former British colonial trading houses still exercise pervasive market influence in Hong Kong, thanks to the breadth and depth of their expertise in providing a range of commercial services. But even here, where they are called *hongs* and managed by a *taipan* as chief executive, their number is dwindling. The most prominent of them, Jardine Matheson and Swire, are still largely controlled by the founding families, who direct these large conglomerates with 200 000 and 85 000 employees respectively, scattered throughout the world through minority share holdings and management contracts. As they have most of their assets invested in Hong Kong, particularly in the real estate sector, their future depends very much on their relationship with China. Jardines decided to diversify out of Hong Kong and even to de-list its shares, indicating distrust. Swire banks on China's future and has entered into numerous joint ventures with state-owned Chinese companies. Its flagship, Cathay Pacific, is already majority owned by the Chinese.

The management style of these firms varies: some of them have kept what was one of the major strengths of the traditional houses, an ability to recruit, train and motivate very bright young managers, hand-picked by the head of the family and trusted to take charge of small-scale business operations all around the region. This practice is typical of the Swire group which has succeeded in keeping hundreds of businesses rolling across the Pacific, ranging from trading, distribution, manufacturing, cold storage, shipping and air transportation to insurance. Some of these firms, like Inchcape, have become global marketing and services companies with widely spread shareholders and have transformed themselves into systems-led profession-ally managed firms. Former colonial trading houses Hutchison, Sime Darby and Hagemeyer have been taken over by local interest groups and have lost their specific European management style.

State-owned enterprises

In most parts of Asia, with the exception of Hong Kong and Japan, state par-ticipation in the business sector has been an integral part of the industrialisation process. State-owned enterprises are involved in a wide range of activities, but mainly in those industries which require large investment outlays. These include plantations, exploitation of natural resources such as oil, steel plants, public utilities, airlines, construction and heavy industrial machines and equipment.

The role of the state in business is perhaps most pervasive in Malaysia, Indonesia and China. In Malaysia the government specifically created firms in order to implement its New Economic Policy in the 1970s (Pernas, Renong), to control a strategic resource (Petronas) or to engage in heavy industries (HICOM). In Indonesia state enterprises have mostly been created as a result of nationalisation. In China, until recently, all enterprises of significant size were owned by either central or local government, but this situation is rapidly changing. In other countries, like Singapore, the government used to control several industrial and services sectors through holdings like Temasek or Singapore Technology.

In Taiwan, the government actively promotes technological development, so state firms are engaged in computer hardware and software development as well as venturing into micro-electronics memory devices and laser technology. In this sense, government firms are some of the more important suppliers of technological know-how to local firms. A similar pattern prevails in Korea with the state participating in steel, construction, shipbuilding and banks.

State enterprises are commonly wrongly perceived as hulking, bureaucratic, inefficient machines which abuse public funds and other state subsidies, make use of special favours and privileges and rely on an entrenched bureaucratic elite. Although this undoubtedly does apply in some countries, many state firms have passed the acid test of market success and bottom-line profitability.

In most cases, state-owned enterprises have been a vehicle for industriali-sation and instrumental in the government's entrepreneurial role in economic development. In Singapore, one of the most market-minded of the Asian NIEs, state-owned firms are nominally run by government officials but are guided by professional business managers and are subject to evaluations based on the profitability of their operations. Singapore Airlines is one of the best examples of a well-managed, government controlled firm. Another good example is provided by China Steel Corporation of Taiwan.

The competitive and business behaviour of state-owned firms varies from pure monopolies in oil, electricity and airlines to pure market-oriented business concerns. Increasingly, governments in Asia are privatising some of their firms (Renong in Malaysia, Singapore Airlines) or deregulating the economy by letting private competitors enter monopolies, particularly in telecommunications and banking.

Chinese state-owned enterprises

Before 1979, state-owned enterprises were the Communist Party's arms of economic management. Their major task was to implement the state's mandatory Five Year Plan; they were pure production units and were not responsible for the distribution of their output. Profits were turned over to the state and all deficits were subsidised by the state.

Since China's opening to the West and the implementation of the economic and management reforms of 1979, the Chinese government has taken steps to ensure that manufacturing enterprises become both more autonomous and more financially accountable.[18] Manufacturing enterprises were progres-sively permitted limited autonomy in certain areas, such as production, marketing and finance. These enterprises were allowed to develop their own plans, based on market needs, and therefore paid more attention to long-term objectives, such as setting prices lower than full cost to capture certain markets. In addition, capital investment funds became loans rather than outright grants. Certain rights were also granted to corporations, including the right to market above-quota production, the right to hire workers and the right to retain a percentage of profits. Since the mid-1980s the traditional managerial pattern has shifted again, as the ultimate objective of the government is to make state-owned enterprises more competitive and market oriented.

Changes taking place in these firms affect all aspects of management, particularly in the domains of resource allocation, decision-making and personnel management. Instead of administrative allocation of funds by the planning bureau, market mechanisms regulate supply and demand and direct the allocation of resources. As a consequence managers of state-owned enterprises set their prices and calculate their return based on market forecasts and on market-based evaluations of the cost of capital, thanks to the modernisation of the banking system and the introduction of stock exchanges. This implies a delegation of authority to those managers who become responsible for their results and no longer rely on 'instructions' coming from 'above'. Bankruptcy becomes theoretically and in some cases practically possible, although during the transition period the government is very cautious in allowing bankruptcies to occur at their normal pace. State-owned enterprises remain artificially alive through the granting of generous loans. On the personnel side, people are recruited more and more on the basis of their professional skills, and no longer on the basis of the party's benevolence. Rewards are attached to performance and job flexibility is encouraged, while the government is trying to remove from enterprises their 'welfare' obligations (such as health insurance, housing and schooling).

This transition will take time to implement because of its social implications; it is estimated that about one-third of the 105 million people employed in the state-owned enterprises would have to be laid off if state-owned firms were run productively.[19]

The role of state-owned firms in the Chinese economy has declined. In 1992 they produced less than 50 per cent of total output and it is expected that this will drop to 30 per cent by the end of the century.

The Asian crisis and the future of the Asian firm

The crisis came as a shock to many Asian players, especially those engaged in major development projects which were partly speculative in nature.

The effect of the crisis has been threefold: a dramatic fall in domestic demand, a credit squeeze, and the spiralling cost of paying for imported goods and servicing over-extended debts in unhedged foreign currency loans. All companies, even the sound ones, have been affected by one or more of these factors. Export-oriented companies, which theoretically should benefit from the massive currency devaluations, were affected by the credit squeeze and have suffered from lack of working capital. Firms who predominantly sell in the domestic market have been the most affected. They have had to lay off personnel, slash budgets and sell assets in order to survive. Firms which borrowed money abroad without fully hedging the risk are hastily trying to reschedule their debts and restructure their balance sheets. The example of Siam Cement, one of the best and most successful companies in Thailand, is a useful illustration of the problem. As its annual report showed, Siam Cement had a debt/equity ratio of 4.5:1 at the end of 1996 (Table 4.5).

Table 4.5 Simplified Balance Sheet of Siam Cement at the end of 1996

Siam Cement *			
Current assets	47.3	Current liabilities	69.4
Property, plant,		Long-term liabilities	
equipment and other	132.5	and others	77.6
		Equity	32.8
	179.8		179.8

* Consolidated balance sheet 31 December 1996, in baht billion.

SOURCE: *Annual Report*, 1996, Siam Cement.

A footnote in the accounts mentions that 61.5 per cent of the long-term liabilities, or close to baht 50 billion, consisted of foreign loans. Assuming that these loans are denominated in US dollars, baht 50 billion would be the equivalent of US$2 billion at the rate of baht 25 per US$1 at the end of 1996. When the baht reached the level of about 50 to US$1 at the end of 1997, the same US$2 billion was now equal to baht 100 billion. Holding everything else constant, the foreign exchange loss of baht 50 billion would have wiped out Siam Cement's entire equity.

The company did indeed report a foreign exchange loss of such magnitude in its annual report for 1997. Total liabilities ballooned from baht 147 billion to baht 289 billion. At the same time Siam Cement revalued very substantially its property, plant and equipment, the latter consisting of much imported machinery, and thereby avoided a decrease in its equity.

Developments like this had dramatic consequences for companies used to double or triple digit growth in the short term. In the long term, however, we may expect some beneficial effects.

First, the time of the ubiquitous conglomerate seems to be over. Firms will have to focus on businesses in which they can gain and sustain competitive advantages in open battlefields. The implication is that they must review their portfolio of activities, divest from non-core businesses and concentrate their investment efforts.

Second, financial controls and management systems will have to supplant, or at least outweigh, opportunism, nepotism and deal-making in the conduct of business.

Third, there should be genuine attention given to the development of expert and performance-based human resource management practices, to replace the more traditional, paternalistic and autocratic management styles.

Fourth, the introduction of accountability at all levels of the hierarchy, starting with senior executives, is long overdue.

Fifth, the design of business strategies should focus more on the 'soft' aspects of competitiveness like innovation, know-how, services and marketing, rather than relying entirely on government contacts or on low factor costs.

Some Japanese *kaisha*, such as Toyota, Canon, Honda, are still dominant in the global marketplace and will stay that way. Similarly one can expect several of the Korean *chaebol*, possibly Samsung or Hyundai, to rise fortified from the crisis. In South-East Asia, large resource-based firms in the pulp and paper or the palm oil industries will emerge as world-class players. We can expect to see the emergence of truly multinational companies coming out of China in the next 20 years in most of the major industrial sectors: automobiles, shipbuilding, chemistry, information technology. Those will be the successors to some of the major state-owned enterprises that survive the present restructuring.

In short, we should expect that the first years of the third millennium will see the emergence of stronger and fitter Asian groups on the global and regional competitive battlefields.

Notes and references

1. An excellent though somewhat outdated analysis of the Japanese firm can be found in Abegglen and Stalk (1985).
2. Hamel and Prahalad (1993).
3. Montgomery (1991).
4. Schütte (1994).
5. Stalk and Hout (1990).
6. Kotler, Fahey and Jatusripitak (1985).
7. Jones and Ohbora (1990).
8. The most thorough analysis can be found in Gerlach (1993).
9. Imai (1987).
10. For references to Korean *chaebol*, see Yoo Sanjin and Sang M. Lee (1987); Steers, Yoo Keun Shin and Ungson (1987); Chang and Chang (1994), and Kim (1996).
11. Ernst (1994) and also *Business Week* (1994).
12. For references to Overseas Chinese, consult: Redding (1990); You (1991); Tanaka, Mori and Mori (1992); Lasserre (1988a); Limlingan (1986); Mackie (1992); Redding (1995); Whitley (1992). This book gives also a very interesting insight into Japanese and Korean industrial structures.
13. *Institutional Investor*, August 1991, p. 30.
14. Limlingan (1986).
15. Tung (1991), p. 18.
16. Yeh (1991).
17. Redding (1995).
18. MacMurray and Woetzel (1994).
19. MacMurray and Woetzel (1994), p. 67.

5 Asian Business Logic

The organisational behaviour and values of Asian business partners, customers, suppliers and employees can differ fundamentally from Western norms and business logic. Western executives are often puzzled by the Asian business contexts in which they operate. Western expatriate managers and executives from corporate headquarters invariably find that they need to decode and understand individual and organisational Asian behaviour before they can even begin to operate and compete effectively in the region. It is therefore crucial to identify the essential traits of Asian business environments and the key institutional and cultural norms that underpin the behaviour of the various business actors (customers, competitors and governments). This chapter examines four key elements of the Asian business environment: the role of governments, the central importance of relationships, the role of ethical and religious cultures, and their implications for competitive and business logic.

THE ROLE OF GOVERNMENT

With the exception of Hong Kong, economic development in Asian countries has been guided by governments.[1] Government intervention has generally been a mixture of what the World Bank refers to as 'fundamental intervention (the encouragement of macro-economic stability, investment in human capital, stable and secure financial systems, limited price distortion, and receptiveness to foreign technology) as well as selective intervention (for example, directed credit, sectorial industrial promotion, trade policies)'.[2] The underlying logic has been to create a business-friendly environment that allows the market to allocate resources, but which can selectively replace the market in order to guide and spur the economy. Without detailing policies of the different Asian countries – which are constantly in flux – it is important to sketch the main consequences and characteristics of this important visible hand in the Asia Pacific region.

Figure 5.1 depicts the views of a sample of Western managers operating in the region regarding the role of government in business and economic affairs.[3] Government intervention must be analysed in terms of development context, development orientation and direct participation.

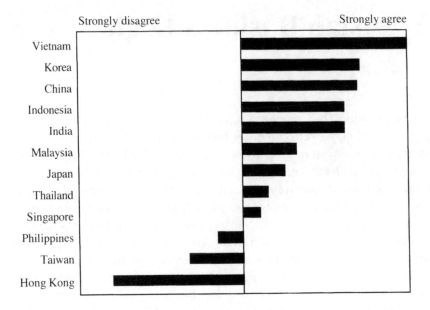

SOURCE: Lasserre and Probert (1997).

Figure 5.1   Government Influence in Business as Perceived by Western Managers

Development context

Asian government involvement in economic development aims to generate public support and an environment conducive to economic growth. Asian governments have been assisted not only by certain societal attitudes and values, but also by political and administrative constituencies that capitalise on them to channel energies towards economic performance. Elements that contribute significantly to this purpose are a broad social consensus for growth, close business – government relationships, pro-business bureaucracies, and the pragmatism and flexibility of public authorities in control of economic management.

Consensus towards growth

Government interventionism in Asia would not have achieved much without a popular consensus about economic objectives and the shared belief that economic growth is good and must be given priority over egalitarian or social welfare goals. For government interventionism to work there must also be a high degree of cooperation between government and the business community. Finally, government officials must adopt a positive attitude towards business and set an example by managing the public sector according to the principles of modern business management.

Until 1998, the Asia Pacific region had often been perceived by the business community as the most growth-obsessed region in the world. This image reflected the social consensus about economic objectives in many Asian countries. In Korea, this took the form of 'the sacrificed generation'[4] of the 1970s and 1980s, who deferred immediate enjoyment of the benefits of their hard work to build the competitiveness needed for future generations to enjoy a better life. In Indonesia, President Suharto referred to himself as 'the father of development' and identified economic growth as the national priority. In China, in the name of the 'socialist market economy', economic growth is given priority over other social values such as democracy and individual freedom. In Asia, as a rule, both elites and the general populace believe that everyone benefits from economic growth, and that it must be shared, though not in a strictly egalitarian manner.

Business–government relationships

Business and government cooperation is institutionalised in certain Asian countries, is informal in certain others and, in some cases, exists as a hybrid of the two. As the World Bank reports, 'the high performing Asian economies tend to have formal institutions that facilitate communication and cooperation between the private and public sector'.[5] In Japan, business–government cooperation is institutionalised in 'deliberation councils', where 'government officials and representatives from the private sectors discuss policy projects and exchange information'.[6] Government activity also often takes the form of administrative guidance (a combination of notification, informal hints, invitations and direct pressure that originates from ministries). Government officials rather than politicians try to persuade and guide corporations to reach a consensus. In most cases consensus means acceding to the will of a particular ministry, and carrot-and-stick mechanisms are commonly used to influence corporate decision-making. Because laws are vague in Asia, government ministries often have great leverage over firms when it comes to implementation. Close links between government and business mean that both sides are in constant contact. This in effect institutionalises the influence of government policy on the corporations, so that it becomes an external governor.

Japanese bureaucrats themselves benefit career-wise from successful cooperation with corporations. (Success is defined here as bringing firms in line with ministerial policy.) If companies are antagonised, bureaucrats may jeopardise their chances to obtain *amakudari* – lucrative positions on the board of a corporation – after their retirement. During their tenure, these retired officials naturally remain in close contact with former colleagues at the ministries, which ensures close business–government cooperation and compliance with state policy.

Close cooperation between business and government exists in one form or another in Korea, Malaysia, Singapore and Thailand. In Indonesia and the Philippines, institutional fora like those in Japan either do not exist or are not very active, but informal relationships do develop between the leading business groups and ministers and their senior staff. In China, state-owned enterprises (both at municipal and provincial level) and relationships with government and party officials are maintained through informal networks (*guanxi*). Business–government cooperation is helped in a culture of economic nationalism, as in Korea or Japan, and when top government officials belong to the same 'old boy' or alumni networks (either university or military), as in Korea or Singapore.[7] Relationships become more complex when top government officials are recruited from one ethnic group and leading businessmen from another.

Pro-business attitudes of the bureaucracy

The third context that has favoured economic development in the Asia Pacific region is the existence of a skilled, business-oriented state bureaucracy. The situation varies, however, from country to country. Singapore, Korea and Japan have promoted a well-educated, well-remunerated professional bureaucracy which understands the needs and constraints of firms. This attitude is enhanced by dynamic public sector management which emulates the private sector. In Singapore, for instance, the government is very careful to ensure that the salaries of Singaporean civil servants do not vary too widely from those in the private sector. In addition, public agencies are adopting management techniques very similar to those adopted in enterprises; hence the popularity of business-school-type training among civil servants. In Singapore, the Economic Development Board (EDB), the public agency in charge of investment promotion, is run like a business, and EDB officials are rewarded for performance and remunerated according to their achievement of precise objectives, as in private enterprise. This is not as true of other Asian countries where civil servants are either less business-oriented, as in the Philippines, or where there is a lower degree of professionalism, as in Thailand. In Indonesia, both situations exist. This does not mean that there are not notable exceptions, since attitudes and skills have improved and spurred economic growth. China, for example, which had one of the least business-minded and most incompetent bureaucracies in the whole of Asia, is catching up rapidly. The popularity of business training for civil servants in South-East Asia and the NIEs is another sign of pro-business attitudes.

Governments in Asia: pragmatism and flexibility

Government intervention in Asia, whether direct or indirect, has created a climate conducive to economic growth. One frequent metaphor used to describe the role of government in Asia is to compare it to the coach of a football team. Instead of managing the economy, governments have emulated market forces and tried to create an environment favourable to business expansion. When necessary, the government's hand has been more visible, but not necessarily ideological, with the obvious exception of China during the years 1949–79. Pragmatic implementation has allowed flexibility, even in the ideological sphere. This applies even in Vietnam and China, both communist countries which embrace the free market economy but which are straining to retain control of the political sphere. China's paramount leader of the 1980s and early 1990s, Deng Xiaoping, perhaps best expressed the pragmatism of the region with his famous adage, 'It does not matter whether the cat is black or white as long as it catches mice.'

Development orientations

The import-substitution countries

Overall, Asian countries can be divided into two distinct groups: those which have traditionally adhered to import-substitution policies and those with an outward-looking, export-led orientation.

In the 1950s, most countries in the Asia Pacific region opted for import-substitution strategies in an effort to accelerate industrialisation. Many governments adopted policies that called for selective trade protection for domestic producers as well as incentives to localise production. While Japan and the NIEs began to deregulate and dismantle their import-substitution regimes in the 1960s and 1970s, South-East Asian countries – notably Indonesia – adhered to them as late as the mid-1980s.

Indonesia, which exhibited the most inward-looking industrial orientation, has a history of large-scale government intervention, state ownership and regulation of the economy. The Suharto government partially dismantled import licensing and exchange controls introduced under the previous administration, but in the 1970s continued to make extensive use of various regulatory instruments which created monopolistic rents. In the late 1980s Indonesia began to deregulate selectively, but overall the country continues to adhere to its import-substitution orientation.

Malaysia has combined an import-substitution orientation with a plan, introduced in the early 1970s, designed to redistribute economic wealth in favour of the Malay population (the *bumiputra*), who are perceived to be disadvantaged by the more entrepreneurial Overseas Chinese population. This plan, called the New Economic Policy, used quotas to guarantee *bumiputra* capital participation and contributions to value-added. When necessary the Malaysian government has intervened directly in the industrial sector in order to ensure the creation of local content, as in the case of the Proton Saga (the Malaysian car manufactured by HICOM, a state-owned company).

Thailand and the Philippines have not relied so extensively on government-supported enterprises but have nevertheless been able to implement a classic import-substitution policy through the manipulation of tariffs and quotas, and the control of production licences.

China's economic policy began to change in 1979, when Deng Xiaoping announced his 'open door' to foreign investment. China is gradually moving away from a centrally-planned economy and has encouraged what is referred to as 'a socialist market economy with Chinese characteristics': an ideologically correct euphemism which has allowed the current Chinese leadership gradually to introduce market forces and elements of a free-enterprise system. Ailing state-owned enterprises, with their bloated workforce and 'iron rice bowl' policies (cradle-to-grave job security and social welfare benefits) are still under government protection, but their importance in the Chinese economy is decreasing every year.

Export-led countries

In terms of industrial policy, the export-led economies of the Asia Pacific region can be divided into two important sub-groups: the middle-of-the-road countries and the wide-open-door countries.

Japan, Korea and Taiwan belong to the middle-of-the-road countries. In the 1950s and 1960s Japan practised a combination of import-substitution, export-stimulation and fierce internal competition. The government has mapped out industrial strategy in which the two most important ministries, the Ministry of International Trade and Industry (MITI) and the Ministry of Finance (MOF), were free to encourage successful companies and discourage those considered dysfunctional. MITI has been specially empowered to channel investment and working capital to those companies whose activities appear to conform to national industrial policy. It should be noted that, contrary to popular perception outside Japan, MITI's role has been considerably circumscribed due to the increasing power and self-confidence of Japan's large firms. Since the 1970s Japan has shed its import-substitution orientation, although invisible barriers are still strong.

The Republic of Korea embarked on an industrialisation policy emphasising the development of heavy and chemical industries. This policy was implemented by the provision of credit at artificially low interest rates, and by strengthening direct government intervention which led to systematic privileges for the *chaebol*. Economic priorities were clear, relationships between business and government were encouraged and the government directed development programmes where private enterprises were designated as the prime engines of growth. Selective government intervention took the form of publicly-announced quarterly export targets, the manipulation of exchange rates, the creation of a free trade regime for exporters, and the granting of credit and direct tax preferences to selected *chaebol*. These policies entailed a close monitoring of the private sector and the current trade situation. Progress towards export targets was reviewed by the monthly trade promotion conference, which was chaired by the president and attended by ministers, bankers and the more successful exporters. The highest export achievements were crowned with national awards. And, in instances where private enterprises were reluctant to respond to the government's promotional efforts, public enterprises were established to initiate exports of targeted goods.

In Taiwan, the essence of government policy was to create favourable conditions for exporters: single (depreciated) exchange rates, removal of import controls for exporters and low interest rates. Taiwan adopted a strategy that aimed to sustain export-led growth through expanded manufacture of standardised products in selected sectors (calculators, watches, colour televisions, apparel, plastics, synthetic fibres). During the 1980s the government targeted high-tech industries (information, biotechnology, opto-electronics, machinery, precision instruments) and offered incentives to firms engaged in those sectors. Finally, the government announced a plan to fund public infrastructure to bring the country into line with the industrialised world.

Given the size of their market, Singapore and Hong Kong, as wide-open-door countries, had little choice but to open their economies. In Singapore the rationale for import-substitution – the prospect of a common market with Malaysia – was dashed when Singapore was expelled from the Malayan Federation in 1965 and became an independent state. Since then, the Singapore government's policy has been free trade. However, it intervenes in other ways to promote industrialisation and export expansion, mainly by offering various tax concessions to exporters and foreign investors. Perhaps the biggest attraction for foreign investors has been Singapore's widely-publicised, large-scale investment in infrastructure such as housing, transport and telecommunications. Furthermore, since the mid-1970s, government has attempted to restructure industry, weaning it away from labour-intensive activities by encouraging wage increases and giving preferential treatment to more capital- and skill-intensive manufacturing.

Hong Kong has always practised an export policy with minimal government intervention. The regulations which do exist are primarily administrative and are essentially intended to streamline and preserve Hong Kong's competitiveness as an industrial/financial/export centre. Economic policy is characterised by balanced budgets, maintenance of fiscal reserves, avoidance of public debt, and interest rate manipulation to regulate financial activity.

Attitudes towards foreign investment

Foreign firms are viewed as important contributors to economic development by many Asian governments and business communities. Most Asian countries expect foreign firms to contribute to technological development, capital formation and job creation. For the import-substitutors, foreign firms have to produce locally and usually in association with a local partner if they want to gain access to the market. Wide-open export-led economies like Singapore or Hong Kong have expected Western firms to bring production platforms, thus creating employment, which in turn is expected to effect technology transfer and generate export income. In these countries, foreign firms enjoy limited constraints on their operations. In the past, Japan and Korea adopted a reserved attitude towards foreign investors. The basic philosophy of bureaucracy and of the business community was to invite foreigners to bring technology into the country on the condition that they share it with local firms. This attitude still prevails to some extent in Korea.

Restrictions on Western firms and ventures vary widely according to the nature of the investment project. As a general rule, the more a foreign firm is geared toward exports, the less stringent the restrictions. If a foreign firm is 100 per cent export-oriented, there will very often be none at all.

In the case of certain large-scale projects such as those in the Philippines, pressures for localisation are still strong. In some countries (for example, Indonesia), foreign investment legislation still requires Western firms to localise progressively by selling off a certain percentage of their shares to locals or to the government within a certain contractual period.

Direct government participation

In addition to their role as policy makers the majority of Asian governments have intervened directly in the economy through the ownership and control of enterprises and through a targeted policy of public procurement. At one extreme are China and Vietnam who, because of their adoption of Marxism, have economies dominated by state-owned enterprises. Then comes Indonesia, which in the 1960s moved to nationalise the majority of foreign firms, especially those in the plantation, oil and petroleum industries. The Thai government still controls many sectors: fertilisers, commodities distribution, air transport, steel, and so on. Malaysia followed suit with Petronas (the state oil company) and Pernas. Singapore controls a large number of firms through state holdings (for example, Temasek and Singapore Technology). Korea and Japan rely less on the ownership of firms than on targeted procurement. At the other end of the spectrum, Hong Kong has a limited number of state enterprises (the Mass Transit system) and has made limited use of targeted procurement. During the 1980s most of the Asia Pacific region moved towards deregulation and privatisation. In China, the proportion of industrial production by state enterprises decreased from 56 to 29 per cent between 1985 and 1996.[8] Malaysia, the Philippines and Singapore undertook privatisation drives.[9] However, state enterprises will not disappear overnight and governments will remain major players for the rest of the century.

THE ROLE OF RELATIONSHIPS

The Asia Pacific region is one of the areas of the world where building and cultivating relationships is crucial to business development. Every society is built around relationships. Networking and cultivating relationships with customers, suppliers, competitors, partners and government officials, and maintaining good and regular contact with them, is standard practice in business all over the world. In the Asia Pacific region, however, there is a greater need to network. The difference between Western and Asian relationships is not only a matter of degree, since the quality and cultivation of relationships is more crucial to business success than their numbers. The nature of relationships in Asia is also different: personal and reciprocal ones are valued over the contractual and transactional type. In Asia, personal relationships are mutually binding and permeate all aspects of the firm. Regardless of the situation – whether it is obtaining a visa, finding information, getting an investment proposal approved or cutting through a maze of bureaucratic obstacles – the natural tendency of Asian managers is to focus on the individual who can best resolve the particular problem or clinch the deal. In China, the *guanxi* is the mutual obligation that derives from being connected to someone through a third person. These individuals are not viewed as disposable, replaceable parts, as they so often are in the West.

The Asian business environment can be best described as a series of interlocked networks: family and relatives, ethnically-based connections, alumni connections, social clubs, industrial connections and finally government–business connections.

Family and blood ties

Figure 5.2 identifies the various levels of relationships in a Chinese society. At the centre is the nuclear family in which relationships are precisely codified by a set of hierarchical Confucian relationships: father/children, husband/wife, elder/younger brothers and sisters. Trust and loyalty among family members is taken for granted and considered absolute; hence the tendency for most Chinese entrepreneurs to appoint family members to top management positions. Within the nuclear family there is no reciprocity, though respect for the hierarchy and obedience are automatically rewarded with protection. Appointments based on family ties, business undertakings and

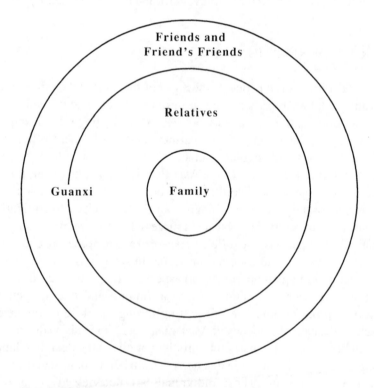

Figure 5.2   Chinese Relationships Heirachy

networks between family members are also prevalent in non-Chinese societies: Korea, the Philippines, Indonesia and Thailand are a few examples.

Outside the inner circle of the nuclear family is a second layer of relationships: the relatives. In this category come the second-degree family members: cousins, uncles and in-laws. Their loyalty is expected, but on the basis of some kind of give-and-take reciprocity. One relative will enter a business deal with another provided that he or she can expect an immediate tangible or future return. This can translate into a moral debt or credit that can be activated in the future. Just as powerful as nuclear family relationships, business networks among relatives form an intricate web of reciprocal obligations referred to as the extended family.

Social, school and club ties

Beyond the extended family lies the domain of friends and connections who expand further the network of *guanxi*. Life-long *guanxi* are cultivated through early, formative shared experiences. Attendance at the same school or the same military academy is a lasting bond, as is having been born in the same village or province. In Confucian societies, friendship can only occur between equals. Consequently, relationships formed during early childhood or young adulthood are the only kind of human bond that escapes the hierarchies of the workplace, marriage and later life. Indeed, some of the most important network structures in East Asia – particularly in Korea and Japan – are the deep, lasting social relationships that bind alumni from the same secondary school or university. Membership of the same clubs or sponsorship of the same charities also creates links far more binding than routine social activities. In Korean business, for example, powerful alumni networks determine hiring procedures. (This kind of network is, of course, also prevalent in the West, but Asian alumni tend to view this particular kind of link as a more systematic obligation, rather than a personal favour.) Another type of network, particularly prevalent in Japan and ASEAN countries, is the practice of allowing senior bureaucrats to leave the civil service and take on top positions in companies, thus providing a direct channel of communication for government and business.

All these networks are regulated by implicit principles. To become part of the network one needs to be connected to someone who is already part of it, and loyalty relies on a complex web of mutually-binding obligations and dependencies. When engaging in a business transaction, a person will check to see if the targeted party is connected to a mutual acquaintance. This link, if sufficiently strong, can create the basis for mutual obligation. If it is not the case, as in a purely arm's length contractual transaction, the strength of

In order to be successful one needs to build up a network of 'contacts'

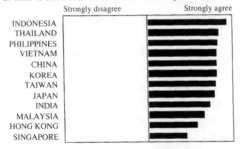

People prefer to work on the basis of personal relationships rather than on the basis of rational arguments

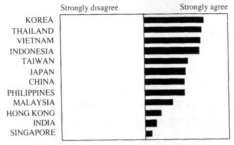

Business relationships based on trust are essential but difficult and time consuming to build

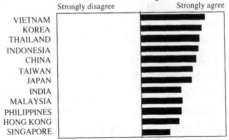

When doing business it is often more important to know with whom one deals than to have technical expertise

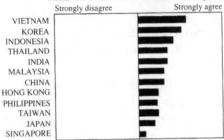

SOURCE: Lasserre and Probert (1997).

Figure 5.3   The Importance of Relationships in Asia Pacific

the mutual commitment will be inferior. Relationships of this sort require cultivation and maintenance through regular personal contacts.

Many Westerners unfamiliar with these practices find this network culture cumbersome and difficult to understand. Building relationships in an Asian context requires more time and effort than it usually takes in the Western world. It requires frequent visits, social interchanges (known sometimes as 'golf course meetings'), the exchange of small presents, and patience. Complaints about nepotism or factional behaviour are common among Westerners, but these are the direct consequences of the network culture. However, the patient and understanding Western manager can penetrate these networks and develop his or her own web of *guanxi*. Access to Asia's complex networks is often crucial to business success, and gaining this access will require far more sensitivity and experience than the usual technical and managerial skills Western firms use as the criteria for their appointments and promotions. Figure 5.3 shows how the importance and nature of relationships is perceived by Western managers.

Corruption

In the West, the cultivation of relationships is often equated with corruption. As a result, the Asia Pacific region has gained the reputation of encouraging and breeding various kinds of corruption. There is no empirical evidence that this region is more corrupt than other parts of the developing or industrialised world. There are, however, differences in definition: customs that most Westerners define as corrupt are considered both acceptable and indispensable to the financing of the state in many Asian countries. Second, there are differences in tradition. In most Asian societies people come to rely on social networks of officials to provide security which is not available from the state. Because of the overweening power of officials in many developing Asian societies, very few civil servants or ordinary citizens see any value in the concept of conflict of interest, or the separation of public and private concerns.[10] Also, because civil servants in many of the developing economies of South-East Asia earn very low salaries, emoluments which would elsewhere be regarded as corrupt are considered simply as perquisites of office, or a kind of social subsidy which keeps them above the poverty line.

Finally, most Asian societies have few social sanctions on corruption.[11] In China and the Philippines, for example, elaborate systems of patronage make investigation difficult, and in Japan the nature of the political system itself ensures that not much social stigma is attached to bribery. Asian societies tend to be regulated by shame, in the sense of public humiliation, rather than by guilt, which is often a matter of private or individual conscience, as in

Judeo-Christian or Western societies.[12] An Asian civil servant will not necessarily feel guilty about accepting a favour, and neither would many Asian societies consider such behaviour shameful; indeed, in some senses this sort of behaviour is encouraged as tribute or as essential maintenance of the social fabric. This may explain why anti-corruption campaigns in Asia have been unsuccessful and why, after a brief period of turmoil during which a certain number of individuals are scapegoated and punished, most campaigns run out of steam. Singapore is one of the rare Asian countries which has fought a successful campaign against corruption.

The essence of the East Asian political model according to Pye, is that 'authority is expected to combine, with grace and benevolence, both elitism and sympathy. Asian cultures revere hierarchy, but they also expect their leaders to be concerned with the livelihood of the masses.'[13] Reciprocity is at the root of most relationships, and social rules require that past favours must be returned. As a result, maintenance of good relationships is normally combined with the ritual practice of gift-giving.

CULTURES AND BUSINESS IN THE ASIA PACIFIC REGION

Various scholars and analysts have shown that culture affects business behaviour and performance.[14] The Asia Pacific region is at the crossroads of several cultural and religious traditions: Confucianism, Taoism, Buddhism, Hinduism, Islam and Christianity. Western political philosophies (such as liberalism and communism) have also had a major impact on the region.

Instead of becoming a cultural patchwork, the region has developed some unique norms and values which are reflected in the behaviour of its economic players. Although some countries are more influenced by one particular cultural trait, like Malaysia by Islam or China by Confucianism, certain traditions have had an impact across the region. These traditions and cultural traits are significantly different from the Western Judeo-Christian values which justify the identification of a distinctively Asian culture.

Across the Asia Pacific region, business is influenced by two dominant cultural contexts: a homogeneous concept of social organisation and the pervasiveness of Confucian values.

The Asian concept of social organisation

From 1967 to 1973 Geert Hofstede, a Dutch social scientist, conducted a series of interviews with 116 000 IBM employees from 72 countries. His intention was to identify the fundamentally different nature of work-related values across national cultures. Hofstede's statistical analysis (Figure 5.4) showed that all Asian countries shared a common pattern of values; they scored high on power distance, and low on individualism. Countries in Northern Europe, North America, Australia and New Zealand had exactly opposite scores. In high power distance societies, people are considered unequal. In organisational terms this translates as a strong respect for hierarchy and autocratic leadership. Low individualism exists when groups and collectivities rather than individuals are considered to be the nucleus of society. Individuals exist only as members of groups, and their duty is to take care of and provide for other higher status members of the group, who in turn offer protection. For Western managers, these differences are highly visible in the way Asian corporations are managed. Asian group orientation is the foundation for the networking described earlier.

The focus on the group – or the individual's membership of the group and obligation to it – rather than individual rights and identity is also manifested in the importance attached to saving face, another dominant feature of Asian societies. In business dealings, face-saving has several applications. In negotiations, it might entail avoiding public humiliation of the opposite party, or making symbolic public concessions. To cite a specific example,

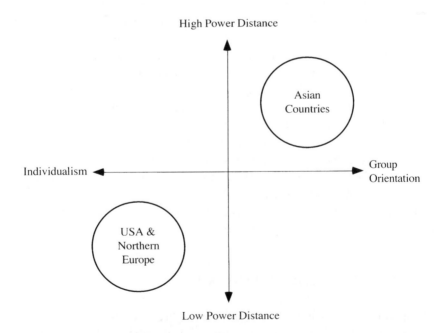

SOURCE: Adapted from Hofstede (1980).

Figure 5.4 Asian Cultures versus Western Cultures

even if the Western manager dominates the negotiation process, it may be necessary to yield in some way to the other party in order to achieve the company's goals. The imperative of saving face also means that conflicts are most often settled out of court through informal and indirect mediation by a third party. Attention to face-saving is particularly important in the sphere of human resource management of local personnel (see Chapter 10). High power distance in business situations is manifested in a punctilious respect of protocol and in the extreme deference paid to hierarchical status. In Asian societies, formalism and due process must be respected.

The pervasiveness of Confucian ethics

Confucian values have had a major impact on Asia's economic activities, directly in the Chinese countries and indirectly in the other countries. In Hofstede's original study, economic success (defined as economic growth rates) had a high correlation with high individualism. This finding was puzzling, since Asian economies have achieved high economic growth while scoring low on individualism. Hofstede explained this paradox by introducing a fifth index that measured the impact of Confucian values (thrift, perseverance, sense of shame, status). This fifth dimension was correlated with economic growth.[15] Even the World Bank in its analysis of the success of high growth East Asian economies concedes that Confucian ethics may have had some positive impact.[16] Confucian ethics can be summarised as a set of values that reward hard work, thriftiness, obedience, benevolent leadership and harmony. These values are achieved through strict respect of traditional hierarchical relationships and the importance of education. Some scholars have argued that not all Confucian values are conducive to economic progress, particularly the respect for tradition. If this had not been the case, China would have probably made even greater progress. It is apparent, however, from what happened in Korea in the early 1970s, in Japan in the early 1950s, in China in the early 1990s, and nearly everywhere in the region where large Overseas Chinese communities exist, that economic take-off and development are accelerated when Confucianism meets Western technology.

COMPETITIVE AND BUSINESS LOGIC

Competitive and business logic refers to the premises and models used by top management for strategy formulation.[17] The term includes the definition of purpose (objectives), the way a firm approaches competition, and the criteria used to make business decisions. The rules of business in Asia Pacific

differ quite substantially from those in Europe or the USA (see Figure 5.5).
Differences emerge in three managerial domains: goal setting, competitive
behaviour and decision-making.

Goal setting

The nature of objectives assigned to businesses varies according to the
economic system in which they operate, the society which has created them,
and the values of the dominant coalition which controls them.[18] In the Asia
Pacific region there are certain countries in which goal setting differs from
the West, although this is not true for the entire region. Three particular factors
form the basis for the differences: time, outcome and social orientation.

In terms of time orientation, Asian businesses tend to position themselves
at the extremes of a spectrum that ranges from a very long-term orientation
(for example, Japanese or Korean firms) to a short-term, opportunistic
orientation, as is the case in Hong Kong and most Overseas Chinese family
firms. The long-term orientation of Japanese and Korean firms has several
causes. First, as indicated earlier, the Japanese and Korean governments
have provided the economy with both a political context and financial
incentives conducive to long-term thinking. Second, nationalism and its
concomitant fighting spirit have given these firms the drive to think in terms
of long-term, rather than short-term, gain. In contrast, Overseas Chinese firms

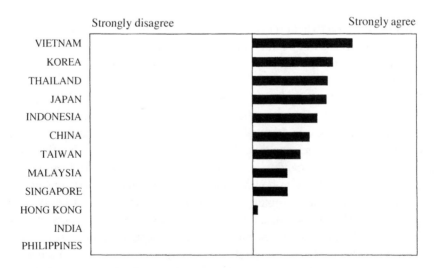

SOURCE: Lasserre and Probert (1997).

Figure 5.5   European or US Business Rules do not Work Here

and managers, who because of their ethnic minority status tend to operate in volatile and adverse political contexts, are more prone to short-term thinking. However, even in a context in which local firms have a short-term orientation, foreign firms operating in the region should bear in mind that they need to adopt a long-term view, due to the time involved in acquiring experience and cultivating relationships.

As far as outcome orientation is concerned, Asian firms place more emphasis on marketing objectives (for example, market share, growth) and tend to perceive profitability as a result of sound marketing strategy. This is in sharp contrast to American or British companies, which emphasise financial objectives.[19] It would be a mistake to conclude that Asian firms neglect financial performance but the stability of their ownership and the long-term view of their stakeholders – whether the firm is state- or family-owned – free them to focus on marketing objectives instead of quarterly returns.

Social orientation in Asian society is the belief that their firms should first fulfil various social and nationalist functions before pursuing individual wealth. There is therefore a greater acceptance of government intervention in business. In Singapore, for example, Singaporean firms form teams that parade on National Day, right after the military parade. This is just one symbol of the critical role Asian governments assign business in national development.

Competitive behaviour

It is not uncommon to hear recently-appointed Western expatriates complain about the unfairness of Asian competition, the price bargaining attitudes of Asian customers for high-tech products, and the copy-cat behaviour of their Asian competitors.

In most Asian countries local businesses are given preferential treatment, particularly when it comes to bidding for government contracts. This is viewed as an acceptable form of government intervention and economic nationalism. Advantages can take the form of preferential supply of credits, granting of business licences, restrictions on employment and protective regulations. Figure 5.6 shows how Western managers perceive this in the region.

With the exception of Japan, most Asian societies adopt a bargaining attitude in their business transactions. Nevertheless, it would be incorrect to assume that Asian customers automatically sacrifice quality for price (Figure 5.7). The most common strategy is first to determine the required level of technological performance and quality, then to select suppliers on that basis, and finally to use competitive rivalry as leverage to negotiate price advantages. This bargaining attitude does not conflict with the need to cultivate relationships,

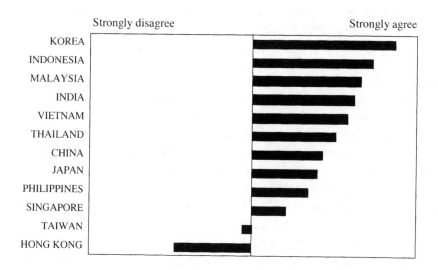

SOURCE: Lasserre and Probert (1997).

Figure 5.6 The Government Grants some Preferential Advantages to Local Firms over Foreign Ones

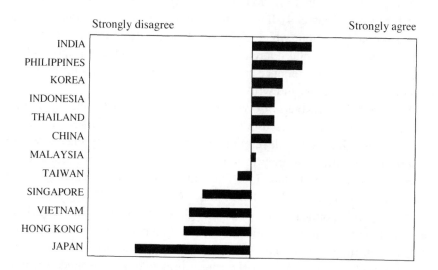

SOURCE: Lasserre and Probert (1997).

Figure 5.7 Quality is More Important than Price

since loyal, long-term suppliers are not expected to abuse their special relationships by overpricing products or services. The bargaining approach is particularly prevalent in competitive bidding situations. In their bids, Western suppliers have a tendency to emphasise technological sophistication and guarantee margins. In Asia, they are often surprised to discover that they have been rejected for a lower-priced bidder, whose strategy is to offer a base price and save additional features for future negotiations.

Although not limited to Asia, imitation is an indisputable part of Asian business life. Imitation can take the form of illegal copying, counterfeiting of trademarks or simply attempts to replicate the success of a competitor by adopting the same product or service concept, or by entering the same market. First mover advantages do not last long unless they are supported by a unique product or competence. The situation is aggravated in many cases by the absence of protective regulations regarding intellectual property rights, or of effective enforcement. Although legislative protection is gradually being introduced in Asia, enforcement is still ineffective and largely unmonitored. The practice of reverse engineering is still common in China, Korea, Taiwan and Hong Kong.[20]

Decision-making

Decision-making is the third domain in which Western and Asian business logic differs (see Chapter 4). It is useful to summarise a few key traits of Asian organisational behaviour which differ substantially from those dominant in the West: an incremental approach to planning, an inductive approach to decision-making, and a reliance on personal interface and commitment rather than on formal systems and written contracts.

There are many reasons why Western-style long-range business planning has not been widely practised in the Asia Pacific region. First, at the early stages of growth in Asia's developing countries, local entrepreneurs tended to seize opportunities as they presented themselves via their contacts (an approach that rendered planning irrelevant).[21] In addition, databases were unavailable. In Japan, at the other end of the spectrum, although data were available and economic planning existed at government level, businesses have preferred to rely on a combination of incremental planning and strong long-term vision. Incremental planning can be defined as a series of short-term, operational plans guided by a set of business principles and inspired by a long-term vision (strategic intent[22]). While traditional Western planning approaches encourage abstraction and deductive reasoning, Asian managers at all levels resist abstract theories about business decision-making. Asian managers tend to prefer a more inductive form of decision-making that proceeds from concrete situations rather than abstract models.

While Western managers adopt an engineering approach to building and regulating organisational behaviour, Asians prefer to view their enterprises as organic, living entities where various individuals and groups obtain mutual benefits through cooperation. This fundamental difference in philosophy has a considerable effect on both decision-making and human interaction within the firm. Western managers tend to favour systems for decision-making and mechanisms for resolving their problems. In many cases, this can lead to a formal or legalistic approach to human interaction that is abhorrent to many Asian managers, who come from cultures that tend to value paternalistic though informal employer–employee relationships. Significant cultural misunderstandings can arise in situations where Western managers, believing that they are being equitable and fair by using contracts and well-defined procedure, actually baffle their Asian colleagues or business partners. In general, Asian managers and employees tend to value the quality of interaction, defined in terms of loyalty, trust and dedication, and therefore often interpret recourse to legal contracts and procedure as a failure of human interaction.

THE ASIAN BUSINESS CONTEXT: AN OVERVIEW

The profile of organisational behaviour in the Asia Pacific region which emerges from this chapter differs significantly from that of Europe or the USA. Taken individually, each of the characteristics which make up that profile bears some similarities to those of more familiar environments, but taken as a whole they make the Asia Pacific region quite distant from what Western managers are used to. A pictorial representation of this distance is mapped in Figure 5.8, based on a 1997 survey conducted with 294 Western managers.[23] The diagram is organised along two axes.

One axis, the *competitive context*, includes characteristics which make business life in Asia Pacific more or less alien to Western players, such as the obligation to enter a complex network of relationships and the obligation to decode intriguing business rules. The second axis, the *political, ethical and legal* context, is concerned with the degree of government intervention, the integrity of business practices and the legal framework of business actions, all of which determine the rules of the game in different countries.

It comes as no surprise that, according to the survey, Singapore and Hong Kong are places where the rules of the game seem clearest and most familiar. The positions of Korea, Vietnam and Indonesia indicate that Western managers operating there experience enormous difficulties in understanding and dealing

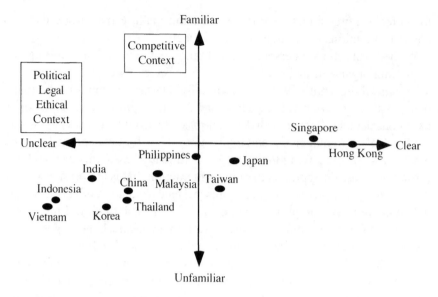

SOURCE: Lasserre and Probert (1997).

Figure 5.8   Perception of the Accessibility of Asia Pacific

with the business environment. The recent boom in the southern Chinese provinces and their proximity to Hong Kong may explain why China, considered to be a difficult country, scores higher than Korea, and not far behind the Philippines and Malaysia. The position of Japan on this map confirms the uneasiness of Western managers in dealing with the complex Japanese industrial environment. Japan, despite its well-developed infra-structure and accessible, reliable data, is still considered an unfamiliar country in which to do business. Although it is difficult to generalise on the basis of one survey, the results would seem to confirm the prevailing idea that, with the exception of Singapore and Hong Kong, Asia is perceived to be complex and unfamiliar to a large proportion of Western managers. This perception may be due to a lack of experience. With time, Asia will undoubtedly lose some of its mystery.

THE FINANCIAL CRISIS OF 1997 AND ASIAN BUSINESS LOGIC

Since the Asian crisis struck Thailand during the summer of 1997, followed by Malaysia, Korea, Indonesia and the rest of the region, many analysts have tried to understand the causes of such a profound disturbance. Beside a number of economic factors such as current account deficits, easy access to cash and the devaluation of the renminbi, it became obvious that some of the characteristics of the business environment which are described in this chapter have played a role in the origin of the crisis and in its evolution. Close government–business ties have prevented governments from exercising the necessary discipline over financial institutions and corporations. Such blindness or laxity on the part of bureaucrats has more often than not been fuelled by corruption. The importance of relationships in business was such that some deals were made without elementary precautions, as was the case of Peregrine of Hong Kong, which lent substantial sums to a business associate of President Suharto. It has sometimes been difficult to disentangle relationships based on trust from cronyism based on political patronage. Lack of planning and reliance on entrepreneurial opportunism when pushed to their limits were transformed into pure speculation. These are the elements of the business environment under attack from Western market-oriented economists and the IMF.

The crisis is forcing change in these practices. After the political changes in Korea, Indonesia and Thailand, and the appointment of a new prime minister in China, the new leaders have declared their intention to move the business environment towards a more open, transparent, market-based context. It is not yet clear the extent to which nepotism, clannishness and networking are rooted in history. The nationalistic reactions in some quarters to the IMF medicine indicate that societies prefer sometimes to find an external scapegoat rather than face harsh reality.

As usual the answer lies somewhere in between: we can expect more transparency and more market-based mechanisms, but probably accompanied by a serious dose of networking.

Notes and references

1. World Bank (1993).
2. World Bank (1993), pp. I–II.
3. Lasserre and Probert (1994a).
4. The term, the 'sacrificed generation', was used by Kim Woo Chong, Chairman of Daewoo, in a public talk given at Harvard Business School in 1984: video 9-885-510, Harvard Business School, 1985.
5. World Bank (1993), p. 181.
6. World Bank (1993), p. 182.
7. Joon Bae (1989).
8. Economic Intelligence Unit, *Country Profile: China* (1997), p. 39.
9. Hensley and White (1993).
10. This is particularly obvious in Indonesia where the armed forces are mandated with a dual function (*dwifungsi*), a military one and a socio-economic one. This has given rise to a complete corporate system run by the army. See Jenkins (1984).
11. Palmier (1989).

12. This distinction between 'shame' and 'guilt' cultures was introduced by Benedict (1976). A guilt culture is developed by a society that inculcates absolute standards of morality and relies on the development of conscience. By contrast, a shame culture relies on external sanction for good behaviour.
13. Pye (1989b), p. 76.
14. Hicks and Redding (1983). See also Brislin (1993); Peterson (1993); and Weinshall (1993).
15. Hofstede (1980).
16. World Bank (1993).
17. Prahalad and Bettis (1986).
18. Cyert and March (1963).
19. Hayes and Abernathy (1980).
20. Reverse engineering consists of copying competitive products by learning the technology and disassembling the product itself.
21. Lasserre (1983).
22. Hamel and Prahalad (1989).
23. A report on this survey can be found in Lasserre and Probert (1997).

6   Competing

STRATEGIC AND MARKET INTELLIGENCE

Reliability and accessibility of information

In the late 1970s, Alcan, a major aluminium producer, planned to build a rolling mill in Malaysia. The company had been present in Malaysia for several years in the downstream side of the industry and was in contact with a network of distributors all over the country. In order to prepare a strategic plan and a capital expenditure request for headquarters, a forecast of the future demand for aluminium was needed. Distributors were interviewed about their sales volume but the results were disappointing as the distributors were reluctant to give figures for fear of tax control. The company was obliged to 'guesstimate' and during the various stages of the projects the forecasts varied considerably.

This example illustrates the difficulties of obtaining information in Asia. A Western firm willing to invest and expand in the region will have to gain an understanding of the rules of the game in such diverse settings as post-industrial Japan, with its formidably intricate network of business connections; Indonesia, where the business climate is dominated by several Overseas Chinese conglomerates; or China and Vietnam, where communist cadres share confidential information with entrepreneurial friends or family members for mutual gain. Given the greater degree of uncertainty arising from differences in culture, business organisation and public policy, the collection and the processing of strategic and marketing information are generally more difficult to perform in Asia Pacific than in the home country or in countries which share similarities with the home country.

According to the results of a survey conducted in 1992,[1] Western managers indicated that, with the exception of Japan, forecasting in the Asia Pacific region was more difficult than in Europe or the USA. The special case of Japan may be related to the higher level of economic development of the country and the sophistication of its information systems compared to the rest of the region. There is a correlation between a country's stage of development and reliability of forecasts, except in the case of Taiwan (Figure 6.1).

An attempt was therefore made to find out what managers thought about the two major obstacles with which they are confronted when collecting and interpreting data: the first is availability and accessibility and the second is

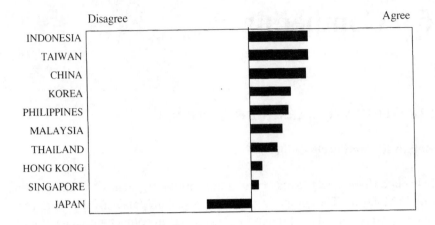

SOURCE: Lasserre and Probert (1993a).

Figure 6.1 Business Forecasting is Less Reliable than in the West

reliability. In both cases, respondents perceived the region to be clustered into three groups of countries (Figure 6.2).

Japan, and to a lesser extent Singapore and Hong Kong, are perceived as information-friendly. In these countries, the multiplicity of sources makes it

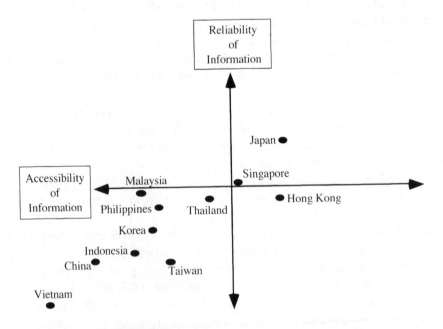

Figure 6.2 The Information Environment in Asia Pacific

relatively easy (although possibly expensive) to get access to information and the information obtained is perceived to be reliable. Japan is without doubt an information-rich country where information is both accessible and of good quality. In fact, respondents found information too detailed in Japan. Japan was not seen to provide less reliable information than Europe and the USA; the only handicap seems to be the cost of acquiring it. Singapore is on the borderline for accessibility and Hong Kong below the zero line for quality of information.

Most of the ASEAN countries, Korea and Taiwan constitute a second group of countries. Expatriate managers in these countries perceived the quality of information as bad and accessibility as also poor due either to the cost of obtaining information, or to the fact that information is kept in relatively small circles. Reliability is poorly rated because in these countries information is perceived to be manipulated or voluntarily truncated by governments or dominant business groups.

Finally come China and, far behind, Vietnam. Neither of these countries is considered information-friendly. This comes as no surprise given the well-known propensity of communist regimes to consider information gathering as a form of political espionage.

Sources of information

Given the mixed reliability and accessibility of data in the region, the most useful sources of information are those collected directly by companies, either from their personal contacts with customers, other business relations, competitors and government officials, or from their own market surveys. Publicly available information from newspapers and magazines, bankers or general surveys are considered of less value by managers operating in the region.

Except for those of Singapore and Japan, government publications and statistics are not an important information source, and that may reflect the view that the realities of business life are not fully represented by official documentation: government regulations are frequently open to generous interpretation by those with the right contacts.

Countries with a relatively strong local press include Japan (the *Nikkei Weekly*, published in English, and *Nikkei Shimbun*, in Japanese), Hong Kong (*South China Morning Post*) and Thailand (the *Bangkok Post* and *The Nation*). The *South China Morning Post* is easily the most widely used local or regional newspaper, with a readership extending throughout much of South-East Asia. The *Business Times* (Singapore and Malaysia) also receives a fairly good rating.

The preference for directly collected information rather than press accounts confirms that business in Asia depends more heavily upon the creation of a network of relationships than on the analysis of hard data collected through public surveys or published information.

There are many reasons for this. They may be political (information is often very tightly controlled by the government), cultural (information has a bargaining value in Asia), historical (information is power), structural (information circulates among small groups of the happy few) or economic (some developing countries of Asia have not yet built the intellectual and physical infrastructure to gather and distribute information).

Another cause of the difficulty in collecting information may be attributable to expatriate managers themselves: their lack of familiarity with the culture and inability to decode the information available, their lack of contacts (*guanxi*), and the fact that they place too much emphasis on hard data. This may explain why, at the end of the day, the information environment appears to be unfriendly and government or journalistic sources either too vague or manipulated.

Managers have no choice other than to make the crucial investment of building their own database, particularly through the establishment of a network of relationships which has to be cultivated, shared with colleagues, and carefully maintained. Information is no longer a commodity that one can buy, but a competence that one builds. This requires more than an individual effort; it is part of a collective, organisational learning effort. Particular emphasis has to be given to the memorising of information and attention paid to considering the problem of succession. Job rotation might result in the successor re-inventing the wheel. A proper and timely introduction of the successor into the network is certainly a preferred solution if organisational memory and intelligence capability are to be built up and exploited productively.

Market research in Asia

When no information can be gathered from secondary sources, or information is needed on very specific product markets and buying behaviour, primary data have to be collected through market research. In Asia Pacific this area is still relatively underdeveloped except in Japan, which represents 9 per cent of world-wide market research expenditure.

Most of the full-service research agencies are local, independent firms concentrating on their domestic market. Not all of them can undertake reliable research to an international standard, though most charge comparatively high fees for their services. Very few can carry out surveys across the region.

The largest regional network, SRG, was taken over by A. C. Nielsen in 1994 and is thus part of a global group.

The problem of finding a reliable agency that does not already work for the competition has forced a number of multinational firms either to build up expertise in-house, as Unilever began to do many years ago in a number of countries, or to rely on their own sales people to feed sufficiently good information back to their marketing or planning departments. Product tests or interviews in these cases are often improvised in showrooms, or near demonstration vans or stalls in markets.

For multinationals, most market research still consists of testing the suitability and acceptability of existing products and services for Asian target groups, though the percentage of testing done on domestically developed goods is increasing. More general usage and attitudinal studies are often carried out with the help of syndicated and omnibus surveys.

There are a number of problems encountered in information gathering across the region which reflect the stage of the development of the various economies involved. Textbook-style probability sampling, for example, is possible only in countries that have strict registration requirements. This makes it necessary to combine primary and secondary data to reach more-or-less reliable estimates of market share. Multiracial and multilingual environments create obvious communication and comprehension constraints. These are amplified when research projects are carried out in several Asian countries simultaneously. Even defining a similar socio-economic profile of a given segment across borders can create serious problems.

While these problems are obvious and largely practical, there are other, more subtle difficulties that are specific to Asia Pacific, or to some Asian countries.

The courtesy of most Asians tends to bring a positive bias into most surveys, thus requiring very careful interpretation of respondents' answers. 'Would perhaps buy' in the West indicates that chances exist for sales, but probably means 'definitely not interested' in an Asian context. Adherence to hierarchy in focus group discussions can lead to deference to the most senior member of the panel instead of expressions of independent opinions. Face-to-face interviews can rarely be carried out in privacy and touch on taboos in multiple-family households where the individual member has to conform to certain expectations and role models. In industrial market research, decision-makers are difficult to identify and even more difficult to get hold of. Batteries of assistants and secretaries tend to keep senior Asian managers out of the reach of the ordinary market researcher or interviewer.

In China as in Vietnam, it is still advisable to get clearance from local authorities. This will make it easier to approach people and will avoid the risk of being suspected of spying. Once properly introduced, the response rate in these two countries tends to be high due to the excitement of being interviewed and asked for an opinion. In both countries market research was completely unknown until recently, though there is substantial know-how for conducting social and economic studies.

In sharp contrast to China and Vietnam, Japanese markets are probably the most researched in the world. Western firms have no difficulty in finding a suitable agency, which will often be one which specialises in a range of industries or research techniques. Data collected and included in reports commissioned by customers are often more detailed than any survey results an expatriate has ever seen outside Japan. On the other hand, agencies will be reluctant to interpret the data. This is left to the ordering firm (not an easy task for a company newly arrived in the country or still looking at the market from outside).

ENTRY STRATEGIES

Selecting and changing entry modes

A generic model for entry strategies for the region has already been discussed in Chapter 2. In a specific country, market attractiveness and the pressure to produce locally are often the most important criteria for selecting the entry mode. Market attractiveness is influenced by economic factors such as market size, market growth, resource availability and the degree of competition. The question of whether customers can be reached through imports or whether local manufacturing is needed depends not only on individual government policies but also on the economics involved.

By and large, governments in Asia prefer foreign firms to manufacture locally, or at least to assemble imported parts and components within the country. This does not apply to Singapore and Hong Kong, or to Japan, but most other countries have introduced a number of regulations favouring local production over imports. Equally, economics will influence the decision on the way a firm wants to start operating. It does not make much sense to transport from a distance low value, bulky products for which raw materials are available locally. A lack of economies of scale, on the other hand, may render local production even of those items infeasible, at least during the first phase of market penetration. The matrix shown in Figure 6.3 uses the two criteria of market attractiveness and pressure for local production and consequently shows four possible entry modes for the foreign firm.

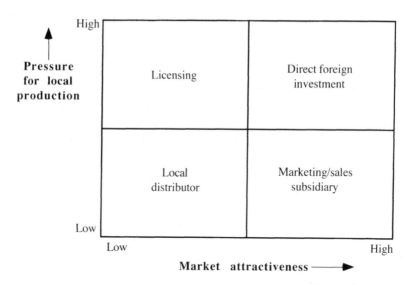

Figure 6.3 Selection of a Mode of Operation

Not all options are open in all countries of Asia. Direct foreign investment in a number of countries is only possible in certain industries and with local participation. Direct exports from abroad to customers in a given market without any local representation are not indicated in Figure 6.3 but theoretically would be another option. The markets in Asia Pacific have by and large become too sophisticated and too demanding for such transactions, except for unique product offerings or very large deals such as the sale of aircraft or power plants (though Westinghouse used a distributor to sell a nuclear power plant to the Marcos regime in the Philippines in the 1970s).

As a rule, decisions on entry mode are made when the firm concerned has only limited knowledge about the opportunities and risks of the market. Decisions have therefore to be made under great uncertainty, even though they may affect the well-being of the firm for many years to come. Foreign firms tend to go for solutions which look less risky: either representation by a local distributor or local manufacturing through licensing. These entry modes limit investment requirements and costs, which are welcome aspects at a time when the volume of local sales is still small.

There are pitfalls in selecting entry modes which do not force the foreign firm to become directly involved in the market. First of all, the essential activities of building up reputation and image are left to an outside distributor or manufacturer. The long-term consequences of the provision of insufficient after-sales service or the delivery of low quality products can be serious and costly. Second, it will be very difficult for the firm to assess the real potential of the market over time as marketing activities are carried out by others. Limited sales can be as much the result of insufficient efforts by the distributor or licensee as of limited demand.

In line with the overall growth of Asian economies the attractiveness of many product markets has improved considerably over time. This can call for a change in entry mode. In other cases new government regulations require a reconsideration of local production. Existing agreements then become major constraints, economically, legally and in some cases even politically.

Decades ago, Japan was seen as too difficult for most foreign firms. Technology was transferred to Japanese licensees, and distribution rights assigned to partners who today have become major competitors in world markets. As a number of large Western pharmaceutical firms realised in the 1980s, taking over these activities themselves was not easy; in fact, it was extremely costly. It would probably have been cheaper and more effective to have made a full commitment years back (though such decision was not always possible due to government policies). In the past, distribution rights for China were often given to small Hong Kong firms with some contacts in China. Today, most foreign multinationals prefer to be in full control of their future in that market.

The French electrical switch gear producer, Merlin Gerin, started to sell its products in China with the help of a distributor in Beijing in the early 1970s. It then felt that local manufacturing would be necessary to exploit the market fully and asked a Chinese company to produce certain switches under licence. But the quality was below standard and sales were not good. In 1985 Merlin Gerin opened a representative office in China. Two years later it started its own factory as a joint venture in Tianjin, having gone through several reassessments of the opportunities that China offered them and all four of the entry modes shown above.[2]

Distribution agreements

The important role of intermediaries in Asian life and the uncertainty of how to manage with their own resources have led many foreign firms to favour a distributor when entering markets in the region. Today there is a trend towards more direct involvement, especially among the larger and more experienced companies and in the more promising markets. Distribution agreements, however, remain crucial for smaller, less experienced firms and for markets or market segments which are presently of secondary importance. In countries like Indonesia, the Philippines, China and Vietnam, foreign firms also experience restrictions in their distribution activities, forcing them to join up with a local partner or to appoint a local distributor. These distributors can act as importers or wholesalers, take care of retailing or combine several of those functions. Their tasks range from taking sole responsibility for all activities in a given market including logistics, inventory control and financing, to facilitating sales by establishing contacts.

Some distribution agreements still weigh heavily in the strategies of the largest multinational firms even though they may have been concluded many decades ago. These companies either do not consider a switch to more direct representation to be feasible yet, or conversely would prefer to cut the existing links with their distributor, but are not able to do so.

Using a distributor is advantageous when a foreign firm does not have the experience, the contacts and the resources it needs to penetrate a new market. As the volume of sales will be limited at the first entry phase, using a distributor's resources will also be cost-efficient. The decision to use a distributor is also influenced by the complexity of the products in question and the availability of local companies in the market with expertise for handling such products. Contacts in some countries are vital, especially in dealing with governments and government-owned corporations or operating in markets which are heavily influenced by government regulation.

The appointment of a distributor may also bypass certain constraints foreign firms have in business ethics and practices. If the arrangement of commissions and other facilitating activities is left to the distributor, these activities remain outside the control of internal auditors. For similar reasons distributors located in Singapore or Hong Kong are used to import products on which high customs duties are levied into markets such as Indonesia, China or Vietnam. The foreign firm will then not be directly involved in bringing the products into the country, thus avoiding problems with customs clearance. Thereafter it may leave the distribution in the country to the importer, appoint another distributor in the country or take charge itself.

The greatest disadvantage of distribution agreements is that they tend to cut off the principal from the market. If the appointment of a distributor initially was made because there was insufficient knowledge about the market in the firm, operating through a distributor may not help the firm to gain market insight and experience. The flow of information from the market back to the manufacturer is often limited, as is the influence of the principal on what is happening in the market. Pre-selling support, price setting and after-sales service are especially difficult to control. Coordination of activities across borders in a region which is tending to become more integrated is difficult when various distributors are involved, each of whom is in charge of only one country or even one market segment in a country.

Despite all the talk about partnership and mutual benefits, it cannot be denied that most distribution agreements are structurally flawed and intrinsically problematic. Multinational firms tend to look at a given country as one among many and pursue their strategies across regions or on a global basis, often considering market share and competition more important than immediate profit. Distributors, on the other hand, tend to look at the products of one multinational firm as only part of their total product portfolio which may contain large numbers of similar, sometimes competing, products. For them sales, margins and payment terms matter more than the long-term market share considerations of multinationals.

Traditional Chinese distributors, dominating most of the ASEAN markets, tend to look at distribution as a cash management business. Foreign firms are often surprised to find them selling their products to retailers at prices below purchasing costs. This does not indicate a loss-making undertaking. Distributors may be granted payment terms of three months, stretching them to four. They will then sell to the retailer either against cash, or demanding very high interest payments when granting terms of a few weeks. In adding interest earnings distributors achieve a positive margin, often without even having to invest in the business themselves. On the contrary, distributors can set up the business as an activity to raise cash, which in turn can be invested in other businesses (such as real estate). It is obvious that under these circumstances the objectives of distributors and the principal are not in line. The demand to give special attention to the introduction of a new product will not necessarily find enthusiastic support from a partner primarily concerned with cash management.

There is another, even more serious, concern which is related to the dynamics of the market and the expectations of the two partners about the duration of their agreement. Distribution agreements are generally considered when sales are small or non-existent. From the point of view of the manufacturer the business at this stage cannot support the very high fixed costs related to setting up and running a marketing or sales subsidiary on its own. The manufacturer therefore appoints a distributor and allows the partner a profit related to the sales in the country. For the manufacturer this basically represents variable costs.

The market may then turn out to be highly attractive and the distributor an aggressive entrepreneur pushing up sales to high volume. Sooner or later the manufacturer as principal will calculate the income generated by its products for the distributor and compare this with the costs of setting up its own subsidiary. A break-even is reached when the costs of the distributor to the principal are equivalent to the costs of running a subsidiary (see Figure 6.4).

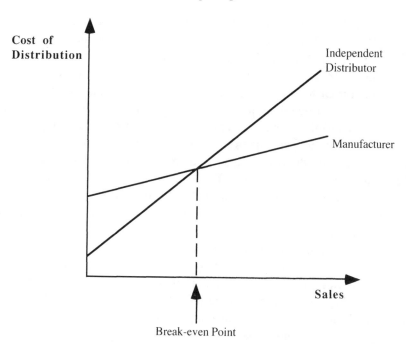

Figure 6.4 Break-even in Distribution

From the break-even point onwards it is more cost efficient for the principal to cancel the agreement with the distributor and to take over. Other strategic reasons, such as taking direct control, may accelerate this move towards divorce. While this may be considered a natural evolution, there is a real danger of preventing the distributor – well aware of the economics involved – from showing full commitment to the business. The more the distributor increases the volume of sales, the higher the likelihood of him or her losing the business. The firm will either deliberately underperform or try to compensate for reduced volume by increasing prices and therefore profits per unit. The Japanese car importer Yanase is a case in point. Over several decades the firm brought Mercedes, BMW and Volkswagen cars into Japan, selling them at grossly inflated prices. For years the German manufacturers did not consider it feasible to set up their own import business and distribution network due to the low volume of sales. When they finally did decide to make the leap, the long-lasting good relationship with Yanase was difficult to dissolve. Mercedes took over the import business but kept Yanase as one of their distributors. The Japanese firm accepted this solution. When Volkswagen followed suit in the 1990s, Yanese, which had imported and sold 600 000 cars for them, balked and walked away leaving the German firm with only a few outlets in Japan. Yanase also decided to distribute Opel cars in future, a further blow to Volkswagen which consequently lost sales and market share.

This case exemplifies the difficulties of evaluating distribution alternatives, foreseeing the reaction of the distributor to a proposed change and estimating the effects on customers when a change is implemented. Understandably distributors will argue that any success in the market is due to their efforts or – more relevant to the Asian environment – their contacts. Distributors will try to be as independent from the principal as possible by making the manufacturer's products only part of their overall operations, by offering additional services which are difficult to replace (such as extending the activities to retailing), by not sharing vital information with the principal and by displaying interest in taking over the business of other competing manufacturers.

The high potential for conflict in these situations necessitates paying more attention not only to signing a distribution agreement, but also to the possibilities of dissolving such an agreement in a mutually acceptable way at a later stage. Distributors are key external resources, requiring years of effort to build and constant, attentive management. Agreements with them represent a commitment which often goes beyond the text of a legal document. Changes in distribution are notoriously difficult and rarely possible within a limited period. This contrasts with changes in the other elements of the marketing-mix which are generally easier and more adaptable to changes in the environment.

Successful partnerships require a fit in strategies, resources, culture and organisation. These issues will be explored in depth in Chapter 7. Several types of partner can be considered for a distribution agreement. A typical local distributor will have better local contacts and possibly a better local sales force, but the establishment of fit with a Western principal can be problematic. Local in the ASEAN and Vietnamese context often means Chinese. Chinese entrepreneurs dominate the distribution sector in these countries. Selecting one of these firms may work well in terms of efficiency, but entails certain political risks due to their uncertain role, particularly in Indonesia and Malaysia. Deciding to join up with a Chinese distributor can be especially disadvantageous when dealing with the public sector.

International distributors are of Western, Japanese and increasingly also of Asian origin. Some Asian distribution companies (such as Sime Darby of Malaysia) have outgrown their own territory and are now offering their services elsewhere in the region. Some Western distributors have been in Asia since colonial times and have developed from traditional trading outposts into modern marketing firms. Others, unable to change their way of doing business, are disappearing. Among the better known survivors are Diethelm, East

Asiatic, Hagemeyer, Liebermann, Inchcape, Jardine and Swire. Foreign manufacturers will find it relatively easy to establish a fit with them. However, some companies may be less well connected and less well endowed with resources than local distributors. The strength of these companies is also spread very unevenly across the region. British firms, for example, are strong in Hong Kong but weak in countries such as Indonesia. Diethelm is very successful in Thailand but has less to offer in other countries. This basically rules out the appointment of an international distributor for the whole of Asia Pacific.

The Japanese *sogo shosha* are the exceptions. Represented in almost all the countries of the world, these distributors have well-staffed offices in all the countries of the Asia Pacific region. With turnovers above US$100 billion in 1997, Mitsui, Mitsubishi, Itochu, Marubeni and Sumitomo are in a class of their own. Their size is a multiple of any other non-Japanese trading company in the world. Their strength lies more in industrial goods, commodity trading and project management than in final distribution or the marketing of fast moving consumer goods. Because of their size and enormous product range, the *sogo shosha* do not offer exclusivity to their principals. This makes Western manufacturers uncomfortable as they are aware of the close links which these firms have with Japanese manufacturers at home. The experience of some Western multinationals has, however, been good, particularly when targeting Japanese companies operating in the region or projects initiated and financed with development aid from Japan. Appointing the *sogo shosha* as importers for Japan, on the other hand, has often failed to come up to expectations. Their dominant role in Japan makes it difficult for a Western firm with limited sales in the country to get sufficient attention. Here the solution is to go into a major, more complex arrangement with a *sogo shosha*, leading to substantial business volume, or to go it alone, or to appoint a smaller distributor.

Choice of location

As with decisions about entry modes and distribution, the choice of location for the firm within a country has to be made at a very early stage of market entry and carries far-reaching consequences. Companies rarely relocate after years in one place, even if the location turns out to be less advantageous than anticipated or if changes in market dynamics or government policies turn an early correct decision into a later wrong one.

In many cases the choice of location seems to be obvious for the multinational firm: in the capital, which in most cases in Asia is also the centre of economic activity. This seems to be appropriate in Thailand, Korea or the Philippines, but is more problematic in Japan, where Tokyo and Osaka represent alternatives, or in Vietnam with both Hanoi and Ho Chi Minh City. In China, Beijing, Shanghai and Guangzhou vie for the prize as the most attractive location for foreign investment.

The choice of location is often related to the selection of a joint venture partner. Once this partner is found, no real choice exists as the location will often be where the partner is already established. This can give the new entrant a bad start in comparison to competitors who have conducted a systematic location analysis and based their decision on an optimisation of those factors which determine the feasibility of a location. Figure 6.5 charts some of the most important factors influencing choice location.

Locating close to customers means savings in transportation costs and can enable the firm eventually to take distribution into its own hands. This is the most important factor for sub-contractors following an assembling firm as its dominant customer. Being close to the customers also means immediate feedback from the market and enables the firm to react rapidly to changes in demand. Rarely, however, is a major market uncontested. Any latecomer locating close to it will encounter fierce competition from entrenched local or multinational firms which have built 'walled cities' in the territory they consider theirs. Having established good contacts with the local authorities, suppliers, distributors and customers, they are determined to fight intruders to an extent they would not consider in other areas.[3] The battles between the beer brewers in Surabaya and Jakarta, or those in Ho Chi Minh City and Hanoi, are good examples of corporate psyche when it comes to the defence of home

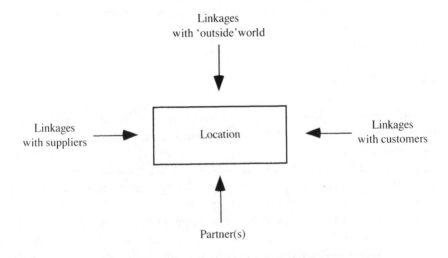

Figure 6.5   Location Decision Factors

territory. Successful invasion of such locations requires major resources and a high degree of product differentiation.

A location close to suppliers of raw materials, parts and components, industrial consumables and ancillary services is equally beneficial. This factor is the overriding consideration for firms exploiting natural resources, but it also plays a very important role in LDCs such as China and Vietnam, where local sourcing represents a major bottleneck in the operations of multinational firms. The activities of existing competitors and their relationship with suppliers also have an impact on the choice of location. Entrenched firms may have already signed up existing suppliers, preventing them from cooperating with newcomers. On the other hand, the emergence of a cluster of manufacturers in close proximity to each other may give rise to the development of ancillary industries which in turn boosts the competitiveness of all the firms in a given area.[4] Location seekers can therefore gain from being close to their competitors, as Western pharmaceutical firms have found when locating in Osaka, or cosmetics firms when locating in Shanghai.

The costs of a location are determined not only by its proximity to customers and suppliers but also by the cost of buying or setting up facilities, the infrastructure around these facilities, the cost of labour and other inputs, as well as incentives from government authorities in terms of tax holidays, subsidies, rents, and so on. Multinationals locating in SEZs like Shenzen or Subic Bay consider these aspects of prime importance. Producing for overseas markets, their links with the domestic economy are often limited, hence their efforts to keep the cost of inputs low. Once located in a zone and enjoying special privileges, sales into the domestic market are not easy, as the products are often considered as imports rather than as locally manufactured. For example, as the domestic market for sports shoes explodes in China, manufacturers in zone locations find themselves at a disadvantage compared to those firms which started production in locations close to the main markets.

Even in the age of electronic mail, links with headquarters, regional offices and other affiliated companies remain important. Receiving instructions and financial data by fax does not give senior management in a remote location the same feel for shifting company policies or changing market trends as face-to-face meetings and visits to key markets. Because of this, proximity to travel centres will remain an important factor in selecting a location. Companies in far-away places will also find it difficult to staff operations with senior managers who do not come from the area themselves. Few expatriates can be persuaded to locate to a plant in Mongolia even if they – as Taiwanese expatriates do – speak the language. This is linked to prosaic issues such as housing and schooling for the children, but is also related to a more general feeling of uneasiness at being cut off from the rest of the world and therefore quickly forgotten.

The selection of a location which takes into account these four decision factors very rarely leads to the choice of what can be termed an ideal location. A compromise is therefore called for. Unfortunately, such a compromise often leads to a solution inferior to that found by existing firms in the country. An alternative lies in decoupling various activities. Instead of thinking about one individual site, operations can be split up. Many Western firms have done this in Japan. Sales, marketing and general administration are located in Tokyo, manufacturing plants in various locations far away in the countryside, and research and development in Tsukuba. In doing this, the locational advantages the company gains over its competitors must be weighed against the disadvantages of the extra costs the company will incur for eventual loss of efficiency and additional coordination and communication efforts.

Local content requirements

In manufacturing the percentage of material and labour input from within the country determines the local content. It varies considerably depending on the industry, country or objective of each specific plant. At one end of the scale are offshore operations for the assembly of consumer electronics or garments in Indonesia or the Philippines, which rely on supplies from abroad and export most of their output. At the other end of the scale are fully integrated manufacturing plants for special machinery in Japan, which operate independently in the domestic market.

In most cases cost will be the overriding factor in determining local content, especially in the more developed parts of Asia Pacific. In China or Vietnam, on the other hand, the absence of reliable suppliers who can deliver quality products on time limits the options.

Investing in in-house facilities and capabilities is not often feasible when the demand from the main plant is not yet sufficient to justify such moves. The alternative of importing from abroad can be restricted by the government. Restrictions are imposed through investment approval documents, through general (and often changing) foreign investment and trade regulations, or through central bank rules limiting the outflow of foreign exchange.

The restrictions are most critical in the countries of Asia Pacific which run a trade deficit or see the potential for a massive outflow of capital. China expects those foreign investors not operating in priority sectors to balance their foreign exchange. This rule basically means that all imports (including that of expatriates as far as their non-local currency payment is concerned) require a foreign exchange equivalent of exports. While shortcomings can be dealt with through swap facilities, these may not always be available, or only at a high cost. Foreign firms interested only in the domestic Chinese market therefore have to develop export businesses.

Limiting supplies from abroad creates other constraints, too, particularly if these are coming from either the home country plant or other affiliated companies. The latter often have a vital interest in supplying plants abroad due to underutilised capacities or to political pressure to generate employment. Any reduction in intra-firm supplies will also limit the opportunities for multinationals to optimise profits and taxes across the globe.

In putting pressure on foreign investors to increase their local content, governments in the region do not only want to control foreign exchange flows and tax payments. Forcing multinational firms to create and develop suppliers within the country fosters the transfer of technology to local firms, a process which would not occur in a pure assembly operation. Employment generation is another welcome effect that comes with the creation of a sub-contracting sector. When building up its first plant in Shanghai, Volkswagen at times had more than half of its expatriate technicians helping sub-contractors to develop and manufacture the parts and components Volkswagen needed to meet local content requirements. After years of major effort the firm now reports a local content of more than 80 per cent. This has not only earned Volkswagen high praise from the government, but has also brought some relief for the export targets that had originally been imposed on the multinational. Meanwhile, formerly unwilling and incompetent local suppliers have developed into reliable and cost-efficient sub-contractors, helping Volkswagen to become the most profitable joint venture in China by the beginning of 1993.

Critical mass and optimism traps

Any entry decision is connected with the question of how many resources should be deployed in the country. The theoretical answer is easy: enough to make an impact on the market, but not so much as to waste capital or human resources which could be used more efficiently elsewhere. In other words a critical mass of resources has to be allocated to succeed in a market, to pay back the investment and also to provide a profit in the future (see Figure 6.6).

In practice the problem lies in the identification of the critical mass threshold where any additional input of resources results in a disproportionately high growth in output. This can normally be found by taking the most successful (often the largest) competitor in the market as a benchmark. For example, a European trading house in Thailand was wondering why it was so unsuccessful in selling textile machinery in the country. The department in charge of this product line was staffed with three local salesmen, supervised

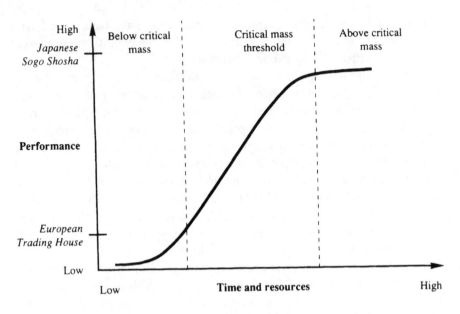

Figure 6.6   Chart of Critical Mass

by an expatriate who devoted only part of his time to this business. Through some intelligence work based on informal networks and relationships the company discovered that its European competitor had eight specialists working in the area, three of them textile engineers. One of the Japanese trading houses had five engineers assigned to the business, plus a large number of local salesmen. The company decided to drop the product line. It seemed impossible to make any impact on the market while clearly operating below critical mass.

Overlapping products, technologies or segments, however, make it difficult to identify the main competitors in many industries. In addition, foreign firms tend to overrate the importance of other multinationals and are often not fully aware of the strength of local firms, or how they deploy their resources.

The dynamic nature of the economies of Asia Pacific, as opposed to the more mature markets in Europe and North America, create additional difficulties in determining the right level of investment. Some of these are related to the environment, while others are home-made in the firm.

Due to the high growth recorded in many product markets, existing and entrenched competitors tend constantly to upgrade their resources, therefore raising the benchmark. New competitors from abroad build additional capacities, often using more up-to-date technology than existed beforehand.

Local firms, especially the large Asian conglomerates, are equally attracted by fast growing markets which apparently offer interesting profit opportunities. As a result, critical mass can no longer be achieved with the resources originally allocated. When incumbents and newcomers simultaneously add new resources, an investment stalemate can occur, turning a market in need of supply into one suffering oversupply and falling prices. Even when profits can still be achieved, these have immediately to be reinvested. This represents a cash trap in which the company cannot expect to see a rapid return on its investment.

This clashes with the high expectations of the managers concerned or senior executives at headquarters. They tend to take an overoptimistic view of deadlines and profits. Competition, especially local competition, is underestimated, as is the subtle underlying nationalism which works against multinational firms in many countries of Asia Pacific. The difficulties of building a network of local contacts, overcoming bureaucratic inertia and developing a capable team of loyal local employees are played down as technical rather than structural problems costing considerable time and money.

Overoptimistic planning and costing can lead to serious and expensive backlashes regarding promises made to governments, customers and suppliers, and the morale of those involved in the project both in Asia and at headquarters. An initially feasible project has run into an optimism trap when overoptimism turns into overpessimism. The reason is often a lack of information and understanding.

Expatriate and local managers in Asia unconsciously contribute to such phenomena. Operating in a high growth, rapidly changing environment and away from the mind-set of their colleagues, there is a great temptation for them to oversell projects at corporate headquarters. Frequently, the new project is hardly approved before a request for additional funding is made. The initial investment has become insufficient due to surprisingly inadequate infrastructure, unexpected pressure from the competition, or promising new investment opportunities in related business areas. Reasons for integrating forward and backward are easily found, leading to further requests for funding.

Investments in real estate are a case in point. These raise capital needs substantially. The value of office buildings, apartments for employees and industrial property has dramatically increased almost everywhere in Asia Pacific over the last few decades. However, this has not always improved cash flow, let alone the flow of money back to the parent firm. As events in Japan at the beginning of the 1990s and later in the other parts of Asia showed, real estate is also not without risks. More importantly, it diverts money away from the core business where it could be used to build brand image or customer loyalty. It also reduces the essential flexibility which the firm needs to maintain if it is to operate in an environment characterised by rapid change and turbulent competitive activity.

ACQUISITIONS

Before the financial crisis of 1997, straight acquisition by a foreign firm of a local Asian company was quite rare. Several reasons explained this. First, legislation was very vague about, if it did not completely rule out, the possibility of making acquisitions. Second, acquiring a company was not culturally acceptable, particularly in Japan where a company is considered as family and to sell out is seen as a public admission of failure. Just selling out to another owner seems to be inappropriate in Asia where a firm is seen conceptually as a social or a political organisation rather than a collection of tradable assets. The Japanese word for take-over, *nottori*, literally means 'hijacking'. Moreover, in both Japan and Korea there is a bitter sense of national disgrace if a company is sold to a foreigner. When Coca-Cola in 1996 tried to buy one of its bottling plants in Korea, workers carried banners protesting against 'American imperialism's treacherous conspiracy to plunder Korea's national assets'. The third reason for the rarity of acquisitions in Asia was that most assets were in the hands of or controlled by family conglomerates or through a complex web of cross-share holdings. In both cases outside shareholders could not exert pressure, even in case of gross mismanagement. As the proportion of shares listed on capital markets was small, investors from the outside were unable to make a take-over bid. Fourth, in many cases businesses in South-East Asia and Korea depended on protected relationships, especially with the government, which could not be transferred to foreigners. Fifth, even when acquisition was a possibility the price demanded by the seller was usually far above the potential economic value that could be generated from the assets.

The only alternatives in the past for a foreign firm determined to make an acquisition were to buy a small or medium-sized company when the owner was willing to sell, or to increase progressively the foreign share holding in a joint venture. The few companies which were publicly on offer were those in need of a bail-out which had been refused support by the local business community. For foreign firms they were in most cases not even worth the trouble of taking a closer look. The slow process of deregulation and privatisation in Asia did open up some acquisition opportunities, such as in the telecommunication sector. However, participation was normally limited to minority shares with no direct influence on management.

The situation has changed since the impact of the Asian crisis began to be felt. Governments, facing the imminent bankruptcy of entire industrial sectors such as in the financial industry, started to change the law to allow foreigners to acquire the whole or part of cash-strapped Asian firms. Closely held conglomerates began to realise the need to sell off parts of their empires as a means of rescuing the rest. Governments in need of cash started to accelerate the privatisation of state-owned companies. The lack of local investors left them with foreign capital as the only available source of funds. Overcapacities in many sectors such as the cement industry forced local owners to search for international firms who could buy into their plants and sell the output through their world-wide distribution network.

Since the autumn of 1997, business journals have been full of reports signalling the latest interest of foreign firms in acquiring Asian companies.[5] Certain key examples have been held out to support the view that Asia is becoming, like the USA or Europe, fertile ground for acquisitions. Table 6.1 gives a list of the major deals announced in the first half of 1998.

However, one should be cautious about all this excitement. Even if it is true that the crisis has opened the door to more acquisitions, the fact remains that the details of their implementation may be problematic. We will discuss the various issues raised in the planning and implementation of acquisitions in Asia Pacific using a framework developed by Haspeslagh and Jemison[6] (Figure 6.7).

Table 6.1 Acquisitions of Local Companies by Western Firms in Asia Pacific January–June 1998

Buyer	Target	Deal	Type
• Daimler-Benz (Germany)	Nissan Diesel (Japan)	60% of Nissan's lorry-making subsidiary	II
• Coca-Cola (Australia)	Coca-Cola (Korea)	Full control of existing bottling operations	I
• Seagram (Canada)	Doosan-Seagram (Korea)	Raising holding from 50% to 77.8%	I
• SNF Floerger (France)	Lyang Chemicals (Korea)	50%	II
• Nestlé (Switzerland)	Haitai Confectionery (Korea)	100%	IV
• AES Co. (USA)	Hanwha Energy (Korea)	100% of Hanwha Energy's power operating division	IV
• Metropolitan Life Insurance (USA)	Korea Life Insurance (Korea)	50%	II
• Johnson & Johnson (USA)	Samsung Insecticide (Korea)	100% of Samsung Pharma's insecticide operations	IV

continued

Table 6.1 *cont.*

Buyer	Target	Deal	Type
• Asia Pacific Brewery (Singapore/Netherlands)	Sino Brew (China)	From 50% to 100%	I
• Danone (France)	PT Tirta Investama (Indonesia)	40%	II
• Lyonnaise des Eaux (France)	PT GDS (Indonesia)	60% to 100% (JV buyout)	I
• Ispat International (Netherlands)	Krakatau Steel (Indonesia)	49%	II
• Intrawest Corp (Canada)	Sandestin Resorts (Malaysia)	100% sale by Sime Darby Bhd	IV
• Holderbank (Switzerland)	Tengarra Cement (Malaysia)	70%	II
• Generale des Eaux (France)	Intal Utilities Bhd (Malaysia)	17.84% with option to raise to 30% stake	II
• AMOCO (USA)	Projek Lebuhraya (Malaysia)	20% stake sold by United Engineers	II
• GE Capital (USA)	Asia Life Assurance (Philippines)	100%	IV
• Holderbank (Switzerland)	Union Cement (Philippines)	40%	II
• International Lottery (USA)	Prima Gaming (Philippines)	52.25%	II
• Orica Ltd (Australia)	Chai International (Thailand)	JV buyout	I
• Ahold (Netherlands)	Central Retail Group (Thailand)	51%	I
• Merrill Lynch (USA)	Phatra Securities (Thailand)	51%	II
• Danone (France)	Yeo Hiap Seng (Singapore)	12.5% to be increased to 51%	I
• ABN Amro (Netherlands)	Bank of Asia (Thailand)	75%	II

Note: Type I is an increase in participation in an existing joint venture or distributorship.
Type II is a participation in a local company where there was no prior business partnership.
Type III is the acquisition of a local subsidiary resulting from the acquisition of the parent company.
Type IV is a 100 per cent straight acquisition.

SOURCE: *M&A Asia*, June and July 1998.

The decision-making process

Finding a firm to acquire

In most cases, acquisitions in Asia even in the post-crisis period have been horizontal (that is, in the same business line) and the targets have mostly been a sub-division of a business unit of a large group. For that reason the search

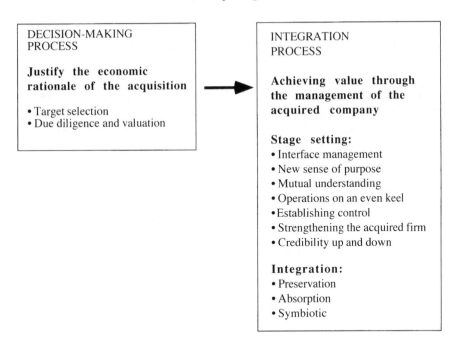

Source: Haspeslagh and Jemison (1991).

Figure 6.7   A Framework for Acquisition Analysis

for a potential target has been relatively easy and the role of the Merger and Acquisition specialist has been more to help companies in their due diligence than to identify targets. Acquisitions have been of one of four types:

1. The first and most frequent is an increase in equity participation in an existing joint venture or distributorship to take full managerial control while a minority share holding sometimes remains in the hands of the local partners.
2. The second type is participation in the capital of an existing company with or without a management agreement to run the company. This type can be approximated to a joint venture, although the capital participation of the foreign partner in this instance enters an existing firm, while in a joint venture the foreign partner participates in the creation of a new company.
3. The third type is the acquisition of a local subsidiary of a multinational company as a result of a deal made between the headquarters of the two parent companies.

4. Finally, the fourth kind of acquisition is the purchase of a controlling majority or full ownership of an existing company with which there was no prior relationship such as a joint venture or distributorship.

As Table 6.1 shows, most of the acquisitions are of type I or II, with few of the acquisitions being straight 100 per cent take-overs. Buyers and sellers have in most cases had previous relationships either as joint venture partners or as distributors. However, since the beginning of the crisis, type IV acquisitions have increased because of modifications to local legislation. In all cases acquisitions are friendly. The main reason is that only a small proportion of capital is listed on local stock exchanges and a potential buyer will always have to deal with the dominant shareholder, whether that be a family or a conglomerate holding.

As more acquisition targets come onto the market, many multinational companies have started to engage in a more systematic search rather than to rely on opportunism. Eager companies like GE Capital have hired local talent, often of senior level, with good insights and networks to identify the best prospects. Developing contacts and preparing the ground at an early stage gives them a competitive advantage over any other foreign firm without roots in the specific country. The search for acquisition targets requires strong collaboration between these local managers, regional headquarters executives and global business units.

Due process and valuation

One of the main obstacles to acquisition in Asia is the proper evaluation of the target company. There are several reasons for this. First, local accounting practices do not necessarily comply with international standards, even in Japan. In Korea the *chaebol* have not had to consolidate their accounts or eliminate inter-company transactions within the same group. Naturally this has led to overstated revenues. In South-East Asia books of accounts are kept specifically for tax purposes and the figures have very little relevance for asset valuation. Finally, as already mentioned in Chapter 4, marketing and strategic information is less accurate and less reliable than in the Western world. The financial crisis has added more uncertainty, making future cash flow analysis more difficult, not to mention complicating the determination of the right weighted average cost of capital to use in discounted cash flows. The major adjustments to balance sheet analysis that should normally be made are the following:[7]

● Many financial statements are kept on a cash basis. Accruals are ignored and must therefore be restated.

- Real estate should be valued at market prices and the necessary tax adjustments made.
- Inventories are commonly overvalued.
- Employees' retirement benefits are frequently under-funded and provision has to be made for future liabilities.
- Directors' retirement benefits are usually off-balance sheet but have to be restated as liabilities.
- Letters of guarantee to affiliated but legally independent companies may also be a source of surprise.

The above adjustments are the most common. There is still the issue of adjustment for any cross-subsidiary transfers which may distort announced profits, as well as verification of whether any licences, distributorships or contractual arrangements will still be valid post-acquisition. Overall, more time and effort are required to validate data than in the West. Detailed interviews with customers, suppliers and financiers, not common in the West, may be part of this due process.[8]

Asian sellers tend to rely on valuation methods based on assets rather than cash flows. The inflated cost of real estate pre-1997 made asset-based valuations more attractive to sellers and, in spite of the financial crisis, most sellers still tend to be overoptimistic about the real value of their business. In China, officials in the various State Assets Bureaux make it clear that they calculate asset prices in such a way that they cover the company's debts as well as the costs of resettling the workers. According to Nicholas Bloy of the Boston Consulting Group: 'On the rare occasion that a seller did emerge, asset inflation often had made market values so far in excess of discounted cash flow values that no amount of synergy could earn back the implied value premium.'[9] Estimating future revenues in Asia's volatile environment at the end of the 1990s is not only difficult due to the uncertainties of market demand. Risks lie also in the rapidly changing government regulations. A protected market today may be an open market tomorrow. Equally, the competitive structure may change considerably, thereby influencing profit opportunities. The number of competitors can change, as can their nature. As weak local competitors are acquired or merge with each other, a formerly sleepy industry may turn into a lions' den.

ABN Amro found an original solution in 1998 to the valuation dispute in its acquisition of the Bank of Asia in Thailand, by using two-step pricing. The pricing calculation was split into two parts. First, there was an initial up-front payment of baht 7.5 billion, giving ABN Amro a 75 per cent stake. Second, in the year 2000, their initial payment will be adjusted based on the evolution

of the net asset value of the company, calculated as the net asset value at the
end of 1999 multiplied by the average price-to-book value of six unnamed
Thai banks, within the limits of a ceiling of 27.5 baht per share and a floor
of 5.27 baht. In this way the price finally paid by ABN Amro will reflect the
state of the Bank of Asia and that of the Thai economy in 1999.

The integration process

The integration process of an acquisition consists of two distinct parts: the
stage setting phase and the integration phase.

a) The stage setting phase immediately follows the take-over. Its purpose
is to establish confidence among the various stakeholders, particularly
employees, bankers, distributors and suppliers, and to reactivate the company's
activities under its new management. This phase consists of seven tasks:

- Establishing interface management
- Instilling a new sense of purpose
- Developing mutual understanding
- Putting operations on an even keel
- Taking stock and establishing control
- Strengthening the acquired organisation
- Building up credibility up and down

Establishing interface management

The purpose of this step is to assure the ability to direct and control interaction
between the organisations. The best way to achieve an efficient interface is
to appoint as managing director of the acquired entity, an executive or a team
of executives capable of understanding the cultures of both seller and buyer
organisations and able to serve as a bridge between the newly acquired entity
and the new owner. When the acquisition is simply the transformation of a
joint venture into a dominant majority share holding or a full ownership, the
interface can be achieved relatively easily since it is likely that managers of
the acquiring company would have been involved in the operation already.
For instance, when Whirlpool took control of its joint venture in Pondicherry,
India, a new management team was installed. This team consisted of two
managers who were already working in the joint venture, as well as a
newcomer, a Sri Lankan who had long experience of working for multinational corporations. This mix of old-timers and a newcomer, all of them either
Indian or Sri Lankan, provided the common ground for effective communi-

cation between the parent company and the local operation. It guaranteed both a certain continuity and the possibility of rejuvenating the activities.

A different solution is to keep the existing top management team and bring in a few specific, experienced people from the acquirer, in order to instil some of the needed key competences. This was the solution adopted by ABN Amro, which maintained the existing president of the Bank of Asia in his post but appointed from the Dutch bank the executives in charge of treasury and credit. The selection of the interface management team is a key feature of the success of acquisitions, particularly in Asia where personal relationships are perceived as more important than procedural or contractual ones. The ability to communicate and to behave in a culturally sensitive fashion are other factors which ease the tension aroused by a change of ownership.

Instilling a new sense of purpose

This consists of establishing credible goals which demonstrate to stakeholders that the acquiring company planned the deal properly and which reassure them about its determination to lead the company along the road to success. One way to do this is, immediately after the acquisition, to set goals for growth in output or for desired market share, or to announce precise cost-reduction targets, and customer-satisfaction and quality objectives. That this is done at once indicates that the acquirer is fully in charge and knows what it is doing. A new sense of purpose can also be communicated through the dismissal of top managers who owe their positions to nepotism and their replacement with managers selected on the basis of merit. This will signal to both insiders and outsiders that times have changed and that performance rather than influence peddling will be valued in future.

Developing mutual understanding

Here the task of the acquirer is to spend time educating managers about each other's organisational and cultural contexts. This can be achieved in several ways. First is to organise a systematic and structured communication campaign. By meeting with managers and employees, through publications or social events, the new management team signals the main messages concerning the acquisition: what are the objectives, what is the main direction the company is to take. At Whirlpool Pondicherry, the new team established monthly question-and-answer sessions between workers and the managing director as well as a daily meeting among senior managers. During these meetings operational matters were discussed, but the new management was also able to sound out the views of all employees and address some of the salient issues which were raised. A second method of developing mutual understanding is to organise specific training sessions dealing with management methods, cross-cultural and behavioural issues.

Putting operations on an even keel

This step consists of focusing the attention on specific operational details and performance targets. This is necessary to erase the uncertainty created by the take-over *vis-à-vis* employees, suppliers and customers. A powerful method of eliminating uncertainty is to create 'integration teams'. These teams, which are also valuable in the context of a joint venture, are task forces appointed from personnel drawn from both the acquirer and the acquired company for each of the key operational activities (accounting, purchasing, quality, and so on). Each working party discusses and proposes concrete solutions to operational issues: what kind of software to use for inventory control, what method to adopt in order to recover outstanding receivables, how to deal with distributors, what the possibility reducing in logistics costs might be, and so on. The advantage of such an approach is that it gives people a tangible sense of involvement and makes them participate in the integration process. It also helps to develop mutual understanding between the employees of the seller and the buyer.

Taking stock and establishing control

In this phase the objective is to introduce control systems from the parent organisation. Despite its apparent motive, this is not a contradiction with the previous step of forming 'integration teams'. The recent crisis has proved the weakness of Asian firms with respect to financial control, and in certain cases with respect to the quality of management as well. Western companies can make a significant contribution to the functioning of the acquired companies by bringing to them tried and tested management techniques.

Strengthening the acquired organisation

The objective here is to correct rapidly the intrinsic weaknesses of the acquired organisation. This means shooting for a rapid turnaround as a method of establishing confidence and demonstrating the benefits of the acquisition. To that end, effectiveness is more important than optimal efficiency. A quick minor gain is more important at this stage than a slow major one. This is why the use of 'integration teams', whose purpose is to implement specific solutions to specific problems, is very useful.

Building up credibility up and down

Confidence is not likely to be established if the various stakeholders do not perceive that what the new owners say and do is credible. Credibility relies essentially on the quality of the people who are put in place to run the company and the perception of their real power within the parent organisation. It is essential that regional managers and global managers work closely together, and with the backing of central headquarters, to make sure that the acquisition receives the support it needs from the centre and that sufficient resources will be provided to make it work.

b) The integration phase is the phase during which the acquired company establishes its permanent role in the organisation of the acquiring company. We can distinguish three modes of integration.

The first mode is the preservation mode. It applies to an acquisition made in a business which has no or limited operational synergies with the business of the acquirer and which operates in such a different competitive environment from that of the acquirer that management practices are also necessarily different. In such a case the managerial autonomy of the acquired company has to be preserved and the acquirer must make sure it does not try to impose its culture and management practices on the newly acquired company. Whatever potential synergies there may be between the acquirer and the acquired will have to be discovered progressively. The only measures the acquirer has to take in such a case is to ensure that the acquired company is run by competent management and that proper financial controls are put in place.

Conversely, the absorption mode applies when there are operational synergies to exploit between the acquirer and the acquired, and when the competitive environment of each is not so different as to justify autonomous management. The rule here is to proceed very rapidly with the achievement of operational synergies by rationalisation and strong coordination of assets. In such cases there is a common management system and the two organisations have a strong operational linkage. This mode applies when the existing plant of a multinational company in a given Asian country is small but is able, after the integration of a newly acquired local firm, to achieve sufficient economies of scale to become a world-class producer.

Finally, the symbiotic mode fits the type of acquisition where the businesses would benefit from synergies but the difference in competitive environment requires some degree of autonomy at the acquired company. The acquirer should not in this case proceed with a hasty integration of operations but should instead proceed by steps. There will be a period of learning and discovery during which it will become clear what specifically can be done to achieve potential synergies, while at the same time a certain degree of managerial autonomy has to be preserved.

This last mode clearly describes the situation in most Asian acquisitions. As mentioned earlier, Asian acquisitions by Western firms have been primarily horizontal: there are potential benefits of synergy to be gained in terms of products, production methods, purchasing, marketing and management systems. But at the same time the competitive environment requires a high degree of flexibility and adaptation, which justifies a degree of managerial autonomy for the acquired firm.

The challenges of symbiotic acquisitions in Asia

While recognising the need to proceed step by step in symbiotic acquisitions, Western acquirers have nevertheless to achieve three challenging tasks: the task of providing the acquired company with a new identity, the task of inserting the acquired company into the knowledge and competence network of the acquirer, and finally the task of exercising control without stifling the entrepreneurial requirements of the local environment.

Providing the acquired company with a new identity means that it must have a specific role in the overall regional or global strategy of the acquirer. Employees, governments and the local community may resent the acquisition as a foreign intrusion reminding them of the old days of colonialism. During the stage setting phase described earlier, the purpose was to give the various stakeholders confidence in the will and capability of the acquirer to contribute to the development of the firm. During the integration phase, it is important to confirm that the acquisition was not made merely for asset trading or because it looked like a good bargain, but that it was a real strategic move in which the acquired firm has a specific role to play. This gives employees a sense of direction and self-esteem to counterbalance the loss of face caused by the acquisition.

The employees of the acquired firm in particular must feel that they are not peons but strategic partners, and that they are part of a strategic vision to which their contribution is essential. One of the best methods of underlining that contribution is to give the firm the responsibility for a strategic initiative in a particular business or product development. Unilever in Thailand made a point of such identity building after the acquisition by Lever Brothers Thailand of Foremost, a leader in the Thai ice-cream market. The combined operations were given the task not only of developing the Thai market, but of taking responsibility for the strategic development of the ice-cream business throughout Asia Pacific.[10]

The second challenging task is to make the acquired company part of the family by plugging it into the existing network of knowledge and competences. This can be done by seconding personnel to other subsidiaries, through participation in conferences and seminars, and by team working in operational areas where the transfer of competences can produce value-added results. Synergies in the domain of technology or marketing transfers need to be developed without arrogance, which requires a high degree of cross-cultural skills among participating managers in addition to their technical expertise. The challenge will be significant in industries such as investment banking in which foreign firms have shown superior performance and many Asian players have failed miserably. Merrill Lynch's take-over of branches and employees from the now defunct Yamaichi Securities is a case in point, where successful integration depends not only on the transfer of new technologies to Japan, but also on the re-establishment of pride among the former staff of the Japanese investment house and brokerage operation.

Finally, control has to be exercised without stifling entrepreneurial benefits. The ideal situation is to rely on most of the existing senior and middle management talents in the acquired company; provide them with adequate education and the tools to put in place good practice in strategic and financial management as well as in operational systems and processes; and let them develop their own business plans.

Combining the integration principles of identity, networking and autonomous control offers the dual advantages of achieving efficiency and encouraging local entrepreneurism. There are also the tremendous benefits of acquiring the loyalty of the people and the consideration of governments and the local community. The acquirer thus is neither an 'intruder' nor an 'invader' but an 'insider'.

COMPETITIVE MOVES

First mover advantage

As information, products and technologies travel rapidly across borders, companies must act fast to stay ahead of competitors and to enjoy the advantage of being the first mover. But being fast often means entering a market that is still small, often too small to make the business feasible. This dilemma has to be weighed against an entry at a late stage when the market is large but competition already fierce.

Large Western multinational firms were already present in many markets of Asia Pacific several decades ago. In some of these markets their early entry still pays off. Unilever still dominates the detergents and toothpaste markets in Indonesia; P&G those of the Philippines. Neither of them has been able to make large inroads into the other's territory, nor have Japanese latecomers succeeded in challenging the incumbents. More recently, Japanese firms have opened up new markets for themselves ahead of Western firms and shaped them to their standards. In Vietnam, motorcycles are already called Hondas, and even the most primitive repair shop along the road proudly calls itself a *Hon-Da* service station.

To be ahead of others enables the first mover to reach the customer easily before he or she is bombarded by masses of conflicting messages. Clear images can be shaped at a time when interest in something new is still high. In emerging markets such as China, advertising is still cheap and does not have to fight hard for the attention of the target audience. For a brand name to be taken over as a generic name for a certain category of products, like Honda, is exceptional. However, to establish the name firmly in the mind of satisfied customers at an early stage is the greatest advantage a firm can achieve and should lead to subsequent brand loyalty.

A first mover will also find distributors and retailers more ready to carry the new products as they have no alternatives. Signing them up denies followers access to established channels. By setting new technical standards, even by having those specifications officially sanctioned, formidable entry barriers can be built against late competitors or imitators.

Very few new products introduced into a market will immediately be sold in large quantities. This means very high marketing costs and low revenues: a heavy investment in the future of the market. Such a strategy requires confidence and full commitment. Japanese watch manufacturers, for example, showed courage when they started advertising their products on huge billboards in Shanghai at the beginning of the 1980s, at a time when their watches were not yet officially available and in terms of price were far beyond the reach of any Chinese citizen.

Early investments of this kind have often paid off. French producers of luxury products, such as Louis Vuitton or Chanel, started to build up images of prestige brands in Japan decades ago. This set the stage for their immense success across the whole region today. Grundig, a European producer of television sets and a marginal player in the world market, still benefits from having been one of the first suppliers of consumer electronics in Indonesia years ago. Early leaders in the hotel business in Asia, the Okura in Tokyo, the Raffles in Singapore or the Peninsula in Hong Kong, can still charge premium prices despite formidable competitors offering more modern facilities.

Of course, an early start does not automatically guarantee continued leadership. Constant upgrading in line with more sophisticated demand and more aggressive competitors is essential. Positioning brands initially at the upper end of the market has its merits. A limited number of customers will be prepared to pay a premium price for a novelty. As soon as competitors give customers a choice and the total demand increases significantly, pricing becomes more difficult. There is a danger of not being able to deliver superior quality while charging a much higher price than the competition. The result may be a stagnating number of customers still loyal to the first mover, but a growing market for the followers. If broadening the customer base is of interest, a careful climb-down from premium prices is possible. For companies coming late to the market, a climb-up against an established competitor is much more difficult (another advantage for the first mover).

Late entry strategies

The things that work in favour of the first mover represent entry barriers to firms which enter a market later than their competitors. They are confronted with the choice of either challenging the incumbents head-on or changing the rules of the game in such a way that they avoid direct confrontation with their entrenched competitors.

A frontal attack by the latecomer requires superior resources, something which few firms can claim when they enter a new territory. While multinational firms may have superior financial and technological resources, they are probably weaker in terms of local human resources, market knowledge and contacts. It is also difficult to make any judgement about real superiority in view of the new, untested products the latecomer brings to the market.

A late entry is advisable when competition is in turmoil because of technological change in the industry or changes in the marketplace. The second situation is found in many Asia Pacific markets due to the transformation of traditional distribution systems and shifts in consumer behaviour. It also helps when the incumbent is a long-established market leader which has become complacent and slow to react to change. If none of the above applies to a situation which a latecomer is facing, the chances of succeeding with a frontal attack are small. As many foreign firms in Japan have learned, bringing me-too products into a stable market guarded by strong incumbents can be a frustrating undertaking.

The alternative to head-on competition is a strategy through which the rules of the game are changed. For this to work the latecomer avoids taking the incumbent as an example to follow. Instead it looks for different ways to bring value to the customer or to identify and sell to new segments in the market. The American company Amway made major inroads in the Japanese market by extensive use of direct marketing techniques. It realised the power of established competitors like Kao over retailers and thus avoided the heavy losses P&G experienced during the same period. At the beginning of the 1990s, US computer manufacturers such as Apple went against established wisdom and decided to compete on price in Japan. The result was a war in the market with the leader NEC losing share against the newcomers. In Japan, BMW offered cheap financing for the purchase of their cars, thereby touching on a taboo topic in the marketing of luxury cars. The pay-off was increased sales in market segments entirely occupied by Japanese competitors. Today, in many markets in China, the rules are changed by putting emphasis on service, an aspect of the marketing-mix totally unknown in the past. This provides a good opportunity for those entering product markets with large local competitors to overcome the disadvantages of a higher cost structure and higher prices.

Late entry strategies look riskier as they deviate from the established norm. This risk is the price that has to be paid for finding a sufficiently large market, but also for being confronted with strong and entrenched competitors. Trying to change the rules of the game and avoiding head-on competition is often less risky than being an unimaginative follower operating below critical mass and therefore very likely to fail.

Marketing across the region

Apart from Japan, most markets in the countries of Asia Pacific are too small for most suppliers of special goods, such as sophisticated machinery or motor yachts, to justify the sort of full-scale operations described above. Even for those Western firms for whom prospects seem most promising, the opening of sales offices in all the countries of the region may not be feasible for a long time. Nevertheless while individual country markets may be too small, the region in its entirety can be very attractive.

Under these circumstances the firm could look for distributors in each country. However, due to the limited volume it will be difficult to find competent partners prepared to look after a small and specialised business. Alternatively, one can consider the various markets as one market and try to cater to the whole through a sales office covering the whole region or major parts of it. Such a strategy diversifies the efforts of the firm and spreads them across borders. Each individual market will get only limited attention. At its most extreme, this strategy means the firm will spread its marketing activities so thinly that it makes no further impact on potential customers. The alternative would be to select only the most attractive markets and concentrate efforts on them, hoping that the volume will eventually grow more significant through these concentrated activities.

There are several criteria one can use to judge whether a diversified or a concentrated strategy is called for. First, the competitive advantage of the firm must be considered. If it is high, efforts can be spread thinly. If it is low or non-existent, concentrated marketing efforts will have to compensate. The activities of and attendant strategy of competing firms should also be considered. If their activities are thinly spread across the region, the new arrival could attempt to do the same; if they concentrate efforts in certain countries, these countries may be excluded then from a regional approach or else the firm may establish direct countercompetition in specific markets.

The way customers respond to marketing efforts in an industry will also influence decisions. Efforts can be spread across many markets when immediate responses can be expected from newly approached customers. If much effort is required before even the first reaction is obtained, and substantial time passes before decisions are taken, a concentrated approach is recommended. The kind of response is dependent not only on the customer profile, but also on the complexity of the marketing process itself. If one product relies on substantial technology which needs to be understood and later on serviced and upgraded, then a concentrated effort is essential. If existing expertise or the simplicity of the product means it may be handled easily, then a diversified approach can be chosen.

Finally, the interrelationships of the individual countries have to be taken into account. If there is a close network between buyers in the region, or pan-regional promotional activities are undertaken, or the customers themselves operate regionally, then a diversified effort is justifiable. If no spill-over effects can be expected, a market-to-market approach is inevitable. Table 6.2 shows the ideal situations for a diversification or concentration strategy.

Table 6.2   Marketing Across the Region

Strategy Criteria	Diversification	Concentration
Competitive advantage	High	Low
Competitors' activities	Regional	Country based
Marketing response	Immediate	Slow
Complexity of marketing	Simple	Complex
Spill-over effects	High	Few

Rarely do all criteria argue for one solution over the other. In most cases some criteria call for a diversified approach, and others for a concentration of efforts. In such a situation a compromise may have to be found. This could, for example, consist of a sales office in charge of ASEAN countries and Hong Kong combined with a distributor agreement for Taiwan and sales offices in Korea, China and Japan.

Countering Japanese competitors

The concentrated attention which Japan has paid to Asia Pacific has made Japanese companies the largest investors in the region and the largest exporters to it. In the 1970s and 1980s their foreign investments and export activities were closely interlinked. Many of their manufacturing activities in Asia Pacific were either screwdriver operations (in which parts and components from Japan were locally assembled to circumvent import restrictions), or operations set up for exports to the USA and Europe, making use of the favourable trade preferences extended to the developing countries of Asia. In addition, Japanese firms also invested heavily in the exploration of natural resources in order to secure a steady supply to their home country.

During the 1990s the emphasis has started to change. Projects are becoming better integrated within local economies, and an increasing percentage of the output produced in the region is going back to Japan, where sourcing from Asia has become one of the strategies adopted to cope with the appreciation of the yen.

Disenchanted with their experience in the USA and Europe, Japanese firms have also started to re-emphasise their activities in Asia. The so-called *Asia-Shifto* in Japan in 1993–4 calls for greater involvement in neighbouring countries offering attractive opportunities in terms of market and cost. It is in this context that Japanese firms, having been slow to invest in China in the 1980s, finally started to move there on a large scale making Dalian their main port of entry.

As a result of their massive engagement in Asia Pacific, Japanese firms have a dominant market share in many industries. In the ASEAN countries, Japanese-affiliated companies have a more than 80 per cent market share in automobiles. Most consumer durables are of Japanese origin, and shopping in Asia is often done in Japanese department stores. The implications are far-reaching: by being well represented in a fast growing region, Japanese firms will grow more rapidly than those competitors who have weak or no activities; by systematically exploiting Asia's resources of labour and raw materials, Japan is strengthening its overall competitiveness. If they remain stuck in traditional, slowly growing markets Western firms will not be able to counter competitors from Japan in world markets, even in industries not yet attacked. In the elevator industry, for example, it is estimated that more than 50 per cent of all future demand will come from Asia Pacific. Otis, Schindler and Kone are the world's leaders in the industry. In Asia Pacific, however, Mitsubishi Electric is number one, followed by Toshiba and Hitachi. Otis, the world leader, is presently only in fourth position. Without appropriate reaction from Western firms, it is not difficult to predict faster growth, higher profitability and therefore increasing global investment capabilities in the long run for Japanese competitors due to their superior regional portfolio.

It is for this reason that Western firms cannot restrict competition with Japanese firms to a defence position in their home market, involving cost-cutting exercises, productivity improvements, and perhaps re-engineering. Similarly, strengthening weak positions through flank defence activities such as a shift of manufacturing activities into neighbouring countries (Mexico in the case of the USA, Eastern Europe for West European companies) is insufficient. Global competition with Japanese firms requires an Asia Pacific response, either in terms of a pre-emptive attack on Japanese competitors who are not yet very active internationally (as Western pharmaceutical firms have done), or a counterattack in answer to Japanese expansion into Western territory (as American personal computer manufacturers have done), or more flexible responses in terms of massive engagement everywhere with the eventual plan of supplying the Japanese market from manufacturing operations located in Asia Pacific (as happens in the chemical field and even in the case of Volkswagen manufacturing cars in China). Figure 6.8 shows the various options.

Designing strategies to counter Japanese competitors in the region requires a clear appreciation of their strengths and weaknesses. One immediate strategy is the full commitment of firms to Asian operations located in their own territory, their own front yard. Related to this is the treatment of market

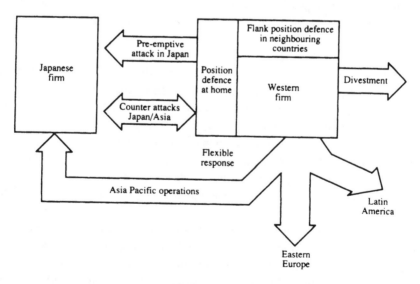

SOURCE: Adapted from Kotler, Fahey and Jatusripitak (1985), p. 156.

Figure 6.8   Regional Defence Strategies of Western Firms

entry costs as investments, rather than expenses, and low expectations of an immediate return.[11] Second, the large number of Japanese investors in the region means that the individual firm is embedded in a Japanese infrastructure in terms of availability of support that is second to none. Support ranges from the provision of information through JETRO, availability of credit from Japanese banks, and supplies and project management furnished by the *sogo shosha*, to more mundane services such as Japanese restaurants, clubs, and so on; in all, a totally reliable network in what are often erratic and risky environments.

As Japan is the largest provider of development aid to Asia Pacific and the Asian Development Bank is Japanese-led, Japanese suppliers often receive preferential treatment. The readiness of Japanese firms to engage in partnerships also gives them an excellent network of local contacts with governments and leading firms in the region. Minority share holdings in numerous projects and offers of financial support also help to cement buyer–supplier relationships.

The view, often aired by Westerners, that the Japanese are disliked by Asians may be wishful thinking. Surveys carried out by the Japanese government show that the perception of the Japanese is very positive throughout the region, with the exception of Singapore and Korea. No doubt the good performance of the Japanese in countless ventures over the last few decades, their flexible attitude towards partners and their apolitical stand on many contentious issues is shaping a positive image of Japan. In addition, the generation with memories of the Second World War is giving way to a generation that grew up appreciating Japanese products and services. Not everything is rosy, though. The notorious reluctance of Japanese firms to transfer technology is well known in Asia, as is the closed nature of their management which makes it difficult for local staff to be accepted in positions of full responsibility. Western firms can exploit this apparent weakness by taking a more open-minded approach to the sharing of knowledge and power.

Bearing in mind the very strong position of Japanese firms in Asia Pacific, half-hearted strategies will prove inadequate to counter them on their own territory. As the Japanese deploy their most promising managers in countries such as China and Indonesia, requiring them to learn local languages and play by the local rules of the game, Western companies must come up with equivalent strategies and leave post-colonial and expatriate-biased personnel policies far behind. And as the Japanese and leading local enterprises build new, world-scale facilities equipped with world-class technology, Western firms have no choice but to do the same if they are to avoid becoming instantly uncompetitive. Outdated machinery intended to supply small, protected markets will be no solution at a time when Japanese competitors are setting up regional production centres even in the heavily protected and regulated automobile industry.

Otis is determined to counter the Japanese challenge in Asia with massive investment in people and facilities and a clear priority set on market share rather than profit. Despite the presently tiny size of the elevator market in Vietnam, Otis signed two joint venture contracts in the country in 1994 in a pre-emptive move intended to block the entry of its competitors.

Few Western firms are prepared to go so far as to consider 'overinvestment' in order to counter Japanese competitors. Others tie up with strong companies from Taiwan or Korea, or at least try to secure market niches from which they hope to expand further. To match the presence of Japanese managers in the region, they have to rely much more on the integration of local executives. It is said that the number of Japanese expatriates in Bangkok alone exceeds that of all European and American expatriates in the five ASEAN countries.

Whether an Asian strategy can work without a strategy for Japan is debatable.[12] Due to the size of the Japanese market, it is indeed difficult to imagine winning the competition without being successful in Japan. Bearing in mind today's entry costs, and the unfavourable cost situation in which many producers in Japan find themselves in the 1990s, the solution may lie in emphasising manufacturing activities in developing Asia, while seriously pursuing market opportunities in Japan.

Notes and references

1. This section is based on a survey conducted by the Euro-Asia Centre of INSEAD in which 167 European marketing and planning executives operating in the Asia Pacific region participated. See: Lasserre (1993a).
2. Schütte (1990b).
3. Williamson and Hu (1994).
4. Porter (1990).
5. Articles such as 'Rich Pickings for the Vultures' by Montagu Pollock and Daniel Yu in *Asiaweek*, February 1998, or 'Asia Provides Golden Buying Opportunities' by Harris Clay and John Ridding which appeared in the *Financial Times*, 26 February 1998, give a flavour of the attitudes prevailing.
6. Haspeslagh and Jemison (1991).
7. 'Deals as Always are Difficult in Asia', *M&A Asia*, January 1998.
8. R. Anandan, A. Kumar, G. Kumra and A. Pahdi, M&A in Asia, *McKinsey Quarterly*, 1998, No. 2, pp. 64–75.
9. Nicholas Bloy, 'Plan to Buy into Asia? Behave Like a Venture Capitalist', *Asian Wall Street Journal*, 8 June, 1998, p. 20.
10. Williamson, Harvard Business School, 1995.
11. Schütte (1993).
12. Abegglen (1994). The author feels strongly about the central role which Japan must have in any Asian strategy.

7 Cooperating in Country-Based Partnerships

PARTNERSHIPS IN ASIA

During the 1950s, industrial partnerships between Western companies operating in the Asia Pacific region and local Asian firms proliferated, mainly in the form of equity joint venture or licensing agreements. Asian firms which lacked technology joined up with large Western multinational firms which offered to provide it. Asian governments introduced legislation which, while encouraging foreign firms to invest and cooperate with local firms, was also intended to protect local firms in their relationships with more powerful partners from the industrialised world. Care was taken to ensure that the agreed technology was transferred at a fair price. Much has changed since then, and the legislation has evolved as well. In recent years, Asian companies have become stronger: more financially sound, more technologically advanced and more sophisticated in their managerial practices. This is particularly true of the more developed countries of East Asia. During the 1970s and 1980s, the emergence of Japanese and Korean firms as global players turned many cooperative agreements between Western companies and Asian firms into partnerships between equals rather than simple one-way transfers of technology or exploitation of local market expertise.[1]

This chapter analyses the process by which Western companies select their Asian partners and enter into strategic partnerships with them, and also discusses the various issues involved in the negotiation, implementation and management of these cooperative ventures. Partnerships in Asia can be divided into two basic types: partnerships for a specific country and partnerships which concern regional or global competitive activities.

Country-based partnerships are set up either to capture opportunities in a particular market (market-seeking partnerships) or to exploit locally-based resources such as raw materials and labour (resource-seeking partnerships). Typical market-seeking partnerships are those established by Unilever and Nestlé in household goods, or by Hoechst and Rhône Poulenc in pharmaceuticals. Resource-seeking partnerships are best illustrated by Shell and BP, who have chosen to cooperate with local oil companies to explore and produce fossil fuel, or by Texas Instruments and Siemens, who manufacture electronics with local Asian partners in order to utilise cheap labour resources. However, it is difficult to draw a clear distinction between these two types of country-based partnership. Shell and BP sell some of the oil they extract in local markets, just as electronics find their way either directly or indirectly to the end consumer in the country of production. Equally, Unilever and Nestlé buy the bulk of their raw materials locally.

Country-based cooperative agreements with Asian partners have recently become more complex as they operate not only in their home country but also as facilitators in other related countries in the region. Taiwanese and Hong Kong firms, for example, offer expertise to their Western partners as they expand into China. The American sports shoe manufacturer Nike uses Korean firms to produce its shoes in Indonesia. Working capital for the venture is provided by a Japanese trading house. Equally, its long-term partners in Taiwan supply Nike from China.[2]

Global partnerships are cooperative ventures in which partners combine their resources, assets and competences to improve their overall competitiveness in major global and regional markets. In this type of partnership, success or failure has a critical impact on the global competitive advantages of participating firms. This type of partnership is analysed and discussed in Chapter 8.

Partnerships come in various legal forms. They can consist of long-term supply or management contracts, and cover licensing and franchising operations. In general, agreements can regulate joint research and marketing activities and set up consortia. More often than not agreements between Western and Asian firms establish a separate legal entity, an equity joint venture, in which two or more partners invest tangible and intangible capital. The joint venture company can conclude other contracts with the individual partners related to the use of brand names or transfer of technology under the umbrella of an overall partnership agreement: licensing, management contract, franchising, and so on.

The legal structure of an agreement is an indication of who is responsible for what, but does not necessarily clarify the distribution of power and control between the partners. For the Western partner in Asia, even a 51 per cent share in an equity joint venture and a majority on the board in an Asian venture does not necessarily ensure that the partnership's activities are managed according to its wishes. Legal agreements should therefore not be taken at face value. Cooperative activities are influenced by pressures from the local environment, by the partners and by the managers who, although thousands of kilometres away from the Western partner's headquarters, help bring them to life. In theory, partners should be most committed to equity joint ventures which, in contrast to other types of cooperative venture, demand up-front investment.

COUNTRY-BASED PARTNERSHIPS

Rationale for partnering

Foreign investors appear to be driven by three major forces in choosing to enter joint ventures in preference to wholly-owned ventures. The first is a political imperative (the will of local governments); the second is a competitive imperative (the need to acquire local resources, assets and competences in order to compete more effectively); and the third is a risk sharing imperative (to hedge against adverse conditions when the stakes in the investment are high).

The political imperative

Although all governments in Asia are actively promoting economic growth through industrialisation, they are particularly concerned that the benefits of this process accrue to their own people, and that nationals rather than foreigners exert some form of ownership over core industries under construction. In keeping with this political perspective, Asian governments have, to varying degrees, sought to limit foreign ownership and influence in firms. Requiring foreign firms to enter partnerships with local Asian firms is seen as an efficient way to build local expertise and to let local shareholders participate in the success of foreign firms in the market.

This political imperative was strongest in Asian countries which adhered to industrial policies based on the logic of import-substitution. This applied to Indonesia, Malaysia and, to a lesser extent, Thailand and the Philippines. In these countries, the choice to retain 100 per cent foreign ownership barely existed unless the foreign investor complied with the requirement to re-export all or a large part of local production. However, recent legislations in those countries have relaxed a certain amount of constraints giving foreign investors more flexibility in choosing against having a joint venture.

Ownership restrictions, however, are rarely applied equally across all industries in the region. Governments are more protective of raw materials and service industries than they are of assembly operations. Indonesia, for example, publishes several lists which variously indicate which industries are totally open to foreign firms, which are restricted to joint ventures or local firms, and which are totally closed to foreign investment. These lists change over time as a function of both local capabilities and national development priorities. Before 1991, distribution in Asia was off-limits to foreigners, but most Asian governments now accept joint ventures. In Japan during the 1950s, foreign investment was forbidden in most sectors. Then, in the 1960s and 1970s Japan invited foreign firms to join up with local companies in selected industries in order to benefit from their capital and expertise. Very few of these restrictions still exist today and as a rule foreigners are not legally bound to conclude partnerships.

Historically, the Asian host governments who have been most successful in imposing partnerships on foreign investors have been those with the largest and most attractive domestic markets. Japan's booming market is a case in point. China continues to use the long-term promise of its populous and rapidly growing consumer market to gain concessions from multinational firms. Until April 1986, the Chinese government refused to approve wholly-owned foreign ventures, but after that date decided to allow 100 per cent foreign-owned ventures for export-oriented operations. In March 1992 the Chinese government opened the door to wholly-owned ventures, legalising what was in fact an already widespread practice. The Chinese government continues to encourage Western companies to choose joint ventures as the preferred form of direct investment.

Another major reason why Western firms have chosen to enter into partnerships in Asia is to gain access to contracts for important government infrastructure projects. Even in Singapore, where no protectionist investment regulation exists, the government chose to adopt a policy of positive discrimination towards foreign contractors with already established local joint ventures. To cite one example, in 1982–3 the Singapore government gave these particular foreign firms preferential treatment in competitive bidding for the construction of the country's MRT mass transport system.

The competitive imperative

The second factor which has tended to favour the creation of country-based partnerships is the need for a foreign company willingly to expand its local presence in order to access critical resources, assets and competences through a local partner. In the large majority of cases, this involves the Western partner searching for a local firm with capabilities in distribution, sales, local market know-how, local production expertise or, more importantly, contacts with decision-makers and business networks. Managerial and human resources are often the most critical resources which can be obtained from a local joint venture partner.

The underlying factor in this competitive imperative is the Western company's need for support in launching its operations and in accelerating the process of market entry through immediate use of the local Asian partner's ready-made distribution networks or production facilities. The more complex the market is and the more relationships matter, the greater the need for learning and local adaptation, in which case a partnership is most likely to shorten the delays involved in market penetration. This approach is really a question of buying time. One example of this is the agreement by the French tyre manufacturer Michelin to enter three separate partnerships, in Japan (with Okamoto), Korea (with Wuon Poong) and Thailand (with Siam Cement), although the Michelin company has never engaged in such partnerships in other parts of the world.[3]

Internationally successful multinational companies with strong expertise in global strategies will be less inclined to tie up with a local partner for competitive reasons. The underlying assumption here is that the market automatically adjusts to them, obviating the need for them to adjust to the local market. Companies entering markets with strong international brands at an early stage of their development may indeed not need local support as much as latecomers with unknown brands. This is also true for firms who are reactive in the field of industrial goods, and where building relationships with customers is an important element of competitiveness.

The risk sharing imperative

Finally, a Western firm may seek out a local partner in order to reduce the risk of its financial investment or human resource commitment to a particular Asian market, or in a particular venture. This risk sharing imperative comes into play either when the investment outlay is very high, or when the ROI is highly uncertain. The desire to reduce exposure comes from three sources: the complexity of a project, the uncertain market acceptance of a product or service, or the country risk in terms of both macro-economic and political stability. An extreme case of risk avoidance would be the use of outside agents or importers to sell products locally, or the conclusion of a licensing agreement to handle local production. These types of partnership, however, considerably limit the influence of the Western firm and carry contingent risks such as insufficient exploitation of the market potential in a given country or the creation of a negative image due to bad quality products or sub-standard provision of services by the local partner. Figure 7.1 summarises the position of the various countries in the Asia Pacific region with regard to political and competitive imperatives.

The decision whether or not to enter a partnership, if the choice exists, is part of the strategic decision about whether to enter or stay out of a particular country. Western firms often have strong views on what form their entry should take. Some companies prefer joint ventures and may even shy away from a potentially interesting market if they cannot enter into a partnership or if they

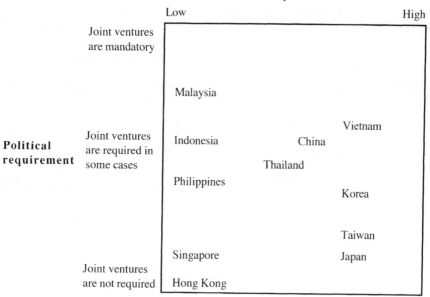

Figure 7.1 Partnerships in Asia Pacific: Positioning Countries with Regard to the Political and Competitive Imperatives in the Manufacturing Sector

fail to find the right partner. Other Western firms are determined to go it alone and consider a joint venture partner a burden rather than a supporting element. Such attitudes are less influenced by specific situations in a given market than by the general philosophy of the firm, the way it operates at home and its experiences in other countries. Japanese companies, accustomed to operating in their home market through an extensive network of cooperative agreements, show a higher propensity to enter partnerships in Asia than American firms. European companies fall somewhere between the two. Another consideration relates to the firm's self-sufficiency in deploying the necessary resources, assets and competences in the country, independently of the local partner. A third consideration is government policy. The type of partner a foreign company should try to attract will vary according to these three factors (see Figure 7.2).

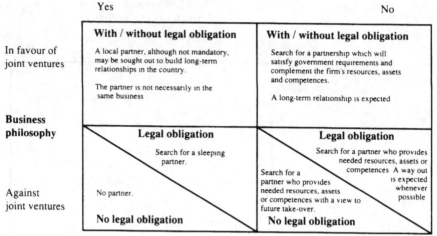

Figure 7.2 Joint Venturing in Asia Pacific: The Western Company's View

Partner selection

The selection process

The selection of a potential partner is the most crucial and difficult decision the Western firm will make, and one which will have long-term ramifications for its future in the target country. Asia offers a wide range of possibilities for potential partners and it is important to find a partner whose qualifications correspond to each particular company's objectives in the region, and with whom it will be possible to communicate and build a stable and lasting partnership. Partner selection is crucial because the foreign firm's expansion and strategic success in a country will depend on the capabilities of the partner, the partner's willingness to cooperate, and the climate of mutual trust which must be allowed to develop between both. Partner selection is difficult because it is usually undertaken at a time when the experience of the Western firm in the target country is limited and when available information is often unsystematic and sketchy. Studies have shown that partner selection in Asia Pacific is very *ad hoc* and that Western firms conduct far too little advance planning of the whole process.[4] At such an early stage, few Western firms have decided whether to pursue a project in the country; hence the parent company is usually reluctant to commit substantial resources to the selection process. This behaviour contrasts sharply with the Japanese approach to foreign markets. As a rule the representative office of a Japanese company will be established far in advance of any investment commitment and will often be staffed with at least one full-time Japanese expatriate manager, whose task is primarily to collect information on market opportunities and potential candidates for partnership and acquisition.

Western multinationals do not usually devote the same amount of time and resources to partner selection. In general, they approach their local agent or the contacts they have established by mail or which have been arranged by a banker or business colleague already residing in the country. In most Asian countries such contacts can be easily initiated. Unfortunately these first arbitrary contacts are often the parties with whom the Western company will choose to negotiate. Little or no screening is conducted, even by companies which under other circumstances would normally require thorough feasibility studies to compare alternatives and investigate the motives and capabilities of the candidates.

In many cases, the Asian partner with whom the Western firm negotiates is already involved with the Western company and may have acted as its agent or distributor for many years. The existence of such a relationship, especially if accompanied by personal friendships, may prevent the Western firm from searching for alternative contacts or from raising critical questions, since this will hurt and endanger existing links. For the multinational firm, the arrangement of another venture, often in addition to the agreement concluded a long time ago, offers the advantage that the Asian partner is already known and is familiar with the company's products. From the perspective of a Western company, the partner's past track record in their mutual dealings seems to reduce the risk of making a wrong decision. However, the fact that a local Asian company has proved to be a decent or outstanding distributor does not necessarily guarantee that it will be as competent in a joint venture which involves complex manufacturing activities.

Successful partnering in Asia must begin with a thorough investigation of potential partners. This is done by requesting information from the firm concerned and by intensive communication, not only with the owner or top managers of the firm, but also with the operating staff in manufacturing and sales. Western companies should ask the potential partner to supply financial data, though these may be of limited value given the lack of reporting requirements for privately owned companies in most Asian countries. Not all balance sheets carry the signatures of internationally recognised auditors, and the tendency of Asian firms to build conglomerates with cross-share holdings and a mixture of publicly quoted and privately held companies makes interpretation very difficult.

Companies should also interview the local firm's other joint venture partners, and carefully explore and analyse any past failures which might be discovered. Banks, suppliers, customers, competitors, diplomats and established foreign investors are important sources of information. Asian and Western consultants in the region may also specialise in matchmaking; however, while they may be valuable in making the necessary introductions, interpreting data and making recommendations on local procedure, they cannot be relied on to be entirely neutral. Their status as established residents often places them inside a network of contacts and relationships which can bias their views. A similar word of caution should apply to bankers and diplomats, whose vested interests in supporting a partnership do not always coincide with the investor's interests. The fact that Asians generally attach great importance to personal relationships can often facilitate the process of information gathering. Links to unknown companies can easily be established through the use of a middleman, or through family business networks. The business community is well-informed about its individual members, their relationships with each other and their reputation with local government authorities. Consistent probing, cross-checking, good listening and sufficient time will allow the Western firm to put together a fairly reliable profile of the various potential partners.

One method often used by companies willing to test a partner before embarking on a joint venture is to establish some sort of 'pre-marital' arrangement, either in the form of a manufacturing contract, a limited distributorship or a licensing agreement. This allows partners to experiment with their working relationship on a small scale. This method, while not entirely error-free, increases the chances of detecting eventual misfits.

Even if the Western partner is not in a position to select a partner independently, due to government pressure or other legal obligations, a thorough inquiry is absolutely necessary. This is especially true for latecomers to an established market, who may find that their choice is limited and that available candidates are not always of first-class material. In any given industry only a small number of local firms exist, and many may already have established ties with other foreign firms. However, as industry boundaries shift, companies may diversify and newcomers may suddenly appear on the scene. In any case, there is no absolute shortage of potential partners in Asia.

Western firms may narrow down their own choices by insisting on a government partner rather than a private one, or by giving preference to certain ethnic groups, such as the Overseas Chinese, who are often perceived to be more entrepreneurial than other Asians. Companies fearful of cultural barriers may want to consider selecting partners of European or American origin who have obtained the legal status of local firms, like Inchcape, the East Asiatic

Company, Diethelm or Italthai in Thailand. A Japanese trading house may also be a suitable partner for firms who are keen to work with one partner in several countries across the region. Other Western firms which operate in politically sensitive areas will stick to a partner with local roots. Preferences of this kind have to be judged in the political and ethnic context of the country.

Companies which are forced by government regulation into partnerships or which wish to operate in industries exposed to heavy government influence have tried to retain managerial control of critical activities by sharing their subsidiaries' capital with 'straw-men' or 'sleeping partners'. These options are of value only for companies who already possess the necessary operational capabilities to conduct business in a particular country.

The term 'straw-man' implies that while somebody officially runs a business, he is in fact only a front man who represents the venture, stays passively in the background and does not influence any important decisions. The Overseas Chinese in Indonesia and in Malaysia have been singularly successful in using these so-called Ali Babas to gain access to highly-guarded privileges reserved for indigenous Malay *bumiputra*. Partners are often senior government officials or retired military officers. Arrangements of this nature can jeopardise a Western company's long-term reputation in the country and become a trap where the foreign investor is perceived as a selfish or exploitative neo-colonial presence, thus damaging its image as a good citizen.

Despite this risk, a sleeping partner arrangement need not imply a hidden agenda. The joint venture partners agree that the Western firm will actively run the business, while the sleeping partner will provide some support and finance. By and large the passive shareholders are banks, insurance companies, government departments and other institutions which do not have the expertise to participate in the actual running of the business. Established Western firms in Malaysia have in many cases successfully sought the investment of the Islamic Pilgrim Funds (IPF) in their locally-established companies. Essentially fund management organisations, the IPF look after capital appreciation rather than management control and therefore do not normally interfere in operations. Wealthy Asian individuals, however, have also taken over the role of sleeping partner from time to time to help Western partners gain access to government contracts and privileged supply networks.

Straw-men or sleeping partners generally belong to two categories. Some are pure investors, like the IPF. In such cases, if foreign investors are capable of running operations and producing results themselves, relatively few problems will arise. However, local Asian partners can turn out to be opportunistic political partners whose motivation is to use their position or ethnic origin to gain advantage in the form of a free share holding and healthy dividends. They may also seek certain other advantages, such as procurement from a sister company or employment for friends. In this case, the partner is no longer sleeping but active, and will create operational headaches without contributing to the business.

The selection criteria

It is difficult to list the features of an ideal Asian partner, since these will invariably depend on the criteria of the Western firm. If the Western firm seeks the acquisition of resources, assets or competences in the local market, it should seek out an active partner who will ideally be financially solid, technically competent and have a good reputation in the local market. The Asian partner's managers should be experienced in dealing with foreigners. The Asian partner should be successful in its home country, but remain open to initiatives from the Western partner. The firm should have good contacts with the authorities, but only use them to get favours for the joint venture, not for itself. The ideal Asian partner should be politically influential, but at the same time neutral enough to survive and manage shifts in power. The local partner should be aggressive without taking too many risks and (most importantly) be reliable and trustworthy.

If, however, the Western firm is only interested in finding a partner in order to satisfy legal requirements, the desired qualities should be a good financial profile, trustworthiness, a record of non-interference, an absence of nepotism and a non-extremist, scandal-free political reputation.

One could add more criteria to these lists but this is already more than enough to indicate that good partners will be hard to find. If they exist, they may already be partnering other firms. The key issue in partner selection is to assess the degree of possible fit to the other partner's profile. As such, the ideal partner for a British corporation will probably be very different from those that join forces with a medium-sized German enterprise or a small American high-tech company. There are basically four different types of fit: strategic, capabilities, cultural or organisational (see Figure 7.3).

A strategic fit exists when the long-term objectives or motives of the partners are compatible. In this case, firms pool some of their assets, resources and competences in order to reach goals which they could not attain individually. In order to assess the potential strategic fit, Western firms should map the strategic motives of both partners.

Assessing strategic fit consists of an analysis of the implicit or explicit motives for partners to engage in a joint venture and of the nature of the benefits they expect to gain from the venture. There are three main types of motive. The first is a venturing one, in which a partner seeks to develop the potential of a given market with the other partner by together creating a new business

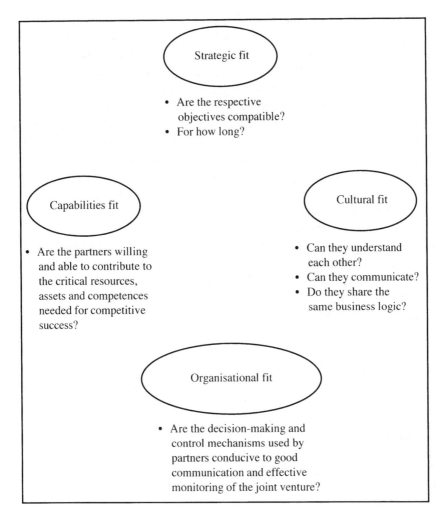

Figure 7.3 Partner Analysis

activity. In this case, the primary intention is not to use the joint venture to exploit the other partner but rather to join forces.

The second type of motive is extractive: one partner identifies a key resource, asset or competence that the other partner possesses and makes plans to obtain it through learning. Asian local partners with an extractive motive would typically seek to acquire product technology in order to become able later on to market their own products, or to obtain process technology, hardware and software from foreign joint ventures in order to integrate vertically or diversify into other industries. Korean firms have gained the reputation in the Western business community of being essentially motivated by the opportunity to extract technology. Some Korean leaders confirm this view: in an interview given in 1984, Chairman Kim of Daewoo stated that his joint ventures with Western partners were designed to gain access to technology and that their time horizon would not extend beyond the year 2000. The pace of recent technological development has shown that the year 2000 was too far away and the relationships were terminated in the early 1990s.[5] Another case in point is that of Sukree Bhotiratanangkul, the head of a textile conglomerate in Thailand, who, some years ago, engaged into a joint venture with the French group Rhône Poulenc in order to acquire continuous polyester fibre technology. After a period of intense conflict, Sukree bought back the shares from Rhône Poulenc and is now a major producer and exporter of fibres.[6] Other extractive motives among local partners may include the desire to gain access to international markets through a network of foreign partners. In Indonesia, where distributorship agreements cannot be broken easily, joint ventures are sometimes started in order to pre-empt competitors from distributing the foreign product. Extractive motives exist also among foreign partners, typically to use the joint venture as a vehicle to learn how to build relationships and win access to the market. Another very frequent extractive motive is for the foreign partner to conceive a joint venture as a means to make up-front profits through high transfer pricing on equipment, components or management services. Finally, some foreign companies are interested only in getting access to a source of raw materials or low-cost labour, and not in promoting the business of the joint venture itself.

A third type of motive from the local partner's point of view is to capitalise on citizenship and political contacts or to seek a financial return in the form of a portfolio investment. This is the motive particularly in the case of the IPF in Malaysia, which is looking for good equity investment opportunities. The foreign partner may be motivated simply by the need to comply with regulations forcing foreigners into joint ventures, or it may even be an unplanned reason such as the desire to enter into a short-term 'deal'. This third category of motive is opportunistic or passive, rather than strategic, in nature.

When entering into a joint venture agreement both partners may have a similar set of motives, but more often than not they have different aspirations. Although the official rhetoric will be that both pursue a venturing objective, the hidden agenda is often that both have some sort of extractive motive. A classic extractive combination associates a Western partner who sees the joint venture as a means of acquiring marketing expertise, and a local partner who sees it as a means of acquiring technological expertise (either product or process). Figure 7.4 presents an assessment of the likely stability of a joint venture according to the original motives of partners.

Foreign partner

	BUILD NEW BUSINESS (Venturing Motive)	EXTRACT MARKET KNOWLEDGE (Extractive Motive)	COMPLY WITH LAW TO MAKE A 'DEAL'
BUILD NEW BUSINESS (Venturing Motive)	Child strategy Basis for long-term success is present	Stable in the short term Potential conflicts arise very rapidly	Asian partner may feel frustrated by lack of clear vision support from partner
EXTRACT TECHNOLOGY (Extractive Motive)	Stable in the short term Potential conflicts arise very rapidly	Short-term stability Conflicts will arrive when a 'learning' period is over	Conflicts will appear very rapidly
BENEFIT FROM POLITICAL RENT (Opportunistic Motive)	Can be successful if the Western partner is self-sufficient High risk of frustration	Western partner may feel frustrated by lack of operational support from partner	High risk of frustrations and misunderstanding
FINANCIAL INVESTMENT (Opportunistic Motive)	Can be successful if the Western partner is self-sufficient	Chances of failure are high, especially if the Western partner is not familiar with the environment	Chances of failure are high, especially if the Western partner is not familiar with the environment

Local partner (label at left of table, spanning rows)

Figure 7.4 Analysis of Strategic Fit

The most favourable strategic fit occurs when both partners approach the joint venture with a desire to build and develop a new business. This is essentially the matching of two venturing motives. There is no guarantee that the partners will not experience serious disagreements within the venture; neither does it imply that both partners benefit equally from their joint undertakings, nor that the partnership is of equal importance to them. As the main preoccupation of the parties involved is to develop a joint activity, each partner should aim for a minimum level of interference in the other company's core activities.

When the motivation of both partners is to gain access to the other partner's resources, assets or competences (two extractive motives), the stability of the joint venture is a function of the length of time that the partners take to absorb or extract what they need from one another. When this process is complete, interest in continuing the collaboration often wanes. While this phenomenon of phased decomposition, also known as joint venture decay, applies to all kinds of partnerships, it is more frequently encountered in extractive partnerships. The most common solution is a termination of the joint venture, generally through absorption by one partner or by renegotiation of the agreement.

As discussed earlier, a type of partnership which may result in a satisfactory outcome (provided that the Western partner has the internal capabilities to operate alone), is one which allies a venturing foreign partner with an Asian local partner whose prime motive is to invest or to earn a political rent. All other combinations are problematic, due to the frustrations which arise from lack of convergence, even short-lived, between the strategic objectives of the partners.

Obviously, motives are often mixed and it may well be that some kind of extractive benefits take place in a venturing partnership or that joint business development may emerge from an extractive venture. Original motives may change over time, but as a rule it is important to remember that the original motivation will be the prime determinant of the future conduct of partners in their association.

In the assessment of strategic fit, the degree of the partner's commitment to the joint venture is particularly important. Of course, much attention is given to a new partnership on the day the agreement is signed or a new factory is inaugurated. Commitment, however, really comes into play when problems occur during day-to-day operations and additional support is needed for which no provision has been made.

For most Western firms who already have major investments in the industrialised Western countries, a venture in one of Asia's developing countries may be given low priority by corporate headquarters. Equally, Asian conglomerates – such as the Charoen Pokphand Group in Thailand, the Salim Group in Indonesia, or Samsung and Daewoo (leading Korean *chaebol* which have hundreds of subsidiaries and dozens of joint ventures with foreign partners) – cannot give priority to all ventures. But even if a particular joint activity is not very important to corporate headquarters, the individual managers assigned to it may be fully committed and able to get backing from top management. However, commitment is problematic in a situation where the conclusion of a cooperative agreement is a purely opportunistic move by one of the partners. This often produces a lame duck venture rather than the ambitious child venture created when a strategic fit exists and both partners are fully committed. There are numerous examples of failure arising from opportunistic partnerships.[7]

Very often Asian entrepreneurs, once they have achieved a certain stature, maintain their growth momentum by constantly expanding into new businesses, a tendency which stretches their cash reserves to the limit. When growth suddenly slows, they may have to disengage themselves from the partnership or even try to divert some funds from the joint venture to their core operations. Equally, Western firms invest resources in ventures either because a particular country is in fashion (for example, China between 1980 and 1985 or Thailand at the end of the 1980s), or because their competitors are actively pursuing new projects which need to be followed. Commitment to a partnership may therefore be weak and shortlived.

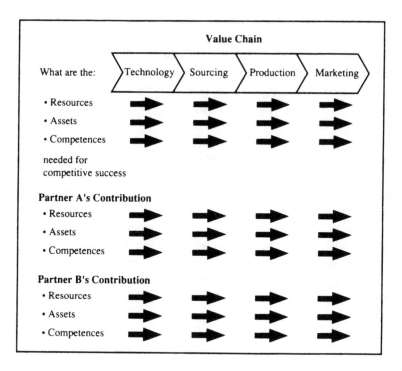

Figure 7.5 Analysis of Capabilities Fit

The mere convergence of strategic objectives is not enough to make a cooperative venture work. Each partner must be willing and able to contribute to the resources, assets and competences needed to ensure competitive success in the joint venture. In particular, potential gaps in contributions should be identified and solutions found to fill them. The methodology for gap analysis is straightforward. Figure 7.5 gives a blueprint for assessing capabilities fit in joint venture agreements.

The starting point is to identify which resources (people, financing, contacts, raw materials, and so on), assets (tangible and intangible) and competences (expertise) are needed to be competitive in the industry in which the joint venture will operate. This analysis is made for the various components of the value chain.[8]

The second stage consists of listing the respective contributions of each partner. The last stage is the identification of any gap which might call for specific plans. A classic mistake is an overly optimistic evaluation of what the partner is likely to bring to the joint venture. Western partners (particularly newcomers) tend to harbour unrealistic expectations of the marketing capabilities of their local Asian partner. Similarly, the Asian partner frequently has an idealistic view of the Western ally as a technological master. Another problem is the question of time and commitment: initial resources, assets and competences are generally insufficient to sustain competitiveness over time. New contributions and reinvestment of profits into the business will be needed. Short-termism, opportunism or simply inconsistency by one or both partners may aggravate a potential resource gap.

Linked to the question of resources fit is the problem of valuation of contributions. Basically, contributions which do not have a market price, such as expertise, intangible assets or non-market based contributions (for example, land in China) are items which can typically cause conflict. Economic theory has always treated the valuation of intangibles and technology as residual, but most of the time these are the most valuable contributions that are brought to a joint venture.[9] Intangibles become a key element in the negotiation of the venture when the time comes to assign an equity value to them.

All empirical evidence on international joint ventures shows that cultural differences lead to numerous problems and conflicts within partnerships.[10] Any cooperative venture between Western and Asian partners is bound to run into cross-cultural problems of various kinds. Societal and economic systems, religions and philosophies, geography and climate, and a host of other influences have shaped people's way of dealing with each other and doing business.

The heterogeneity of Asian peoples has prevented the emergence of a monolithic business culture. If there is anything all Asians have in common and which differs from the West, it is the high degree of importance attached to personal relationships in preference to contractual ones. The establishment of a cultural fit therefore requires the Western partner to plan for a more personal involvement by its managers.

Partners assessing cultural fit must address the following questions: can we understand each other; do we speak the same business language; do we share a common logic; can we communicate with each other? In an international joint venture there are three types of possible cultural difference: corporate culture, industry culture and national or ethnic culture.[11] These differences in culture influence three major aspects of management of particular relevance in joint ventures (Table 7.1): business objectives (what are the priorities of the venture, and what should the time horizon be?); competitive approaches (how do we compete, and what are the critical capabilities to invest in?); and management approaches (how should authority be defined and exercised, and what type of control should be used? What kind of people management?).

Corporate culture is shaped by influences which derive from the history of the corporation, the imprint left by strong past leaders and the ownership structure (private, public, family), as discussed in Chapters 4 and 5. A Western partner should expect to encounter corporations with a tradition that differs markedly from the classic, publicly quoted Western corporation.

Table 7.1   Assessing Cultural Fit: The Three Dimensions of Culture

Management issues	Potential cultural differences
Objectives	
• Role of business in society	• Social role: shareholders' satisfaction
• Time horizon	• Long-term versus short-term
• Criteria emphasis	• Profit versus growth
	• Shareholders' value versus stakeholders' value
• Use of cash flow	• Reinvestment versus dividend
Competitive Approaches	
• Role of government	• Market price versus 'managed' competition
• Advantage factors	• Price versus value
	• Economic versus political
	• Competition versus monopolies
	• Competition versus 'relationships'
• Role of expansion	• Organic versus acquisitions and alliances
Authority/Interaction	
• Power	• Autocratic versus democratic
	• Hierarchy versus technostructure
• Formation	• System-led versus people-led
• Performance	• Individual versus group
• Individual relations	• Paternalistic versus contractual

Generally speaking, there are two salient differences between Asian and Western corporate culture. In South-East Asia in particular, many firms still tend to be overdependent on the decisions of the person at the top, who often is the founder or owner of the company. This entrepreneurial culture contrasts sharply with the managerial culture of Western firms and their attendant checks and balances. Second, local firms (particularly in East Asia), tend to emphasise both the firm's and the employee's duty to contribute to society and to strengthen the domestic economy. This nationalist orientation can make it difficult for Western firms to cooperate with Asian firms on the basis of mutual benefit. Not surprisingly, joint ventures with Korean firms show a high number of problems.

Differences in industry culture should also be considered. If the joint venture takes place between partners in the same industry, there is potentially a degree of mutual understanding. Very often, Western partners choose to link up with Asian partners who come from a trading tradition but are in the process of diversifying. Asia's rapid economic growth and fast-paced business environment have led many Asian firms to adopt a short-term orientation and to concentrate on closing a deal quickly. With the exception of Japan and certain of the NIEs, Asian firms seldom invest in developing human resources or research and development. The momentum of Asia's growth and the relative ease with which its protected markets can be exploited have delivered profits to Asian firms who would have been unable to compete in other markets. This can-do atmosphere in many Asian companies stands in sharp contrast to the cautious, industrious approach of the majority of Western firms. Notably, there is a sharp contrast between some Asian trading mentalities which can be very short term and opportunistic, and the Western industrial view which favours analytical, long cycle investments. Developing Asia differs markedly in this respect from Japan, where long-term-oriented companies find it difficult to achieve a cultural fit due to the perceived impatience and short-sightedness of potential Western partners!

National and ethnic cultures are also shaped by the differences which arise from sociological, religious and philosophical norms and beliefs. As mentioned earlier, partners in Asia differ considerably with regard to their value systems, beliefs and business logic whether they are Muslim Malays, Overseas Chinese, Japanese bureaucrats or members of the Korean elite.[12]

The success of a joint venture is to a large degree determined by the way the partners communicate with each other and deal with the joint venture as individual firms. The way communication is organised among the various parties is influenced by the management systems and procedures used in the companies involved. A small Asian firm without any procedures will have difficulty cooperating with a bureaucratically organised Western multinational company. The entrepreneur who heads a large Asian conglomerate, accustomed to making all the important decisions himself, will resist negotiating with a middle manager of a Western firm, even one empowered to do so by the parent company. Accountants at the headquarters of a Western multinational often expect a variety of monthly reports which the Asian partner may consider unnecessary. Production people may be seen as vital by the Western partner, while they may not be accorded a very high status in the Asian organisation.

While organisational practices are often part of the heritage of the firm, they can be changed in order to establish organisational fit. Western firms should consider a more flexible attitude towards the application of certain strict internal procedures and avoid imposing all of them on their Asian partner's own joint ventures or subsidiaries. The Asian partner, however, may also have to make an effort to adapt by becoming more formalistic in order to manage the relationship with the Western firm successfully. Both parties must agree on details of the various interfaces and not shy away from discussing operational issues.

The Western partner will probably be forced to take the lead and set minimum standards for decision-making and the establishment of financial reporting systems. Organisation fit, however, is more difficult to establish when it comes to integrating the local joint venture into a network of other subsidiaries of the Western multinational which together pursue regional or global strategies. Equally, the integration of the joint venture into the network of the Asian partner's other companies has to be regulated. In both cases transfer pricing can be one of the main causes of disputes among partners, if no clear guidelines have been developed.

The transfer of technology is another area which needs to be carefully structured. As this rarely consists of simply shipping blueprints from the Western partner to the local joint venture, but actually brings technical people together in one way or another, details have to be carefully worked out to achieve organisational fit. The early involvement of operational managers is essential in resolving these issues. Detailed training packages should be drawn up and included in plans to ensure the smooth and effective transfer of the required competences.[13]

NEGOTIATING PARTNERSHIP AGREEMENTS

Negotiating and structuring a partnership agreement is a complex and multifaceted task anywhere in the world. Many of the negotiation approaches used in Europe or the USA can be used in Asia as well. Good preparation through systematic information gathering and consensus building among all members of the negotiation team about objectives, strategy and tactics are as essential in Asia as elsewhere. There are, however, certain peculiarities of the Asian mind which merit special attention from the Western negotiator.[14]

Asians are reputed to be good negotiators, to enjoy bargaining, and in the process to display considerable patience and perseverance in extracting additional information from the other side. Rarely is a deal closed without giving in to some extent in order not to let the other party lose face. Compromise is thus part of a successful negotiation. Bargaining on credit, a technique of giving away an advantage in order morally to oblige the other party to give something back at a later stage, is a more sophisticated way to build relationships, if not dependencies. These relationships are always of a personal nature and cannot normally be transferred from one individual to another or to the organisation the individual represents. Western firms should therefore provide continuity in their team once relationships have been established. This takes time and requires a much higher level of personal effort from the manager concerned than would ever be extended to a potential partner in the West. It is often said that in Asia what matters is not so much what you negotiate but whom you negotiate with.

A good relationship will bring a high degree of trust to the negotiation table. It obliges both parties to be reasonable, act in good faith and respect the other's opinion; hence any overly contractual or legalistic approach is frowned upon. That does not mean that contracts should be dispensed with or that one should avoid recourse to lawyers. Rather, it means that a general agreement on principles should be arrived at first, before lawyers look at the details. This Asian way of moving forward does carry risks for Western representatives. A vague declaration of a mutual agreement to a partnership does not carry much weight in legal departments of large Western corporations, which only recognise the conclusion of an agreement when every last detail has been sorted out and proper signatures have been appended to a voluminous contract.

In Asia, agreements are rarely concluded within short time periods. Often the need to clear certain issues with the government or other parties invisible at the negotiation table slows the decision process considerably. While to the Western mind time is money – especially when a representative is sitting idle in an expensive hotel in Shanghai waiting for an answer – time usually counts less for the local partner. This may be part of a negotiation strategy or an unconscious ploy to get to know the foreign partner better, or a way of slowly overcoming doubts about the project. In Japan, the local partner's need to obtain commitment from everybody in the management of his firm can add considerable time to the negotiation process.

For the Western partner, a single-minded focus on closing the deal quickly – which often means concentrating on purely legal and financial issues and neglecting technological and operational problems or considerations – does not always pay off. In fact, most joint venture failures are caused by disagreements over the implementation of the transfer of technology, the organisation of marketing responsibilities, rules concerning transfer pricing, and other operational issues, rather than the overall structure of the initial agreement.

Both partners would be well advised to work on these details together and to conduct joint feasibility studies and sales plans. In doing so, they should stress active communication and cross-checking of different sources of communication. The French company Merlin Gerin left the market research for its new joint venture in China entirely to its local partner, assuming that it would be very knowledgeable about the sales potential in the country. The partner came up with totally unrealistic figures, recommended the wrong product and a lower price than the market would have accepted. This cost

Merlin Gerin dearly. A joint market survey could have reduced the risk, reassured both parties, and established a relationship among operational managers, one of the most vital aspects of a successful long-term cooperative undertaking. Even better, though this may be wishful thinking, would have been a form of pre-marital agreement: a trial run of limited range to test each other in working towards a common goal.

Negotiations never end in Asia. A signature on a contract does not start a relationship; achieving a successful fit in a joint venture in Asia Pacific requires constant energy and attention from both partners. Negotiating joint venture agreements in the Asia Pacific region requires an unusually high degree of flexibility from the Western partner accustomed to signing a contract and then fulfilling it to the letter. The Asian approach, on the other hand, may be better adapted to the region's often dynamic and volatile business environment which demands frequent changes and the reinterpretation of contracts to make them work in favour of the joint venture. The Asian sense of flexibility explains why Asian firms emphasise finding the right partner rather than putting the right words on paper.

The negotiation of a joint venture is not limited to agreeing on the financial and legal clauses regulating the partnership. A strategic business plan should normally be part of the agreement between partners. The advantage of this is that both parties are forced at this stage to spell out what they expect from the joint venture. Elements such as expected market share, the market segments in which the company is going to operate, the anticipated future investment effort and its mode of financing are matters which need to be discussed prior to the implementation phase. Partners should test the degree to which they share a common vision about the business, as well as their ability to identify potential sources of future misunderstanding.

MANAGING PARTNERSHIPS

The conclusion of negotiations in Asia is often marked by some sort of ritual social celebration (banquets, for example) during which abstract goals such as harmony and perpetual friendship are evoked. In Thailand, the opening of the joint venture premises is sometimes accompanied by a religious ceremony, while in Chinese communities the choice of the physical layout may be referred to a geomancer. These practices should be taken seriously, since they are part of the Asian tradition, but not overemphasised. The task of managing joint ventures starts with the design of an organisational structure, the staffing of the management team, the setting up of mechanisms for controlling the operations and the design of communication channels between partners.

Organisational design

The type of organisational design to be adopted will depend upon two major parameters. One is the initial strategic motive of the partnership: venturing or extracting. In a venturing partnership whose mission is to create and develop new businesses, the joint venture company is expected to have a high degree of autonomy. If it is extractive, the joint venture company will be an organisation entirely dependent on the parents.

The second parameter is concerned with the development of operational capabilities within the joint venture. On the one hand the joint venture is endowed with its own operational means: product development, production and marketing. On the other hand the joint venture plays the role of a broker whose function is to coordinate operational activities which are performed by the parent companies.

Four patterns emerge from the combination of the two parameters (Figure 7.6). The first one is a self-contained joint venture which is an autonomous subsidiary either possessing its own assets and resources brought in by the

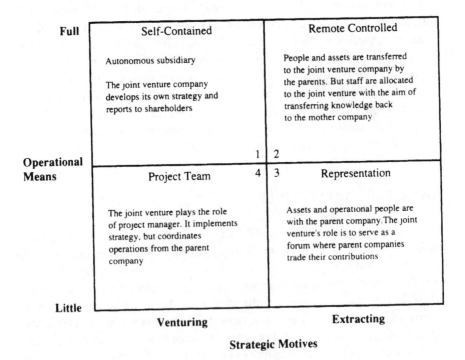

Figure 7.6   Four Different Organisational Designs in Joint Venture Companies

parent companies at the start, or created as a greenfield investment. The joint venture's charter is fixed by the shareholders, but the implementation is left to the entrepreneurial talents of the managers. Except for the top managers, who are appointed by the partners, the staff are recruited for the joint venture and their loyalty is to the joint venture company.

The remote controlled joint venture is a subsidiary with its own operational means, brought in by the shareholders, but whose operations are staffed by employees from the parent companies. The objective of the overseas expatriate staff is to accumulate learning and experience from their interactions with employees from the other party. The label 'sandwich' comes from the fact that each key position in the company is staffed by two people, one head and one deputy, each coming from the partner-shareholders.

The representation joint venture is a company which has only limited or no operational means. For most of its activities it uses resources, assets and competences which belong to one of the parent companies. A typical example would be an automobile joint venture, assembling completely knocked-down (CKD) kits coming from the Western partner, whose marketing and distribution are handled by the local partner. The employees assigned to the joint venture company represent the interests of the parent companies and their main task is to learn from the other party.

The project team joint venture is also a subsidiary which uses the capabilities of the parents, but in order to develop the business. The employees are rewarded for their talents and have a large degree of autonomy in management. One of their key tasks is to negotiate with their parent company the necessary capabilities required to make the operation a success.

Staffing

Managers involved in the management of joint ventures will need more than normal technical competences; they should also possess political and cultural skills enabling them to fulfil their dual role as managers and representatives of the parent company. When the foreign staff who choose to be involved in joint ventures are insufficiently prepared for the cultural complexity of the Asian business environment, their lack of preparation can cripple the Western partner's ability to handle critical situations and impede its ability to pass on the lessons from which the Western partner could benefit. Managers and other personnel assigned to joint ventures are too often chosen according to their technical qualifications and not for their cultural or political talents and sensitivities. This is one of the most crucial lessons illustrated by the experience of Rhône Poulenc in Thailand. More than 40 European engineers were assigned to the Bangkok site, all qualified technicians, but few of them sensitive to Thai culture. A number of cultural blunders in the handling of both the local partner and employees combined to exacerbate and fuel conflicts.

Another possible mistake is to assign to joint ventures those managers who are not part of the core international managers group, and who therefore lack internal prestige or power in the parent company. The other partner may see such appointments as a signal that the company does not give high priority to the partnership. The worst attitude would be to consider partnerships as an exile for undesirable personnel.

Finally, one task which joint venture managers will have to perform, particularly when the strategic intent is to extract knowledge from the local environment, is to be capable of synthesising and transmitting learning experiences to the institutional memory of the Western parent company. A systematic synthesis of information obtained from the joint venture experience has to be documented and transferred to the relevant department in the parent company.

In the direct recruitment of local personnel, a critical question concerns identity and loyalty. Do the local employees feel that they belong to the parent company or to the joint venture? Most of the time, because of knowledge of the environment and an established presence, the local partner is responsible for recruiting and appointing local employees and workers. Western partners should monitor carefully such practices in order to ensure that employees' loyalty is to the joint venture and not merely to the local Asian partner.

Control

The control of joint ventures is exercised through the board of directors. Boards of directors are composed of executives who represent shareholders. In addition, certain locally selected Asian personalities can be invited to sit on the board in a non-executive capacity. In the Asia Pacific region non-executive board members (bankers, say, or local personalities) may be very useful as go-betweens in cases of conflict with the local partners.

Western companies tend to be more comfortable with a majority stake in a joint venture, rather than with a 50-50 or a minority joint venture. Empirical evidence produced by A. T. Kearney with the American Chamber of Commerce in Japan and in Hong Kong, and with the European Business Council in Japan, tends to support this view. In their research, the most successful operations out of 55 US and European multinationals were the wholly-owned subsidiaries, while the highest proportion of unsatisfactory performances were found among the 50-50 or minority joint ventures.[15] However, majority ownership is not always possible, hence the usefulness of finding a second local partner, whose role is both to provide the missing local majority and to act as a buffer with the active local partner. Non-executive board members have to be selected carefully and treated with deference. One should avoid confronting them with *faits accomplis* which may cause them to lose face, and transform their goodwill into hostility.

Communication

In 1996, an INSEAD Euro-Asia Centre study on joint ventures showed that cultural and strategic fit are the crucial factors for success.[16] (See Figure 7.7.)

The respondents in the survey answered questions such as 'What lessons did you learn?' and 'What would you do differently?', focused on the need to build a strong understanding between partners (40 per cent), and the importance of taking time to prepare the joint venture from a business point of view and defining the role of each partner (22 per cent) at the implementation stage. Patience, commitment, flexibility and the ability to re-negotiate and to develop local human resources scored third (20 per cent), ahead of

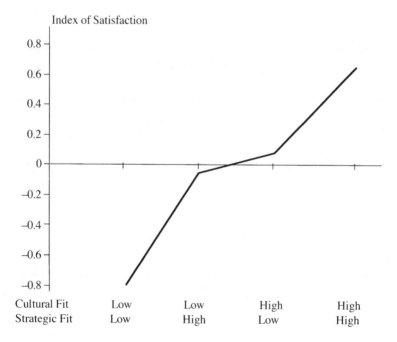

SOURCE: Lasserre and Probert (1977).

Figure 7.7   The Effects of Strategic Fit and Cultural Fit on the Perceived Satisfaction of Western Managers with Joint Ventures in Asia

the more legalistic approach to controlling the joint venture through a majority shareholding or through a rapid buy-out. A respondent in Indonesia stated: 'While multinationals tend to be legalistic and structured in approach, here we must be willing to make "deals" with the partner.'

In practical terms this means that preparing and negotiating joint ventures requires more than legal, marketing or financial skills. It requires first a thorough understanding of what the company wants to achieve with the joint venture, and on that basis the development of a strong and clear message to be conveyed to potential partners. In reaching this stage the time taken to evaluate, talk and communicate with potential partners should not be counted. A respondent in Indonesia indicated: 'Don't underestimate the time to develop the relationship to reach the agreement. The local partner, even after reaching the agreement, may not go into bat for the project until he is sure that it is likely to be successful.' Another manager based in Thailand stated: 'Instead of negotiating a joint venture during business visits, one should spend several months in the host country.' A good cultural and strategic assessment of the partner's capabilities and objectives is imperative. A general manager in Korea insisted: 'Focus on shared objectives; do not have a hidden agenda, it will not work. Do not look for the majority at any cost; look for the right partner.'

This demonstrates that an ongoing dialogue with the local partner is a necessary condition for success in the management of partnerships. Specifically, instead of formal reporting, face-to-face communication needs to be institutionalised. This includes frequent meetings between high-level directors from headquarters; an annual conference of the licensees or joint venture partners; and even the organisation of internal training seminars between employees of both companies.

Of particular importance is the preservation of regular high-level contact between the chairman (or one of the top-ranking executives) of the Western firm and the chairman of the local group or company involved in the joint venture. The expatriate in charge of the joint venture is normally the interface between the Western firm and the local partner, and should be empowered to make decisions on behalf of the company. Expatriate managers rotate and their hierarchical status is not the same as the local chairman's. Local entrepreneurs want a certain parity of recognition with their Western counterpart.

JOINT VENTURE DECAY AND FAILURE

Joint ventures seem to have a lifecycle which resembles the one illustrated in Figure 7.8. After a period of relative stability lasting from five to six years there is a sudden decrease in mutual interest leading to a crisis which can degenerate into conflict and a disruptive split. This phenomenon, known as joint venture decay, has been documented by various researchers in the USA and Europe.[17] At a certain point in the lifespan of the joint venture, the high level of mutual interest which prevailed at the time of its formation grows weaker. This is the point at which both partners often feel they have acquired whatever expertise or gained whatever competitive advantage they sought from their association with each other. As mentioned earlier, the partnerships undertaken with an extractive motive are more likely to experience joint venture decay because, by definition, what is expected from the venture is learning and learning takes place over time. It is precisely at this moment that the impetus for further collaboration can dissipate and the entire joint venture partnership can degenerate into a crisis. This crisis can be recognised as signifying a breakdown in the relationship, in which case both partners should prepare

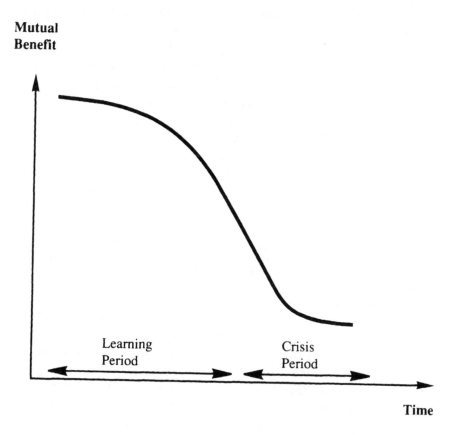

Figure 7.8   Joint Venture Decay

for a divorce or dissolution of the partnership. However, if both partners wish to avert the divorce, it is essential to anticipate and revitalise the association by the infusion of new products or the contribution of new expertise.

In general, the experience of Western companies in joint venture partnerships in Asia has not been happy. Most companies have become quickly disillusioned by the number of unforeseen problems which have arisen in the course of both the setting-up and the operation of their partnerships.

There are several principal causes of failure or difficulty in joint venture partnerships in Asia. The absence of strategic vision is perhaps the determinant factor in the failure of partnerships and one that can skew the course of subsequent decision-making. It takes the form of a precipitous, impulsive desire to launch a joint venture founded on short-term considerations or for purely defensive or opportunistic reasons.

The failure to evaluate the intentions and capabilities of the local partner often leads enterprises to underestimate or overestimate their partner and hence leaves them vulnerable to disappointment. The first mistake arises in partner selection. A classic error is often made in the choice of a distributor in an industrial partnership: nothing guarantees that the distributor will possess the corporate culture appropriate to a slow cash-flow cycle, or that he or she will not simply bring a trading mentality to a few rapid cash-flow deals instead of developing a long-term approach to the product.

Another error is believing without seeing. The art of appearances can be highly refined in Asia and many a Western investor has fallen into this snare, mistaking elaborate ceremony for a real commitment.

A third error is to fail to understand the strategic logic of one's own partner. In many cases a thorough investigation would reveal the real intent of the local partner (for example, to achieve vertical integrations to appropriate technology or simply to enter into an opportunistic deal).

Haste in negotiation constitutes another source of failure. Very often, the desire to conclude a deal rapidly leads the negotiators to concentrate solely on financial or legal clauses and to neglect key technological or operational issues involved in the actual management of the venture. It is not enough to use a legalistic approach in negotiations in Asia; it is essential that the contractual stage is preceded by an overall planning session for the project, a point at which the partners will agree on the objectives and strategies of their common enterprise. This implies a minimum investment in understanding the logic of the partner, as emphasised earlier. One effective method, often difficult to implement, is the technique of advancing by small steps through a limited, or staged, commitment: a licensing contract, for example, can often serve as a good prior test of the durability of a long-term joint venture agreement. The goal of this pre-marital arrangement is to assess the real capacities of the other party before engaging in a more serious, and hence more risky, partnership.

Insufficient preparation of staff to deal with the political and cultural complexity of the local environment is more often than not a source of difficulties. In failing to understand the logic of their partners and employees, unprepared expatriate personnel can exacerbate tensions. Careful selection and cultural training are not absolute guarantees of success, but their absence is guaranteed to cause problems.

Finally, failure can often be linked to the lack of organisational support. This aspect of partnership failure is discussed in more depth in Chapter 8, but it is important to outline it briefly here.

In the daily practice of exchanges with headquarters or the technical services department, the joint venture is often poorly served. This may be reflected in a variety of ways: delays in technical assistance; deliveries of poorly adapted products; exorbitant transfer pricing; or exaggerated administrative rules or constraints which fail to take local conditions into account. The lack of visibility of Asian operations in many Western organisations is a well-known problem which goes beyond the simple framework of joint venture partnerships; in fact, it affects the totality of the firm's operations in the region. As the director of the Singapore subsidiary of a major French company put it, 'I have more trouble communicating with headquarters than I do fighting my competitors.'

The problems which can arise from the lack of proper staff selection for Asian postings can have a deep and irreversibly negative effect on the way both the joint venture and the Western company are perceived by the Asian host country and key Asian business figures. In Asia, local partners are often highly respected businessmen in their own country, and when they suffer what they consider improper treatment at the hands of unsophisticated foreign staff, or from having to deal with foreign counterparts who are often very low in the hierarchy of the Western partner company, they can quickly become disillusioned or unenthusiastic about future ventures with the foreign firm.

These five causes of failure or difficulty in joint venture partnerships are very often interrelated and contribute to a vicious circle of misunderstandings which can degenerate into open conflict and end in frustration, loss of market share, and sometimes even legal action. Any Western enterprise which seriously considers setting up in Asia, either in the short- or long-term, and chooses the partnership route, should devote all the necessary resources and effort for the careful preparation and monitoring of the process of partner selection and joint venture management.

A SPECIAL CASE: JOINT VENTURING IN CHINA

The political and legal context

In any part of the world, foreign investment is both an economic and a political phenomenon. In China, however, a history of colonial exploitation has left a deep-rooted mistrust of foreigners. Moreover, the pervasive influence of the communist party in virtually every sphere of public and private life has only exacerbated China's traditional lack of distinction between political and economic goals. Consequently, China's foreign investment legislation and policy implementation have been shaped and assessed with respect to political objectives. In short, economic reform and business transactions are all considered inseparable from national political stability.[18]

The vagueness of China's foreign investment legislation gives Chinese government and party bureaucrats substantial leeway. From the viewpoint of the Western firm this creates both problems and advantages; for the Chinese side, a contract is viewed as a starting point for negotiation and not as a final binding agreement. This is an obvious source of conflict. However, the advantage of this flexibility for the Western party is that influence and political connections can be used to obtain what legal agreements fail to guarantee.

China's foreign investment legislation defines two types of joint venture: the equity joint venture and the contractual joint venture. In the equity joint venture both the foreign and the Chinese partner provide capital and management and share the risks and profits of the venture according to their respective equity share. In contractual joint ventures no separate legal entity is formed; instead, the partners contract their contribution to a joint activity. Although this arrangement is more flexible, it should also be regarded as a more temporary type of relationship.

Western firms have preferred the equity joint venture, largely because it provides a more structured form of cooperation with a Chinese partner. The contractual joint venture, on the other hand, has tended to serve better the needs of Hong Kong entrepreneurs, many of whom conduct offshore manufacturing in China, providing raw materials and machinery in exchange for manufactured products.

Investment incentives and regulations are primarily influenced by the Western investor's choice of location for the joint venture, but can also vary according to the choice of product to be manufactured. In the latter case, investment incentives and rules depend on whether the Western investor chooses advanced technology, or produces for export or for import-substitution.

The choice of location is crucial to the success of the venture. Although Beijing is considered attractive because of its proximity to national decision-makers, locating a joint venture in a town or province can have advantages. Very often, secondary areas benefit from the attention of provincial officials and managers who are increasingly considered to be the real force behind China's economic growth.

China has designated certain regions as target areas for foreign investment. These include the 5 SEZs, the 14 Open Coastal Cities (OCCs), the Economic and Technical Development Zones (ETDZs) and the Shanghai Pudong Area. Conditions at these sites vary considerably in terms of the availability of skilled employees, wage levels, transportation, infrastructure, work attitudes, and so on.

Entering a joint venture

In 1986, the Chinese government began to allow 100 per cent foreign-owned ventures in the country.[19] Originally those Wholly Owned Foreign Enterprises (WOFE) were essentially located in Shenzhen, but since 1995 their importance has grown and spread over all sectors and provinces. During 1996–97, WOFEs have outmatched joint ventures in both number and value. It has been argued[20] that a WOFE is now the preferred choice of entry into China because it gives foreigners better control of their strategic development without enduring conflictual relationships which plague many joint ventures. A survey conducted in 1998 on 229 projects, by A. T. Kearney, found that 62 per cent of projects in WOFEs were profitable, while only 42 per cent in joint ventures were.[21]

Partner selection in China is difficult, and for those Western firms willing to enter into a joint venture it will be one of the most problematic aspects of the venture, since it is a highly politicised issue and the freedom of choice is severely restricted. The political imperative is the key consideration in partner selection, since the most important resource that Chinese partners have is their close connections with relevant authorities (both local authorities and the central ministries in Beijing).

Joint venture negotiation in China is a time-consuming and arduous process. A typical negotiation time for a contract is two years or longer. On the Chinese side, the consensus building required for decision-making is complicated by the communist bureaucracy and political system. The Chinese often regard joint venture negotiations as vehicles for training and information gathering for higher-level authorities rather than as a decision-making session. Chinese negotiators are in many cases frontline scouts or representatives for absent, higher authorities. The multitiered administrative structure of the Chinese government, the existence of various state, provincial and municipal ministries, and the fact that, as a general rule, no one individual has decision-making power, are factors which slow the process of negotiating a joint venture considerably.

Conducting a feasibility study as part of the negotiation process puts the foreign firm in a less adversarial position and allows it more access to detailed information on potential markets and expected costs. To their detriment, many foreign firms rush through this process to get to the contract signing. The foreign firm should also be prepared to abandon negotiations. Even months of sunk cost should not pressure the foreign negotiating team to accept less than the best terms.

It is crucial for any Western firm that considers entering a joint venture in China to understand the role of *guanxi*: in the Chinese economy, where prices are not always market-determined and profits are not a goal, interfirm and interpersonal relationships are paramount. Connections based on personal relationships and mutual obligations are often crucial determining criteria for resource allocation decisions.

Creating and managing the fit

Chinese and Western partners enter joint ventures from very different cultural orientations and backgrounds. The Chinese side is government-owned, or at least strongly government-oriented, and its thinking will be influenced by China's macro-economic and political objectives. The Western side, as a rule, comes from the private sector, is not subject to government constraints or influence, and will pursue profit objectives. As a result, there is substantial room for cultural misunderstanding and strategic misfit. Generally, the fit can be assessed as follows.

Considerable conflict has arisen from the fact that the Chinese party generally aims to obtain technology and earn foreign exchange through exports, while the Western partner generally seeks to tap the domestic market. China has not forgotten its history of foreign exploitation; consequently, when attractive local market opportunities emerge, the Chinese government has tended to favour local over foreign firms. These differences represent a major strategic misfit. The Western partner is also less keen to export (in order to earn foreign exchange) from China, since low labour costs are offset by other high operation costs. These considerations make alternative sites (exports from Indonesia, Singapore) viable options. Another strategic fit issue is technology transfer: the Western partner is reluctant to transfer technology to the Chinese side because of the Chinese tendency to copy or re-engineer technology. In the past, Western firms have encountered considerable difficulties in protecting their technology against piracy outside the venture, either in the Chinese market or abroad.

In terms of resources fit, the inherent difficulty in valuing resources, assets and competences in China also poses problems for the foreign investor. Contributions which do not have a market price, such as expertise, intangible assets and land, are frequently sources of conflict in joint venture management.

Radically different child-rearing and educational systems, political traditions, and enormous disparities in incomes and standards of living have created considerable psychological gaps between Western expatriate managers and local Chinese employees. Additionally, the clash between the more generally international Western perspective and the more introverted, ethnocentric Chinese world-view often becomes apparent. The lack of cultural fit brings about considerable scope for misunderstanding. While training can be used to overcome this, it is doubtful, for example, that Chinese managers would take the side of the Western joint venture partner in a conflict. In general, and given the current political system, the creation of a shared corporate culture in joint ventures in China and other residual communist countries in Asia, like Vietnam, is highly problematic.

The Western investor and the Chinese joint venture partner come to the cooperative venture from very different types of parent organisations. Both parties will also be represented by very different kinds of managers and board members. The Chinese often have a broad political mandate representing 'the people' or very large bureaucracies, while in Western firms the objectives, responsibilities and decision-making powers are clearly defined. An organisational fit is therefore difficult to achieve.

Problems with staffing represent another common misfit. Many Western firms have discovered that, for the Chinese partner, staffing decisions are often influenced by political considerations. Western partners, on the other hand, insist on finding the most capable person for the job.

Early entrants' advantage

During the first half of the 1980s, very few joint ventures in China were able to report any real success stories. Joint ventures were then in their infancy and had to cope with numerous operational problems and considerable uncertainty about China's direction. Both Chinese and Western joint venture partners had to learn how to work with each other, often through painful experience. Western firms which had done well often skirted publicity and avoided reporting high profits for fear that the Chinese government might levy an additional tax or fee on them.

The situation has changed since then; more and more Sino-Western joint ventures which initially reported problems are now doing quite well. Two well-known examples are Shanghai Bell and Beijing Jeep. During the first years of local production, Shanghai Bell's output was considered too expensive by the Chinese, who preferred to buy from the parent company in Europe. Beijing Jeep had gained considerable attention by speaking to the press about their initial difficulties and what they considered unfair treatment by the Chinese government.[22] In both cases the companies were able to overcome their problems: however, in contrast to other countries in Asia Pacific, China does not seem to offer any particular advantages to early entrants. In fact, latecomers have found the legal system more refined, the infrastructure more developed and their partners more familiar with Western business systems. Many of these more recent joint ventures have turned quick profits (for example, Avon, Pepsi, P&G).

Whether a joint venture is a success or a failure cannot be judged within the first few years. This is especially true during years of exceptionally high growth in which almost all new ventures prosper.

On the whole, Western companies which came to China with a limited investment and a cautious approach to joint venture cooperation have tended to do reasonably well. These firms were often realistic and took a firm approach to the initial negotiation process with both the Chinese government and their potential Chinese partners. In most cases, they also had the backing of a senior board member at headquarters.

Notes and references

1. For more information on this subject see Gomes-Casseres (1991b).
2. 'The China Connection', *Far Eastern Economic Review*, 5 November 1992, p. 60.
3. *Financial Times* (1988).
4. Lasserre and Boisot (1980).
5. Aguilar and Sung Cho (1984; video interview with Chairman Kim).
6. Lasserre and Fouraker (1989).
7. Lasserre and Boisot (1980).
8. Lasserre and Boisot (1980).
9. For further information on the valuation of technology see Contractor (1981); and Teece (1976).
10. Lasserre and Boisot (1980). See also Harrigan (1985).
11. Schneider (1988).
12. Laurent (1986).
13. Lasserre (1982).

14. R. Tung (1984); Graham and Sano (1984); Hendryx (1986); Pye (1983), and Pye (1986a); Weiss (1987).
15. A. T. Kearney Inc. (1992).
16. Lasserre and Probert (1997).
17. Franko (1971).
18. Wagner (1990).
19. In March 1983, 3M became the first wholly-owned foreign enterprise in China.
20. Vanhonacker (1997).
21. *Business China*, June, 1998, p. 1.
22. Mann (1989).

8 Cooperating in Global Partnerships

THE REACH OF GLOBAL PARTNERSHIPS

Global partnerships and strategic alliances

Global partnerships have been defined as cooperative ventures in which independent partners combine resources, assets and competences to improve their overall competitiveness in global or regional markets. The majority of strategic alliances in Asia to date have been with Japanese, Korean and Taiwanese firms; only firms from these countries are deemed to possess the capabilities necessary for global partnership with Western firms. Partnerships with even large firms in other Asian countries have been restricted to market access, and thus have to be considered country-based ventures. Many of the issues related to global partnerships are similar to those of country-based partnerships: the rationale for partnership, the selection and negotiation process, the management of the partnership itself. The emphasis, however, is very different. Since global partnerships are concerned with the international arena rather than with national markets, the political imperative is less dominant. Also, since most global partnership agreements are concluded between large multinational firms with abundant resources and assets, the main interest is normally in sharing competences. And as these firms operate several partnerships with various companies in a number of different countries at the same time, the management of these relationships is more complex.

Global partnerships include everything from spot transactions (that is, buying and selling without further commitment) to mergers and acquisitions, where independent firms evolve into unified organisations. They also include informal partnerships, mutual agreements regarding consortia and associations for intelligence gathering and lobbying; and contractual agreements covering, for example, OEM supplies and equity investments, and occasionally cross-share holdings. No reliable statistics exist on cooperative agreements, since they are not bound to any legal form, do not have to be made public and cover a wide variety of projects. However, a number of surveys document the rapid increase of agreements between Japanese and Western firms starting in the early 1980s.[1] No comparable data exist for partnerships between

216

Korean or Taiwanese firms and Western companies, but a large number of agreements concluded with Samsung, Daewoo, Goldstar, Acer and Tatung have since been made public.

The trend towards global partnerships shows that even the largest Western multinational firms cannot market all their products equally well everywhere in the world, and neither can they sustain state-of-the-art research in all areas important to the firm's development. Many find it difficult to remain fully competitive in all parts of the value-added chain. Global partnerships allow these firms to concentrate on their core competences and to borrow or rent the right of use of a partner's expertise without a major commitment, a shift in focus which is particularly useful in times of down-sizing. Compared to acquisitions, which are even more difficult to make in East Asia than in many other parts of the world, global partnerships have been called a soft option.[2]

Cooperative ventures which are of such importance to the partners that their success or failure has a direct impact on the partners' competitiveness are called strategic alliances. Their weight influences the fundamental independence of the firms involved. In strategic alliances, agreements are negotiated and supported by the very top management levels and can embrace several activities and several divisions. A medium- to long-term planning horizon is the norm. Technology sharing is frequently accompanied by some cooperation in production and marketing operations across the globe.

Global partnerships are driven by the need to strengthen the competitiveness of the partners through cost and risk reduction or revenue increase. Cost reductions can be achieved by pooling resources in order to gain scale effects or by shifting manufacturing to the lowest cost producer in the partnership. Risk reduction is achieved by sharing the development costs for a new product. Joint development and rapid commercialisation of innovative products across borders can lead to the shortening of time and consequently to an increase in revenues. All these reasons for entering a partnership are expected to bring mutual benefits to the participating firms. However, from the point of view of the Asian firm, the acquisition of market expertise and technologies from the partner and the consequent improvement of the parent firm's competences usually play a far more decisive role. Fear of the extractive motive on the part of the Asian partner has often led Western firms to adopt a cautious approach, or actually to exclude their own core competences from partnerships (at least during the initial period).

In some cases global partnerships are clearly second-best, defensive solutions that are concluded not so much to achieve greater efficiency as to coopt a partner or to prevent it from cooperating with a competitor. Western firms have also entered global partnerships in Asia in order to overcome government opposition (for example, in cases where a foreign firm is attempting either to sell locally or to invest in highly visible industries). The majority of the partnerships between Western firms and Japanese telecommunication, computer or automobile companies falls into this category. NEC's partnership with Bull of France was based on a similar rationale, although it involves more than a single market and includes technology agreements and an equity investment in Bull NH in the USA.

Japanese, Korean and Taiwanese partners

Many partnerships between Western firms and Japanese, Korean and Taiwanese partners are considered strategic alliances because of the importance of these firms in the world market. A partnership which assists the Western firm only by allowing it to enter the Japanese, Korean or Taiwanese market is not usually considered a strategic alliance as it lacks global reach. However, because of the size and dynamics of the market and the technological competence of the Japanese partner, a market entry partnership in Japan may lead to far-reaching consequences for the world market. For example, the joint venture between Rank Xerox and Fuji Film created Fuji Xerox, a company that was initially only in charge of Japan. Today Fuji Xerox has taken over responsibility for most of Asia and is a source of innovation that has enriched Xerox's global operations with new product developments and supplies from Japan. Fuji Xerox also sells its own products directly to American customers under OEM agreements without the involvement of its US parent, Xerox.

Partnerships with the Japanese can include aspects of manufacturing, marketing and technology. The contribution of Korean and Taiwanese firms is mainly limited to manufacturing. This helps the Western partner to reduce production costs and the Asian partner to gain volume and eventually access to markets too difficult to enter at this stage.

In terms of research and development, Korean and Taiwanese firms are still considered junior partners who are likely to appropriate technology from the Western partner rather than develop it jointly. Despite the stereotype, there are many positive examples of partnerships that have led to considerable mutual benefits in terms of research and development for both firms. Goldstar's purchase of a minority stake in Zenith, for example, is more than an equity investment; it pools the development capabilities and efforts of both firms in high definition television (HDTV), gives Zenith low cost manufacturing capacity in Korea and Goldstar additional marketing clout in the USA. To cite another example: Samsung brings its manufacturing expertise in semiconductors into Texas Instrument's plant in Portugal.

From a global perspective, it is interesting to note that Japanese, Korean and Taiwanese firms have concluded far more partnerships with American than with European firms. A multitude of agreements have also been made between American and European firms. However, the number of global partnerships between European and Asian firms remains relatively low.

Competitive collaboration and networks

Stand-alone companies that do not have the opportunity of jointly creating value with their partners are finding it increasingly difficult to compete. Kao's lack of global reach and global partnerships made it impossible for the firm to market its Japanese innovations in nappies and detergents world-wide. Thomson of France finds it difficult to remain competitive in consumer electronics without an alliance with a Japanese firm in product development. In the computer industry, even IBM and DEC, both firms that had previously insisted on total self-reliance, have recognised their limits and entered a large number of partnerships.

In the electronics industry the multitude of partnerships which each player in the market has set up in recent years has led to a constantly changing network of relationships. Gone are the days when firms believed they could cooperate with only one Japanese partner: IBM is developing the next generation of semiconductors with Toshiba and Siemens, but cooperates with Hitachi and Mitsubishi Electric in the systems area; Sun works with Fujitsu and Matsushita at the same time, as does Philips with Matsushita and Sony; Hewlett-Packard cooperates with Mitsubishi Electric and Fujitsu, while simultaneously buying chips from Samsung of Korea.

Firms will only enter into global partnerships when they are sure of the other firm's capacity to make a valuable contribution to the cooperation. Consequently, most partnerships are concluded between firms that either are already competitors in the same or similar businesses, or expect to become competitors in the future. For diversified firms the relationship can be even more complex because they may buy and sell certain products with the partner, while competing with it in a third business. In highly political undertakings such as the FSX project (the development of a new generation of fighter planes), the interests of the main contracting partner firms Mitsubishi Heavy Industries and General Dynamics, as well as those of their sub-contractors and of their governments, all had to be taken into account. Competitive collaboration therefore requires the utmost attention. On the one hand, the partners have to share knowledge to achieve results; on the other, they should not share too much knowledge or engage in exchange of highly strategic information if they are to avoid strengthening their competitors, who can often turn out to be their own suppliers and customers.

SUCCESS AND FAILURE OF GLOBAL PARTNERSHIPS

Western perceptions

Many global partnerships that were originally concluded with high hopes end in a premature break-up or linger on without ever achieving anything substantial. These are obvious failures. When one partner emerges as a clear winner and reaps more benefits than the other partner, the cooperation has similarly failed to fulfil objectives (at least for the losing partner).

There are several reasons why partnerships fail. Some fall victim to insufficient preparation and negotiation, while others suffer from incongruity in the partners' objectives which leads to the strategic misfits of culture, organisation and resources. A disparity in the partners' ability and motivation to learn from each other and their alliance may also be a decisive cause for failure, and one which may specifically arise in the clash (interaction) between the enterprise cultures of Western and Asian firms. Finally, external factors such as a change in the market, in technology or in government regulation can also lead to failure.

The existence of unsuccessful ventures is therefore not surprising. However, at the end of the 1980s came the perception in the West that partnerships, particularly those formed with Japanese firms, are difficult or work only in favour of Japanese partners.[3] It is in fact relatively easy to cite examples of partnerships in which the Japanese have apparently benefited more than the Western side. Decades ago, Siemens and Furukawa founded a new venture called Fuji Electric, out of which were born Fujitsu and subsequently Fanuc. The long-term transfer of technology made a significant contribution to the success of all three Japanese companies. However – and despite Siemens having been present for a century in Japan – the cooperation has not helped the German company to penetrate the Japanese market. During the 100 years of Siemens' operations in Japan, their dependency on Japanese supplies, and more recently on mainframe computers from Fujitsu, has steadily increased. To cite another example: years ago, the Japanese firm NEC obtained technology from Honeywell and then helped the American firm to market their computers in Japan. Meanwhile, the balance of power shifted and even the fact that Honeywell's top machines were from NEC did not prevent the decline of the American partner. Today, Honeywell Information Systems is called Bull HN and has NEC as a 15 per cent shareholder. Another agreement between Honda and British Leyland/Rover included plans for the sale of Honda cars in Europe and of Rover cars in Japan. Rover never succeeded in Japan but Honda is now firmly established in Europe. Despite being out-manoeuvred later on by BMW which bought Rover, Honda achieved its goal. In the 1990s, partnerships have become more balanced as in the case of IBM and Toshiba in flat panel displays, or in several alliances in the pharmaceutical industry.

Assessment and measurement of success and failure

Neither individual cases nor statistics can provide a comprehensive view on whether global partnerships with Japanese firms lead to success or failure. Xerox would probably have ceased to exist without its joint venture in Japan. On the other hand, IBM and Nestlé, both 100 per cent foreign-owned in Japan and both very profitable over a long period of time, could have managed even better with a Japanese partner. Both Rover and Honeywell have survived due to their link with a Japanese partner. While Siemens found it difficult to penetrate the Japanese market despite its close relationship with various partners, it may not have succeeded in that market on its own.

The above examples show the limited value of statistics and individual cases in assessing partnerships. Not all costs and benefits from a cooperation are manifest, even to insiders. As interviews with managers prove, personal views differ considerably, even within the same venture.

Due to the complexity and the long-term nature of the agreements, a clearly defined measure of the success or failure of global partnerships does not exist. Figures on sales, market share and profits can provide indications but have to be related to the time horizon and to the geographical importance of the specific venture. While difficult to quantify or evaluate, the improvement of technologies, growth of organisational capabilities, or the spread of brand images are soft criteria which may be more significant than hard data. The transfer of knowledge in the broadest sense may often be the underlying motive for entering a cooperative venture; if this is the case, then any assessment of the quality or intensity of joint activity becomes superfluous.

More importantly, the success or failure of the cooperative venture may be judged differently by the partners, and as a rule will have a very different impact on their own activities. Finally, for the partners involved in an alliance, the success or failure of the partnership may be strongly correlated to the strengths or weaknesses which the respective partners initially brought into the venture. The assumed weakness of Western partners compared to strong and self-confident Japanese firms would explain in part why the Western side often reaps fewer benefits from such alliances. However, despite the growing international competitiveness of Japanese firms, there is no proof that they necessarily demonstrate a corresponding superior strength in partnerships. For example, Rover may be no match for Honda, but Siemens is certainly a larger and more profitable firm than Fujitsu. After several years of cooperation, the American chain 7-Eleven was taken over by its Japanese licensee Ito

Yokado, but Motorola has gained additional strength from its partnership with Toshiba in telecommunication equipment.

STRUCTURAL DIFFERENCES BETWEEN PARTNERS

Trading of contributions

Contributions to a partnership come from the areas of research and development, manufacturing and marketing. Apart from rare cases in which the partners make identical contributions in identical or similar areas, one partner's contribution has to be traded against a different type of contribution from the other.

It is generally accepted that Japanese firms excel in process technology, a competence which enables them to produce competitively high quality, complex products in large scale and great variety. Korean firms employ economies of scale to drive down the production costs of standard products, while Taiwanese firms are quick to churn out down-scaled innovative products at lower cost. Japanese firms are also good at turning new developments into marketable products, and all of them are better at marketing their own products in their home markets. Since Western firms claim to be more creative and therefore stronger in product technology, and since they also invest more in basic research and offer more customised products and services, they should theoretically be in a better position to manage their own Western markets.

While some of these points are arguable, the overall difference in strengths and weaknesses is apparent. Given the different histories and cultures of Japanese, Korean, Taiwanese and Western firms, this is not surprising. It also explains why the number of partnerships in which the same or similar contributions are pooled is relatively small. In most cooperative agreements with Asian firms, the strength of the Asian partner in one area is complemented by the strength of the Western partner in another.

Any number of different combinations of complementary contributions is possible. Three types of agreement, however, stand out. In the first type, the Asian firm obtains technology from its Western partner, manufactures the product at home and markets it, either domestically or regionally, in Asia. The Western firm enters this type of partnership either because it considers the Asian markets too difficult to penetrate or not important enough, or because it feels unable to adapt its products to Asian customers' needs. In the past such agreements have dominated in the pharmaceutical industry and are now increasingly used in core technologies, such as new materials and service industries.

The second type of agreement exploits the manufacturing strength of the Asian partner. Product design and specifications come from the Western partner who is responsible for marketing the products, usually under its own brand name (OEM agreements). The Asian partner is allowed to sell the output in its own market, often under its own name. The Western side is interested in sourcing from Asia mainly for cost reasons. For the Asian partner the partnership provides access to foreign markets for which it has no market expertise. Such agreements cover large parts of the international trade in computers and peripherals, office equipment and consumer electronics.[4]

As a result, Asian partners import more technology than they export, manufacture more products at home than they source abroad, and allow the marketing side to be handled by the most suitable partner in the relevant market. This division of labour has important implications for Western firms, especially those that consider their Asian partners actual or potential competitors.

By obtaining technology from their Western partners Asian firms are able to make up for their lack of investment or success in research. Licensing fees or lump sum payments for technology transfer are often welcomed by the Western partner, even though they invariably do not make up for the time or investment needed for independent innovation, and can hence lead to cost savings for the Asian side.

The particular strength of Japanese firms in developing, improving and adapting certain technologies gradually reduces their dependence on the Western licensee. Historically, the transfer of technology from the Western partner has been a launch pad for Asian development activities. In addition, the Japanese partner's ability to refine obtained technologies and to apply them to a diverse range of products that had not initially been conceived, strengthens its own competitiveness to the detriment of the Western partner. As a result, Western firms often find themselves in the unenviable position of competing with products offered by their own Japanese partners which, while originally based on the Western partner's technology, have been made superior either in quality, performance or attractiveness to the mass market.

By manufacturing for its partner, the Japanese, Korean or Taiwanese firm is able to increase its volume, move into larger-scale production and, as a result, further reduce its costs. Opportunities for generally improving production capabilities often follow. The Asian partner is likely to benefit most, since the advantages gained will not only apply to the Western partner's products, but will also affect the branches of the Asian firm with which the Western partner may eventually compete. Confronted by the growing competitiveness of its partner, the Western firm will be induced to shift production from its own factories to Asia. And the dependency is increasing: as Westerns firms produce less and less in-house, the vital link between production, development and the market is progressively weakened. The hollowing-out of the Western partner begins when it considers delegating to the Asian firm still further links in the value-added chain.[5] As a result, instead of fostering the Western firm's own long-term manufacturing capabilities, short-term sourcing opportunities may actually endanger its long-term viability. At the same time, close cooperation and the continuous demand for additional supplies will inevitably encourage the Asian firm to compete with its Western customer/partner.

In all the partnerships described above, one kind of contribution is traded against another. In the first, research and development expertise is traded against marketing; in the second, manufacturing is traded against marketing; and in the third, marketing expertise in one market is exchanged for market access to another market. In all these partnerships Western firms allow Japanese partners to cater to Japanese or Asian markets, while Japanese firms ask the Western partner to market their products in the West, or in certain Western markets. (Korean and Taiwanese firms rarely become involved in this type of cooperation.) Superficially, this third type of agreement represents a balanced approach to the world market, though market sizes and competitive climates may differ from region to region. Both sides expect to benefit from offering a broader product range to their customers and spreading their fixed marketing costs over a larger volume.

However, the more success local Asian firms have in selling the products of their foreign partners in their own market, the more likely the foreign partner is to want direct involvement. This instability is inherent in all international marketing agreements, as the foreign partner inevitably becomes more acquainted with the market and an image of its products has been built up. Once a sufficient volume is reached to make the operation financially viable, the Western partner will generally want to take over distribution. Japanese firms, among others, are pursuing this path in many Western markets. Theoretically, Western firms should be able to apply the same strategy to their operations in the Japanese market. However, in the particular case of global partnerships between Western and Japanese firms, what appears to be an initially fair or symmetrical exchange inevitably tilts in favour of the Japanese firm. Sales in Japan are primarily based on direct and often non-transferable buyer/seller relationships, and only secondarily on the attractiveness of the offer. As a result, a Western firm with an established marketing partner in Japan will find it difficult, if not impossible, to implement such a strategy.

Western firms that dare to break an existing marketing agreement have to replace established relationships with new ones, an almost impossible task given the difficulties involved in recruiting sales personnel, of trying to take over the existing partner or, alternatively, finding another distributor. In the

1970s, Beiersdorf of Germany and Kao of Japan went into two very similar marketing joint ventures in the German and Japanese markets. The German venture Gulil now has its own sales force and is under Kao's influence and direction. The Japanese venture, called Nivea-Kao, is successful, but continues to rely heavily on Kao's strong distribution network in Japan. Because of its name, many Japanese believe it is a subsidiary of Kao, although Beiersdorf is the majority shareholder.

It has been argued that firms which are not actively represented in all three key markets (the USA, Europe and Japan) will gradually lose out in international competition.[6] This argument posits that firms aiming at a global role must expand from their own territory into the other two parts of the triad, and recommends that if entry is difficult they should turn to cooperative agreements with partners from other parts of the world. For Japanese firms cooperation with American or European partners may be unnecessary, or only required at the beginning, and for a limited time. Western firms, on the other hand, rightly or wrongly assume that entering the Japanese market without a Japanese partner is almost impossible, or at least very difficult. In choosing a partner their global activities consequently include a cooperator/competitor who may influence their decisions and ultimately their competitiveness, not only in Japan but world-wide.

Asymmetric strategies

To achieve in a global partnership the participating firms must have the capacity to align their objectives. While objectives do not have to be identical, they must be compatible. Even if they are identical, the firms' parent organisations will have their own agendas and assign them different priorities. This is particularly true for firms that sell a large number of products across the globe, or are simultaneously involved in several different partnerships. Because the activities of partnership are separated from each of the partners' core activities, the outcome of joint activities is rarely an end in itself, but must be seen in light of the expected flow of benefits to the partner firms involved. The expectations of Western and Japanese firms vary considerably. Generally, the Western partner, after negotiating the cooperative agreement, is interested in making the venture work. The explicit outcome of the joint undertaking, financial benefit in particular, is the criterion by which the success or failure of the partnership is judged (see Figure 8.1).

Obviously, the Japanese partner is also interested in achieving positive results for the venture. However, Japanese firms seem to be equally (if not more) keen to learn from the Western partner's contribution to the partnership and from the way joint activities are carried out. In transferring expertise from

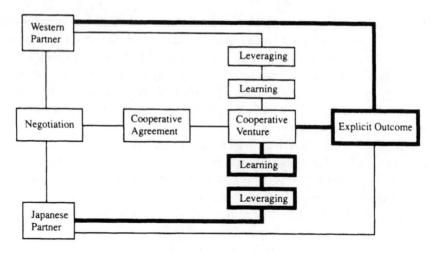

Figure 8.1   Explicit Outcome

the joint undertaking to other parts of the Japanese partner's firm, it tries to strengthen its competences and competitiveness. This process of leveraging may well provide the Japanese parent firm with far greater indirect benefits than the outcome of the cooperative venture itself.[7]

If the indirect benefits it will receive dominate the thinking of the Japanese partner, its interest in the joint activities will continue to exist only as long as the Western partner's contribution continues to be seen as a source of learning. When the Japanese partner perceives that no further expertise can be exported from the partnership into its parent firm, the *raison d'être* for the cooperative venture disappears. Paradoxically, it is the long-term interest of the Japanese firm in strengthening its own competences which reduces the partnership with its Western partner to an intermediate venture with a limited life span. To keep up appearances, however, the cooperation may continue forever, particularly if it is based in Japan where face-saving is important.

There are two major reasons why Western and Japanese firms tend to have different expectations from their partnerships with each other. They are structural and lie in the different strategic logic and the different strategic intent of the partners.

As described in Chapter 4, the strategic logic of the Japanese firm differs markedly from that of the Western firm. As an organisation, the Japanese firm defines itself as an association of people fighting against competitors for survival.[8] To secure the survival of the firm and its stakeholders the Japanese firm has to grow and long-term growth can only be achieved by building up competences. These, in turn, can be developed internally through efforts in research and development and training. Externally, competences can be built up by learning from others. Global partnerships are part of this learning effort and are managed accordingly.

In contrast to this, the Western firm is considered an aggregation of assets, and its purpose is the creation of value for the shareholders in order to give them a satisfactory ROI. The firm's survival and growth are not judged by comparing the acceptance of its products and services in the market with those of its competitors, but by comparing the firm's ROI with the standards set in the financial markets. Consequently, the Western partner in an alliance is almost forced to pay more attention to the financial results of the venture. Competence building is not rejected by Western managers, but learning from the alliance simply does not have the organisational or structural priority it has in Japanese firms. This is especially visible in equity joint ventures, where the measurement of returns on investment can easily be calculated and compared with the firm's capital investments in other ventures.[9] If the return is insufficient, the Western partner may decide to sell out to the Japanese partner, as Dow Chemical, McGraw-Hill, International Harvester and several other firms have done.

Strategic intent has been defined as the ambition, if not the obsession, of a firm to gain long-term leadership in a given industry. This trait is ascribed particularly to Japanese firms,[10] which over the last few decades have invested heavily in many industries and have achieved major gains in world market shares.[11] The success of many Japanese firms stems from the deep commitment of Japanese employees to this strategic intent, which represents an offensive approach towards new markets and new technologies to be acquired. Global partnerships are only one of many stepping stones to leadership. The various partnerships in information technology between Japanese and Western companies concluded in the 1970s have helped Japanese firms, which initially had very limited competence, to emerge as major players in world markets. Sumitomo Chemicals entered 12 alliances with foreign partners to strengthen its competences. Four of them were formed with pharmaceutical companies before Sumitomo Pharmaceuticals was established as a separate company. The other partnerships included Akzo, Bayer, Dow, Hercules, ICI and Rohm & Haas.[12]

Few Western firms have shown a similar strategic intent. Most of them view alliances with Japanese firms as a short-cut to new markets that saves investment in assets and resources. Alternatively, partnerships are concluded as a defence against encroaching competition, often from other Asian firms. OEM agreements that secure supply of lower-cost products, or milk an existing market expertise or technology for as long as possible, fall into this category. In all these cases there is neither full commitment from the Western partner nor a willingness to build up further competences.

Managerial behaviour and learning

Both Western and Japanese firms have altered their organisational structure to allow for the allocation of resources to different groups according to the priorities of top management. These groups, which enjoy some degree of independence, are frequently referred to in the West as strategic business units (SBUs), while in Japan they generally consist of divisions. Western SBUs have to fulfil objectives laid down in business plans or budgets, and the performance of SBU managers is judged according to their ability to reach those financial targets. The purpose of this organisational structure is to delineate responsibilities clearly and to foster intrapreneurship. As a result, there is no incentive for Western managers in these SBUs to leverage obtained competences across the parent company, or to sustain high investments in core technologies which may benefit not only their specific business unit but the firm as whole. Make-or-buy decisions are also taken on a business level. If all SBUs could collectively evaluate the long-term implications of becoming dependent on supplies in important product technologies, perhaps the Western firm's orientation would be different. As it stands, however, the SBU structure militates against the leverage of technologies across the firm. In such a business structure, where single country units insist on their own autonomous decision-making power, international coordination of competitive activities becomes difficult.

In general the SBU structure does not exist in Japanese firms. Here, budgets serve primarily to facilitate cash flow planning rather than to link objectives rigidly with the performance of the division or the individual managers concerned. For Japanese managers it is equally important to contribute to the parent firm as a whole and in a way which is compatible with its strategic intent. In bringing staff and different parent firms from different cultures together in a partnership where learning is important, the gap between Western and Japanese management behaviour and practices tends to work against the Western partner. The benefits that accrue to the Western parent firm from its individualistic and compartmentalised business structure will be more limited than those in a Japanese firm, where the staff try to maximise benefits for the entire corporation.

The organisational structure of the firm is not the only influence on learning and leverage. The attitudes of individuals and their expectations of the firm also have an important impact. In their contact with Japanese partners, many Western managers and engineers do not show the same interest in their partner's work and expertise as is shown in theirs by their Japanese counterparts. By and large, Westerners do not walk through factories camera in hand, do not ask detailed questions and do not take note of everything they see and hear, though this is expected of their Japanese counterparts. In a typical operations meeting between Western and Japanese partners, the Japanese representatives will invariably be more numerous and better prepared than the Western side.

Even today, many Western managers tend to underestimate their Japanese partners. The myths of 'Japan Inc.', unfair trading practices, accusations of Japan stealing technology from the West rather than developing its own, the difficulties in decoding the strategic intent of the Japanese partner: all these factors have led many Western managers to the conviction that the strength of their Asian partners does not come from their own technological capabilities. Hence the conclusion is that there is not much to learn. To make matters worse, learning – even in the framework of a global partnership – is rarely part of the Western job description. There are also external constraints: time for learning is simply insufficient, and in a situation where managers feel hard pressed to achieve concrete objectives, learning from their partners is viewed as a secondary, or even an unaffordable, academic exercise. In many Western firms, the diffusion of knowledge is problematic and few methods for systematic collection and transfer exist. The parent company rarely shows any interest in the task, because of the psychological and geographical distance from Japan, and in many cases due to an even more serious underestimation of the Japanese partner.

The Western representative him- or herself may not consider the transfer of knowledge to the parent firm helpful for his or her own career. In Western firms information means power and influence, and sharing information is viewed as a loss of control or influence. This attitude usually enhances the representative's position in the organisation, due to the myth that the Japan expert is indispensable and that the firm will be unable to operate without 'the person who knows'. In no other country but Japan do Western representatives get away with the argument that their business environment is totally unique and much more difficult than in other parts of the world. As a result of the monopolisation of knowledge these managers do become indispensable; when they leave or retire, valuable information is totally lost, since the firm has never paid sufficient attention to organisational learning.

This Western managerial behaviour, often individualistic and defensive in nature, contrasts sharply with the Japanese attitude to learning. Deeply ingrained in the Japanese counterpart is the desire to search for information, to explore, to ask questions and to listen. Constant improvement is expected for the benefit of the individual as well as for the organisation.[13] Japanese managers are expected to share the information obtained, and they do so as they perceive themselves to be first of all members of the group and only secondly as individuals. The evaluation of someone's performance is, in fact, based on how much information that person has brought into the group, not on how much more knowledge he or she individually possesses compared to the peer group. Diffusion of knowledge takes place easily and automatically in this information-sharing environment. Constant communication by phone or fax across continents, immediate information exchange in open space offices, the constant contact between Japanese managers and their head office, and even informal contacts through frequent socialising after work: all of this works to the advantage of the Japanese partner, who sees the advantage of leveraging knowledge throughout the organisation.

Not all knowledge can easily be obtained, absorbed and transferred. Some knowledge is deeply rooted in the social fabric of the firm, has grown over the years and is embodied in people's skills and routines. This type of knowledge is difficult to observe and even more difficult to describe. Systems innovations, new production or distribution processes, and the delivery of service quality belong to this category. Migratory knowledge, on the other hand, can be more easily decoded and understood. Product expertise, for example, can be gained through reverse engineering, as can design through careful observation.

In global partnerships between Japanese and Western firms this can lead to a gap in the transfer of competences. This is especially relevant when the contribution of the Japanese partner consists of production expertise, that of the Western partner of product expertise, and the manufacturing activities take place in Japan. But this disadvantage may also apply to the Japanese partner. To cite one example: Boeing's cost-efficient aircraft assembly capability has never been challenged despite close cooperation with various Japanese partners. Despite many Japanese attempts to learn from their respective partners and to transfer competences to their parent firms, state-of-the-art software development is still concentrated in the loosely-structured, entre-preneurial environment of American firms, and France still holds the leading position in the creation of fragrances and flavours.

ORGANISATIONAL REQUIREMENTS

Setting up a global partnership

In the context of an alliance, structural differences between Japanese and Western firms tend to afford certain advantages to the Japanese partner. Notwithstanding, the outcome of a cooperative venture depends to a large degree on the way the partnership is set up and managed; otherwise partnerships would automatically work in favour of the Japanese partner and examples of mutually successful ventures, such as the Toshiba-Motorola cooperation, would not exist. Certain other partnerships, for example in pharmaceuticals, have provided great benefits to the Western partners by giving them access to the Japanese market without any loss of their strong position in research and development and the world market.

Good management of a partnership starts with a thorough analysis of the firm's own objectives and then of the objectives of the prospective partner. In negotiating and concluding an agreement it seems advantageous and profitable to be as specific as possible regarding the delineation of tasks and responsibilities, even though the actual contract may only vaguely outline the scope and implications of the joint activity. This is particularly true for joint research projects in which the outcome or follow-up work cannot be specified at the outset. Broad declarations of willingness to cooperate alone do not get activities started, as Daimler-Benz experienced with its widely-publicised partnership with Mitsubishi. To reduce the risk of running into conflict and to enhance trust between the partners, core technologies should not be at stake in the alliance.

Moving into neutral territory – that is, related businesses or new geographical markets – has been shown to improve chances for mutual success. Cooperating in one part of the value-added chain and relying together on the output of this joint activity cements the close relationship between the partners. BASF and Nippon Oil and Fats, for example, carry out joint research and development and production of special chemicals in Japan, but each sells them separately in the world market.

The selection of a neutral location for the joint activity is equally important, especially if the partnership is to be set up as a separate, autonomous entity. Ventures in Japan, even if designed for the world rather than the home market, are generally only seen as extensions of the Japanese partner's activities, even when the Western partner holds the clear majority of the equity. This is due to the fact that most of the personnel tend to come from the Japanese partner's parent company and will identify more with their parent than with the Western firm.

In general, autonomous ventures have fared better by distancing themselves from their parents, by remaining flexible, by building up their own corporate culture and by making their own decisions. This contrasts sharply with OEM alliances in which the relationship tends to be more contractual and where the interaction between independent entities with different cultures mainly consists of bargaining. In the long term, unequal or dependent partnerships – for example, those between strong and weak, large and small companies – have rarely worked out.[14]

Trust can only be established over time. Competence and reliability have to be proven and require close interaction. Playing golf together or socialising after work may help, but this level of contact is not enough. Without trust the issue of control will dominate the thinking of the partners, and the transaction cost will be high. Obviously, trust is easier to establish when the partnership leads to a new independent venture which is encroaching on no one's territory. As soon as the extraction of knowledge from each other becomes a more important or the most important reason for the partnership, the relationship needs to be more carefully regulated with clearly defined boundaries and functions. In the JVC-Thornson partnership in video recorders in Europe, a clear understanding was reached to share the manufacturing operations but it did not extend to exchanging product development expertise. This strict delineation did not prevent the emergence of trust; on the contrary, trust was established because all parties were able clearly to identify and discuss areas of mutual and conflicting interest.

Relationships matter, especially in Asia. They matter even more in partnerships with a lot of interaction and high expectations from both parent firms. The selection and briefing of the right representatives working in cooperative ventures is therefore crucial for the success of the partnership. The managers and engineers involved will face a multitude of challenges: differences not only in national but also corporate cultures, even industry cultures; the need to satisfy not one but two parent firms which may have conflicting interests or hidden agendas; the inability to use power in relationships between hierarchically equal partners; and the pressure to make the joint activity work while feeding back information to the parent firm.

It is not surprising that career-minded executives shy away from these tasks, particularly in view of the perception that partnerships with Japanese firms often founder. But the complexity of the task requires high calibre personnel, especially those who consider an assignment to an alliance as a long-term commitment rather than a short-lived step in a fast-track career. By and large, Japanese representatives in cooperative ventures tend to stay in the job much longer, if not for life, while their Western counterparts rotate quickly and have difficulty solving problems before their next transfer. The exceptions to this are German and Swiss partners, who in their alliances with Japanese firms have sought to assign their managers to ventures for considerably longer periods than other Western partners.[15]

In the final analysis, highly qualified and ambitious Western managers can only be convinced to take up a less structured, more difficult, and perilous position in an alliance when they see a clear commitment from their own top management.

Equally important is the provision of support for the representatives in the partnership. They should be given enough room and time both to achieve and to learn. For the Western partner, support in this sense consists of sufficient staffing of the venture, of taking the Japanese side rather than normal Western subsidiaries of a similar size as a benchmark, and of good back-up services in the parent company. An alliance manager in charge of several partnerships may be part of this set-up as long as he or she wields sufficient power and influence within the parent firm.

Organisational learning

Organisational learning is a process through which knowledge gained by individuals is shared with others and used throughout the organisation. It does not take place automatically, at least not in Western cultures dominated by individualistic behaviour, where it needs to be initiated and nurtured. Organisational learning requires first, a positive attitude to learning from the individual members of the organisation, and second, a systematic approach to collecting data. A third step lies in sharing information, followed by organisational synthesis and interpretation, and finally action and change in the parent firm. All five steps are essential (see Figure 8.2). Too often information is collected in one part of the organisation without ever being channelled to others.

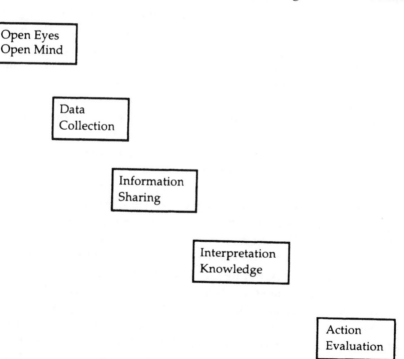

Figure 8.2 Organisational Learning

In a global partnership the first step is the creation of an awareness that there is something to learn from the other side. This is no easy undertaking for Western firms, which are successful in their own markets and proud of their past technological achievements. The attitudinal change is most likely to take place in a situation where the Western firm feels threatened by Japanese competition, particularly in its home market. The Americans were the first to troop to Japan in large numbers to study Japanese manufacturing technology because they were the first to witness Japanese successes in the USA. The Europeans, who have been less exposed to Japanese competition in their home markets, have shown markedly less interest in learning from Japan.

Systematic data collection is a precondition for reaching any conclusions or for converting data into useful information. This requires clear briefings and assignment of tasks. Data can come from internal or external sources and cover both hard, tangible facts and intangibles. The use of outsiders often raises questions about their integrity; insiders, on the other hand, may be loyal to their firm, but either fail to see information gathering as a priority or simply lack skill at intelligence gathering.

For information sharing to happen, clear communication channels and regular reporting systems have to be defined and established both within the partner firms and between the cooperative venture and the parent firms. This planned approach differs considerably from sporadic and informal exchanges, which often receive inadequate attention from top management. Establishing a working communication system is a major task in multinational, multidivisional firms, and one that very few companies have come to grips with. Not only do the disparate parts of the parent firm have different information needs and attitudes towards learning, but these are all in constant flux.

Communication also takes place in meetings between various groups within the Western firm, the partnership venture and the Japanese partner. Task-oriented Western engineers tend to align themselves easily with other experts in their field and do not hesitate to disclose technical details even if they are proprietary. Western experts often see no contradiction in cultivating a dual loyalty to their profession and to their firm. For their Japanese counterparts, however, professional loyalty is not similarly divisible: in Japanese corporate culture, loyalty is exclusively to the Japanese firm. Information flows without involvement from people directly charged with the collection and channelling of data. Moreover, the Japanese partner's staff pay visits to various parts of the Western firm which may be unaware of the multitude of contacts taking place. For the Western firm, the challenge in these situations is to brief and debrief the managers involved so that information is widely shared across functions, departments, divisions and countries. Several Western firms have experimented with the establishment of a gatekeeper or alliance office in charge of all communication with the Japanese side. However, this system only works if all participants see the advantages of a coordinated approach and benefit from it. Total control of information flows is otherwise impossible.

The centre for gathering, pooling and distributing information can also synthesise and interpret it in order to produce useful knowledge for the firm. This process should be shared among the various interested parties in the partnership at the parent firm and include some representatives directly involved in the cooperative venture. For the Western firm, the process of synthesis ideally leads to self-reflection and an examination of its established practices. This comparison of the Western firm's own business and technology with that of the partner is vital for the last, decisive step in organisational learning: the implementation of change through obtained knowledge.

Organisational learning does not happen without substantial management guidance and without a positive attitude at top management level. To take this process out of the sphere of fashionable management recipes and bring it into the world of reality, consultants now recommend annual cost-benefit analyses of the organisation's learning from the partner.[16]

Provisions for exit

Monitoring a firm's progress in the acquisition of knowledge and experience of organisational learning is important, but does not encompass all aspects of a partnership. Progress made in the market, research and development spending and output, financial results and many other factors have to be evaluated to see whether the partnership meets expectations on both sides. But such evaluation rarely leads to clear-cut conclusions. For example, it is difficult to weigh advances in the market against a potential loss of technological advantage to the partner. The benefits derived from organisational learning are difficult, if not impossible, to quantify. Different stakeholders in the parent firm may have divergent views on the partnership and varying time lags may pre-empt proper judgement for a number of years. If, for example, the Western partner contributes technology to the partnership, the transfer can take place rather quickly; in exchange, the Japanese partner may promise access to its market. But providing market access only means opening the door, not guaranteeing market success. This may be years away or never come.

In evaluating the partnership, all potential sources of conflict that may arise from the external environment and from the relationships between the various actors should be taken into account (see Figure 8.3).

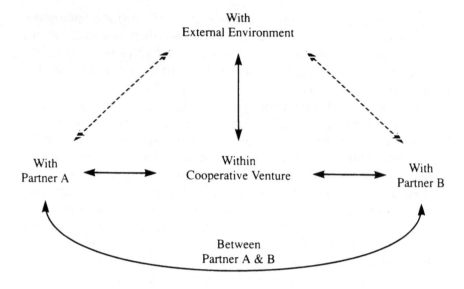

Figure 8.3   Sources of Conflict

These difficulties should not prevent the partners from institutionalising regular evaluations of the partnership to clarify their costs and benefits, the actual and expected conflicts and the advantages and disadvantages of continuing the relationship. One way to enforce a systematic evaluation of an important partnership is to require an explicit decision-making process to mandate its continuation. While such a process may seem cumbersome, it ensures the regular attention of top management. It also implies that clear provisions for leaving or dissolving the partnership should be made at the time of the initial partnership agreement. Obviously, the dissolution of an OEM agreement is much easier than that of an equity joint venture, particularly one that has existed over a long period and has produced new technologies which are jointly developed and jointly owned.

Even if the Western and Japanese partners get along well and no conflict exists among other parties directly involved in the partnership, the interaction of the individual firms with the external environment will lead to changes in their position in their specific markets and technologies. This may cause substantial shifts in the balance of power between the two partners, eventually leading to the total dependency of one partner on the other. This is very often the first step towards the full acquisition of the partnership by the stronger partner. Alternatively, the partnership reaches a point where it has fulfilled its purpose and should be dissolved. Partners either sell out or share the benefits, and continue working on their own without the constraints of the partnership agreement. (Dissolving one agreement may also open the way to a partnership with another firm.)

The outcome of the dissolution of the Philips-Matsushita partnership is a case in point. In 1993 Philips and Matsushita ended their 31-year global partnership in semiconductors and cathode ray tubes. The large joint venture operated plants in Japan, the USA, Singapore, Malaysia and China. Both firms felt that their partnership had become too complex to be managed jointly but it was also apparent that the expansion of the venture outside Japan had created increasing conflicts with Philips' own semiconductor and picture tube business. Matsushita bought out its Western partner, thereby helping Philips to overcome its weak financial position.[17] This outcome is not exceptional. A survey of 700 alliances between Japanese and non-Japanese companies indicated that Japanese partners were acquirers in approximately 70 per cent of all terminated ventures.[18]

Dissolution of a partnership or full acquisition by one of the partners is often seen as a failure by those who consider partnerships as marriages. But this understanding is fundamentally flawed; partnerships, even if launched as eternally-binding relationships, are in fact affairs rather than marriages: exciting, difficult to manage and very prone to divert the interest of the partners from their long-term ability to survive and prosper on their own.

Notes and references

1. The most comprehensive Japanese survey was carried out by Hirotaka Takeuchi of Hitotsubashi University. It identified more than 6000 cooperative agreements between Japanese and foreign partners which were announced during the period 1982–6. Twenty-two per cent of those agreements were joint ventures, 44 per cent with an American partner. Forty-six per cent took place outside Japan, 41 per cent inside Japan, and the rest both outside and inside Japan. See *Japan Economic Journal*, 7 May 1988.
2. Doz (1992).
3. Hamel and Prahalad (1989).
4. Schütte (1990a). See also Gomes-Casseres (1991a).
5. Reich and Mankin (1986).
6. Ohmae (1985).
7. Hamel and Prahalad (1989).
8. See Chapter 6.
9. Ohmae (1989).
10. Hamel and Prahalad (1989).
11. Franko (1991).
12. Jones and Shill (1993).
13. Warner (1992).
14. Bleeke and Ernst (1991).
15. Jones and Shill (1993).
16. Amponsem and Rutenberg (1992).
17. *Financial Times*, 1–2 May 1993, p. 22.
18. Bleeke and Ernst (1991).

9 Organising

Western firms seeking to expand their presence in the Asia Pacific region are confronted with two kinds of organisational problems. Initially, they will have to decide to what extent their firm's structure must be tailored to the Asia Pacific region. Second, they must decide whether a specific regional structure should be designed to lead and coordinate country strategies. To a large extent, traditional organisational practices have hampered the strategic development of Western firms in the region. This chapter looks at three companies which demonstrate some of the organisational characteristics conducive to facilitating and supporting Asian strategies, and discusses how organisational structure and processes can be adapted to fit regional characteristics.

ORGANISATIONAL VICIOUS CIRCLES

The failure of some Western firms to establish a presence in Asia Pacific commensurate with the region's strategic potential has often stemmed from their inability to adapt to different managerial cultures and competitive climates in Asia. Although this might be true for any company operating in any culture, the Asia Pacific region presents certain fundamental differences for the Western manager.

The main causes for the relatively weak presence of Western companies in the Asia Pacific region are depicted as two interrelated vicious circles (Figure 9.1). Inadequate financial allocation and inappropriate human resource management are both related to Asia's low internal visibility in the corporate organisational structure.

Internal strategic visibility depends on the Asia Pacific perspective being represented in a company's central corporate fora and supported by influential executives who lend it their prestige. Asia Pacific represents a relatively small proportion of the global corporate activities of Western firms and the region has had limited internal visibility and, at best, an exotic image. Within the parent company's organisational structure, the Asia Pacific region is frequently underrepresented or given inadequate attention. Only a limited number of Western companies have appointed board members to supervise and represent Asian operations. Often, unless the Asian perspective is championed by a

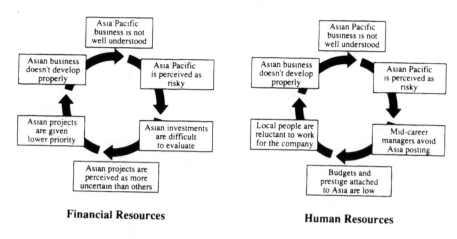

Financial Resources

Human Resources

Figure 9.1   Organisational Vicious Circles

powerful senior board member, Asian strategies fail to receive adequate attention. This in turn prevents the firm from developing Asian operations and contributes to the poor visibility of the region. The annual reports of several major public US and European firms reflect the poor visibility of the region. Western firms rarely list their percentage of sales in Asia in geographical breakdowns, lumping them instead in the 'rest of the world' category. Finally, few Western board members have ever actually served in Asia.

The first vicious circle is linked to the allocation of financial resources. Financial resource allocation is usually made through planning, budgetary and capital investment systems. For planning and budgeting, as well as capital appropriation, projects and plans are prepared at the operational level while decisions are made at higher levels. Proposals are supported by market data, sales projections, cash flow and profitability analysis. Project acceptance depends on the confidence top management has in the information provided, profitability, the payback period and personal considerations such as the profile and the reputation of the managers involved.[1] Asian-related investments are generally perceived to be more risky than comparable investments in Europe or the USA, largely due to the scarcity and perceived unreliability of data. Even when high quality information is available, as in Japan, senior managers are still uneasy about interpreting data. As a result, managers operating in Asia Pacific are often more hesitant to forecast than their colleagues in the USA or Europe. As the vice-president of a leading European firm with two plants in Japan recently indicated, 'When I present a project proposal in Japan to my board, I have to be very convincing; when my colleague from the United States presents a project, he gets it.' Very often, Asian investment is seen as a low priority and this projects an attitude which creates another vicious circle:

given the weak strategic posture of Western companies in the region and the perceived uncertainties involved in operating in Asian markets, investment projects are considered risky and only capable of producing long-term pay-offs. As a result, top managers in most Western companies, especially when they are unfamiliar with Asia, have less confidence in Asian projects than in their equivalents in Europe or the USA. Consequently, Asian projects are gradually perceived to be less important, an attitude which reinforces the weakness of the Western company. The result is a self-fulfilling prophecy where the uncertainty of future investment is reinforced by lack of support from top management.

The second vicious circle is linked to the management of human resources. Proper regional development requires the support of both local and expatriate managers who have the necessary entrepreneurial capabilities to develop successful Asian strategies, the cultural and political skills to implement them, and the internal drive needed to push projects through the maze of corporate systems and procedures. However, since the region has such relatively poor internal visibility and financial support, managers have tended to perceive it as risky for their careers and have avoided volunteering for posts there. Local graduates tend to see these Western companies as providing only limited opportunities for long-term career advancement. As a result, the overall drive and commitment of both expatriate and local managers has been weak and has led to mediocre results.

ORGANISATIONAL FACILITATORS IN ASIA PACIFIC

In order to understand how certain Western companies either perpetuate or succeed in breaking the two vicious circles, in 1992 the Euro-Asia Centre at INSEAD undertook an in-depth study of three major companies: Unilever (UK and the Netherlands), L'Oréal (France) and Wella (Germany).[2] All three companies have improved their presence in the Asia Pacific region, to different degrees and with different objectives. However, despite these differences, the similarity of approaches reveals the existence of some important facilitators for operating successfully in Asia Pacific markets. These three European companies also appear to share key organisational features that constitute an effective approach to Asia.

Five interrelated salient characteristics, called Asia Pacific facilitators, emerge (Figure 9.2). They are regional legitimisation, regional drive, corporate adaptation versus transformation, commitment through people, and informal networking.

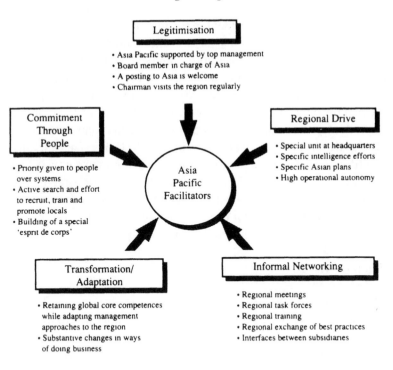

Legitimisation

- Asia Pacific supported by top management
- Board member in charge of Asia
- A posting to Asia is welcome
- Chairman visits the region regularly

Commitment Through People

- Priority given to people over systems
- Active search and effort to recruit, train and promote locals
- Building of a special 'esprit de corps'

Asia Pacific Facilitators

Regional Drive

- Special unit at headquarters
- Specific intelligence efforts
- Specific Asian plans
- High operational autonomy

Transformation/ Adaptation

- Retaining global core competences while adapting management approaches to the region
- Substantive changes in ways of doing business

Informal Networking

- Regional meetings
- Regional task forces
- Regional training
- Regional exchange of best practices
- Interfaces between subsidiaries

SOURCE: Lasserre and Butler (1993).

Figure 9.2   Asia Pacific Facilitators

Regional legitimisation

In each of the companies the emergence of an Asian strategy followed a recognition of the region's strategic importance at the centre of the firm. This process of legitimisation was not necessarily large scale, and neither did it imply a sudden miraculous enlightenment about the region, but it was a definite and conscious trend.

Unilever had always considered the region to be strategically important, but until the end of the 1970s gave it little attention in its portfolio. Investment in Asia was at best sporadic. In the 1980s, the need to globalise, combined with the recognition of Asia Pacific's growing economic importance, led to Unilever's decision to expand its presence in the region. In this case, legitimisation was followed by a reorganisation at head office to focus the group's efforts better. This was backed by a considerable investment programme which signalled to other parts of the group that the region had become a priority. This perception has been reinforced both at the centre and in the region by the frequency of subsequent visits to Asia by board members.

At L'Oréal, a change of president in the mid-1980s, and the realisation by top management that the company was walking on two global legs instead of three, led to a heavy investment programme designed to make up for the firm's past neglect of the area; this was largely a defensive response to competitors. This in turn signalled to other parts of the group that Asia Pacific had become an area of strategic importance for its top management.

For Wella, legitimisation and the emergence of an Asian strategy were the result of a search for new growth areas in the late 1960s. This led initially to the identification of Japan as an important market. A manager was sent there with the mission to make it. His success led to the centre's recognition that the country was potentially its second most important market and to the decision to relocate a corporate director to Japan. These signals had important repercussions for the company's internal recruitment policy.

Regional drive

All three companies demonstrated similar approaches. Unilever had a traditional belief in the local power of its operating subsidiaries; L'Oréal developed entrepreneurial managers called 'missionaries'; while Wella sent a newly-recruited manager to Japan to set up an operation. In all three cases the early years of business expansion were marked by a high degree of local autonomy. This gave the expatriate managers free rein to accumulate knowledge, contacts and operating experience throughout the region.

During the late 1980s, all three companies began to move away from this remote control approach towards a greater direction by the centre of their regional drive. In only one of the three cases did this drive lead to the establishment of administrative structures, or an attempt to stimulate synergies among different regional operations. Regional drive was also demonstrated by the companies' efforts to collect and disseminate information between their subsidiaries. All three carried out specific intelligence efforts in the region. For Unilever, information gathering was part of corporate procedure, but the 12 operating companies in the region were also encouraged to share intelligence, stimulated by the circulation of reports between them. There was a sense at the centre that there should be an attempt to conserve learning from past experiences and expertise by documenting the evidence, rather than losing it in the heads of expatriate managers likely to move on. L'Oréal assiduously collects information on products and competitors' moves, relying on word-of-mouth and personal contacts to pass on expertise. Wella also routinely collects information and encourages the pooling of experience at its home training centre.

Adaptation versus transformation

During the interviews undertaken as part of the 1992 survey, a manager stated: 'One problem that all our divisions face is the degree of difference in the Asian markets that should be taken into consideration when formulating their strategies. Are these differences of substance or of context?' This represents the dilemma between simple adaptation or a complete change in strategic thinking and approach. All three companies were able to balance the need to retain their global core competence while transforming approaches at the regional level. At Unilever, for example, the chairman of the Hong Kong subsidiary found that in China the evolution of the market did not correspond to any of the norms or graphs normally used to predict future products and sales. These results caused the centre to break with its traditions, re-evaluate its marketing strategy and reinterpret data.

One important aspect of this problem is the conflict between global integration and local autonomy. How should the company manage the balance of power between the manager who focuses on country strategy and the global manager who looks at broader product strategy? The three companies studied began with decentralised operations, where the autonomy of the local chief executives meant products were adapted to local market needs in a way which was later perceived to be excessive. In part the reasons for this *laissez-faire* approach were historic, but they also reflected the prevailing ignorance about Asia at the centres, which tended to focus their attentions on the more familiar European and North American markets.

Market adaptation was carried to the greatest extreme at Unilever, which was very much locally-led. Since the late 1980s, the company has modified its approach and has moved away from its tradition of extreme local autonomy. For example, there is an attempt to create personal products with a South-East Asian concept and then adapt this marginally for other countries in the region.

The experience of these companies indicates that Asian strategies call for both substantive and contextual adaptation, at least in a learning phase. However, this must take place in such a way that the company is not forced to abandon its core technological competence. Such a balance is difficult to achieve and cannot be codified into a set of procedures; in the words of one of the managers, it has to be 'people-processed' rather than 'system-processed', and requires a high degree of flexibility both at the centre and in the field.

Commitment through people

In all three cases, Asia Pacific strategies were formulated to create a body of committed people rather than elaborate marketing plans. This did not preclude rigorous market surveys or thorough product testing, but these activities were already considered routine practice. What was unusual and crucial, however, was the ability to build a corps of talented, competent managers who could generate local initiatives without diluting the corporate identity. Here a distinction must be made between the internal recruitment of home-grown managers, sent out on three- to five-year postings to Asia, and the recruitment, training and promotion of local managers to maintain continuity.

The central issue of expatriate management – how many and for how long? – is one that all three companies found difficult to resolve. In the early stages of their growth in Asia, the problem lay in finding managers of the required calibre. For human resource managers in all three companies, the ability to recruit high flyers only followed the company's legitimisation of Asia and its recognition as an important posting for expatriate managers. In none of the cases was there a specific recruitment policy for the region, or any difference in reward and evaluation criteria. In all three companies, Asia is now considered a good ladder for career advancement, and ex-Asia hands are now increasingly visible among top management.

As the businesses of these three companies developed, management began to focus more on the problem of local managers. All three preferred to reduce their dependence on expatriate managers and improve their ability to attract and retain skilled local managers; this was seen as crucial for sustained performance and future growth in the region. When Wella's first Asia director began to build the business in Japan, he made the assembly of a local team one of his earliest priorities. He now attributes the success of the business to his ability to recruit such a force.

Since 1991, Unilever has offered special training programmes to attract skilled local managers. Its Hong Kong subsidiary has made a special effort to develop as many Mandarin speakers as possible and '*roll them through China*' in the hope of building a pool of Chinese managers for the future. At L'Oréal, corporate '*missionaries*' are given the task of recruiting and training local people.

In the long term, an important factor in the struggle to retain managers will be their visibility in top management. Two contingent issues are the training and development of these local managers, and the implications of their promotion for each company's corporate culture. Although all three companies say they would like to promote local managers to the highest levels, Unilever, L'Oréal and Wella have very strong corporate cultures and operate on networks of personal contacts and a shared European style of doing business. At Unilever there now seems to be a general acceptance within the company that the club style must change, and that Asian managers must be encouraged to '*do it their way*'.

The Asian director for Wella, while distrusting any tendency to go native, also believes that companies must build a different, hybrid corporate culture between Europe and Asia. L'Oréal, on the other hand, is determined to maintain the purity of its own culture, and believes it can only succeed by having managers who are '*true men of the company*', steeped in its particular strategic logic. It expects its local managers to be '*vaccinated*' in this culture first by being missionary-trained, and afterwards through indoctrination training courses in France.

Informal networking

None of the three companies has sought to apply a single or standard approach to the operations of all its subsidiaries in the region. Subsidiaries have opted for varying degrees of local autonomy, ranging from countries which operate independently to a system of regional strategies, products and management. This is a natural stage in the businesses' evolution. As they grow and the companies' presence expands, there is a search for synergies and opportunities for cross-fertilisation in order to reduce costs and increase regional muscle. This trend has already been demonstrated with regard to products, and it also applies to the sharing of human and financial resources.

Such a move is presaged by attempts at informal networking between the subsidiaries in the region. The role of these informal networks is to achieve synergies without building layers of bureaucracy and to create and reinforce a regional identity.

Unilever, which of the three companies studied has been longest in Asia, has made the most progress towards the creation of synergies, something which is viewed as a departure from its traditional manner of running regional operations. Unilever's various subsidiaries now concentrate on stimulating a multicountry approach, to get more push behind products or better resource allocation. The company's regional strategy has two key elements: task forces, which play an important role in the transfer of know-how and experience from one subsidiary to another, and the regional mobility of senior, product and marketing managers, who meet regularly to exchange information.

The change has been reinforced by top management, which is receiving more information to be analysed and later used for benchmarking. Another dimension has been the move to stimulate the adoption of 'best practices' throughout the region. At the same time, the increased emphasis on group-wide coordination is a further blow to the traditional local autonomies. The company is 'struggling to take a regional view'. As the country barriers crumble, the central group has actively applied a multicountry approach to organisation and management.

Comparisons and conclusions are made and transmitted via the network. Wella already had a tradition of strong regional coordination through regular regional conferences, and this has continued under the latest director, who hopes to coordinate the marketing of products in the different countries of the region from his Tokyo base.

THE EFFECT OF GLOBALISATION ON ASIAN OPERATIONS

During the 1980s, many multinational corporations moved to a global approach in managing their operations. This shift profoundly affected the way companies managed their international networks; while some had previously used the traditional system of a multicountry federation of subsidiaries, others had experimented with matrix organisations. In both cases the move towards globalisation shifted the power structure from one of geographical hierarchy to one which favoured the managers in charge of global businesses. This move, known as globalisation, was counterbalanced by the need for companies to be flexible enough to adapt their strategies to local conditions. This dual strategic requirement, the global/local tension, was widely discussed in the academic and management literature of the 1980s and led to the emergence of different management models,[3] as illustrated in Figure 9.3.

Against this background, multinational companies have become increasingly divided in their views on regional management. Some have retained or built their regional headquarters in parallel with global products organisations, while others have assigned the supervision of regions to key corporate level executives. Still others have delegated regional management to the global products divisions, hence creating several regional centres within the same corporation.

The management of Asian operations is obviously very much affected by these transformations. However, it rapidly becomes obvious (even to the most global-minded manager) that the sheer heterogeneity, strategic distance and specificity of the Asia Pacific competitive climate requires a regional perspective to enable companies to gather intelligence, mobilise forces and focus their energies in the region. Throughout this book we argue that the Asia Pacific region is both strategically important and contextually different. In order to succeed, one needs to develop some sort of regional perspective. But adapting a structure is not good enough, because the essence of

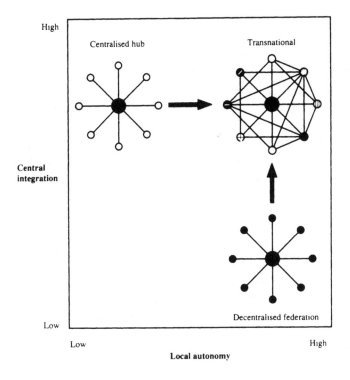

SOURCE: Bartlett and Ghoshal (1989).

Figure 9.3 Global and Local Structures in Multinational Corporations

management problems in Asia Pacific lies in the breeding of attitudes as well as the enhancing of specific competences, such as the building of relationships, which are the result not so much of organisational structures but rather of internal processes. The experiences of Unilever, L'Oréal and Wella suggest that commitment, attitudes and information sharing are important ingredients of success. None of these is due to formal structures or systems but to the way decisions are made, how priorities are set, how investments are approved and implemented, the manner in which information is gathered and distributed, how manpower is recruited, trained and promoted, how control is exercised and, finally, how strategies are debated and formulated.

Four processes require particular attention: strategy formulation and budgeting processes, people management, evaluation processes and learning processes. Of these four, people management processes are so important for the success of companies in Asia that a full chapter is devoted to them and therefore the discussion of their many aspects is contained in Chapter 10.

Strategy formulation and budgeting

Strategy formulation consists of translating strategic ambition into actions requiring specific allocation of financial and human resources. To do this, a variety of tasks must be performed. On an analytical level, these include structuring and interpreting information, forecasting and calculating possible outcomes, generating alternatives, designing sets of choices and militating internally to obtain acceptance and resources. In a multinational corporation, this process takes place at three levels: the business level, the country level and the corporate level. Three main factors militate in favour of a regional perspective in strategy formulation. First is the region's rapidly changing business climate, and second, the strategic distance of the marketing and competitive climates. This can lead to significant delays in the time it takes for global managers to grasp the importance of events there. Companies cannot afford to disregard the importance of grey imports from one country to another, or to ignore the ramifications of the shifts in the Overseas Chinese family network across the region, or to underestimate the potential benefits of an ASEAN joint venture. Third, the fragmented nature of the different markets makes it difficult for country managers to sell their ideas to executives at the centre.

It is therefore important that a regional strategy tying together the various country strategies should be elaborated. There are a number of ways in which this can be achieved: through the formulation of a regional strategic plan, consolidating country and product strategies and presenting them in a coordinated way to corporate headquarters; through the systematic addition of a regional plan to global product plans; through the scheduling of regional strategic meetings where global product managers meet with regional executives and confront their own global plans with specific local requirements; and through the establishment of a review and appeal process by regional managers for global product plans before they are finalised at corporate level.

The resource allocation process which translates into budgets for capital (capital budgeting) and operating budgets is normally well codified in companies. Planning and budgeting procedures define the criteria for capital investment approval and set out the rules for budget preparation. In multinational corporations, rules and procedures tend to be standardised and the criteria by which projects and plans are evaluated and approved tend to be the same for every product line and country. If no corrective element is brought in to adjust for specific regional characteristics, there is a risk of considerable bias in the allocation of resources. This is particularly true in the Asia Pacific region, where the business environment is often perceived as more risky than in the USA or Europe, with a long-term pay-off and a strong need to spend time and effort on building relationships. Research on several companies in the region shows a strong resistance to adapting rules and procedures, but in practice they exhibit a nuanced perspective when it comes to allocating resources.[4] What counts is the overall Asian ambition of the corporation and also the power of the executives in charge of Asia. However, as we argue consistently in this book, with the multiplicity of opportunities arising from the region, corporations need to establish a different perspective from the one they adopt in their Western markets when it comes to making decisions about investing in Asia Pacific.

Evaluation processes

The classical criteria for evaluating business performance do not always reflect the peculiarities of Asian environments. For instance, a quick marketing success may be a good yardstick for evaluating a marketing manager in Europe or the USA but may be totally inappropriate to the Asia Pacific region, where business cultures often require a gradual acquisition of a network of contacts before a company can expect to see progress reflected in sales. Political and negotiation skills as well as the ability to develop team work and to recruit and motivate local staff are more relevant criteria than return on business assets. The argument here is not that managers should neglect return on assets but that if one focuses and rewards people only on this criterion one is unlikely to build a base for long-term success. To mention one example, Merlin Gerin, the French producer of electrical equipment, set up a joint venture in Tianjin in 1987. In 1990, the company was doing very poorly and on the basis of return criteria should have closed. Today it is working very profitably and growing. A similar example can be found in the Xian-Janssen joint venture in the pharmaceutical sector in China or the Bell-Shanghai Telecom operation.

Learning processes

For Western managers, the experience of doing business in Asia and the lessons learned are assimilated on an individual level. The problem for Western firms is that because these managers are highly mobile, their knowledge of Asia and Asian enterprise cultures is often difficult to institutionalise and retain. The challenge for Western firms operating in Asia is to find concrete structures for translating individual experience and knowledge and incorporating it into a continuing process of organisational learning and renewal. To cite just a few examples of successful methods: certain Western firms have found it useful to prepare videos on Asian corporate culture, or to circulate case studies on their firm's experiences in Asia. Another way to conserve organisational learning is to ensure a better handover between expatriates and their successors, so that the expertise of experienced Asia hands is recycled and institutionalised. After expatriate managers are moved back to headquarters they should be debriefed, and asked to share and pass on their Asia Pacific experience in some way.

REGIONAL HEADQUARTERS

Many multinational corporations have established regional headquarters (RHQs) in Asia Pacific. The motivation was either that the region was becoming too complex, too large and too far away to be handled from corporate headquarters, or that it was too different from other parts of the world.

In contrast to other investment decisions, the establishment of an RHQ by the MNCs is rarely preceded by in-depth analysis, but often based on the gut feel of the president or other senior managers. Alternatively, a team may be sent to the region to carry out some trouble-shooting, later evolving into a permanent institution with RHQ status. Such 'ad hoc-ism' is probably attributable to the limited initial capital outlays involved, which simplifies internal approval procedures. In most cases, however, the decision is driven by very ambitious strategies for the region which need to be implemented with the help of an RHQ. This desire must be strong at a time of de-layering and lean management in many corporations. The lack of planning may be one reason why so many RHQs either have failed or been dissolved, or have been restructured.

Regional headquarters actively manage integration and coordination across the region, and provide a link with the corporate centre. In this respect they differ from a representative office, a holding company set up for fiscal reasons, or a regional organisational unit that provides services and a regional infrastructure on behalf of headquarters. Companies typically set up a RHQ when they feel that the benefits of regional integration are greater than the costs of setting up an additional organisational unit and those associated with the loss of independence (and responsiveness) for national units. These costs and benefits, however, are often difficult or impossible to measure.

This may be one of the other explanations why RHQs of Western MNCs in Asia have such a chequered track record and are largely unstable organisational phenomena. Of 15 RHQs surveyed in 1994/5, the majority had undergone a dramatic change in their regional organisation. Only a small number had not seen a substantial change.[5] The number of RHQs playing a truly managerial role is still low, but increasing. Most of the larger, diversified MNCs with substantial operations in Asia have such an RHQ already established.

The role of regional headquarters

Regional headquarters have two main sets of roles:

- strategy development and implementation, which are directed towards headquarters: budgeting and control, strategic stimulation, intelligence gathering, new business development, and more generally providing a channel for demands from local operations, and ensuring attention from headquarters in competition with other regions;
- integrative, administrative roles more directly involved with local operations: pooling resources for greater efficiency and effectiveness; benchmarking and spreading best practices; coordinating activities across borders and business divisions. The aim here is to achieve synergies and consistency.[6]

The role of regional managers is frequently challenged at other levels in the company by corporate, business, functional and national unit managers who feel that their power to influence their specific territory has been curtailed (Figure 9.4):

- corporate managers fear that the region may go astray and therefore try to keep the RHQ in line with other parts of the world;
- business managers argue that product specific knowledge counts more than regional market know-how;
- functional managers believe that their expertise is best leveraged across the world without any modification;
- national unit managers maintain that their specific market is different, and is best left alone.

To overcome resistance from the various stakeholders, some Western MNCs have decided to assign very senior executives to head their RHQs. In ABB, Otis, Raychem, Schindler, Unilever and Volkswagen main board members have been appointed to manage the RHQ. Other MNCs have despatched managers just one level below the board to direct the regional activities. Data show that where less senior managers are transferred to the RHQ, they tend to be less effective.[7]

The organisation of regional headquarters

Both the leverage and the effectiveness of an RHQ depend on its organisation. It is often a reflection of the organisation at headquarters and consists of two

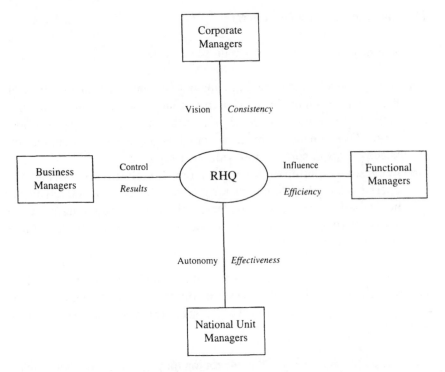

Figure 9.4   Stakeholders in RHQs

aspects, that is, the structure in terms of formal linkages specifically between the RHQ and HQ, and the managerial approaches or styles applied to the relationship between the RHQ and the subsidiaries.

Organisational structure

The *global RHQ* is characterised by a strong alliance of its staff with the headquarters. This alliance is influenced by the dominant mind-set in the MNC; the commitment of the head of the RHQ; and by the emotional attachment, the bonus system and/or career opportunities of the regional staff. Global RHQs tend to be in charge of a limited number of global businesses and report to a senior manager who is responsible for these businesses on a world-wide basis. The RHQ can therefore be considered as an extension of the corporate HQ, set up for the purpose of convenience in order to be in easier reach of the subsidiaries in the region. It is staffed primarily by managers dispatched from HQ, who see themselves as enforcers and controllers.

While the dominant organisational logic of the MNC is that of global businesses, the RHQ introduces a further, though secondary, geographic dimension. Within its domain the RHQ will undertake the coordination of functional activities such as finance and human resource management, and can represent headquarters in board meetings of the subsidiaries and during discussions with governments. It will, however, be less involved in synergy development between different businesses. It will also be relatively weak in representing regional concerns at headquarters.

The advantage of the global RHQ lies in its simplicity: the organisation is streamlined and focused. The managers involved basically believe in the credo that the similarities of the markets are greater than the differences and, thus, pursue efficiency. To make it work, and to avoid ambiguity and overlapping responsibilities, a clear allocation of tasks between the centre, the region and the local subsidiaries is needed. In the case of Seagram, for example, sales are driven by the local subsidiaries, prices are set by the RHQ, and brands are managed at the HQ level.

There are three problems associated with the global RHQ. First, while tasks can be allocated across the three levels of the MNC in a flexible manner, there may be a tendency to accumulate too much power and influence at the centre (normally at the HQ, but not necessarily so), downgrading the role of regional and national managers to implementors. This can lead to demotivation, and the loss of local initiative and reduced feedback from the region.

Secondly, the global bias will influence career patterns and human resource management policies. Regional managers will try to please their peer group, which consists of managers representing the businesses. Regional managers taking a regional perspective or managers without the backing of such a peer group at home have fewer career opportunities and will consequently either underperform or leave. Loyalties to the head of the RHQ to whom managers in the region may officially report can be weak when, in case of conflicts of interest, the globally operating businesses represented at HQ take the final decision. Disciplinary and actual reporting lines therefore diverge. Figure 9.5 shows the power structure of a typical global RHQ with only dotted lines going to the head of the RHQ.

Thirdly, the reduced friction between businesses due to the streamlining of the organisation along business lines may generate fewer contacts, less mutual interest and less commonality between the different product divisions. Synergies within the region in these circumstances become almost impossible to achieve, and opportunities for cost sharing (such as using a common infrastructure) are limited. There is even the danger that a confusing picture is presented towards governments, partners and customers.

The attractions of a simplified organisational structure in a large MNC nevertheless remain high. It can be ideal in a situation where local subsidiaries have for a long time existed independently without much control and interest

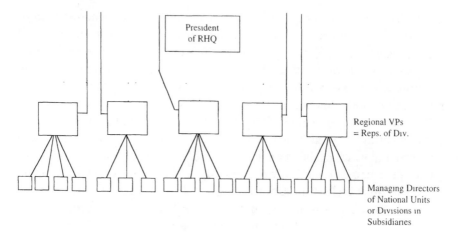

Figure 9.5   The Global RHQ

from HQ. However, a global RHQ seems best suited to MNCs with a limited product portfolio and a corporate culture which allows for the clear delineation of tasks within the organisation.

The staff of a *transnational RHQ* feels a strong commitment towards corporate HQ and considers that pressures for the globalisation of businesses are legitimate. At the same time there is recognition that the characteristics of the region distinguish it from other regions and that an appropriate approach is required. The transnational RHQ is therefore a prototype of an organisation exposed to tensions arising from the dual pressures for integration and responsiveness, but operating at the regional rather than the global level. It is, however, not only the RHQ as an organisational unit that has to balance the pressures brought to bear by both the HQ and the operating units in the region, but also the individual regional manager who is asked to be a 'glocaliser' (that is, global + local manager) with regional responsibility.

For practical reasons the transnational RHQ has to have an organisational structure which allows both the global and local forces to exert influence on decision-making at the regional level. The matrix organisation offers such a structure, with geographical concerns represented by sub-regions or countries and business concerns by product divisions or strategic business units (SBUs), as shown in Figure 9.6. Despite all the criticism vented against it, the matrix remains widely used at present by companies such as BASF.

The matrix structure can be used very flexibly. Only those product divisions and SBUs which are important should be represented. They can be added to or dropped from the matrix without any difficulty. Individual countries can be grouped together in sub-regions according to common interests and char-

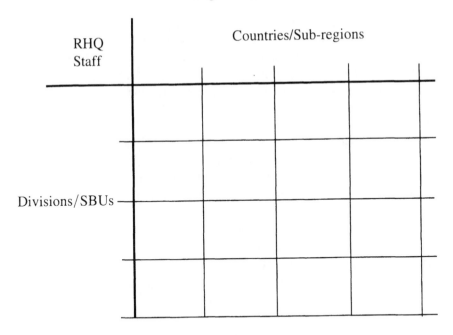

Figure 9.6 The Transnational RHQ

acteristics. To fulfil the role of arbiter and buffer, the core of the RHQ staff
has functional responsibilities, with the head of the RHQ ideally coming from
a neutral background, that is, also from a functional area.

The advantages of the transnational RHQ operating through a matrix
organisation are obvious. It serves as a regional forum where conflicting
interests can be brought together for negotiation and solution. Over time, this
experience leads to better understanding and a common spirit within the region.
Synergies are possible between the businesses and the countries as well as
across businesses and countries. When sufficient delegation takes place at
HQ, the transnational RHQ emerges as a powerful organisational unit where
decisions for the region are made without recourse to HQ.

However, the experience with matrix organisations in general is not wholly
satisfactory. Trade-offs have to be made, and these may be difficult to achieve
in the absence of adequate data or a sound accounting system. Balancing
pressures can degenerate into horse-trading on the one hand or stalemates
on the other when the interests of individual managers are influenced by one-
sided incentive schemes or reward systems. At the extreme, collegial
cooperation may turn into adversarial relationships. Such shortcomings can,
however, be overcome with experienced and disciplined managers.

A second drawback of the transnational RHQ relates to the tendency to create a large, if not overblown, regional organisation in order to accommodate all interested parties. In the extreme case an existing matrix at HQ level is simply replicated in the region, an arrangement which will not be well received in times of lean management and de-layering. Only restraint and cost consciousness can keep organisational growth under control, once it has started.

Bearing in mind its advantages and disadvantages, the transnational RHQ emerges as a suitable model for large, experienced and diversified MNCs with mature regional managers. Through its flexible structure, it admits a multitude of perspectives, and maintains the balance between global and local needs without allowing one to dominate the other.

The *multi-domestic RHQ* operates in a geographical environment which is perceived to be different from other parts of the world. The staff of the RHQ feels strongly committed to the region and obliged to fight for the region or defend it against pressures for globalisation originating from HQ.

The multi-domestic RHQ acts as a representative body of the operating units in the region and of their concerns. It therefore relies heavily on consensus between them and on their support. Its main purpose is to amplify the views of these local subsidiaries, which individually are too small to carry much weight at HQ.

The advantage of this particular RHQ model lies in the devotion of the managers to the cause of the region. The organisation chart as depicted in Figure 9.7 shows the unambiguous nature of relationships, though weak dotted lines back to the businesses at headquarters may exist. Establishing linkages between the operating units and achieving synergies between the different businesses will be easier than in global RHQs as long as regional staff can convey the message that cooperation works to the benefit of the entire region. Regional managers act as advocates for the region and as mentors and supporters for the national units in the region. Ideally, the staff working in a multi-domestic RHQ will include managers from the region or at least expatriates with a long track record in the region.

The single-mindedness of this model of RHQ makes it vulnerable and could, in the extreme case, lead to its own undoing. Vulnerability stems from the need to represent the whole region, that is, all national units and all businesses. Where certain businesses in the region follow a more global logic due to technological or competitive pressures, friction with the other businesses may arise. Similarly, individual country units may outgrow the need for support from a mentor and develop a preference for directly representing their case at HQ. This has tended to happen with the Japanese operations of Western MNCs which do not like to report to an RHQ but prefer a direct rapport with

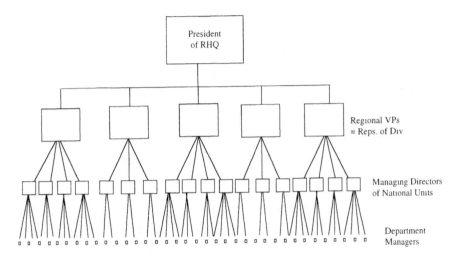

Figure 9.7 The Multi-domestic RHQ

HQ. Similarly China holding companies, which pool MNCs' ever-increasing numbers of joint ventures in the country, already represent an intermediate layer between the local unit and HQ, and they do not want to report through another layer such as an RHQ.

Strong advocacy of regional concerns may also lead to a view of the world which is too one-sided and therefore not in the overall interest of the MNC. Such a single-mindedness risks antagonising those corporate managers for whom the region in question represents only one part of the world and who are in favour of a more standardised approach to markets as a means of reducing complexity. Too strong a push on behalf of the region can give rise to negative consequences, whether the isolation of the RHQ, or its dismantling in order to re-establish an equilibrium between the region concerned and the rest of the organisation.

The multi-domestic RHQ is a suitable model for an MNC needing to build a closer network in the region and win more recognition at HQ. It may be ideal for MNCs in which the region is not yet fully positioned on the mental map of the world or is still considered peripheral. The structure has the potential of creating a strong organisational unit in the corporation.

Managerial approaches

Whichever organisational structure of the RHQ is chosen, there is still flexibility in the way an MNC decides to manage the relationship between the RHQ and the subsidiaries. The decision is, however, not entirely without constraints. First, to some extent, the determination of a specific structure limits the choice of how to manage. Second, even when MNCs are just in the process of establishing and managing an RHQ, they rarely start with a blank sheet of paper as far as their regional activities are concerned. A corporate history already exists, as do traditionally grown management practices and a certain style of management which has been consciously or unconsciously adopted in the past. All of these issues will have an impact on the first actions of a new RHQ and the expectations of the subsidiaries.

The RHQ can manage its relationship with the national units in three distinct ways. The *vertical RHQ* model is based on the idea that direction and control of all activities in the region are derived from the RHQ as an organisational unit. The relationship between RHQ and local units is strictly hierarchical. The RHQ is the only unit in the region with authority and there are no direct links between national units and headquarters.

Theoretically, in this model the region is treated as if it were a single country operation, such as in the US, where separate local units have no autonomy and function as cost centres with their accounts consolidated at the centre. In practice, such treatment is impossible due to the existence of national legislation and to the requirement that managers in charge of national units take care of the concerns of other stakeholders such as local employees and their unions, national governments and their demands for payment of taxes, customers and suppliers, and outside shareholders.

The reporting lines drawn are clear and leave no room for ambiguity. This is the greatest advantage of the vertical RHQ. However, as discussed in the context of the structural model of a global and a multi-domestic RHQ, regional vice-presidents (VPs) can be in charge of businesses or countries/sub-regions, eventually even of functions. This raises the immediate issue of double reporting lines at the departmental level in the national units for functional and business managers, who are subordinate both to the director of the national units and to a regional VP of a specific function or business.

Nevertheless, organisational complexity is limited, enabling the MNC to take difficult decisions relatively easily when competing interests are at stake. This applies particularly to MNCs in capital intensive industries in which resource allocation and the need to rationalise manufacturing operations across the region are dominant issues. Similarly, clear reporting lines may be of advantage in fast moving industries when MNCs are exposed to regional competitors.

The disadvantages of the vertical RHQ are embedded in the classical centralisation-decentralisation dilemma. Too much centralisation strangles local initiative and entrepreneurship, while too much decentralisation leads to inefficiencies and a loss of control. The dangers of demotivation are particularly critical as managers in the national units tend to be local managers, while those in the RHQ are mainly expatriates. Any power dispute can, thus, deteriorate into emotional arguments between locals and expatriates, with all the attendant consequences on local recruitment, alienation of staff, and the ability of the MNC to become an insider.

To avoid such risks a very clear delineation of tasks and responsibilities between the various levels of the hierarchy has to be observed. This requires rules, procedures and management information systems, and an awareness of the dangers of the stifling effects of too much bureaucracy in the organisation. Certain tasks can remain under the responsibility of the national units within agreed budgets and policies. Other activities should be kept under the exclusive domain of the RHQ, such as regional manufacturing or research and development, central warehousing, or key account management. Managers of these activities will report directly to the vertical RHQ independent of their location.

The second model, that of the *virtual RHQ*, relies on input from national units. It does not, however, exist as a separate organisational unit with its own office and dedicated staff. The responsibilities and functions of the traditional RHQ are distributed to existing national units. As such, the RHQ continues to fulfil its tasks, though only in a conceptual sense through the activities of dispersed local/regional managers.

In the virtual RHQ, some local managers have taken over regional tasks in addition to their jobs in the given country and are therefore connected with all other units. These tasks carry responsibility for certain functional or business activities in countries other than their own, while the regional responsibility for some of the activities in their own national unit is carried by a local/regional manager from another country.

The proper functioning of the virtual RHQ depends on a number of conditions which are primarily related to the managers concerned and the corporate culture in which they work.

1. Managers must be competent and willing to carry out both local and regional tasks. They must also have enough time at their disposal to manage the two functions, a rather unlikely situation when local operations are run on the basis of lean management and regional tasks are demanding.
2. Managers must be mentally flexible and less concerned with the trappings of status. Hierarchies in the virtual RHQ are structured along tasks, not traditional seniority. In their regional function they will be in charge of certain aspects of the activities of their colleagues. On the other hand they will have to accept that certain parts of their own local activities are subordinated to other colleagues who may be their juniors in terms of status.

3. Managers with regional responsibilities must be willing and able to cooperate closely with each other, and they must subscribe fully to a corporate culture which values open and informal information sharing, long-term commitment and trust. Otherwise the difficulties of communicating across distances cannot be overcome and a traditional (physical) RHQ will not be replaced.

4. Local/regional managers must be able to live in a state of ambiguous accountability, although a certain degree of clarity can be introduced, as in the case of the horizontal RHQ.

Even if managers can comply with all these conditions, other problems remain. Communication and cooperation among the local/regional managers of a virtual RHQ takes place in an international, multicultural environment. Misunderstandings are bound to happen and can create havoc.

Conflicts of interest among the managers concerned are also difficult to solve within the framework of a virtual RHQ. The absence of a head as in the traditional RHQ set-up can be compensated for by the appointment of one of the local/regional managers as the regional representative. Power may also be given to the representative to solve conflicts in the region. Alternatively, major disagreements have to be brought to the attention of senior management at headquarters with a request for a decision from that level. This, however, is not in the spirit of the model which is based on the input of the region alone.

The non-existence of a physical RHQ office may also raise doubts about the commitment of the MNC to the region, with regard both to external contacts such as governments and partners, and to the internal organisation. The declaration of a *de facto* RHQ attached to a national unit carries limited credibility and undermines the idea of the virtual RHQ in the eyes of the other national units.

To overcome these difficulties of the virtual RHQ some companies have started to set up a small RHQ as a physical unit mainly staffed with functional managers, and to surround them with managers carrying both regional and other responsibilities. These 'double-hatted' managers are, however, not located at the RHQ. The lines between RHQ and subsidiaries becomes blurred through this concurrence of interests of two organisational levels which often tend to be in conflict with each other.

The term 'double-hatting' was probably coined by BP when it introduced such a system at the beginning of the 1990s. The MNC decided then that all managers should belong to profit centres, and that almost all purely staff functions would be eliminated. The resulting cost savings were significant but, more importantly, people began to find it easier to understand and

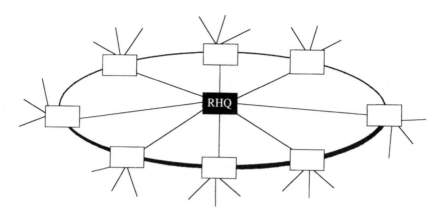

Figure 9.8   The Horizontal RHQ

appreciate each other's point of view. Wearing two hats became synonymous with having two perspectives, a welcome development in the MNC. Henkel adopted this system with the appointment of the senior head of their local Malaysian operations to a major regional responsibility without asking him to join the RHQ physically.

Overall, a semi-virtual RHQ with blurred lines leads to a flatter hierarchy through the combination of local and regional functions. It is appreciated by managers in favour of taking on more responsibilities and those in charge of reducing overheads.

Similar to the virtual RHQ, the *horizontal RHQ* is primarily driven by the will of the national units. The system operates on a consensus basis, with the authority of the RHQ dependent to some extent on the national units. The horizontal RHQ maintains the integrity of the national units, while at the same time unifying their activities for the common objectives of the region. It allows the local directors to become local barons or local heroes, while moderating their individualism through mechanisms which demand collegial approval and enforce close cooperation.

Figure 9.8 shows the model of the horizontal RHQ. The box in the centre representing the RHQ is purposely drawn to the same size as that of the national units, signifying the dispersion of the centre throughout the region. Everything else being equal, the size of an RHQ of the horizontal model should be smaller than that of the vertical type.

There are several ways to organise the horizontal RHQ. They basically differ from each other by the degree to which the RHQ as organisational unit still holds power and influence over the national units. Table 9.1 outlines three types of horizontal RHQs and their characteristics.

Table 9.1   Types of Horizontal RHQs

Type of regional organisation	Objective	Decision-making	Role of RHQ
Debate club	Consensus building	Non-binding	Stimulating
Committee	Use of regional expertise	Recommendation	Final decision
Council	Distribution of RHQ's power	Joint decisions	*Primus inter pares*

In its weakest form – the debate club – managers from the region are occasionally brought together for meetings during which information is exchanged and attempts are made to reach a consensus among participants over major decisions. Executive power, however, remains with the RHQ. The role of the RHQ in this type of model is to take initiatives and stimulate the debate.

This arrangement contributes positively to the development of a common purpose and a strong team spirit. Yet it can also backfire and demotivate national unit managers when meetings are misused to impose on the audience decisions already taken, rather than to discuss new ideas with them. This is often the case in annual regional meetings which bring together corporate board members, divisional heads, RHQ staff and local managers. On these occasions senior managers seem to 'descend' on the region to spread the gospel, but not to listen.

The second type relies primarily on committees, task forces and project teams which are charged with clearly defined responsibilities, or with solving specific problems. Functional committees, for example, could be concerned with the coordination of regional research and development activities, and task forces with the development of rules for transfer pricing or the analysis of a new business opportunity for the region. Otis uses committees extensively and calls them pan-regional forums. Similarly, Unilever's senior managers in the region meet regularly to work on marketing or investment problems. Membership of these groups is designed in a flexible manner and brings together managers from both the RHQ and the national units. Their work will result in recommendations to the RHQ.

The formation of regional councils represents the third type of horizontal RHQ. A limited number of senior managers from the national units, as a rule the managing directors of the largest operating units, are coopted in a more formalised way by the RHQ to join the head of the RHQ and the regional VPs in a decision-making body. The head of the RHQ acts as the chairman of that council and therefore carries substantial weight. Raychem has introduced such a regional council in Asia.

The presence on the regional council of managers from the national units forces the RHQ to be more responsive to their needs. Equally, once they perceive the regional as well as the local perspective, managers from the national units in the council may give up unreasonable opposition to measures which threaten to have a negative impact on their operations, but serve the whole of the region well.

The horizontal RHQ model relies on a bottom-up system and a more participative style of management. It will therefore be more attractive to MNCs whose senior managers have no difficulties with sharing power and where the diversified nature of the businesses requires a high degree of coordination among them. MNCs with a concentrated power structure and stand-alone businesses which do not rely on synergies between them will feel better served by the managerial style of the vertical RHQ.

Unfortunately, within the same MNC, what is the ideal organisational solution for one business may be less acceptable for another. There are two ways to handle diverging interests. The obvious solution is to allow the dominant business to determine the way the RHQ is run since it will normally be carrying the costs. The disadvantage of this course of action is that it may prevent the smaller businesses from succeeding, thereby perpetuating the leadership of the larger business. Alternatively, the RHQ could allow the various businesses sufficient room to achieve a fit for themselves, with the provision that a certain degree of commonality in organisational features remains to foster integration. This may, however, result in complex and cumbersome solutions which turn out to be very costly. Unilever, for example, ran its chemical division on a global basis without the intermediary of an RHQ, while its main businesses (detergents, toiletries and food) were organised regionally. Rhône-Poulenc and ICI have separate RHQs for their various businesses, and not all of them are physically located in the same countries of the region.

Boundaries and location

The first move towards regionalisation and establishing regional headquarters is to decide how many regions a multinational firm will need to manage global operations. Most MNCs have adopted a 'triadic' structure – Europe, Asia, the Americas – complemented by a fourth region which covers their home market. They usually adopt a pragmatic attitude in defining the boundaries of these regions, and distances and transportation links apparently matter more than political linkages and cultural similarities.

In almost all Western MNCs the region 'Asia' comprises Asia Pacific as defined in this book and Australia and New Zealand. It is the extension to the West where MNCs differ in their interpretation of Asia. Heineken's Asian region represents the broadest scope and even includes Israel. For several other MNCs the Asian territory reaches as far as Pakistan. Most European MNCs now include India in the region, though not all are committed whole-heartedly. Several of them are starting to explore this market more seriously under the leadership of their Asian RHQs, but are uncertain whether to group this large country together with the other countries in the Asian region, or to create a new region called 'South and Central Asia'. Both BP and Unilever exclude India from the ambit of their Asian region due to long-standing special relationships between national units and their headquarters.

The more broadly the region is defined, the more urgent is the question of whether one single RHQ can do justice to the increasing variations in the region, and is able to exercise such a span of control. The answer is in the affirmative, at least in the sense that Western MNCs try to operate on the basis of one Asia. Some MNCs, like BASF, have however introduced sub-regions that then need to be coordinated, most likely by a board member. The cost of managing this additional complexity has to be weighed against the potential costs of losing specificity and control.

Western MNCs in Asia are exposed to a further issue, namely the inclusion of Japan today or, in future, other major countries like China and India in a region otherwise consisting of small and medium-sized countries. Discussion of the issue is difficult due to the often strong desire of the representative of a major country to follow a different strategy than the other countries and to report directly to headquarters rather than first to the RHQ.

This is more prominent in the case of Japan. The country's own identity and status as the region's economic leader poses a serious obstacle to its inclusion in a RHQ. The Japanese consider, with some reason, that to group them with the other developing South-East Asian countries in the region would be tantamount, in European terms, to grouping France with Hungary, or any of the other former Eastern bloc countries. In the same context, a large subsidiary in Japan reporting to an RHQ in Hong Kong or Singapore would be comparable with a US operation reporting to the Bahamas or Barbados.

To reach an effective solution to the problem, two points must be taken into consideration. The first concerns the extent to which the specific country business is related to the region. Factors to take into account include, among others, differences in technical standards and the presence of regional customers. Secondly, the importance of the country operation itself for the global success or overall competitiveness of the MNC has to be determined.

The matrix in Figure 9.9 takes the example of Japan and describes the effect of its inclusion in or exclusion from an MNC's Asian regional organisation.

In the case of a close relationship between the country activities and the region, the units in Japan should be included in the region and be used either

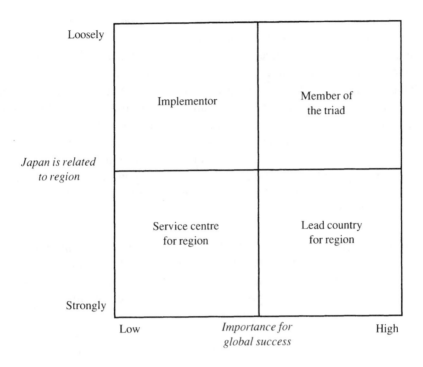

Figure 9.9 The Role of Japan in Asia

as service centres or to lead operations which depend on the overall importance of Japan. Both IBM and P&G have chosen the latter solution and rely on their Japanese subsidiaries continually to create new ideas and products. If the local units in Japan are only loosely connected with Asia and are less important for the MNC's global success, they can be dealt with on a case-by-case basis. No strong argument speaks in favour of or against their inclusion in the region. However, when Japan is important, for example due to its market size or the technological capabilities of the local units, but is less related to the region, a separate strategy and organisation are called for. Several pharmaceutical firms have opted for this solution.

China represents an even more complex case in that its scale and momentum are sufficiently great for it to be considered as a region in itself. It is closely linked with many other parts of the region, but technologically or in volume terms has for many MNCs not yet reached the stage that it is important for global success. At the end of the 1990s, several MNCs had between 10 and 20 ventures in operation in the country and several more under negotiation. Under such circumstances the distribution of an MNC's activities across the whole Asian region is thrown out of balance. The formation of a China holding company as a new legal entity adds to the uncertainty over the organisational treatment of the country. If the various China ventures are first bundled under a China office which in turn reports to an RHQ which in turn reports to headquarters, lines of communication clearly become too long. If all these ventures report to the RHQ directly, it will turn into a disguised China office itself. The alternative is to establish a direct link between the China office and headquarters – a clear signal that a common regional strategy and a unifying regional organisation for Asia are coming to an end.

Most Western corporations locate their Asian RHQ in Asia; a few have it at headquarters, where its main task is to secure support for the region at the centre of the organisation. Four criteria influence the decision of where to locate an RHQ:

- *Geographic location*: by and large, a central location is preferred; for this reason, few Asian RHQs will ever be based in Australia;
- *Convenience and infrastructure* have a direct impact on operations (facilities and staff, supporting services, legal environment, business mentality) and determine the well-being of expatriates (quality of life, language, schooling facilities);
- *Costs* – including taxation – are a consideration, although cheaper locations may have drawbacks in terms of convenience and infrastructure;
- *Proximity to business*: RHQs may be located either where the main market opportunities lie, or, conversely, where the business is small and vulnerable and needs support.

Most RHQs are located in Singapore or Hong Kong. In the case of Otis Elevator, the local Japanese operation, Nippon Otis Elevator Company, which accounted for nearly 50 per cent of total regional revenues, was not keen to see the RHQ located in Singapore and claimed a more active role for itself in regional management.

Two important factors, however, militate against locating RHQs in Japan: first, the lack of English-speaking Japanese personnel, and second, the highly sophisticated and specific nature of Japanese markets and technologies which makes their transferability to less developed countries in the region somewhat difficult.

Many companies that do not have an RHQ have nevertheless succeeded in building a regional culture. Examples are Siemens and Shell. These companies have tried to create an internal culture which facilitates business development in Asia along product lines. Individual networking through regional meetings, exchange of favoured management practices and regionally-oriented task forces are systematically encouraged. This type of coordination through people is regarded by these companies as a more effective way of managing regionally than a bureaucratic organisation. One example of its implementation is the rotation or temporary exchange of Asian managers (for instance, having an Indonesian manager sit on the board of a Malaysian subsidiary, and vice versa). Regional meetings, conferences and training sessions are also useful for cementing these networks and for sharing organisational learning. The use of a project team to improve the regional computer system would be another such network-building measure.

Finally, a very powerful method of networking is the use of regional training seminars. BP, Nokia, Henkel, ABB, Swire and Cable & Wireless are examples of companies which have used this method systematically.

Regional headquarters as change agents

There are three main stages of expansion for multinational firms in Asia Pacific (Figure 9.10):

- As *explorers*, they seek to exploit local opportunities. Their operations are limited and self-contained; they are directed from headquarters, whose commitment to the region is ambivalent;

Stage	Explorer	Strategic Investor	Global Consolidator
Objectives	• Exploit local opportunities	• Build regional presence • Pre-empt	• Balance global portfolio
Operations	• Limited • Self-contained	• Regional linkages • **RHQs**	• Global linkages
Commitment to the Region	• Ambivalent	• Very high	• High

Figure 9.10   The MNC in Asia

- The next stage is that of *strategic investor*: this is where many Western firms are now in Asia, after the need for a more systematic and regional approach became apparent in the 1980s and 1990s. RHQs were set up to channel initiatives and turn them into action. Founding an RHQ increases attention to Asia, replaces opportunistic activities with a more systematic regional strategy, takes power away from headquarters and the national units, and is a reflection of a much higher level of commitment to the region;
- A further step, which few Western multinationals in Asia Pacific have taken as yet, will take them to the *consolidation* stage. Once a sufficient regional presence and efficient regional linkages are in place, the RHQ acts as a decentralised headquarters and enjoys more power. However, as globalisation becomes a major driving force, the RHQ's independence starts fading away, and power moves back to the HQ.

Notes and references

1. Bower (1972).
2. Lasserre and Butler (1993). See quotations from interview as reported in italics.
3. Prahalad and Doz (1987), and Bartlett and Ghoshal (1989).
4. During the research conducted at the three companies mentioned in this chapter, respondents indicated that they did not modify their budgeting systems to account for Asia, but still it was possible to make 'strategic investments' there. This is confirmed by many other contacts that the authors have developed in the region over the years. It shows that formal systems are only a minor element of the actual decision-making mechanisms in a corporation (a fact that is well known by organisation theorists).
5. Schütte (1998).
6. Lasserre (1996).
7. Schütte (1997).

10 Managing Human Resources

Most surveys of Western companies operating in the Asia Pacific region identify human resource management as one of the most complex and difficult challenges to business development.[1] A scarcity of skilled managers, a highly mobile managerial population, and the reluctance of local managers in certain countries to work for foreign companies have been the major obstacles to the recruitment, training and development of local personnel which is so widely advocated by Asian governments. The need for local business expertise and experience, the spiralling costs of maintaining non-national staff, the reluctance of certain international managers to accept long-term postings in some countries, and the challenge of balancing career and family have all increased the complexity of appointing, rotating and rewarding expatriate managers. Finally, Asia's unique social, historical and religious traditions require special attention to cultural traits in the exercise of authority, control and interactions.

Human resource management problems can be grouped into four broad categories: the recruitment of local staff; the retention of local staff; the management of expatriates; and cross-cultural integration and differentiation.

The nature of those problems will differ from country to country, as shown in Table 10.1. This chapter, rather than detailing each country's specific human resource characteristics, will pinpoint the key strategic and managerial issues that Western firms have to deal with in managing people in the region.[2]

RECRUITING LOCAL STAFF

In most of the countries in Asia Pacific, recruiting local staff is problematic, either because there is a shortage of qualified personnel for technical and managerial positions, as in most ASEAN countries (with the exception of the Philippines), or because locals are reluctant to work for foreign companies (which is the case in Japan).

Scarcity

The scarcity of skilled personnel covers the whole range of specialities, but each country has its own shortfall (see Figure 10.1). China has perhaps the

269

Table 10.1   Human Resource Characteristics: Salient Issues in Human Resources
Management in Asia Pacific

	Recruitment	Retention mobility	Culture/behaviour (as perceived by Westerners)	Expatriates
SINGAPORE	• High educational standards • Some shortage of technical skills • Willingness to work for foreign firms	• Uncertain loyalty • Some relunctance for overseas assignments	• Social conformity	• High costs • Easy adaptation
JAPAN	• High educational standards • Overall shortage particularly for foreign-owned firms • Female population is an opportunity	• Low turnover • Reluctance for overseas assignments • Networking	• Team work • Precision • Paternalism	• High costs • Very difficult adaptation
KOREA	• Manager shortage • Political and military connections important • Language problems • Engineering skills available	• Reasonable loyalty to foreign firms • Overseas assignments difficult: language constraints • National pride	• Discipline • Networking	• High costs • Difficult adaptation
CHINA	• Shortage of qualified managers • Language	• Low mobility • Conflict of loyalty	• Unpredictable motivation • Opportunism • Political and family nepotism	• High costs • Difficult adaptation
HONG KONG	• Skilled and trained managers	• High turnover • Shallow loyalty • Willingness to work overseas	• Flexibility • Opportunism • Short-termism	• High costs • Easy adaptation

TAIWAN	• Strong technical skills	• Some turnover • Willingness to work overseas	• Flexibility • Hard working	• High costs
THAILAND	• Language problems • Shortage of technical personnel • Low skills in sciences and technology	• High turnover with young personnel	• Paternalism	• Cultural adaptation
INDONESIA	• Shortage of managerial and technical skills	• Government pressure for localisation	• Paternalism • Motivations difficult to assess • Obedience	• Cultural adaptation • Easy material life
MALAYSIA	• Relative shortage of technical skills	• State enforced ethnic balance • Uncertain loyalty	• Flexibility	• Easy adaptation
PHILIPPINES	• High level of skills	• Willingness to work overseas	• Motivations difficult to assess	• Easy adaptation

SOURCES: *Business International* (1991); Lasserre and Probert (1994b).

most severe shortages of adequate personnel, particularly in managerial jobs.

In developing Asia (that is, the ASEAN 5 and China), educational systems have not traditionally favoured careers in business and production management. Humanities and legal studies are preferred to accounting, and medicine and/or general scientific studies are preferred to engineering. During Mao's Cultural Revolution in China in the 1960s, secondary and university education were completely disrupted by mass movements and political turmoil.

Where vocational training has been encouraged, as in Singapore, it is usually theoretical with very little practical content. Where business education curricula have been developed, students tend to opt for soft disciplines like marketing or business rather than accountancy or engineering.

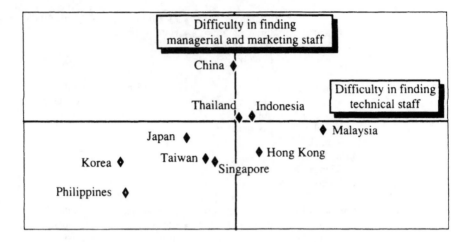

SOURCE: Lasserre and Probert (1994b).

Figure 10.1 Recruiting Local Personnel

Throughout the developing countries, business training and particularly the MBA degree became fashionable in the early 1980s. With the help of American or European schools a large number of local universities have proposed formal business training. In many instances second- or third-rate European or North American institutions have taken advantage of the Asian desire for MBA status by offering quick-fix degrees. While the general level of business training has improved over the past ten years, it remains rather academic.

In practice there is a significant gap between the business qualifications of Asia's younger generation (people in their twenties or early thirties) and those in their forties. Young Asian managers tend to have solid business education, but lack the experience and the seniority to gain access to given managerial positions. Senior Asian managers have the seniority so crucial to managerial authority in Asia, but often lack the relevant international experience or education. This problem is particularly acute in China, and to some extent Indonesia. To compound the issue, in China local partners often tend to consider joint venture companies as golden retirement homes for old comrades.

In the hope of overcoming this problem, some companies are encouraging job hopping, which in certain countries like Singapore, Hong Kong or Malaysia is more or less a way of life and is becoming a serious problem in China (Figure 10.2). Banking, hotel management and sales management are jobs for which there is a fast rotation. Job hopping is obviously self-defeating and companies which succumb to the temptation to enter the job hopping

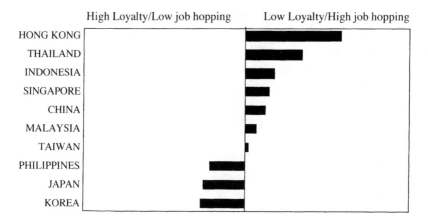

SOURCE: Lasserre and Probert (1994b).

Figure 10.2   Job Hopping and Loyalty

spiral by hijacking managers with a few extra dollars will soon find that the other side of the coin is that they lose their talents to another predator.

In order to overcome this problem of scarcity, companies can rely on three complementary practices: image building, training and consistency.

Image building consists of promoting the company within the local Asian university and educational system, as well as in the host communities and media. Philanthropy in the form of grants, the sponsorship of artistic or athletic events and regular visits to universities or local institutes, can all help to build a positive corporate image.

Asian personnel usually attach a high value to opportunities for additional training. Large Western companies with a reputation for their training policies, like Philips or Shell, have enjoyed an easier entry to the skilled personnel market. For smaller companies that cannot afford such programmes, personal relationships, teamwork and informal or personalised recruitment practices are all effective measures.

Finally, a consistent policy of career development will establish the reputation of the firm and help its recruitment effort.

Reluctance to work for foreign firms

This problem is particularly acute in Japan and to a lesser extent in Korea. In Japan foreign firms employ less than 1 per cent of the workforce. Foreign companies have experienced difficulties in recruiting both young graduates and mid-career managers. The obstacles in recruiting young graduates are caused by the fact that most foreign firms are perceived as small and lacking in dynamism, and are therefore unable to offer attractive career opportunities. For the mid-career manager, this effect is compounded by the fact that traditionally Japanese managers do not change employers. Although life-long employment is gradually disappearing, this is still a highly resilient attitude, particularly with regard to foreign companies.[3] Japanese managers who join foreign firms have essentially renounced the possibility of joining mainstream Japanese firms later on.

In order to palliate this disadvantage, some foreign companies are recruiting Japanese women, though not in sales and rarely in line positions. Another strategy is to offer higher salaries than Japanese firms in comparable businesses. The problem with poaching mid-career Japanese managers is that the pool is essentially limited to managers who already work for foreign firms. A third strategy is to offer a more interesting job, either in terms of a foreign posting, working with more advanced technologies, or an accelerated career path. All these incentives have limits. Foreign assignments are only of interest to the Japanese if they are of limited duration. Technological superiority over Japanese firms is a difficult proposition, and career advancement opportunities are perceived as limited by the size of the Japanese operations within the foreign firms. On the whole, these palliative measures are valuable, but none is an absolute solution to the problem. The answer to recruitment problems lies in the constant effort and long-term commitment to offer challenging and stable careers to local managers.

RETAINING LOCAL STAFF

After recruitment, the second most acute problem Western firms face is the retention of local staff. Job hopping is a serious problem in Hong Kong and in some sectors in Singapore, Thailand or Indonesia. It is linked to two major factors: the first is scarcity (particularly in Indonesia and Thailand); the second is the volatile short-term political situation of the environment, which undermines incentives that stress loyalty to the firm (as is the case in Hong Kong). For obvious reasons staff turnover decreases with length of tenure. Motivation to leave is linked to the perception that the foreign firm does not offer opportunities for future development, or that compensation granted to local personnel is unfairly lower than that granted to expatriate personnel for an equivalent level of responsibility and expertise. Under these circumstances, it is not surprising that companies like Shell or IBM, which take a long-term view of personnel development, have fewer retention problems.

In order to retain local staff, foreign firms must establish the perception that personnel policies are fair; reward (or punish) people within their cultural norms; generate a sense of belonging to the group; and show that the firm has a consistent long-term human resources policy.

Fairness

Definitions of fairness, or the perception that one is justly treated in relation to one's peers, vary from country to country. In Asia, justice is defined more in terms of the perception that one is treated with the respect due to one's rank, and with the expectation of a kind of paternalistic benevolence, than in terms of Western egalitarianism. However, when two individuals of the same rank are treated differently, the situation is perceived as unfair. A thorny issue is the disparity in compensation between local and expatriate personnel, especially those with identical qualifications. It is increasingly possible to find within the same Asian subsidiary a local engineer with the same degree – in some cases from the same school – as an expatriate engineer. If the disparity in compensation levels is too great, the sense of fairness will be eroded and local staff will spread the word that the Western company is not for the locals. Although local managers accept the idea that an expatriate must be compensated for a certain amount of hardship and additional expenses, they often feel that differences in compensation for a similar level of responsibility should be kept to a minimum.

Rewards

Rewards and punishments are among the most powerful management mechanisms. In the Asia Pacific region, it is expected that both rewards and punishments will be granted by superiors, and in private. The preoccupation with saving face requires that the events should have no public exposure. This is always true for punishment. In the case of rewards (promotion or exceptional compensation for particular achievement), minimum individual public emphasis should be given unless they are part of a company ceremony. Asian personnel generally appreciate the reward of a team performance, and in such cases public recognition is not only accepted but welcomed. Promotion and recognition need to be not only celebrated but also rewarded with financial compensation, such as a bonus. In several instances, local personnel much prefer to be rewarded on the basis of behaviour (loyalty, honesty) rather than on quantifiable performance criteria (Figure 10.3).

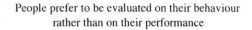

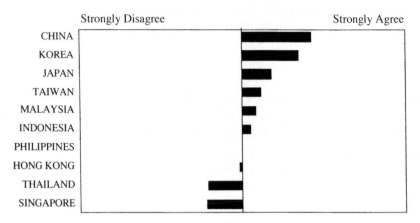

SOURCE: Lasserre and Probert (1994b).

Figure 10.3   Behaviour Rewards

Sense of belonging

A family-style work atmosphere is generally appreciated by Asian personnel. This is reflected in the fact that in nearly all Asian countries superiors are expected to take an active role in the management of personnel problems. Types of arbitration which would be considered interference with privacy in the West are often welcomed in family-centred Asia as marks of benevolence and caring. Paternalism is viewed positively (Figure 10.4).

Long-term view

Finally, a consistent, long-term career development policy – in which local staff can sense the company's commitment to integrate and promote them – will determine local attitudes and loyalties to the Western company or subsidiary. A traditional diagram of the international staffing of multinational companies is represented in Figure 10.5. Multinational firms organise their management in two concentric layers. The core is constituted of international managers whose careers entail assignments in various international subsidiaries, alternating with postings at corporate headquarters. In the second circle are local managers whose careers evolve within the structure of their domestic company. While such local managers may take international assignments at a corporate office or in other subsidiaries for short periods of

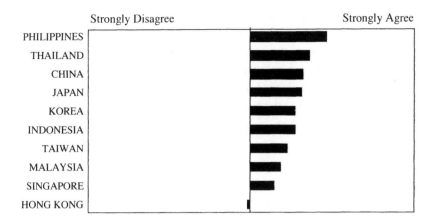

Source: Lasserre and Probert (1994a).

Figure 10.4   Paternalism: 'Employers have a Paternalistic Responsibility'

Figure 10.5   Typical International Human Resources Policy in Multinational Companies

time, their professional future lies in their local country. In both cases, a successful long-term human resources policy must convince locally-recruited staff that they can climb the career ladder within the firm. It must be clear that Asian staff, if they have the necessary skills and ambition, can rise to join the core of international managers. Even those who prefer to remain local must clearly see a future and must not be barred from opportunities by competition from expatriates.

EXPATRIATE MANAGEMENT

The examples of Unilever, Wella and L'Oréal illustrate how expatriates, by acting as pioneers, recruiters and developers, have been instrumental in corporate regional development. Problems associated with the management of expatriates are not limited to Asia. Once a company increases its international presence it must develop an international management team which is able to rotate across businesses, functions and countries. Many problems related to managing expatriate management are common all over the world: motivating expatriate personnel, job performance and family adaptation.[4] Other problems are specific to the Asia Pacific region, such as the fit or misfit of Western managerial skills with Asia's cultural and business contexts, the problem of tenure, and extreme cultural assimilation (going native).

Common expatriate problems: motivation and performance

Figure 10.6 depicts the results of a survey conducted among 198 European expatriates operating in South-East Asia.[5] Of the factors which most motivated the respondents, the challenge of the job came first, before salary benefits, personal and professional development and long-term career opportunities. For most Western managers Asia was not the preferred post for career development. Despite changes since 1988, certain Western managers still see an Asian posting as a dead end or retirement posting rather than the fast track. Dominant expatriate concerns are the reintegration issue and the fear of being forgotten. This is not specific to Asian postings but Asia's geographical and cultural distances have exacerbated, for certain expatriates, the sense of loneliness within the global corporate structure.

Responsibilities linked to the management of a business unit and a feeling of greater independence or autonomy were viewed as the most satisfactory factors. While autonomy is generally viewed positively, there is a negative side to it. Autonomy from the core allows expatriate managers, particularly those with general management responsibility, to have a direct impact on the

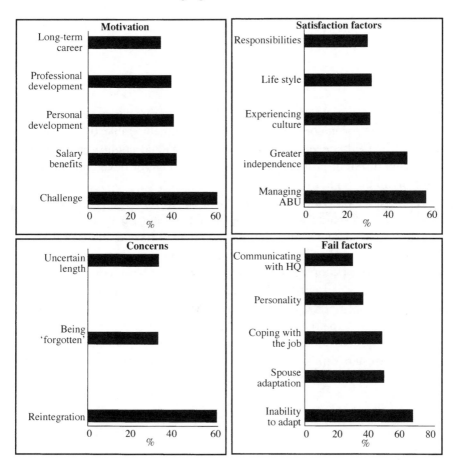

SOURCE: Conway (1994).

Figure 10.6 Expatriates in South-East Asia: Successes and Failures

results of the business without the administrative and bureaucratic burdens that tend to plague headquarters or major operating units. On the other hand, autonomy can be a warning sign that corporate headquarters undervalues or ignores the local subsidiary. In this case, autonomy and independence are synonymous with unimportant.

Finally, of the factors identified as leading to failure, the one most often stated is the inability to adapt and cope with the job and/or the inability of the family (spouse) to adapt to the culture of the host country. Again, this problem is not unique to Asia, and certainly there are rougher environments (notably Saudi Arabia or certain African countries). Nevertheless, Asia's business and cultural environments are sufficiently complex to cause problems, and therefore require Western firms to undertake a careful selection and cultural preparation of their expatriates.

Expatriate skills

The kind of expatriate management skills required depends very much on the individual Asian country's stage of development. Table 10.2 illustrates the kind of skills needed to match each individual country. Figure 10.7 represents different profiles according to the stage of development of the company in the region.

Of the many skills which are required, the ability to build and maintain relationships is an essential asset in nearly all Asian countries. In the early stages of a Western company's entry and development of its operations or markets in Asia, it is critical to have first a pioneering or missionary generation of expatriates with cultural and political skills. Once basic contact networks have been established and the Western company has started to gain experience, traditional managerial and technical skills become progressively more important. At a later stage, expatriates from head office can be kept to a minimum and gradually replaced by locals, or by rotating international managers. In the final stages of a Western firm's establishment in the Asia Pacific region, it is no longer appropriate to speak of expatriates, but of international staff.

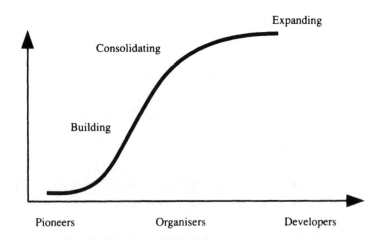

Figure 10.7   Different Profiles of Expatriates

Table 10.2 Expatriate Skills for Asia Pacific

	Language skills	Cultural skills	Relationship skills	Political skills	Technical skills
	Mastery of local language, 'social level'	Understanding of and sensitivity to etiquette, social norms, religions, ethnical characteristics. Knowledge and references to arts and literature	Ability to build and maintain a network of contacts. Ability to call on 'friends' when needed. Ability to negotiate. Ability to demonstrate leadership	Ability to understand the local political context and subtleties. Ability to get close to leaders and high ranking officials	Knowledge and expertise in product technology. Ability to demonstrate logically the characteristics and performances of products and processes
Countries in which the particular skills are of particular importance	China Korea	China Japan Philippines Malaysia Thailand	Everywhere	China Malaysia Philippines Vietnam	Japan Korea Taiwan
Countries in which the particular skills are of importance	Indonesia Thailand Vietnam Japan	Korea Indonesia Taiwan Vietnam	Singapore Hong Kong	Indonesia Korea Thailand	Everywhere else
Countries in which the particular skills are of lower importance	Hong Kong Philippines Singapore Taiwan Malaysia	Hong Kong Singapore		Hong Kong Japan Singapore Taiwan	

Cultural assimilation

In the days of Western colonial involvement in the Far East, some Europeans and Americans went to Asia as expatriates or soldiers, fell in love with the Asian people and their culture, and progressively 'went native'. This kind of extreme cultural assimilation presents a dual danger: a loss of credibility with local personnel and business partners, and a loss of credibility with the parent company, each of these perceptions being mutually reinforcing. Although Western firms should look for a degree of cultural sensitivity and familiarity with the local culture in their expatriate managers, extreme cultural assimilation should be discouraged. This danger is obviously present everywhere in the world, but some of the more hermetic or culturally distinct Asian environments, such as Japan, are particularly seductive. A sound expatriate management policy can use routine and timely rotation to discourage this phenomenon. The exception would be during a Western firm's entry stage, when long-term expatriate tenures may be necessary for relationship building. As soon as the pioneer stage is over, however, rotation should be reinstated and rigorously enforced. The length of expatriate tenure is a function of the skill requirements of the country in question. One rule of thumb is: the greater the need for relationship building, the longer the stay.

CULTURAL DIFFERENTIATION AND INTEGRATION

The religious and civic traditions of Confucianism, Buddhism, Islam and Hinduism have transmitted a legacy of behaviour, attitudes and beliefs which have a deep and constantly evolving impact on Asian entrepreneurial culture. Culture affects government policies, social norms, consumption patterns, business transactions, management practices and labour relations. Cultural traits vary according to ethnic, religious and national groups. However, it is possible to identify certain enduring characteristics of Asian social organisation and group behaviour which are present across the region.

GROUP REFERENCE
- Group belonging is asserted before individual instinct
- Compliance with group norms is expected
- Individualistic behaviour is condemned
- Individual transactions are based on intra-group affiliation leading to networking

CONFLICT AVOIDANCE
- Overt conflicts are perceived as highly disruptive

- Most social etiquettes prohibit the manifestation of anger
- Harmony is sought

IMPORTANCE OF FACE
- Most societies are regulated by shame, as opposed to guilt
- Public shaming is unacceptable and can lead to revenge
- Stress is often translated by a smile

RESPECT FOR AUTHORITY and SENIORITY
- Leaders are expected to be benevolent and virtuous
- Formal authority is not openly discussed
- High social distance, even in societies where wealth is evenly distributed
- Age brings a fatherly aura

PATERNALISM
- Leaders are expected to be attentive to the personal life of employees

RESPECT FOR ACADEMIC CREDENTIALS
- Hunger for diplomas

ATTITUDE TOWARD WOMEN
- Certain Asian societies do not value the professional role of women

SUPERSTITION
- Belief in cosmology or supernatural forces

EXTENDED FAMILY and NEPOTISM
- Family support is considered the norm
- Organisations are seen as an extension of the family support structure and hence as providers of social welfare
- It is considered proper behaviour to give preference to family members in business dealings

Organising and managing people in the region requires that Western managers operating there have a thorough understanding of these traits and pay attention to them. This should be matched by a corresponding understanding within product divisions and at corporate headquarters. Differences in management practices must be reflected in the exercise of control and authority as well as through interpersonal relationships. The following section discusses certain common Asian cultural characteristics and what they imply for human resource management in the region.

Group versus individual identity

Inherent in most Asian cultures, whether Confucian, Buddhist, Islamic or Hindu, is the individual's very deep attachment and sense of belonging to social groups, beginning with the family and the extended family. In large part, this stems from the monolithic organisation of Asian societies, where all organisations, including the state, have been seen for centuries as an extension of the family.

In Asia, the maintenance and development of a person's membership in a group – whether a family or a firm – takes priority over the assertion of individual identity. Compliance with group norms is expected and individ- ualistic behaviour is discouraged and sometimes condemned outright. Individual transactions are often based on membership of groups or networks. This particular and deeply ingrained trait has important implications for human resource management. Expatriate managers who encourage one-on- one competition between their local managers, or reward individual performance rather than group or team performance, may encounter resistance. This does not mean that individual performance should be left unrewarded. In Hong Kong and Singapore, individual performance is expected to earn a pay-off. The difference lies in the way in which the reward is granted; in general, individual rewards (or punishments) should be handled in private, while team rewards are always public or ceremonial. These categories are mutually reinforcing; in Asia, even the most self-centred and ambitious person will still do things on behalf of his or her team or organisation.

Conflict avoidance

In most Asian cultures, overt expression of conflict is systematically avoided. Buddhist, Confucian and Islamic societies particularly value the maintenance of harmony, even if it is only superficial. It is crucial to the self-esteem and public reputation of an Asian organisation to avoid open conflict or expression of anger. This contrasts starkly with Western cultural and entrepreneurial norms which often encourage or initiate overt conflict – or open disagreement – from a dialectical point of view (that is, thesis, antithesis, synthesis.) Although Asian cultures, particularly the Chinese, also have a dialectical view (the Ying and the Yang) the opposition of elements is seen as symbiotic rather than conflictual: opposites co-exist and in some cases even cooperate, and if they do fight harmony is broken. Unlike Western cultures, where confrontation is often used by managers to solve conflicts or reinstate authority, and where open debate of a controversial issue is a strategy used to reach consensus, Asian cultures favour indirect conflict resolution (for example, via a third party, or via intense private discussion and lobbying). In Asia, if an issue is seen to be potentially conflictual, public debate will be avoided.

Anger, when expressed in public, is considered humiliating to the person who displays it. Rather than enhancing the authority of the manager, it undermines it (the logic being that the reputation of a leader or authority figure should be reflected organically in the harmony of the society or the company he or she manages). The need to maintain a facade of harmony has its price. Tensions still exist even if hidden, and a conflictual situation which is not expressed openly (as in the West) or solved indirectly (as in Asia) may lead to accumulated frustration which may erupt in violence. The Indonesian expression for this – running amok – has been absorbed into the English language. In political life, running amok can mean riots, as in 1965 in Indonesia, or 1968 in Malaysia; in the business context, the result could be an unexpected strike or a sudden manifestation of bizarre or violent behaviour. In these situations, a dormant conflict must be addressed, although in an appropriately indirect and private manner.

Another subtle manifestation of conflict avoidance is the non-committal answer to express negation. In Indonesia, for instance, disagreement is almost never expressed directly with a blunt, categorical 'no'; instead, the neutral formula of 'maybe' is the equivalent. This kind of non-committal answer has the advantage of protecting the feelings and reputation (face) of the other person. It is also the perfect expression of the Asian avoidance of negative, and hence potentially conflictual, behaviour.

The importance of face

Underlying the avoidance of anger and attachment to the group is the Asian respect for face. Face can be defined as an individual's public reputation *vis-à-vis* one's family, one's company, and one's society as distinct from a private or individual sense of self-esteem. A person's face can be diminished or enhanced by the perception of one's actions. Most Asian societies are regulated by shame, in the sense of public disgrace, as distinct from guilt, which carries a sense of individual responsibility and conscience. The concept of face is pervasive, deeply affects interpersonal relationships and has important implications for human resource management, since there is a deep taboo against the public shaming of employees in Asia (Figure 10.8, part (a)).

A Western manager who decides to discipline an Asian employee by singling that person out in front of his or her peers may find that this leads to a search for revenge. Negative feedback should be shared with caution and discretion, and whenever possible in a one-on-one context rather than in front of a peer group. Face-saving implies careful interpretation of certain behaviour. Local employees tend to prefer to tell a story or to find external causes to explain their mistakes (see Figure 10.8, part (b)) or to mask their embarrassment under a smile. The Chinese, for example, tend to regard presenting a problem to their managers and asking for help as an admission of failure or incompetence, a sign of their own inability to do the work. Therefore when

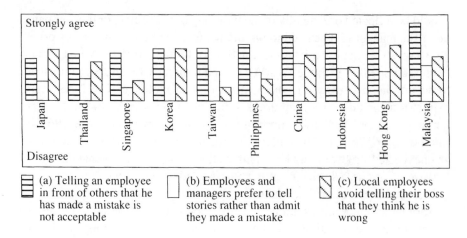

SOURCE: Lasserre and Probert (1994a).

Figure 10.8 Asian Employees and Conflict Resolution

difficulties arise, they invariably try to solve the problem themselves instead of asking for help. This attitude is not uncommon in other countries in the Asia Pacific region and is an expression of the fear of losing face. Loss of face can have considerable disruptive effects, and managers should avoid behaviour that could lead to a loss of face for an Asian peer or subordinate.

Respect for authority

Formal authority has to be respected in Asia; this is part of harmony. Contesting authority is perceived as rebellious, and therefore challenging a boss is considered improper conduct, even if the subordinate thinks the boss is wrong (see Figure 10.8, part (c)). Expatriate managers new to the Asian environment are often perplexed by the fact that they consistently receive positive official feedback despite simmering tensions or an explosive social and political climate. When the problem comes to the surface, generally in a very extreme and unpleasant fashion, and the Western manager asks, 'Why didn't you tell me?', the answer is often an embarrassed smile.

The Asian respect for authority should not, however, be taken at face value. A bad leader can be corrected or contested, but by indirect means: pressure directed towards a third party, anonymous letters, passive behaviour and resistance camouflaged with excuses, repeated illness, and even irrational behaviour such as panic attacks or mystical hysteria. Feedback is often cryptic and the Western manager will have to learn how to decode or interpret indirect signs of discontent.

Respect for seniority

The organisational manifestation of this quasi-universal trait is more pronounced in Asia than in other parts of the world. Age is not only supposed to bring wisdom, but also gives a natural right to command. Respect for seniority is one of the basic principles of the Confucian philosophy. Islamic and Chinese cultures also accord high respect to the aged. Local personnel would be more comfortable in dealing with mature, middle-aged superiors than with younger ones. In practice, however, this does not mean that young local or expatriate managers are barred from the top of the corporate hierarchy. Rather, a younger person is expected first to demonstrate a higher degree of technical competence than older ones in order to be accepted. Despite their reverence for the aged and the deference paid to them, Asian employees place a higher value on proper behaviour than on seniority. One advantage younger Western managers may have over older ones is a better command of the language. Chinese or Japanese studies are more popular now in US and European universities than they were 20 years ago. However, if a Western manager is faced with a choice between two people with equal education qualifications and experience, it is preferable to choose the more senior.

Paternalism

Paternalistic behaviour is not uncommon in Asian cultures where political and corporate leaders are expected to embody certain religious or family values. Organisations and corporations are often seen as an extension of the already broad family structure and are expected to provide accordingly. This has important implications for corporate leadership and human resource management, and in particular for the behaviour of Western expatriate managers. Benevolence and an unusually high degree of attentiveness to the personal life and welfare of employees is often expected in Asia. For Western expatriate managers, especially senior managers, this can mean adopting a paternalistic or maternalistic role, and will require a greater sensitivity to the personal welfare of employees than would be expected or even deemed acceptable in the West.

Reverence for academic credentials

Academic credentials and diplomas bring respect but also raise expectations. This is an expression of the traditional respect for education that prevails in

Asian societies, both Confucian and Muslim. An obvious implication for the management of human resources is that Western firms may find that providing opportunities for their Asian managers to acquire or work towards these credentials is an important means of retaining these staff. Training seminars in a reputable foreign institution are also highly valued by local staff.

Attitudes towards women

Although many Asian societies are deeply patriarchal, women, especially of a certain age, are respected. While Western firms may hesitate to hire or send Western women to Asia as expatriate managers for fear of their encountering sexism, there are advantages in doing so. In China and Japan, for example, Western women, simply because of their foreignness, are often treated with a respect that might not always be accorded to their ethnic local female counterparts in similar positions of authority. Korea is an extreme example of male chauvinism, with women virtually absent from higher managerial levels.

Superstition

The prevalence of certain traditional mystical or superstitious practices in China and South-East Asia may come as a surprise to the unprepared Western manager. Even in the more industrialised and Westernised Chinese societies, notably Hong Kong, Taiwan and Singapore, certain traditional practices still prevail and should not be overlooked. To cite one example: geomancy, also known as *feng shui*, or the divination and interpretation of certain landscape features and sacred sites, is still widely practised in the Chinese world. In practical terms this means that real-estate purchases and building sites must first be approved by a geomancer. Whether Western expatriate managers approve of this process or not, they should not disregard the fact that their Asian staff and colleagues will consider it an important procedure.

Extended family and nepotism

Finally, one of the most sensitive issues in managing human resources that managers will face is the difference between Western and Asian definitions of nepotism and corruption. Due to the importance of the extended family in Asia, nepotism – far from being perceived as corrupt behaviour – may even be encouraged as part of the moral obligation to support one's family. Therefore one can expect to see local employees who occupy managerial positions giving preference to relatives when hiring, purchasing or contracting.

In China, this Confucian obligation to the extended family has been nearly institutionalised in state-owned enterprises, which to Westerners have an unusually high degree of officially encouraged nepotism.

Pressure from government officials or key government clients, who see it as their duty to place their family members in key positions in joint ventures with Western companies, may be difficult to resist and even harder to explain to Western corporate headquarters. The practice seems to be slowly changing, and in Japan and Singapore it has disappeared from modern corporations. More difficult to handle is the practice of giving commissions to employees who buy services or products externally. This internal corruption can be difficult to detect, but it may ultimately undermine the effort made by a company to instil a culture of quality, openness and fairness. Western managers need to understand that the borderline between gifts and graft is often blurred. However, if the Western company provides an adequate and fair compensation scheme, such practices should not be tolerated.

Notes and references

1. A. T. Kearney Inc. (1991).
2. Several figures and tables have been prepared on the basis of a survey carried out at the Euro-Asia Centre of INSEAD in 1992: Lasserre and Probert (1994b). References are also extracted from *Business International* (1991).
3. This paragraph is based on a series of research by Philippe Debroux: see Debroux (1993).
4. Adler (1987); Gersten (1990); Hiltrop and Janssens (1990).
5. Conway (1994).

11 The Future of the Asia Pacific Region

GROWTH VERSUS DEVELOPMENT

In Chapter 1 we discussed the track record of Asia Pacific's economies, the Asian crisis and the prospects of growth beyond the crisis. Growth in this context referred to the increase in economic output, measured in terms of GNP or GNP per capita. The difficulty of working with GNP figures and the growth of these figures with regard to the adjustment to PPP has also been discussed in Chapter 1.

There are additional problems with GNP figures, however, in that they only represent the creation of material wealth; they fail to measure, or measure only partly, the extent to which human lives are enriched. It is only this broader concept of increase in quality of life which leads to what one may call development. In other words, high growth rates do not necessarily lead to substantial development of societies or nations, though they certainly can help. Depletion of natural resources and exploitation of cheap labour can result in high growth rates, as can the accumulation of wealth through corruption among the elite. Such phenomena, which have been observed in certain Asian countries, will not, however, lead to sustainable growth as it is not accompanied by development.

The vision of governments as regards the future of their society, and the way they invest in their development and take care of the needs of their people and of their environment are therefore of utmost importance in assessing the sustainable growth potential of any country. The observation and analysis of growth rates, GNP figures, government budgets or current accounts is insufficient for this purpose. But any broader perspective leads the observer into uncharted waters. If the definition of development in a broader sense is the improvement of the quality of life for everybody, how does one measure this quality of life? How does one weigh the limited availability of space in Japan against a low crime rate and compare these two aspects with those in the USA? What roles are played by factors such as climate, traffic conditions, the chance of a fair trial, the quality of services?

For some years the UNDP has been trying to get to grips with this topic. In its annual reports, UNDP points out that any positive and sustainable

290

development has to be pro-people, pro-environment, pro-jobs and pro-women. It also stresses the importance of an equitable distribution of the benefits of economic growth and the sharing of opportunities between individuals and generations.[1]

The UNDP further argues that the creation and accumulation of wealth do not necessarily lead to the fulfilment of important human choices. These may be expanded by economic growth, but not necessarily. It is the use of wealth, not the wealth itself, that determines the quality of life. Certain benefits – such as respect for the law, maintenance of minority rights, or the equal treatment of men and women – are not really dependent on wealth. Nevertheless, some countries in the region do not grant these conditions to their people in practice, although they claim to do so.

Table 11.1 HDI Ranking versus GDP per capita Ranking

	HDI* (1994) *world ranking*	*GDP per capita (1994)* *world ranking*
Japan	7	7
Hong Kong	22	5
Singapore	26	11
South Korea	32	37
Thailand	59	51
Malaysia	60	47
Philippines	98	110
Indonesia	99	92
China	108	111
Vietnam	121	147
India	138	143

*This is a composite of three parts: longevity (measured by life expectancy), knowledge (measured by adult literacy and years of schooling) and standard of living (measured by GDP per capita adjusted to PPP).

SOURCE: *Human Development Report* (UNDP, 1997).

In a daring attempt to compare countries with each other the UNDP has created a Human Development Index (HDI; see Table 11.1). It has only three components: longevity, education and standard of living. It is a crude measure in that it picks subjectively certain aspects of development and leaves others aside, but conversely it is also relatively precise as it tries to measure those selected aspects objectively. Longevity is taken as an indication of health care, education as an indicator of providing people and society with an opportunity to improve themselves, and standard of living as an indicator of well-being. (Standard of living takes into account income and price levels and therefore relates to PPP calculations, as discussed in Chapter 1.)

The UNDP then proposes two rankings of a total of 173 countries around the world. One ranking uses the HDI, the other uses conventional income per capita statistics not adjusted by purchasing power. Among the Asian countries, Japan comes out as the leader, ranking as number seven in the world on both accounts. Four countries in the region improve their standing in the world community when the HDI is applied but six look less promising. This means that, according to the criteria used, Asian countries have been comparatively less successful in pursuing development in a broader sense than they have been in simply pushing growth by improving their people's income in dollar terms. This result is a reflection of the considerable income increases in Hong Kong and Singapore which were not matched by an equivalent improvement of the selected social indicators.

GROWTH, DEVELOPMENT AND INTERNAL STABILITY

Long-term growth and sustainable development cannot be realised without a certain degree of internal and external stability. China, for example, was politically extremely volatile between 1949 and 1979 and therefore did not exploit its economic potential fully. Indonesia, under the flamboyant Sukarno, did not show much economic progress; this only appeared after Suharto, very much a symbol of stability, had taken over. Cambodia, Laos and Myanmar still suffer from political turmoil, and are unable to develop. Any breakdown of public order in Hong Kong following the return of the former colony to China will negatively affect economic growth. Internal stability depends on the leadership structure of the country, the degree of social cohesion within the country, and on the institutional and legal framework within which the country functions.

In Asia, the debate about internal stability is dominated by a deeply-seated belief in the need for a strong government rather than the need for a stable constitution or a firmly grounded ideology. A strong government is seen as essential to the initiation and pursuit of successful development policies. According to this view, political liberalism is incompatible with economic growth, as governments face policy choices (such as investment over consumption) which are difficult to make when confronted by pressure from special interest groups. China, Hong Kong, Indonesia, South Korea, Singapore and Taiwan find or have found themselves in this position. All have prospered extraordinarily over long periods under authoritarian governments, thereby outclassing almost every other country in the world. On the other hand, the Philippines and India, with their inherited democracies, have fared poorly in comparison.

However, this point and these examples need some qualification. China and Indonesia prospered, but only during certain periods of authoritarian rule. Shortcomings in development may also have been covered up by government controlled media and biased official statistics. Hong Kong on the other hand does not have a democracy, but a legal system that works well and protects individuals from the arbitrary actions of government officials. The Philippines has experienced swings between democratic and authoritarian rule, but even during the worst times it probably provided more public services and more justice for its people than, for example, China did. India enjoyed political freedom, while economic activity was hampered by endless controls. Its stagnation therefore may not be the result of its democratic form of government. Even if one accepts the given examples as valid, how does one explain the economic success of other democracies in Asia such as Japan and Malaysia, or the failure of other authoritarian regimes such as North Korea, Myanmar and, until recently, Vietnam? One may also add that nearly all of the world's rich countries are democratic, while most of the poor are not.

There are two lines of thought that result from this often ideologically tainted dispute between supporters of democracy and authoritarianism. The first argues in favour of a staged approach. Authoritarianism is needed to catapult poor, agriculturally-based countries rapidly into industrialisation and a certain degree of prosperity. It is only at the industrialisation and specialisation stage that societies become more complex and the shortcomings of authoritarian governments – often cornered in a closed political system by big business, the military and bureaucracy – become apparent. The better educated workforce and the emerging middle class also face more demanding jobs. These can only be filled by participating and motivated people who gain self-confidence while they contribute to the continued economic success of their country. This active involvement will inevitably spill over into society and government, as even Singapore's former prime minister, Lee Kuan Yew, concedes.[2]

This change seems inevitable and is accelerated by the media and through increased contact with Western political culture. Germany experienced the transition to democracy during its phase of industrialisation. Similarly we have witnessed changes towards political liberalisation in South Korea, Taiwan and Thailand. These countries have laid the basis for a stable future where their citizens can actively participate in their further development.

The second line of thought steers clear of all ideological arguments and states that it does not really matter whether a government is authoritarian or democratic as long as it is good. The question then is how to define 'good'. A good government should care about its people and ensure that food, health services, housing and schooling are available at affordable prices. It should be honest and competent, and safeguard its people's security. It should also acknowledge the civil rights of the individual and the individual's right to own property. Otherwise, there will be little incentive to accumulate material assets.

So far, neither the authoritarian nor the democrat would disagree with this. The role of law and the independence of the judiciary are more controversial subjects. Supporters of authoritarianism see these as undue limitations of the power of the government. Democrats argue that such a system of checks and balances is still insufficient and call for freedom of expression, freedom of the press, a multiparty system and an elected Parliament. Authoritarians in Asia consider these requirements unreasonable restrictions imposed on leaders who are trying to do their best for their people. They add that good governments listen to their citizens and non-benevolent leaders are automatically phased out by their peers. Apparently, in Asia, where a fundamental appreciation of authority is deeply ingrained, the accountability of governments was not widely thought essential, at least until the beginning of the Asian crisis.

Unfortunately, even a long-serving benevolent leader may change his mind and turn against his people. He may also die unexpectedly with his succession unresolved, and chaos will follow. Blind belief in authoritarian leaders therefore does not help the establishment of internal stability of countries in Asia, any more than it does in the rest of the world. Ethnic and religious divisions, economic disparities and other critical aspects of life in contemporary Asia demand continuous and responsible government. This is best anchored in a strong legal and institutional framework, and must include some provision for accountability. In the long run it is laws and institutions, not individual leaders, that give citizens trust in their future and entice them to identify themselves as a nation rather than with their racial or ethnic group. It is this aspect of internal stability, rather than the question of the remaining life expectancy of a particular current leader, that should be taken into account when assessing the risks associated with foreign investments in countries such as Indonesia or China.

EXTERNAL STABILITY AND SOURCES OF CONFLICT

The potential for growth and development is dependent not only on a country's internal stability, but also on its relationship with others, what might be called its external stability. This includes territorial disputes, ideological differences with neighbouring countries and great power rivalries.

Between internal and external stability lies an area that concerns the integrity of country boundaries. Not long ago, the boundaries of countries seemed to have been drawn for eternity. Then the world watched the disintegration of the Soviet Union and Yugoslavia, the foundation of a large number of new states, and the reunification of Germany. None of these has affected Asia Pacific directly. However, the inviolability of countries or nation states has once again been called into question. The upheavals in Europe also serve as a reminder that a sense of common history and ethnic grounding is still alive among people who live in countries that have not developed naturally over long periods, but have been artificially arranged or created in the aftermath of war or colonialism. The present boundaries of several Asian countries are the result of historical accidents that on the one hand have thrown together different ethnic groups, and on the other have separated homogeneous groups. As recent history shows, neither separatist movements nor unifying forces should be underestimated. Indonesia, Malaysia and the Philippines come to mind in this context, though none of these countries is under imminent threat. Korea's reunification is only a matter of time.

China is a special case due to its size and history. In contrast with the ASEAN countries it is racially rather homogeneous with tightly controlled minorities, and religion has no important role. This, and the strong desire of the Chinese leadership to regain its former glory and re-establish itself as a superpower, argues strongly against the probability that the same kind of break which occurred in the former Soviet Union will happen in China. The small percentage of minorities in the population, however, still total rather large absolute numbers of dissidents who may be prepared to fight for independence. Economic disparities between the coastal regions of China and the hinterland could equally threaten the country's unity in the long run.

With potential disintegration looming in the background, China is actively pursuing the integration of Hong Kong, Macao and Taiwan in its boundaries. Hong Kong returned to the mainland politically in 1997, but will remain a Special Administrative Region (SAR) for 50 years. Macau will similarly return to China just before the end of the twentieth century. Of the three territories, only Taiwan remains apart and represents by far the most critical issue for China in terms of sovereignty and the self-determination of the people of this island. Taiwan's fate will also have a strong impact on its own stability and on that of the whole region. Although it has never been formally recognised as an independent state, Taiwan – unlike Hong Kong and Macao – can feed, govern and defend itself. It is also geographically separated from mainland China. Any integration with China, and by implication further extension of China's territory, will only be possible with the overwhelming consensus of the people of Taiwan. This will remain a rather unlikely scenario for some time to come.

Eventually the borders separating North and South Korea will disappear. While South Korean government officials draw up plans for a slow and smooth transition, crisis management will probably be needed once the physical and ideological barriers which have kept one homogeneous people totally apart for so many decades are dismantled. A united Korea will thus become internally unstable and externally weak, a welcome relief for its neighbours who fear the over-swift emergence of an assertive and militarily strong united country.

There are a number of territorial disputes in the region, some of them between ASEAN neighbours, others between China and its neighbours. Most of them are rather insignificant, although they can be blown out of proportion and misused for political purposes. The most important disputes concern islands in the north of Japan and another group of islands in the China Sea. The so-called Northern Territories (better known as the Kurile Islands) are currently occupied by Russia, but belong historically to Japan. The stalemate in the discussion of their future is responsible for the cool political and economic relationship between the two countries. The Spratly Islands (best known under this name, but actually consisting of several separate groups of small islands) in the middle of the China Sea are claimed by several countries, but have been partly seized by China and officially declared part of Chinese territory. This and other aggressive moves have not only embarrassed Vietnam and the Philippines, but have also set a precedent. In addition, such action raises suspicions about other expansionist moves by China, including those towards Myanmar.

Ideological differences between countries in the region have lost significance since the end of the Cold War. Thus, with the exception of North Korea, the probability of a conflict between communist and non-communist nations has become remote. There are two reasons for the decline of ideological conflicts between countries. First, pressure to improve the economic well-being of their people has pushed governments towards pragmatism. As a result, technocrats within the ruling elite often carry more weight than ideologists. Second, the major communist powers have withdrawn their support from smaller countries and those underground movements in the region that share their beliefs. For example, China long ago reduced, then cut entirely, its support of the Communist Party in Indonesia and of guerrilla groups in other parts of South-East Asia. Since the collapse of the Soviet Union, Russia has stopped subsidising Vietnam and North Korea and cut its links with its former allies almost entirely. Vietnam, in turn, faced international pressure and withdrew from Cambodia.

Internally, however, ideological antagonism continues to exist. In China and Vietnam the authorities rigorously persecute those who openly question the monopoly of the Communist Party. Hard-line anti-communist countries, such as Indonesia, harshly suppress any movement vaguely leaning towards socialist and communist ideology. A civil war based on ideological differences continues to rage in Cambodia. None of the remaining communist countries in Asia has moved towards greater participation of its people in government as Eastern European countries have done. Equally, the many staunch anti-communist countries in the region have made no conciliatory moves towards the integration of the remaining communist or socialist splinter groups, preferring to keep them in obscurity or even as illegal elements in the political landscape.

Great power rivalries continue to shape the foreign policies of the Asia Pacific countries, though in different ways from those of a decade or two ago. The former Soviet Union – one of the superpowers in Asia – has faded away. Although Russia remains geographically an Asia Pacific country, its influence on the future of the region has become negligible, even taking into account the Pacific fleet stationed in Vladivostok.

The decline of Soviet/Russian influence is more than compensated for by the re-emergence of China. Theoretically, China has already been an Asian superpower for decades. The country became a nuclear power in the 1960s and a permanent member of the Security Council of the UN at the beginning of the 1970s, but internal turmoil and ideological warfare with its neighbouring countries prevented it from taking a truly leading role in the region. Today, China is undoubtedly a superpower that pulls Hong Kong, Taiwan and the Overseas Chinese into its orbit.

Its influence is somewhat balanced by Japan, which is often described as an economic giant but a political dwarf. The subliminal rivalry between these two leading Asian powers rarely comes to the surface, but clearly exists. It is complicated by the long history of their relationship and the bitter memories of the Japanese invasion of China in the 1930s and 1940s. Since the Japanese emperor's visit to China in 1992 – an important diplomatic event in Asia's recent history – the mutual economic dependence of the two nations has been openly acknowledged. The relationship between the two governments has warmed considerably, and Japanese capital has finally begun to pour into China.

China's recent political assertiveness, however, and the conversion of its military from a defence orientation into a forward projecting force makes Japan wary. The actions of the Chinese government are considered totally unrestrained both by the Chinese population and other countries. In contrast to this the Japanese government is weak, and embedded in a pacifist, inward-looking society opposed to open conflict with other nations. Its political options are limited to collective action with the USA, which represents the third superpower in Asia.

The USA fulfils several vital roles in Asia. The US market represents the most important export destination, and its business community is linked through manifold direct foreign investments and technology agreements with the region. It maintains large military bases in Japan and South Korea, and also a naval fleet in the region for which Singapore is one of the centres. This military presence provides a security umbrella for the whole of Asia Pacific, and could be mobilised to intervene in any internal or external conflict in the region. Politically, the USA has close bilateral ties with a number of Asian countries and uses them to direct their governments towards American ideals such as democracy, human rights or market liberalisation. Through its membership of APEC, the USA has found a way to extend its influence multi-laterally in a basically Asian body. Culturally, the American influence ranges from Hollywood films and Hard Rock Cafés to baseball, hamburgers and chewing gum. More importantly, when Asian families consider educational options for their brightest children, they think of Harvard, Stanford or MIT (Massachusetts Institute of Technology). In none of these dimensions can the influence of the USA be matched by the two Asian superpowers.

Perhaps it is this predominance and the tendency of the USA to impose its own values on Asian societies which from time to time leads to outbursts against the USA. But such anger never goes far. Asia realises the important role of the USA as a stabiliser in its fast moving and unstable world. Japan simul-taneously opposes and appreciates its interdependence with the USA. China rejects Americans meddling in its affairs, but at the same time admires its enormous financial, military and technological power. Deep down, the other Asia Pacific powers trust neither Japan nor China to secure their future. The USA as a neutral, non-Asian superpower in Asia thus remains welcome, if only as a lesser evil.

THE MOVE TOWARDS ASIANISATION

As the end of the twentieth century approaches, Asia finds itself dominated by one non-Asian and two Asian superpowers. It is doubtful whether this con-stellation can provide the stability which the region needs to continue its rapid economic development. All triangular relationships breed the suspicion that two of the players will collude to undermine the position of the third.

Bearing in mind the growing consciousness of being Asian and the increasing criticism of the West in Asia, the influence of the USA on the region may therefore not be sustainable and may one day be flatly rejected. It has been argued forcefully that future conflicts will be primarily rooted in cultural differences, and will thus occur between different civilisations.[3] If this holds true, the Asian power triangle is in for trouble and the disputes between the USA and Japan over economic and technological issues and the more recent clashes between China and the USA over human rights and weapons prolif-eration may just provide a foretaste of a coming clash of civilisations.

A civilisation in this context is defined as a cultural grouping at the broadest level with which people can identify. It therefore goes beyond the village or religious community, race and nationality, but remains below the level which distinguishes human beings from other species.[4] As ideological and economic differences become smaller, interactions between different civilisations increase, and consciousness of differences in cultures between people again become obvious, it is argued that people will return to their roots through language, history, religion, customs and institutions, and identify themselves as part of a distinct civilisation. By definition the borders of these civilisa-tions are difficult to draw, and they overlap. They may match the borders of nations, cross them or unite several nations under one umbrella. They may also be divided into sub-civilisations.

If one follows this line of thought the question becomes whether there is a single or several Asian civilisations, and where to detect commonalities and differences within the region, or between the region and the West. Among the seven or eight major civilisations which Huntington has identified, Confucian, Japanese and Islamic groupings originate from or reach into Asia Pacific. Hindu civilisation is a separate civilisation dominating the Indian sub-continent.

The division of Asia between various civilisations has serious consequences for any attempts to integrate the region economically and politically. Considering that the EU requires a common civilisation to overcome the difficulties of deep nationalism, the chances for an all-embracing Asian bloc are small. As long as Japan considers itself unique and different from the rest of Asia, it will not be able to integrate fully with the region and will therefore fail to emerge as a leader in Asia. By joining the OECD (the club of the rich countries) and the G7 (the group of the seven most influential economic powers) Japan has anyhow already set itself apart from the rest of Asia and become an associate of the West.

China, on the other hand, has the opportunity to become the new epicentre of the region through its Confucian roots which naturally connect the Chinese to the territories of Hong Kong and Taiwan and to the Overseas Chinese in South-East Asia. Should Confucian thought regain influence in China in the future, common ground will also be found with Korean and Vietnamese cultures. At this level of abstraction, the differences between a Confucian-oriented, but Chinese-led, civilisation and the Japanese world become arbitrary and give way to the commonalities between the two civilisations. One could then speak of one joint Asian civilisation with, however, East Asian characteristics. It could provide a solid underpinning for a process of far-reaching regionalisation in Asia under Chinese leadership.

Such an East Asian civilisation would leave others stranded. India would not join the region, not only because of its own size and distance from East Asia, but also because it clearly represents a different civilisation. Australia would also remain apart. What choices, however, are there for Christian Filipinos with a civilisation resembling that of Latin America? And where do countries with several civilisations such as Malaysia, Singapore and Thailand see their destiny in a world threatened by clashes between civilisations?

In Asia itself the present debate puts more emphasis on commonalities than differences in the region. The strongest advocates of Asianisation today come from neither China nor Japan but from Singapore and Malaysia. Led by Lee Kuan Yew, the so-called Singapore school of thought stresses Asian values and depicts them as superior to those of the West. The term 'Western decadence' has consequently become part of the standard vocabulary of this group. Malaysia's prime minister Mahathir argues from a political point of view. For him APEC as a Pacific rather than an Asian community was hijacked by the Americans for their (Western) purposes. Instead of supporting this movement he still argues for his former idea of the EAEC (East Asian Economic Caucus) which would bring together only Asian nations: a caucus without Caucasians. Not surprisingly, Malaysia emphasises good relationships with Asian neighbours, even with China (a less obvious friend bearing in mind the situation of the Overseas Chinese in the country and the quarrel over the Spratly Islands). At the same time it loses no opportunity to complain loudly about supposedly Western interference in internal affairs, a policy pursued equally strongly by the Singaporean government. In 1994 Mahathir joined Shintaro Ishihara, the right-wing politician from Japan, in publishing a book called *The Asia That Can Say No*, subtitled *A card against the West*.

It is through manifestations like this that the process of Asianisation is accelerated in the political arena. In daily life such a trend towards Asianisation has long been visible. Asians may admire the outrageous behaviour of some Western pop stars, but still prefer Asian music. Japanese, Chinese and even Indian soap operas are staple evening entertainment across much of Asia. Karaoke bars dot the urban landscape throughout Asia and holidays abroad are increasingly taken in neighbouring countries.

The growing feeling of Asianness raises, of course, the issue of how to define the Asian values which provide a common thread across the various societies in the region and can explain their success over recent decades. Tommy Koh from Singapore has provided a list of ten values ranging from the role of the individual in society to the responsibility of the press.[5] His points are summed up by Lee Kuan Yew, who claims that the West has turned the inviolability of the individual into a dogma, while in East Asia the individual exists in the context of family and society only. In contrast to European welfarism, East Asian societies rely on the mutual support of families. Asian thriftiness and the deferment of present enjoyment for future gain preclude American-style overspending and indebtedness.[6] All this is possible through the individual's efforts in educating him or herself and working hard in a morally healthy and consensus-oriented environment.[7]

For liberals in the West, these explanations neither represent values, nor are they Asian. They consider them a set of rules which enable authoritarian rulers to pursue their pro-business policies of economic development undisturbed by opposition from individuals and the demands of society. Even if one dismisses these arguments as ideologically loaded, it remains an open question whether the balance between freedom and order, and between government and family responsibility, is really influenced by the entrenched values of Asian societies or rather by the expedience of their specific stage of development. In other words, will these so-called Asian values still be valid once Singapore or Malaysia has reached the same standard of living as Switzerland or Japan? And how much of a morally healthy and consensus-oriented environment do we find in China or Indonesia today?

This raises the third, even more difficult, question about Asian values: how much are they really Asian in the sense of being truly accepted across the diverse cultures and religions of Asia? If they are equally valid and ingrained among Confucian Chinese, Buddhist Thais, Shintoist Japanese, and Muslims from Indonesia and Malaysia, what is so special about them? Would it be so difficult for Christian Filipinos to identify with them? If not, why should American Christians not be able to make them their own values, or Muslims living in France or atheists in Russia? The point, then, is whether it is possible to define truly Asian values which are broad enough to be appreciated across the whole of the region, but are nevertheless not so universal as to be taken as simple common sense by everybody in the world. One just has to think of the large Sicilian or Lebanese families to see that the family as the nucleus of society is alive and well in areas outside Asia.

In defence, Prime Minister Mahathir in 1996, on the occasion of the first Asia-Europe summit, asserted that Asian values are, indeed, universal ones, whereas European values are not. The picture has become even more confusing since the Asian crisis. Much of what has led to the developments in 1997–8 can be interpreted as the proof of Asian values. Reliance on the family turned into nepotism, the emphasis on personal relationships translated into cronyism. Consensus was achieved through wheel-greasing and corruption. Respect for authority became lack of courage to speak up when things were definitely going wrong.

The Asian crisis has nevertheless failed to silence those who propagate Asian values and consider them superior to those of the West. They can even be seen gaining ground as a cultural defence mechanism against the globalisation of economic and financial systems that favour a more pronounced if not dominant role for the West. Alternatively, or in addition, it may generate more internal discussion in Asia between authoritarians and liberals, governments and non-governmental organisations (NGOs), and between democratic governments like the Philippines and those allowing less individual freedom.

LEARNING ABOUT AND LEARNING FROM ASIA PACIFIC

Whatever doubts the West may have about the validity of Asian values, whatever the impact of the Asian crisis on the psychology of Asia, self-confidence and assertiveness, if not arrogance, are growing in the region. This represents a great challenge to the Western business community to whom this book is primarily addressed. In Chapter 1 we stressed that the colonial times are over. This may seem too obvious a point to need stating at the end of the twentieth century, but scratch the surface and one finds post-colonial firms still paying fat expatriate remuneration packages to those coming from Europe or America, while refusing to do the same for an equally qualified Singaporean sent to China or a Filipino despatched to Indonesia. Firms still talk about transfer of technology rather than best practice, implying a handing down of know-how from the knowledgeable to the ignorant; and often they insist on 51 per cent ownership in a joint venture in order to keep things under (their) control.

Granted, as the Asian crisis has shown, much of this view still may be appropriate and is in line with reality, particularly in the developing parts of Asia Pacific. But even if it is feasible and logical for the Western multinational to take the role of senior partner, in the perception of the Asian firm it smacks of patronising behaviour which is less and less acceptable.

Increasingly, Western managers and multinationals will be confronted with demands for equal partnership at any level and in any aspect of economic exchange. This will require – as we argued in Chapter 2 – a simultaneous modification and adaptation of management practices, leading to a transformation of the Western firm's ways of thinking and acting.

The West will get used to what it perceives as growing assertiveness, but still has to discover how far it can go in trying to impose its own values on the region. It has to accept that human rights will continue to be defined differently in the West and Asia Pacific for some time to come, and that economists in Asia will not swallow the virtue of market mechanisms slavishly, but continue to favour a strong government role in the economy. The West will be exposed to a growing flood of negative comments about its moral decline and will be expected not only to learn about Asia, but also to listen to and learn from the region. In geopolitics it will witness the emergence of China as a military power which will create anxiety, but will only match the country's status as a political superpower. And sooner or later it will give in to Japan's request for a permanent seat in the security council, recognising that times have changed.

What all this means is that Asia Pacific wants to be taken seriously – economically, politically, technologically and culturally – on equal terms with the USA and Europe. It resents being told what to do, and is beginning to express its own ideas more openly and in a more critical fashion than ever before.

The region is changing and modernising rapidly, but it is a Western self-delusion to equate modernisation with Westernisation. As Japan's development over the last 100 years or so has shown, it is possible to modernise without losing one's own identity and culture. Managing this change in Asia is an enormous task and will bring setbacks and disasters. Its confidence in its own newly-found strength, however, will make it possible for the whole region to overcome the many obstacles that lie ahead. Constantly challenging their own perceptions and attitudes will be crucial for those managers and firms which desire to be successful in Asia Pacific in the future.

Implementing global strategies in the region will not always be easy and will create problems for those who believe in a simple, uniform world. Not many global consumers are at home in Asia Pacific. Only on a superficial level do we witness a convergence in beliefs and practices. Bearing in mind the successful development of Asia Pacific over the last few decades, it cannot be expected – even in the face of the crisis – that the region will move towards Western societal, economic and management models soon, if ever. As Rudyard Kipling said at the end of the nineteenth century: 'Asia is not going to be civilised after the methods of the West. There is too much Asia, and she is too old.'[8]

Notes and references

1. *Human Development Report* (UNDP, 1997).
2. Lee Kuan Yew (1991).
3. Huntington (1993). This article has sparked off a vivid debate about a new 'civilisation paradigm' replacing the former division of the globe into the first (free) world, the second (communist) world, and the third (developing) world. See the various comments on Huntington's thoughts in *Foreign Affairs*, September/October 1993, pp. 2–26 and the author's response, *Foreign Affairs*, November/December 1993, pp. 186–94.
4. Huntington (1993).
5. Koh (1993).
6. Zakaria (1994).
7. Koh (1993).
8. Kipling (1891).

References

A. T. Kearney Inc. (1991)   *Trade and Investment in Japan: The Current Environment*   Tokyo

A. T. Kearney Inc. (1992)   *Capturing The Asian Potential: Insight for Western Multinationals*   222 West Adams Street, Chicago, Illinois, 60606

Abegglen, J. C. (1994)   *Sea Change*   Free Press, New York

Abegglen, J. C. and G. Stalk (1985)   *Kaisha – The Japanese Corporation*   Basic Books, New York

Adler, Nancy (1987)   'International Dimensions of Organizational Behavior'   Kent Publishing Co., New York

Aguilar, Frank and Doug Sung Cho (1984)   'The Daewoo Group'   *Harvard Business School* case study No. 38J-014

Amponsem, H. and D. Rutenberg (1992)   'A Process Guide to Accelerate an Organization's Learning'   Paper presented at the 12th Conference of Strategic Management Society, London, 17 November

Bartlett, Christopher and Sumantra Ghoshal (1989)   *Managing Across Borders: The Transnational Solution*   Harvard Business School Press, Boston, MA

Benedict, Ruth (1976)   *The Chrysanthemum and the Sword*   Meridian, New York

Bleeke, J. and D. Ernst (1991)   'The Way to Win in Cross-Border Alliances'   *Harvard Business Review*, November/December, pp. 127–35

Bower, Joseph (1972)   *Managing The Resource Allocation Process*   Richard Irwin, Homewood, Illinois

Brislin, Richard (1993)   *Understanding Culture's Influence on Behavior*   Harcourt Brace Jovanovich, Boston, MA

Business International (1991)   *Managers for Asia Pacific: Recruitment and Development Strategies*   Report No. Q107, Hong Kong, March

Business Week (1994)	'Samsung: Lee Kun-Hee's Management Revolution'	28 February, pp. 4–37
Chai, Joseph C. H. (1992)	'Consumption and Living Standards in China'	*The China Quarterly*, pp. 721–49
Chang, Chan Sup and Nahn Joo Chang (1994)	*The Korean Managment System*	Quorum Books, Westport, CT
Contractor, Farok (1981)	*International Technology Licensing: Compensation, Costs and Negotiations*	Lexington Books, Lexington, MA
Conway, Bryony (1994)	'Expatriate Effectiveness: A Study of European Expatriates in South East Asia'	London Guildhall University, London
Cyert, Richard and James March (1963)	*A Behavioral Theory of the Firm*	Prentice-Hall, Englewood Cliffs, NJ
Debroux, Philippe (1993)	'Human Resource Management in Foreign Companies in Japan'	Paper presented at the 8th Louis Vuitton Moet Hennessy (LVMH) conference, INSEAD Euro-Asia Centre, 5–6 February
Doz, Yves (1992)	'The Role of Partnerships and Alliances in the European Industrial Restructuring' in K. Cool, D. Neven and 1. Walter (eds), *European Industrial Restructuring in the 1990s*	Macmillan, London, pp. 292–325
Ernst, Dieter (1994)	'What are the limits to the Korean Model? The Korean Electronic Industry under Pressure'	B.R.I.E. Berkeley Roundtable on the International Economy, Research Paper, University of California, Berkeley
Fields, George (1989)	*Gucci on the Ginza*	Tokyo and New York, Kodansha, pp. 235–55
Financial Times (1988)	Industry Survey	15 December
Franko, Lawrence G. (1971)	'Joint Venture Divorce in the Multinational Company'	*Columbia Journal of World Business*, Vol. 6, No. 3, June, pp. 13–22

Franko, Lawrence G. (1991) · 'Global Corporate Competition II: Is the Large American Firm an Endangered Species?' · *Business Horizons*, November/December, pp. 14–22

Gerlach, Michael (1993) · *Alliance Capitalism: The Social Organization of Japanese Business* · University of California, Berkeley

Gersten, Martine Cardel (1990) · 'Intercultural Competence and Expatriates' · *The International Journal of Human Resource Management*, Vol. 1, No. 3, December, pp. 341–62

Gomes-Casseres, Benjamin (1991a) · 'International Trade, Competition, and Alliances in the Computer Industry' · Working Paper 92–044, Harvard Business School

Gomes-Casseres, Benjamin (1991b) · 'Xerox and Fuji Xerox' · *Harvard Business School* case study, No. 9-391-156

Graham, John L., and Yoshikuro Sano (1984) · *Smart Bargaining* · Ballinger, Cambridge, MA

Hamel, Gary and C. K. Prahalad (1989) · 'Strategic Intent' · *Harvard Business Review* May–June, pp. 63–76

Hamel, Gary and C. K. Prahalad (1990) · 'The Core Competence of the Corporation' · *Harvard Business Review* May–June, pp. 79–91

Hamel, Gary and C. K. Prahalad (1993) · 'Strategy as Stretch and Leverage' · *Harvard Business Review* March–April, pp. 75–84

Hamel, Gary, Y. Doz and C. K. Prahalad (1989) · 'Collaborate with Your Competitors – and Win' · *Harvard Business Review*, January–February, pp. 133–9

Harrigan, Kathryn Rudie (1985) · *Strategies for Joint Ventures* · Lexington Books, Lexington, MA

Haspeslagh, Philippe and William Jennison (1991) · *Managing Acquisitions: Creating Value Through Corporate Renewal* · The Free Press, New York

Hayes, Robert and W. J. Abernathy (1980) · 'Managing our Way to Economic Decline' · *Harvard Business Review*, Vol. 58, No. 4, pp. 67–77

Hendryx, Steven R. (1986) · 'The China Trade: Making the Deal Work' · *Harvard Business Review*, July–August, pp. 74–84

Hensley, Matthey and Edward P. White (1993)	'The Privatisation Experience in Malaysia'	*Columbia Journal of World Business*, Spring, pp. 71–82
Hicks, G. L. and S. G. Redding (1983)	'The Story of the East Asian Miracle: The Culture Connection'	*Euro-Asia Business Review*, Vol. 2, No. 4, pp. 18–22
Hiltrop, Jean Marie and Maddy Janssens (1990)	'Expatriation: Challenges and Recommendations'	*European Management Journal*, Vol. 8, No. 1, March, pp. 19–26
Hofstede, Geert (1980)	*Culture's Consequences: International Differences in Work-related Values*	Sage, Beverly Hills, CA
Huntington, Samuel P. (1993)	'The Clash of Civilisations?'	*Foreign Affairs*, Summer, pp. 22–49
Imai, M. (1987)	*Kaizen: The Key to Japan's Competitive Success*	Random House, New York
Jenkins, David (1984)	*Suharto and his Generals – Indonesia Military Politics 1975–1983*	Cornell Modern Indonesia Project, Cornell University, Ithaca, NY
Jones, K. and T. Ohbora (1990)	'Managing the "Heretical" Company'	*The McKinsey Quarterly*, March, pp. 20–45
Jones, K. K. and W. E. Shill (1993)	'Japan: Allying for Advantage' in J. Bleeke and D. Ernst (eds), *Collaborating to Compete*	Wiley, New York
Joon Bae (1989)	'Ex-Bureaucrats and Ex-Military Men in the Financial World', *Sin-Dong-A*, August 1986, p. 403, quoted in Steers, Richard, Yoo Keun Shin and Gerardo Ungson, *The Chaebol: Korea's New Industrial Might*	Harper & Row, New York
Kipling, Rudyard	'The Man Who Was', *Life's Handicap*	first published 1891, available as a Penguin Classics series paperback
Kim, Eun Young (1994)	*A Cross-Cultural Reference of Business Practices in a New Korea*	Quorum Books, Westport, CT
Koh, Tommy (1993)	'The 10 Values that Undergird East Asian Strength and Success'	*International Herald Tribune*, 11 December, p. 6

Kotler, P., L. Fahey and S. Jatusripitak (1985) — *The New Competition* — Prentice-Hall, Englewood Cliffs, NJ, p. 156

Krugman, Paul (1994) — 'The Myth of Asia's Miracle' — *Foreign Affairs*, November/December, pp. 62–78

Lasserre, Philippe (1982) — 'Training: Key to Technology Transfer' — *Long Range Planning*, Vol. 15, No. 3, pp. 51–60

Lasserre, Philippe (1983) — 'Strategic Planning in South East Asia: Does it Work?' — *Euro-Asia Business Review*, Vol. 2, No. 2, April, pp. 37–41

Lasserre, Philippe (1988a) — 'Corporate Strategic Management and the Overseas Chinese Groups' — *Asia-Pacific Journal of Management*, Vol. 5, No. 2, January

Lasserre, Philippe (1988b) — 'Why are Europeans Weak in Asia?' — *Long Range Planning*, Vol. 21, No. 4, pp. 25–35

Lasserre, Philippe (1993a) — 'Gathering and Interpreting Strategic Intelligence in Asia Pacific' — *Long Range Planning*, Vol. 26, No. 3, pp. 56–66

Lasserre, Philippe (1993b) — 'The Strategic Role of Regional Headquarters in Asia Pacific' — *INSEAD Euro-Asia Centre Research Series*, No. 15, Fontainebleau, April

Lasserre, Philippe (1996) — 'Regional Headquarters: The spearhead for Asia-Pacific markets' — *Long Range Planning*, Vol. 29, No. 1, pp. 30–7

Lasserre, Philippe and M. Boisot (1980) — 'Transfer of Technology from European to Asean Enterprises: Strategies and Practices in the Chemical and Pharmaceutical Sector' — *Euro-Asia Research Paper*, No. 2, Fontainebleau

Lasserre, Philippe and Charlotte Butler (1993) — 'Strategic Development in Asia' — Paper presented at the 8th LVMH conference, INSEAD Euro-Asia Centre, 5–6 February

Lasserre, Philippe and Elisabeth Fouraker (1989) — 'Thai Polyester Company', — *INSEAD Euro-Asia Centre* case study

Lasserre, Philippe and Jocelyn Probert (1994a) — 'Competing on the Pacific Rim: High Risks and High Return' — *Long Range Planning*, Vol. 27, No. 2, pp. 12–35

Lasserre, Philippe and Jocelyn Probert (1994b)	'Human Resources Management in the Asia Pacific Region: A Comparative Assessment'	*INSEAD Euro-Asia Centre Research Series*, No. 25, Fontainebleau, January
Lasserre, Philippe and and Jocelyn Probert (1997)	'Foreign Direct Investment in Asia'	*Financial Times Newsletters and Management Reports*, Hong Kong
Laurent, André (1986)	'The Cross Cultural Puzzle of Global Human Resource Management'	*Human Resource Management*, Vol. 15, No. 1, pp. 91–102
Lee Kuan Yew (1991)	'A map up here, in the mind'	*The Economist*, 29 June, pp. 18–19
Lee, Chol (1990)	'Modifying an American Consumer Behavior Model For Consumers in Confucian Culture: The Case of Fishbein Behavioral Intention Model'	*The Journal of International Consumer Marketing*, Vol. 3, pp. 27–50
Limlingan, Victor (1986)	*The Overseas Chinese: Business Practices and Strategies*	The Vita Development Corp., Philippines
Mackie, J. A. C. (1992)	'Overseas Chinese Entrepreneurship'	*Asia Pacific Economic Literature*, Vol. 1, No. 6, pp. 41–64
MacMurray, Trevor and Jonathan Woetzel (1994)	'The Challenge Facing China's State-owned Enterprises'	*The McKinsey Quarterly*, No. 2, pp. 61–73
Mahbubani, Kishore (1995)	'The Pacific Way'	*Foreign Affairs*, January/February, pp. 100–111
Malayang, Ruth. V. (1988)	'The Distribution Industry in Asian NIEs and ASEAN Countries and the Effects of the Entry of Japanese Retailers'	*Management Japan*, Vol. XXI, No. 2, pp. 15–28
Malnight, Thomas W. and Michael Yoshino (1992)	'Otis Pacific Asia Operations' (A), (B)	*Harvard Business School*, case study Nos. 9-393-009 and 9-393-010
Mann, Jim (1989)	*Beijing Jeep: The Short Unhappy Romance of American Business in China*	Simon & Schuster, New York
Mintzberg, Henry (1990)	*Mintzberg on Strategy*	Free Press, New York

310 *References*

Montgomery, D. B. (1991)   'Understanding the Japanese as Customers, Competitors, and Collaborators'   *Japan and the World Economy,* March, pp. 61–91

Ohmae, Kenichi (1985)   *Triad Power*   Free Press, New York

Ohmae, Kenichi (1989)   'The Global Logic of Strategic Alliances'   *Harvard Business Review,* March–April, pp. 143–54

Palia, Aspy and Keown, Charles (1991)   'Combatting Parallel Importing: Views of US Exporters to the Asian Countries'   *Industrial Marketing Review*, Vol. 8, No. 1, pp. 47–56

Palmier, Leslie (1989)   'Corruption in the West Pacific'   *The Pacific Review*, Vol. 2, No. 1, pp. 11–23

Pascale, Richard (1990)   *Managing on the Edge*   Simon & Schuster, New York

Peters, Tom (1987)   *Striving on Chaos*   Alfred Knopf, New York

Peterson, Richard B. (ed.) (1993)   *Managers and National Culture: A Global Perspective*   Quorum Books, New York, and Westport, CT

Porter, Michael E. (ed.) (1986)   *Competition in Global Industries*   Harvard Business School Press, Boston, MA

Porter, M. E. (1990)   *The Competitive Advantage of Nations*   Macmillan, London

Prahalad, C. K. and R. A. Bettis (1986)   'The Dominant Logic: A New Linkage Between Diversity and Performance'   *Strategic Management Journal*, Vol. 7, November–December, pp. 485–501

Prahalad, C. K and Yves Doz (1987)   *The Multinational Mission: Balancing Local Demands and Global Vision*   Free Press, New York

Probert, Jocelyn (1992)   'The Investment Climate in the Asia Pacific Region'   *INSEAD Euro-Asia Centre Research Series*, No. 9, Fontainebleau, April

Pye, Lucien (1983)   *Chinese Commercial Negotiating Style*   Oelgeschalger, Cambridge, MA

Pye, Lucien (1986a)   'The China Trade: Making the Deal'   *Harvard Business Review*, July–August, pp. 75–80

Pye, Lucien (1986b)   'The New Asian Capitalism: A Political Portrait' in Peter Berger and Hsin-Huang Hsiao (eds), *Search of An East Asian Development Model*   Transaction Books, New Brunswick and Oxford

Redding, Gordon S. (1990)	*The Spirit of Chinese Capitalism*	Walter de Gruyter, Berlin
Redding, Gordon S. (1995)	'Overseas Chinese Groups in Pacific Asia; Their Origin and Influence'	*Long Range Planning*, Vol. 28, No. 1, pp. 61–9
Reich, R. B. and D. D. Mankin (1986)	'Joint Ventures with Japan Give Away our Future'	*Harvard Business Review*, March–April, pp. 78–83
Roberto, Eduardo L. (1987)	*Applied Marketing Research*	Ateneo de Manila University Press, Manila
Roth, Kendall and Allen Morrison (1992)	'Implementing Global Strategies: Characteristics of Subsidiaries Mandates'	*Journal of International Business Studies*, fourth quarter, pp. 715–35
Schneider, Susan (1988)	'National vs. Corporate Culture: Implications for Human Resource Management'	*Human Resources Management*, Vol. 27, No. 1, pp. 133–48
Schrage, Michael (1991)	*Old Assumptions, New Markets: Doing Business in a Changing Japan*	Japan Society, New York, pp. 5–8
Schütte, Hellmut (1990a)	'Euro-Japanese Cooperation in Information Technology' in F. Meyer-Krahmer, J. Müller and B. Preisse (eds), *Information Technology: Impacts, Policies and Future Perspectives*	Springer, Berlin, pp. 99–130
Schütte, Hellmut (1990b)	'Tianjin Merlin Gerin'	*INSEAD Euro-Asia Centre* case study
Schütte, Hellmut (1993)	'Competing and Co-operating with Japanese Firms'	*United States-Japan Program Occasional Papers*, Harvard University
Schütte, Hellmut (1994)	'Corporate Governance in Japan'	*INSEAD Euro-Asia Research Series* No. 30, Fontainebleau, July
Schütte, Hellmut (1997)	'Strategy and Organisation: Challenges for European MNCs in Asia'	*European Management Journal*, Vol. 15, No. 4, August, pp. 436–45
Schütte, Hellmut (1998)	'Between Headquarters and Subsidiaries: The RHQ Solution' in J. Birkinshaw and N. Hood (eds), *Multinational Corporate Evolution and Subsidiary Development*	Macmillan, Basingstoke, pp. 102–36

Schütte, Hellmut with Deanna Ciarlante (1998)   *Consumer Behaviour in Asia*   Macmillan, Basingstoke

Schütte, Hellmut and Ishida, Eriko (1990)   'Club Med – Japan'   *INSEAD Euro-Asia Centre* case study

Shaw, Stephen M. and Jonathan R. Woetzel (1992)   'A Fresh Look At China'   *The McKinsey Quarterly,* No. 3, pp. 37–51

Stalk, G. and T. H. Hout (1990)   *Competing Against Time*   Free Press, New York

Steers, Richard, Yoo Keun Shin and Gerardo Ungson (1987)   *The Chaebol: Korea's New Industrial Might*   Harper & Row, New York

Tanaka, Yozo, Minako Mori and Yoko Mori (1992)   'Overseas Chinese Business Community in Asia: Present Conditions and Future Prospects'   *RIM, Pacific Business and Industries*, Vol. II, pp. 1–24

Teece, D. J. (1976)   *The Multinational Corporation and the Resource Cost of International Technology Transfer*   Ballinger, Cambridge, MA

Tung, Paul (1991)   'The Taiwanese Presence in Europe'   *INSEAD Euro-Asia Centre Research Series*, No. 3, January

Tung, Rosalie (1984)   *Business Negotiations with the Japanese*   Lexington Books, Lexington, MA

Turcq, D. (1995)   'The Global Impact of Non-Japan Asia'   *Long Range Planning*, Vol. 28, No. 1, pp. 31–40

UNDP (1994)   *Human Development Report 1994*   Oxford University Press, New York

Vanhonacker, Wilfried (1997)   'Entering China: An Unconventional Approach'   *Harvard Business Review* March–April, pp. 130–41

Wagner, Cecilia L. (1990)   'Influences on Sino-Western Joint Venture Negotiations'   *Asia-Pacific Journal of Managment*, Vol. 7, No. 2, pp. 79–100

Warner, Malcolm (1992)   'How Japanese Managers Learn'   *The Journal of General Management*, Vol. 17, No. 3, Spring, pp. 56–71

Weinshall, Theodore (ed.) (1993)	*Societal Culture and Management*	Walter de Gruyter, Berlin/New York
Weiss, S. E. (1987)	'Creating the GM-Toyota Joint-Venture: A Case in Complex Negotiation'	*Columbia Review of World Business*, Vol. 22, No. 2, pp. 23–37
Whitley, Richard (1992)	*Business Systems in East Asia: Firms, Markets and Societies*	Sage Publications, Newbury Park, London
Williamson, Peter (1995)	'Lever Brothers Thailand'	*Harvard Business School* case study
Williamson, P. and Hu, Q. (1994)	*Managing the Global Frontier*	Pitman, London
World Bank (1993)	*The East Asian Miracle: Economic Growth and Public Policy*	Oxford University Press, New York
World Bank (1994a)	*East Asia's Trade and Investment*	Washington, DC
World Bank (1994b)	*Global Economic Prospects and Developing Countries*	Washington, DC
Wortzel, Lawrence H. (1983)	'Marketing to Firms in Developing Asian Countries'	*Industrial Marketing Management*, No. 12, pp. 113–23
Yeh, Ryh-Song (1991)	'Management Practices of Taiwanese Firms: As Compared to those of American and Japanese Subsidiaries in Taiwan'	*Asia Pacific Journal of Management*, Vol. 8, No. 1, pp. 1–14
Yoo Sanjin and Sang M. Lee (1987)	'Management Style and Practice of Korean Chaebols'	*California Management Review*, Summer, pp. 95–110
Yoshino, Michael (1990)	'Procter and Gamble in Japan'	*Harvard Business School,* case study No. 391-0031990
You, Zhong Xuin (1991)	*Seikai no Chainisu (Ethnic Overseas Chinese: Their Expanding Economic Power)*	The Simul Press, Tokyo
Zakaria, Fareed (1994)	'Culture in Destiny – A Conversation with Lee Kuan Yew'	*Foreign Affairs*, April/March, pp. 109–126

Index